China's Changing Economy

One of the most dramatic events in the global economy over the past few decades has been the rise of China as a global economic power. From humble beginnings in the late 1970s, the policy shift in China from a planned to market economy has led to economic growth of tremendous speed.

This book examines the changes taking place in China's economy today and the impacts of these changes in China and abroad. The central theme is that the rapid economic growth has come at a cost, as many problems have emerged as a result in China's economy and society, including a dramatic rich–poor gap, labour issues, problems in the banking sector and severe inflation in the cost of housing, as well as challenges with respect to China's external trade. The Chinese government recognizes these problems and is taking steps to rebalance its economy and society. This book takes a political economy perspective in order to investigate the interplay between the political system in China and the way in which the economy is structured, and the manner in which economic changes take place. Demonstrating that in order for China to achieve sustained economic growth and social improvement it must undertake serious policy changes, it also highlights that if countries are going to deal with China in a stable and productive manner, a thorough understanding of key contemporary developments in that country is vital.

Covering a range of the most pertinent issues facing China today, this book will be of interest to students and scholars of Chinese economics, economic development and political economy.

Curtis Andressen holds the Marubeni Chair in Social Sciences at Qatar University.

Routledge Contemporary China Series

China's Changing Economy

Trends, impacts and the future

Edited by Curtis Andressen

Routledge
Taylor & Francis Group

LONDON AND NEW YORK

First published 2016
by Routledge

2 Park Square, Milton Park, Abingdon, Oxfordshire OX14 4RN
711 Third Avenue, New York, NY 10017

Routledge is an imprint of the Taylor & Francis Group, an informa business

First issued in paperback 2018

British Library Cataloguing in Publication Data
A catalogue record for this book is available from the British Library

Library of Congress Cataloging-in-Publication Data
Names: Andressen, Curtis A. (Curtis Arthur), 1956– editor.
Title: China's changing economy : trends, impacts and the future / edited
by Curtis Andressen.
Description: Abingdon, Oxon ; New York, NY : Routledge, 2016. | Series:
Routledge contemporary China series ; 150 | Includes bibliographical
references and index.
Identifiers: LCCN 2015047069| ISBN 9781138945975 (hardback) |
ISBN 9781315671062 (ebook)
Subjects: LCSH: China–Economic conditions–2000– | China–Economic
policy–2000– | China–Foreign economic relations.
Classification: LCC HC427.95 .C45553 2016 | DDC 330.951–dc23
LC record available at http://lccn.loc.gov/2015047069

ISBN: 978-1-138-94597-5 (hbk)
ISBN: 978-0-367-02672-1 (pbk)

Typeset in Times New Roman
by Wearset Ltd, Boldon, Tyne and Wear

For my wife, Blanca Bolanos and my son,
Andreas Bolanos Andressen
Familia est omnia

Contents

Figures

Tables

Contributors

Curtis Andressen holds the Marubeni Chair in Social Sciences at Qatar University. Over the past 30 years he has written widely on the international relations of Japan, China and Southeast Asia. He is currently engaged in research on Middle East–East Asia relations.

Kai Du is Visiting Research Fellow in the Entrepreneurship, Commercialisation & Innovation Centre at the University of Adelaide, Australia. One of his research interests is the intersection between the financial reform in China and efficiency and productivity analysis.

Lei Feng is Senior Research Fellow and Director, Research Department of International Trade and Investment in the National Academy of Economic Strategy, Chinese Academy of Social Sciences.

Jeffrey Gil is Lecturer in the Department of Languages and Applied Linguistics at Flinders University, Adelaide, Australia. He obtained his PhD in Asian Studies from Griffith University. His research interests include: China's soft power; the promotion of Chinese language learning; the global use and status of Chinese; the use and status of English in China; ethnic minority languages and cultures in China; and environmental issues in China. He has published refereed journal articles and book chapters on these topics.

Steve Goodman is the Program Director of Higher Degrees by Research and a Senior Lecturer at the University of Adelaide Business School. He is an active researcher in the area of marketing – specifically consumer choice and business decision-making in the wine supply chain context. His current research interests involve choice modelling in both the consumer and business-to-business contexts.

Christopher Graves is Senior Lecturer at the University of Adelaide Business School and teaches financial literacy and family business management to managers undertaking the school's MBA programmes. Chris has a particular interest in the management and growth of small-to-medium-sized enterprises (SMEs) and family businesses.

Gerry Groot is Senior Lecturer in Chinese Studies and Head of the Department of Asian Studies, University of Adelaide, as well as Convenor, Ninth Biennial

International Convention of Asia Scholars, ICAS9. Gerry Groot teaches, researches and writes on Chinese politics, particularly united front work, social change, soft power and Asian influences on the world both past and present.

R. John Halsey is Professor of Rural Education and Communities in the School of Education at Flinders University, a Senior Associate of the Center for RelationaLearning, Santa Fe, New Mexico, and Non-Executive Director of the Primary Industries Education Foundation Australia Board. His current research interests include leadership and teacher formation for rural contexts, relational leadership, sustainability and rural communities, and re-conceptualizing rural education and schools.

Ai-Ying Jiang is an Associate Professor of the Shandong Institute of Business and Technology, engaged in research on the multilateral trading system.

Mervyn K. Lewis is a Fellow of the Academy of the Social Sciences in Australia and Professor in the School of Commerce, University of South Australia.

Han Lin is a PhD student in the School of Politics and Public Policy, Flinders University, Adelaide, Australia. She is currently working on her PhD thesis which proposes an alternative climate change-related energy policy for China. Her master degree thesis, 'A Confucian approach to China's environmental governance: A case study of China's atmospheric pollution problem', proposed an innovative solution to China's pollution problems based on Confucian principles. Her research interests include sustainable energy policy, climate change mitigation and adaptation, sustainable urban living and Confucian philosophy. She has presented conference papers and published in these areas.

Noel Lindsay is Professor of Entrepreneurship and Commercialisation in the Entrepreneurship, Commercialisation and Innovation Centre and Academic Director Singapore Operations of the University of Adelaide's Singapore Ngee Ann Adelaide Campus. His research interests are in the area of business and social entrepreneurship. In addition to his academic pursuits, he has widespread practical experience as a successful entrepreneur, venture capitalist, and corporate insolvency practitioner.

Jiajun Liu is Assistant Professor at the National Academy of Economic Strategy (NAES) of the Chinese Academy of Social Sciences (CASS), Beijing. His research interests include industrial distribution, regional eco-economics, resource economics and regional sustainable development, regional eco-economic development planning, recycling economic plans, tourism planning, eco-city planning and new rural construction planning.

Helen Jaqueline McLaren is the Director of Studies for the Master of Social Work degree at Flinders University, a member of the Flinders Institute of

Public Policy and Management, and in 2012 was Visiting Fellow at the Chinese Academy of Social Sciences. Her current research interests are on child and family wellbeing in a global context, including how that may traverse policy and practice, private and public domains, and across service sectors and disciplines.

Michael Schiavone has published extensively on the labour movement and is the author of *Unions in Crisis? The Future of Organized Labor in America* (Praeger Publishers, 2008) and *Sports and Labor in the United States* (SUNY Press, 2015). He has a bachelor's degree (Honours) in International Relations from Flinders University and a PhD from the Australian National University. He is a visiting scholar at the School of International Studies, Flinders University. He also teaches labour studies at the University of Illinois (Urbana-Champaign).

Pi-Shen Seet is Associate Professor at the Flinders Business School, Flinders University, where he is also coordinator of the research higher degree programmes. His current research interests include knowledge-based innovation, entrepreneurial decision-making and family business succession strategies.

Hui Situ is a PhD candidate in Flinders Business School. Her research focus is the motivations behind the increasing trend of corporate environmental disclosure in China. Her chapter in this volume is the preliminary finding of her whole project.

Wee-Liang Tan is Associate Professor of strategic management at the Lee Kong Chian School of Business at the Singapore Management University. His current research interests lie in the domains of entrepreneurship, family business, international cooperation and corporate governance.

Jing Tang is Assistant Research Fellow in the Institute of Finance and Trade Economics, Chinese Academy of Social Sciences, Beijing, China. His key research area is international trade in services and WTO rules, especially in regional economic integration.

Carol Tilt has worked at Flinders University since 1993. Prior to that she worked as a teacher and in retail business. Her research interests are in social and environmental accounting and she is a member of the Centre for Social and Environmental Accounting Research (CSEAR) in Scotland. She is also on the editorial board of a number of leading journals, including the A*-rated *AAAJ*.

Zhiqiang Xia is Director of Graduate Programs at Nanyang Technopreneurship Center (NTC), Nanyang Technological University (NTU), Singapore. His PhD dissertation received the Dean's Commendation for Doctoral Thesis Excellence from the University of Adelaide in 2012.

Lei Xu is Lecturer in the School of Commerce, University of South Australia. Lei (Theodore) came from the banking sector and joined academia in the field of Finance. He is keen to contribute to the understanding and impacts of modern finance concepts, practices and policies in the business and wider community. In addition to being a Justice of the Peace for South Australia, Fire Warden and First Aid Officer for the school, he has actively engaged in various social services.

Po-shan Yu is in the School of Commerce, University of South Australia. His research interests include Chinese real-estate financing and infrastructure development.

Acknowledgements

I would like to express my thanks to my employer, Qatar University, and specifically to the College of Arts and Sciences, and the Department of Social Sciences, in which I am located. At all levels of the university the support of staff and the collegiality is impressive. The financial generosity of Qatar University is also a great stimulus for academics to undertake research.

The work environment at Qatar University has been wonderful. Staff and students are polite, respectful and supportive, and I have never experienced anything like this in my working life. It is truly a great place to work.

Special thanks in particular to Professors Abdulnasser Saleh M.S. Alyafei, Elrayah A. Osman and Daniel Varisco of the Faculty of Arts and Sciences at Qatar University for their support, warmth and collegiality while I was editing this book.

Working in Qatar is a tremendously stimulating experience. The rate of economic growth is nothing less than overwhelming, and one is caught up in the excitement of seeing a city and country grow before one's eyes. The university is central to this rapid development and I am very proud to be a part of it, particularly at this stage of its growth. I wish Qatar University and the people of Qatar all the best in the future.

Finally, thanks to Mary Lyons for helping with the organization of the early chapter submissions.

The genesis of this book was a conference – the 4th Sino-Australian Forum entitled 'Changing Economies' held in Adelaide in November 2013. Hosted by Flinders University, the conference was jointly organized by the Centre for United States and Asia Policy Studies in the Faculty of Social and Behavioural Sciences at Flinders University, and the National Academy of Economic Strategy at the Chinese Academy of Social Sciences (CASS).

1 China's changing economy

Trends, impacts and the future

Curtis Andressen

Perhaps the most dramatic event in the global economy over the past few decades has been the rise of China as a global economic power. From humble beginnings in the late 1970s, the policy shift in China from a planned to market economy has led to economic growth that has been nothing short of spectacular.

Much has been written about this dynamic economic shift. Consider a few selected statistics. China is the world's second biggest economy. Its GDP in 2013 stood at US$9.4 trillion (Roberts, 2014), up from about US$2 trillion in 2004 (World Bank, 2013), and China's GDP could overtake that of the US in under 15 years (Lubin, 2010). Per capita GDP (PPP) has increased commensurately, from just over US$4,000 (PPP) in 2005 to over US$9,000 in 2012 (OECD, 2013). In 2010 China became the number one exporting country in the world. From 2000 to 2010 China's economy grew seven times faster than that of the US (Lubin, 2010). Finally, in 2013 mainland China overtook the US to become the world's largest trading nation (*China Daily*, 2014).

But, this is only part of the picture. The reality is that China's economy, like most others in the world, is dependent on other countries. Its growth over the past three decades has relied heavily on foreign investment. For example, approximately 60 per cent of Chinese exports to the US are from foreign-owned companies in China (Hughes, 2005: 1). This is, of course, a major benefit for the US. Not only are American companies making profits that are repatriated to the US, but the low cost of goods means that industrial inputs are of lower cost as well (the loss of jobs notwithstanding), thereby boosting American competitiveness. The sheer size of the trade in this respect is noteworthy. As Hughes (2005) points out, 'Wal-Mart alone purchased $18 billion worth of Chinese goods in 2004, making it China's eighth-largest trading partner – ahead of Australia, Canada, and Russia.' Today, China is no longer just a recipient of investment, either. Its corporations are beginning to buy into resource and technology companies from the US to Australia to various South American and African countries. The Chinese government is active as well, via the China International Investment Corps (CIC), its sovereign wealth fund and state-owned enterprises (SOEs). Chinese companies are also manufacturing offshore, and brands such as Huawei, Lenovo, Great Wall and Geely are becoming as well known as the Japanese brands became in the 1960s and 1970s.

This interdependency means that increasingly China has to interact with the rest of the world in a responsible manner, in political as well as economic terms. The US is China's largest trading partner and obviously this dependency means that the two countries have much to gain through a cooperative approach. China's other trading partners show an interesting pattern. Australia (seventh), Brazil (ninth) and Russia (tenth) are predominantly providers of raw materials for China's export industries. Hong Kong (second) and Taiwan (fifth) are, more or less, a part of greater China. Japan, the third spot, has a fractured relationship with China, with economic dependency but political difficulties (as in the case of Taiwan). The Republic of Korea is fourth, enhancing the importance of the region of north-east Asia to China. Finally, Germany comes in at number six, with that country's high-technology products being important for China's own industrial growth.

From this pattern we can deduce a range of issues. Regional cooperation is very important, but the political history of the region creates problems, from the lingering effects of Japanese militarism to various islands claimed by more than one country. Importing of raw materials is critical, but the countries providing these materials have a delicate relationship with China, whether it is the history of Sino-Russian conflict or the fact that China is Australia's number one trading partner but has a defence agreement with the US. China's high-technology exports create problems with Germany and other European countries, such as the recent issue of Chinese-made solar panels. China must therefore practice a high level of regional diplomacy and slowly build political bridges, such as its steady push into Southeast Asia via the China–ASEAN Free Trade Area. On the other hand, the US and its allies are attempting to balance this influence by their own political and economic structures, such as the proposal for the Trans Pacific Partnership (TPP), a regional trading agreement that, at present, excludes China.

The reverse scene shows a similar pattern. China is now a very important player on the international scene, using its economic clout to influence economic and political events beyond its borders. In some respects this is welcomed, such as countries looking to China during the Global Financial Crisis as an economy that grew rapidly while others were (and to some extent still are) mired in difficulties. On the other hand, the Chinese government is using some of its new wealth to build up its military capability. Of the US$17 trillion spent on the military worldwide in 2012, 39 per cent came from the US, but China was at the number two spot at 9.5 per cent (Shah, 2013). China is now a country to be reckoned with in terms of military capability, a fact no doubt making its neighbours nervous, and leading to an arms build-up in those countries.

What lessons can we take from this? We are increasingly in a multi-polar world. China will play a very significant role in the economy and political shifts in the world over this century and beyond. It is now centre stage along with the other major powers in the world.

But, all of this growth in wealth and power has come at a cost. There has been much written about China's miracle economy, in a similar vein to that written about Japan in the 1980s. But, as with Japan, there are many problems in China that can slow down if not derail its growth, and foreign companies in China as well as China's trading partners anxiously watch for signs of political and economic difficulties.

It is clear that China's growth cannot be sustained indefinitely. Any economy that has gone through such a growth spurt, and in the region this would include Japan in the 1960s and the newly industrializing economies (NIEs) in the 1970s and 1980s, demonstrates that social and economic fundamentals become seriously skewed over time. The same has occurred in China. Some of the more well-known issues include an economy overly dependent on infrastructural spending, a wealth gap, lack of adequate social services, corruption and environmental degradation.

The Chinese government, well aware of these issues, has recently decided to make substantial changes to its economy and society. First among these is the shift from an economy dependent on exports to one that is increasingly driven by domestic spending. From the consistent 10 per cent annual growth in GPD in recent decades, China's leaders are now aiming for a more reasonable and sustainable growth in the 6–7 per cent range. Of course, sudden changes are to be avoided in order to maintain employment and associated economic benefits, not to mention political stability. Indeed, the legitimacy of the Chinese government is dependent on delivering increasingly higher standards of living to its people. Hence, in 2013 China's growth rate was still a relatively high 7.7 per cent, a slight increase over the target of 7.5 per cent (Yan, 2014).

The growth in China's economy cannot, in part, be sustained because of the nature of its labour force. Its success as an exporter has been based on low domestic labour costs as well as increases in productivity. But, China's labour force will soon decline in size and will continue to do so into the future. As Haltmaier (2013) argues:

> The GDP growth rate is the sum of the growth in employment and the growth in output per employee. China faces challenges in both of these categories. The rate of working-age population growth has fallen from 2½ percent in 1979 to less than one percent in 2011, and is expected to turn negative before 2020. With nearly 80 percent of the working-age population already employed, there is not much room for employment growth to exceed working-age population growth. Thus, in all likelihood, virtually all of the increase in Chinese GDP over the next couple of decades will have to come from increased output per worker, or labor productivity.

Productivity is based on investment and the capability of the labour force. With respect to the former, China's growth has been driven in large part from government investment in infrastructure and manufacturing. It is clear that investment in infrastructure is on the decline (and indirectly affecting trading partners such as Australia) and one cannot expect further large increases in productivity in this respect. In terms of manufacturing, China is focusing less on low value-added exports as wages increase and products become less competitive.

This will be offset to some extent by domestic demand, but overall the secondary sector is not likely to be as vibrant into the future as it has been in the past. Moreover, manufacturing in China has been in part driven by rural to urban migration, but much of that labour has now been used, and the proportion of the workforce in agriculture is now approximately 35 per cent, compared to 70 per cent in 1978 (World Bank, 2014). Finally, education plays a key role in productivity, and though the education levels in China are rising, real problems remain, including vast discrepancies between rural and urban areas, problems with the examination system, and the level of education compared to other advanced economies (Zhou and Andressen, 2013: 65–76).

A problem underlying the issue of labour productivity is the change in the population structure of China. China's one-child policy has been successful in slowing its population growth, but the flip side is that there is less labour available and, ultimately, there will be a substantial burden of a large number of elderly on a relatively small group of young people. Providing for a growing number of elderly is a challenge facing China in the future, along with most developed countries in the Western world.

There are other severe problems facing the government and people of China. First, there are the clear environmental issues. One can scarcely read the news today without noticing that China's rapid economic growth has been at the expense of the environment. Air pollution is terrifying the larger cities in China and in some of the secondary ones as well. Even foreign tourism is down, a reaction to the air pollution in China. In this respect a comparative perspective is useful, given that China faces similar challenges to many other countries, especially in the developing world. India, for example, has similar pollution problems, with New Delhi recently taking the unfortunate position of global leader in urban air pollution.

The health implications of heavy pollution are obvious, and this carries both a human and financial cost for China, but its government is clearly having difficulty grappling with this issue. Food safety, for example, has become a prevalent topic in China. This is intrinsically linked to the health of Chinese, directly in terms of eating healthy food and indirectly with respect to problems of virus control. In recent years the world, though particularly Asia, has experienced SARS, swine flu and bird flu, the latter outbreak being under current investigation. The way in which China governs food safety is therefore an issue of global concern.

China also faces growing discontent with the gap between rich and poor. It was only last year that the Chinese government officially released its Gini Coefficient figures retrospectively for the past decade. With perfect inequality at 1, China comes in at 0.474 (*The Economist*, 2013). While this is a small improvement over previous years, China still has a very wide income gap.

All of this threatens both the political and economy stability of China itself and, because of its role in the global economy, how the Chinese leadership deals with these problems has effects far beyond its shores.

The core question of this book is, therefore, what are the changes taking place in China's economy today and what are the impacts of these changes in China and abroad? The central theme is that China is facing massive challenges resulting in large part from its rapid economic growth, and is taking steps to rebalance its economy and society. In order for China to achieve sustained economic growth and social improvement (not to mention political stability), it must undertake serious policy changes. But this will not be an easy task given the array of competing forces within the existing political and economic structures of China today.

This book takes a political economy perspective. There is a close interplay between the political system in China and the way in which the economy is structured, and the manner in which economic changes take place. Given that while the economy is, for the most part, a capitalist one, the leadership must also deal with the fact that it is an authoritarian government that allows restricted choices in the way in which it manages economic and social policies.

At the same time Chinese leaders are aware that they are, so to speak, hanging on to the tiger's tail. They are attempting to control something that is not completely under control. They must deal with a population that is increasingly globalized and aware of the political, social and economic policies and developments in other countries. The growth in the use of the internet and associated social media means there are alternative means of communication within China, even while the government seeks to limit the capacity of the population to organize itself into pressure groups.

The book begins with one of the most critical aspects of China's changing economy, namely the shifts produced by rising labour costs. Michael Schiavone delves into this issue, pointing out that there are advantages and disadvantages to this inevitable shift as China's economy grows and develops. On the one hand, its status as the 'world's factory' is under threat with increasing wages, where foreign investment looks for better returns elsewhere. On the other hand, with increasing wages the Chinese economy can move away from an export-oriented model of development and shift increasingly to a domestic demand-driven one. Chinese companies can also use their industrial expertise and strong currency to invest in other countries, thereby bringing both financial and political benefits for China. In any event, given that China accounts for nearly one-quarter of the world's economic growth, these shifts will have impacts far beyond China's borders.

Linked to China's labour costs, Helen McLaren investigates China's reliance on rural–urban migration for its economic growth. This has provided a much-needed source of low-cost labour for the factories in the eastern parts of China. Within Australia a less substantial though still important development over the past 15 years has been the movement of workers to the booming mines in outback Australia. McLaren offers new insights into this geographic labour mobility, comparing Australia and China. In particular, she looks at how the trade in minerals has led to migration (either circulation or permanent) within Australia from the cities to the rural mine sites, and compares this with China's rural–urban migration experience. McLaren looks at the different economic systems in China and Australia and the way in which both of them deal with workers having to move to find employment and how this affects the families left behind. She argues that the benefits of economic development in both countries are unevenly distributed, and that the human costs of development have yet to be thoroughly researched. It is within this context that labour migration takes place.

One of the many sources of this labour is the Xinjiang Uyghur Autonomous Region, in the far west of China; while a recipient of substantial funds for regional development, it has recently been a hotbed of political unrest. Gerry Groot focuses on the social and economic problems of this region, arguing that its development by the central government has not had the intended consequences. Instead, there are severe inequities, widespread discontent and political instability.

Following the theme of regional development, Jiajun Liu uses a spatial analysis approach to investigate the way in which industry has restructured in China in order to create greater regional energy efficiencies. He notes that the role of energy is critical in production costs, and indeed is related to China's domestic economy more generally, the profitability of its external trade and also, of course, to the environment. He uses a mathematical model to examine industrial energy use in China's 31 provinces. His findings are interesting, with industrial restructuring along the east coast of China not bringing significant improvements in energy efficiency. But, in the north-west and south-west of China, where industrial development took place later, there have been improvements in energy efficiency. Furthermore, the central and north-eastern areas of China have a low level of industrial structure and energy efficiency, in part because of their historical role as providers of raw materials. As with the east-coast cities, as well as Beijing, they must have industrial restructuring as a goal to improve their use of energy.

Along with issues of labour in China, and the efficient use of energy and industrial restructuring, one of the most visible issues within China's economy today is the role of the banking sector. China's growth rate in general, as well as sub-issues of efficiency of production, the role of SOEs, the cost of creating industries and inflation in housing prices, among others, are linked to the banking system in China, whether in formal terms or informally via the shadow banking system. In this respect the spotlight has been on China's banking sector for some time. Especially since China joined the WTO and foreign banks have been allowed to progressively compete in the domestic Chinese market, there has been a focus in the literature on the sustainability of Chinese banks. Kai Du examines 145 commercial banks in China from 2000 to 2009 and asks the question 'did the efficiency of the banks in the Chinese banking sector increase after WTO accession?'. The short answer is yes, though the results are complex, with city banks being outperformed by state-owned banks, though the former are rapidly improving in terms of efficiency.

Also within the ambit of the financial system is the chapter by Zhiqiang Xia, Noel Lindsay, Pi-Shen Seet and Steve Goodman on the way in which venture capital operates in China. They argue that this sector is becoming increasingly important in China as it is expanding in line with an increasingly complex capitalist economy. Based on a survey of 50 senior venture capitalists operating in China, they find that decision-making differs from that in other countries. In particular, the standard factors of an entrepreneur's track record, competition in the marketplace and proprietary protection are not considered to be as important as they are in other countries. Instead, there are uniquely Chinese norms, customs and traditions that are taken into account when making decisions about the provision of venture capital. These include, among other factors, an entrepreneur's social networks, integrity and customer focus. Hence there are particular cultural characteristics that must be taken into account when one is attempting to understand the role of venture capital in China's economic system.

Continuing the theme of availability of finance for Chinese enterprises, Pi-Shen Seet, Christopher Graves and Wee-Liang Tan have written a chapter on the use of private equity by inter-generational family businesses. They use data from Singaporean cases and apply the findings to China and Australia. They note that entrepreneurial family businesses have been a fundamental part of the development of many Asian economies, but that the generation that built these businesses are experiencing succession difficulties. Their chapter sets out alternatives for these small business owners in the form of private equity firms, and argue that, although there are some real advantages to be had here, current business owners are not well prepared to deal with private equity companies. In this respect their chapter sets out some valuable findings that connect with the larger themes of the book, namely economic restructuring in China within the context of an ageing population.

Moving from issues within the economic system in China, the book turns to some of the more critical social problems in China today though, of course, these are inherently linked to China's economy. In this respect there is no greater issue today than the destruction of China's environment as a result of its dramatic economic growth. It is well known that air pollution in many of the larger and medium-sized cities is a major problem. Moreover, there is an increasing cost to environmental destruction. Han Lin and Jeffery Gil quote a report by the Chinese Academy of Environmental Planning that gives a figure of nearly US$200 billion annually as the cost of the country's environmental destruction. Lin and Gil take an alternative perspective on ways to deal with China's environmental disaster – that is, they argue that Confucian principles can provide a framework for dealing with this problem. Given that Confucian principles originated in China, they stand a greater chance of broad acceptance in the country. Moreover, this philosophical tradition holds some key values, including broad-based (environmental) education, moderation in development and a careful and steady investigation of complex problems so as to produce valid solutions.

Han Lin adds a chapter that looks at a specific framework for dealing with China's pollution problems, namely the Clean Development Mechanism (CDM), a flexible market mechanism set out under the Kyoto Protocol. She argues that this is a way in which developing economies can raise awareness of environmental issues and promote renewable energy. As a market mechanism, the CDM was slow to take off in China, but as the European Union raised its allowance of carbon trading credits, the CDM became very popular. Initially China invested heavily in industrial gas projects as they are responsible for a large proportion of greenhouse gases. This did not, however, solve the problem of China's dependency on fossil fuels. But, a second goal of the CDM is to raise public awareness of environmental issues, and this has had an impact in China. Finally, the CDM promotes renewable energy and this has been the area of most impact, (nearly three-quarters of all Chinese CDM are related to renewable energy). In short, market mechanisms have driven the development of the CDM and this has made a real impact in helping to resolve China's environmental problems.

A final chapter in the environmental section deals with the way in which environmental reporting in China as well as the influence of stakeholders has helped to change corporate practices in China. Hui Situ, Carol Tilt and Pi-Shen Seet examine the environmental reporting of 50 Chinese firms listed on the Shanghai Stock Exchange, and argue that because the state in China is relatively powerful and environmental awareness is relatively low, government directives can force Chinese corporations to quickly change their environmental practices. However, the other side to this argument is that corporate environmental reporting (CER) can also become unreliable in the face of this pressure. Moreover, where the usual pattern in the West is for stake/shareholders to have a substantial influence in CER, the strong state in China can move authority away from these groups.

Along with the environment as a broad social (and economic) problem, and inherently connected with it, is the education of Chinese. Education is clearly a topic that relates to others in this book, whether it is educating people on the impacts of pollution or developing their skills for an increasingly advanced economy. It is also one of the problems facing China in terms of its income gap, with rural incomes being much lower than those in rural areas. In this respect R. John Halsey's chapter examines rural education in China and Australia, and finds distinct commonalities, key among which is the exodus of rural youth to the urban centres and the impact of this on rural communities. It is clear that China is not alone in its challenges to address the problems of rural communities.

While education is one of the core social issues facing the Chinese government and people today, another is housing. The Chinese government has been struggling with this issue for some years, attempting to control bubbles in the real-estate market while concurrently using a free market approach to housing costs. The result has been substantial social unrest among those finding themselves priced out of the housing market, and this has been a real concern for the government. Po-shan Yu, Lei Xu and Mervyn Lewis take on these issues in their chapter on housing in Beijing and the government's role in attempting to deal with problems in this sector. They find that there is friction between sub-national governments that are overly dependent on the sale of local land the central government that is attempting to limit the rise in the cost of housing. It is a telling story of the difficulties in governing China during a time of rapid change, the self-interest of capitalism and the problem of the wealth gap in China.

The final part of the book moves to an examination of China's place in the international scene – that is, it focuses on issues pertaining to trade and the complexities that surround China's international trade and its impacts domestically and internationally.

Lei Feng looks at the broad picture of China's trade within the context of how the country is transforming its development mode.

> In the new mode China should be positioned to be a trading power, seek the equilibrium of imports and exports, pay attention to the balanced development of the effective utilization of resources and environmental protection and keep a balance between scale, structure and benefit.

He argues that there are two basic requirements in this regard. First, China must reduce its dependency on exports and instead focus on improving the quality of the domestic economy. Second, rather than relying on cheap labour and low-cost resources, it should boost its offshore FDI and increase its imports of goods, thereby using the resources and labour of other countries. In this respect he argues that China will have more of a win–win situation with its trading partners. This new development mode will also reduce China's environmental problems and more evenly distribute the benefits of China's growth.

Jing Tang follows Lei's chapter with a focus on China's outward foreign direct investment (OFDI). He looks at China's trade in services and three industrial sectors to determine the effect of OFDI on the performance of domestic Chinese industry. Using time series data from 2003 to 2011, he applies grey relational analysis (GRA), a technique used where the available information is relatively incomplete and uncertain. His findings indicate that OFDI in the services sector has had the greatest impact on the quality of industry in China. By investing abroad Chinese can learn state-of-the-art practices in the use of advanced technology, and the design, marketing and sales of domestic products. Gradually, then, Chinese industries can enhance their competitiveness in the export of higher value-added products as well as services.

Lei Feng concludes the book with a thematic review of the chapters. He points out that China has had a rather different development path from other countries and that comparisons must be done carefully. He adds the important point that, as China's economy has been changing, so too have China's social, political and cultural landscapes been shifting. Hence one must study China within an ever-changing context.

This book therefore covers a range of the most pertinent issues facing China and Australia–China relations today. The problems facing China are many, and they are complex, with changes in one sector affecting others. There are vested interests that inhibit change or promote change in one direction, while others are opposed. There are political issues to be resolved at every step, and the interests of the many different regions of China, and different economic sectors, must be balanced while at the same time maintaining political and economic stability. Given China's interdependency with the global economy, many of these issues are affected by forces outside of the government's control. It is a challenging time, therefore, for China in both domestic and international terms. What is clear is that if countries are going to deal with China in a stable and productive manner, a thorough understanding of key contemporary developments in that country is vital.

References

China Daily. 'Top 10 trading partners of the Chinese mainland'. 19 February 2014. [www.chinadaily.com.cn/bizchina/2014-02/19/content_17290565.htm].

The Economist. 'Gini out of the bottle'. 26 January 2013. [www.economist.com/news/china/21570749-gini-out-bottle#sthash.gjTFoHeN.dpbs].

Haltmaier, Jane. 'Challenges for the future of Chinese economic growth', Board of Governors of the Federal Reserve System, International Finance Discussion Papers, Number 1072, January 2013. [www.federalreserve.gov/pubs/ifdp/2013/1072/ifdp1072.pdf].

Hughes, Neil. 'A trade war with China?'. *Foreign Affairs*, July/August 2005.

Lubin, Gus. '17 facts about China's economy that will blow your mind'. *Financial Post*, 22 December 2010. [www.financialpost.com/related/topics/facts+about+China+economy+that+will+blow+your+mind/4015130/story.html].

OECD, Country statistical profile: China, 2013. [www.oecd-ilibrary.org/economics/country-statistical-profile-china_csp-chn-table-en].

Roberts, Dexter. 'China's dodgy data is under scrutiny again, with latest GDP release', *Bloomberg Business Week*, 24 January 2014. [www.businessweek.com/articles/2014-01-24/chinas-dodgy-data-under-scrutiny-again-with-latest-gdp-release].

Shah, Anup. 'World military spending', *Global Issues*, 30 June 2013. [www.globalissues.org/article/75/world-military-spending#WorldMilitarySpending].

World Bank. World DataBank, 2013. [http://databank.worldbank.org/data/views/reports/tableview.aspx].

World Bank. 'Employment in agriculture (% of total employment)', 2014 [http://data.worldbank.org/indicator/SL.AGR.EMPL.ZS].

Yan, Sophia. 'China's 7.7% GDP growth beats official target', *CNNMoney*, 20 January 2014. [http://money.cnn.com/2014/01/19/news/economy/china-gdp/].

Zhou, Guan Qi and Curtis Andressen. 'Education and change in China today', in *Sustainable Development in China*, edited by Curtis Andressen, A.R Mubarak and Wang Xiaoyi, New York, Routledge, 2013.

2 Rising labour costs in China

A problem or an opportunity?

Michael Schiavone[1]

After decades of very high growth, the Chinese economy has begun to cool off at such a rate that it has an increasing number of economists and political pundits concerned. Of course, it must be remembered that the economy is still growing at over 7 per cent per year; a rate that many governments around the world would be ecstatic over. One reason suggested for the decline in the growth rate is a reduction in exports due to the fragile global economy. As many economies are suffering, this has resulted in companies cutting back on costs. However, at the same time that many companies are cutting back on costs, labour costs in China are rising at a substantial pace. This has led to a fear that many companies will begin to move out of the country and China will no longer be the 'world's factory'. Of course, for overseas governments the fear is that if China's economy slows even further this will have a major negative impact on their own country's economies. The might of the Chinese economy is demonstrated through the following statistic: almost 23 per cent of the world's economic growth for the period 2000–2013 was due to China. In contrast, the US was responsible for approximately 12 per cent (Angang, 2015). There is such a fear of rising labour costs that it is almost impossible to see an article, blog, news report, etc. on China without it mentioning the increased costs to do business.

This chapter will look at the labour costs in the country and determine whether this is necessarily a bad thing. It will also provide an overview of the response to increased labour costs by both Chinese companies and the government. I will conclude that contrary to prevailing wisdom, rising labour costs has the potential to benefit the country as a whole; as such it should be welcomed.

Labour costs in China

For decades it was accepted as fact that it was cheaper for companies to manufacture goods in countries such as China rather than in developed countries like the US, the UK and Australia. However, due to rising labour costs in China, among other factors, such prevailing wisdom is no longer necessarily true. It must be remembered, though, that the spectre of rising labour costs in China has been 'haunting' manufacturers for a few years. In 2012 *The Economist* ran an article entitled 'The end of cheap China'. The article (2012) notes that

'It's not cheap like it used to be', laments Dale Weathington of Kolcraft, an American firm that uses contract manufacturers to make prams in southern China. Labour costs have surged by 20% a year for the past four years, he grumbles. China's coastal provinces are losing their power to suck workers out of the hinterland. These migrant workers often go home during the Chinese New Year break. In previous years 95% of Mr Weathington's staff returned. This year only 85% did.

The article goes on to state that

When the American Chamber of Commerce in Shanghai asked its members recently about their biggest challenges, 91% mentioned 'rising costs'. Corruption and piracy were far behind. Labour costs (including benefits) for blue-collar workers in Guangdong rose by 12% a year, in dollar terms, from 2002 to 2009; in Shanghai, 14% a year. Roland Berger, a consultancy, reckons the comparable figure was only 8% in the Philippines and 1% in Mexico.

Citing a member from the European Chamber of Commerce, *The Economist* claimed that by 2015 due to rising labour and shipping costs, as well as currency fluctuations, it would be just as expensive to produce goods in China as it would be in the US.

The prediction has almost borne fruit. Wages have risen to such a level that it is almost as cost effective to manufacture in the US as it is in China. Harold L. Sirkin (2014), a professor at Northwestern University's Kellogg School of Management, argues that as

Chinese labor costs rise, American productivity improves, and U.S. energy expenses fall, the difference in manufacturing costs between China and the U.S. has narrowed to such a degree that it's almost negligible. For every dollar required to manufacture in the U.S., it now costs 96¢ to manufacture in China, before considering the cost of transportation to the U.S. and other factors. For many companies, that's hardly worth it when product quality, intellectual property rights, and long-distance supply chain issues are added to the equation.

Moreover, a large number of companies are failing to understand that the globalized marketplace has resulted in many countries that were once low-cost havens now being anything but, while countries that were once not competitive now are. Sirkin states that

Many companies continue to make manufacturing investment decisions based on conditions a decade or more ago. They still see North America as high cost and Latin America, eastern Europe, and Asia, especially China, as low cost. The new data show there's a competitive marketplace of manufacturing opportunities today, with high-cost and low-cost countries virtually everywhere.

Indeed, if one includes wage levels with employer social insurance contributions, for Asian countries (outside of Japan and Singapore) only Malaysia has higher labour costs than China (106 per cent of the Chinese level). In contrast, Thailand (95 per cent of the Chinese level), Philippines (49 per cent), Vietnam, (47 per cent), Indonesia (36 per cent) and India (22 per cent) have lower overall labour costs than China. Quite simply, it is indeed cheaper to manufacture in many other Asian countries rather than China. It must be remembered, though, that if the Chinese government wanted to contain labour costs it could. While the government does not want labour costs spiralling out of control, it wants higher wages for Chinese workers – especially those workers on the bottom rung of society. It is these workers that are usually employed in manufacturing plants. Reflecting the government's plan, for the first six months of 2014 the minimum wage increased by an average of 11 per cent in Beijing, Chongqing, Gansu, Guangdong, Qinghai, Shaanxi, Shandong, Shanxi, Shanghai, Tianjin and Yunnan. However, rising wages have seen companies lay-off staff in an attempt to remain profitable. A recent CMA survey of 274 firms found that rising labour costs were impacting 95 per cent of them. As a result, the 'average staff size of the companies polled had gone down to 599 in 2014 from 703 in the previous year, while the labor shortage rate had risen from 10 percent to 13.6 percent'. Likewise, an American Chamber of Commerce survey found that 15 per cent of its members planned to move production and/or investments out of China due to high labour costs (Devonshire-Ellis *et al.*, 2014; Li, 2015; *Shanghai Daily*, 2015a).

Despite the 'doom and gloom', Chinese exports have remained relatively stable and in some months have been increasing. In January 2014 the Chinese trade surplus was US$259.75 billion; a 12.8 per cent increase compared to the previous year and the highest level since 2008 and the Global Financial Crisis. One reason why exports have remained relatively strong is that productivity, while declining, is still reasonably robust. For the period 2001–2008, productivity increased by an average of 11.8 per cent per year; the average increase was 8.8 per cent for the period 2008–2012, and 7.4 per cent for 2011–2012 (the latest statistics available). While there is concern that productivity is declining, the simple fact is that the double-figure growth was not sustainable. Moreover, the current level of productivity combined with manufacturing overcapacity due to increased domestic investment means that Chinese exports are still cost-effective even with increased labour costs. The *New York Times* notes that the 'average prices for American imports from China have actually dropped 0.9 percent in the last year even as the renminbi has risen and Chinese wages have soared' (Bradsher, 2014; Yongding, 2015).

However, Chinese exports for March 2015 saw a decline by 14.6 per cent compared to the previous year and a massive decline from the 48.3 per cent increase for February. A *Reuters* survey of 90 small and medium enterprises found that only 3.1 per cent of the firms expected an increase in sales in 2015, with 24 per cent expecting that it will take six months or more for exports to rebound, and 33 per cent expecting the rebound to take over a year. Moreover,

40 per cent of respondents 'were pessimistic about their factory's prospects, while 59 percent were neutral'. While the decline may be an aberration due to the much larger than expected increase in February, the later than usual Spring Festival holiday (it fell on 19 February and it is common for businesses to be closed for upwards of two weeks; a Chinese spokesperson claimed that if the holiday fell on 31 January as it did in 2014 the decline would have only been 4.8 per cent) or a symptom of a slowing economy (in which rising labour costs are playing a role), is uncertain (*CNBC*, 2015; Pomfret, 2015).

What is undoubtedly true is that the Chinese economy is slowing, but it must be remembered that its previous growth is without peer. Writing in *Foreign Affairs* Hu Angang (2015) states that

> As a latecomer to the modern economy, China has followed what one could call a 'catch-up growth' model, which involves rapid economic growth following years of lagging behind. From 1870 to 1913, for example, the U.S. economy followed precisely this path, growing at an average rate of four percent. Between 1928 and 1939, Russia's GDP grew at an average rate of 4.6 percent. And from 1950 to 1973, Japan's economy grew at an average rate of 9.3 percent. Yet none of those countries came close to matching China's record from 1978 to 2011: an average GDP growth rate of nearly ten percent over 33 years.

Hu goes on to claim that if the Chinese economy grew by 10 per cent for 2014 this would have resulted in its economy increasing in size by US$1 trillion; a figure larger than the economy of Saudi Arabia. In other words, such growth was not sustainable forever. Nevertheless, what is certain is that the Chinese government and business have been preparing for a slowing economy and increased labour costs for a number of years

Overcoming rising labour costs?

One way to deal with increased labour costs is to follow the same path that almost all, if not all, developed countries have done to deal with the issue – namely, outsource. While often associated with globalization, outsourcing has existed in some form since before 1945. For example, throughout the early twentieth century large American companies often had fully owned subsidiaries make non-essential components for its products. Outsourcing was not part of business lexicon, it was simply known as organizational decentralization. The crucial aspect of the early stages of outsourcing was non-essential functions being contracted out, and usually to subsidiaries. However, the functions being outsourced gradually expanded to include essential functions being contracted out to independent businesses; this is especially true in manufacturing.

The origins of outsourcing began in the 1950s. Rather than concentrate on one thing, businesses began to diversify. Such a strategy initially was done 'in-house'. However, beginning in the 1970s and with the onset of globalization, companies began to find it difficult to be the best at everything. This led them to focus on their strengths while embracing the idea that non-essential functions could be farmed out. As a result of the new business mentality and globalization there was a dramatic increase in outsourcing during the 1980s and 1990s, with non-essential and essential aspects being contracted out. For example, half of all American firms not outsourcing in 1987 were doing so by 1991, while only 58 per cent of firms were outsourcing in 1992, 86 per cent were doing so by 1995 (Griffiths and Schiavone, 2007; Hoplin and Hsieh, 1993; Schiavone, 2006).

Of course, it is not just companies in developed countries that outsource; there is an increasing trend for companies in developing countries to do so. Initially, countries such as Japan and South Korea were favoured destinations of Western companies to outsource to. However, as these countries gained economic power and wages rose, Western companies moved production facilities to other peripheral countries. What also happened was, as local companies expanded, they also outsourced. This happened in Japan and South Korea. The same has also been occurring with China.

As I have noted, since the opening of its economy, China has been the preferred outsourcing destination of Western companies. However, with increasing wages and the Chinese government less willing to provide tax breaks for foreign investors, there has been a move away from China. This is to be expected and one that the Chinese government, for better or for worse, is not overly concerned with. Indeed the government has been encouraging Chinese companies to follow the same path as developed-country companies, and therefore outsource. While some may believe that Chinese companies outsourcing is a recent development, it has been occurring for at least a decade. They are outsourcing to such countries as Vietnam due to rising wages at home; the average wage in Vietnam is only one-third of the average wage in China. Chinese foreign direct investment (FDI) in Vietnam has seen a steady growth. It increased from US$66 million in 2005 to US$312 million in 2006. Since then the level of FDI has increased even more dramatically. In 2013, the combination of 89 new projects and 11 existing ones saw Chinese investment in Vietnam increase to more than US$2.3 billion (*China Daily*, 2014). An example of such investment is the Huafu Company's decision to 'invest US$136 million in a textile and dying plant. This project is expected to break ground … [this year]. The plant will occupy 20 hectares and manufacture 300,000 tons of fiber and dye 20,000 tons of cotton annually' (*Vietnam Briefing*, 2014). In the past, the company would have been looking to mainland China to open such a plant. However, it now makes greater economic sense to locate the plant in Vietnam due to cheaper labour costs, tax breaks for foreign companies, as well as being able to access the US market tariff-free.

In addition to Vietnam, Chinese companies are looking to outsource to countries such as India due to substantially cheaper labour costs (as noted above, total labour costs in India are only 22 per cent of the Chinese level). However, this is not a new development. Since 2000 Chinese companies have invested approximately US$410 million in India. While this is obviously a small level of investment, the Chinese government and companies have begun to view India as a source of cheap labour. In June 2014, the Chinese and Indian governments signed an agreement that will result in China establishing industrial parks in India. In September 2014 it was announced that the first two will be set up in Maharashtra and Gujarat, with the total investment being approximately US$6.8 billion; a figure that dwarfs the previous level of investment by the Chinese. As part of the investment, a number of goods that India used to import from China will now be produced at the industrial parks (*Hindustan Times*, 2014; Rapoza, 2014).

Africa is also on the radar for Chinese companies as an outsourcing destination. China–Africa trade was worth US$210 billion in 2013, with over 2,500 Chinese companies having a foothold in the continent. Since 2009, Chinese FDI to Africa has increased by approximately 20 per cent per year and is now worth US$2.52 billion. The Chinese government plans for itself and Chinese companies to invest more than US$1 trillion in the continent within the next decade. As part of the increasing investment in Africa, there is a China–Africa development fund in which China 'agreed to invest $2.385bn in 61 projects in 30 African countries' (*Al-jazeera*, 2014). While the Chinese government is largely focused on securing natural resources from African countries in return for building infrastructure across the continent, Chinese companies are using the burgeoning ties to outsource to Africa. An article in *Bloomberg* notes that 'China's average manufacturing wage is 3,469 yuan ($560) per month.' In contrast, wages at a Chinese shoe factory in Ethiopia 'ranges from the basic after-tax minimum of $30 a month to about twice that for supervisors. By contrast, average manufacturing wages in South Africa, Africa's biggest manufacturer, are about $1,200.' The article goes on to state that the shoe factory's '3,500 workers in Ethiopia produced two million pairs of shoes last year'. Located in one of the country's first government-supported industrial zones, the factory began operating in January 2012, only three months after the factory owner decided to invest there. Also, the factory 'became profitable in its first year and now earns $100,000 to $200,000' (*Al-jazeera*, 2014; *Bloomberg*, 2014; Johnston, 2015).

It is interesting to note that unlike governments in developed countries that discourage outsourcing, at least publicly due to job losses, the Chinese government wants firms to set up subsidiaries abroad. In late December 2014 the

> ruling State Council announced that China will further promote 'going global' by Chinese firms, including with financial assistance. As described by the State Council, the goals are two-fold. First, China is keen to see its flagship firms become internationally competitive.... Second, bankrolling such overseas expansions is a signal that China wants better returns – in the form of profit and political influence – on its considerable foreign exchange reserves.
>
> (Minter, 2014)

In other words, the Chinese government sees outsourcing as part of a 'soft power' strategy. It is willing to undertake such an approach even though outsourcing will lead to job losses on the mainland.

Another strategy Chinese companies and local governments have begun to follow to overcome rising labour costs is to invest a substantially greater amount in robotics. In Shenzhen, one of the manufacturing hotspots in China, and also the city with the highest minimum wage in the country, the local government has a 500 million yuan (US$81 million) fund to help companies invest in robotics. Likewise, in March 2015 the Guangdong government announced the formation of a 943 billion yuan (US$151.7 billion), three-year plan for local companies to invest in robotics and newer, more advanced machinery. The Dongguan city government has a 600 million yuan ($96.5 million), three-year fund to help local companies install robots in their factories and a 4.2 billion yuan ($675.5 million) robot replacement programme that will result in the loss of approximately 30,000 jobs. A reduction in jobs is one way to deal with higher labour costs. In addition to wanting Chinese manufacturers to increasingly use robotics and automation, Christina Larson (2014), writing in *Technology Review*, argues that the government wants manufacturers to move towards high-tech goods. She writes that the

> Chinese government has pushed manufacturers to adapt, focusing government investment on advanced industries and boosting R&D spending on science and technology. According to data from the U.S. National Science Foundation, between 2003 and 2012 Chinese exports of high-tech products climbed from just over $150 billion to more than $600 billion, making China the largest exporter of such products in the world. Ernst & Young forecasts that by 2022, the country will produce a third of the world's electrical goods.
>
> (Larson, 2014; see also *Shanghai Daily* 2015b, p.A6;
> *Want China Times*, 2015).

The increasing use of robotics in the manufacturing sector should boost productivity and help overcome increased labour costs. This is especially true considering that while China is the largest producer of robots, the country lags well behind in the number of robots per worker. In South Korea there are 396 robots per 10,000 workers in the manufacturing sector; in Japan there are 332; in Germany 273; in the US the number is 141; and the global average is 58 robots for every 10,000 manufacturing workers. In contrast, in China there are only 23 robots for every 10,000 manufacturing workers. As such, even a small commitment to increase the number of robots in factories will see increased productivity. Of course, in China things are very rarely done on a small scale. In addition to the hundreds of millions of dollars earmarked by local Chinese governments to increased automation in factories, companies are already or planning to make the switch to robots. For example, the Foxconn Technology Group, which produces goods for Apple and Samsung, among others, plans to invest heavily in machines; so much so that in three years the company wants 70 per cent of assembly-line work to be done by robots. The company, which employs over one million people in its Chinese factories, has been adding approximately

30,000 industrial robots per year over the last few years (Kan, 2015; *Wall Street Journal*, 2014). As wages increase, it is to be expected that more companies will follow suit.

A shift in priorities

While companies are increasingly outsourcing to deal with high labour costs, the government wants the Chinese economy to move away from export-led growth to one where domestic consumption drives the nation forward. It has come to the conclusion that an export-focused strategy is not feasible in the long term and is reliant on the strength of other countries' economies. Instead, the Chinese government believes the best approach to sustain economic growth, which will preserve its power and help its citizens, is one that looks inwards.

Chinese citizens' income is at its highest point in history; 'disposable income of urban residents … [increased by] 9.7 per cent last year [2013], or 7 per cent when factoring in inflation. Rural residents' net income rose 9.3 per cent when adjusted for inflation' (Wassener, 2014). Urban disposable income increased by a further 9 per cent or an inflation-adjusted 6.8 per cent in 2014. At this stage, domestic demand is only slowly increasing, in large part due to the Chinese mentality of saving for their child and or health-related crises, and property being the favoured form of investment. Indeed, with slowing growth there has been a decline in the growth of retail sales – a key performance indicator when analysing domestic demand. For the period 2010–2014, retail sales increased by an average of 14.32 per cent; for the first three months of 2015 retail sales have increased 10.2 per cent compared to the corresponding period in 2014. In other words, while still growing, demand is not increasing to such an extent as in previous years. Likewise, car sales only increased by 3.7 per cent in April 2015 compared to the previous April. In contrast, car sales rose by double digits throughout 2014 and by over 9 per cent in March 2015. However, in a positive for Chinese automakers, their market share increased to 41.1 per cent in April 2015; a 3.8 per cent increase compared to the previous April (Murphy, 2015; *Salt Lake Tribune*, 2015; *Trading Economics*, 2015a, 2015b; Wassener, 2014; Yini, 2015).

While Chinese people like to spend, and 10 per cent increase in retail sales is still relatively impressive, they also worry about their and their child's future. Changing this mentality to increase domestic demand will be challenging for the government. However, this shift in priorities is beginning to bear fruit. This is illustrated by the type of FDI coming into the county. The United Nations Conference on Trade and Development found that inbound FDI to China in 2014 was largely linked to the service sector. In contrast, FDI earmarked for manufacturing declined, with a sharper than average decline of FDI in industries vulnerable to higher wages. According to official statistics from China's Ministry of Commerce, the trend is gathering steam:

> FDI inflows to China's service sector grew 30 percent year on year in the first two months of this year and their share in the total FDI inflows reached

61 percent. On the contrary, the FDI inflows to China's manufacturing sector grew at a smaller pace of 7.1 percent and only accounted for 33.3 percent of the total FDI inflows to China.

(Shanghai Daily, 2015a)

In contrast, the service sector only accounted for 24 per cent of FDI in 2001. Moreover, domestic consumption accounted for 51.6 per cent of GDP for the January 2015 quarter – an increase of 3.4 per cent compared to 2014. Such a trend should continue as companies that are only searching for a cheap workforce redirect investment and manufacturing to low-wage countries like Vietnam, India and Ethiopia. In the end, though, there is unlikely to be a large-scale abandonment of China as a manufacturing hub due to the simple reason that the size of the country's population and the might of the Chinese economy means that companies will always want a presence in the country. Companies pulling all manufacturing out of the country, at this stage, would not be viewed in a positive light by the Chinese government and the Chinese people (Jennings, 2015; *Shanghai Daily*, 2015a).

The future beckons

As this chapter has demonstrated, wage costs are indeed on the rise in China. While for manufacturers looking for cheap labour this is a bad thing, for the rest of the country increased labour costs will be a benefit in the long run. The only way that labour costs could remain low is if the government artificially limited wages. However, one of the priorities of the Chinese government, along with maintaining reasonable economic growth and reducing pollution, is to lessen inequality in the country. Such a thing would not be possible if wages did not rise substantially. Rising wages in China have seen it overtaken by many countries as a source of cheap labour. This has led to an increasing number of Chinese companies outsourcing, a practice that is supported by the government. Quite simply, the Chinese government does not want the country to be seen as a cheap source of labour. In addition, there is a push to modernize Chinese factories through the increased use of automation and robotics. Considering that the current use of robots is quite low compared to the worldwide average, any push to increase their use should benefit manufacturers and the country as a whole.

Of course, with a shift in priorities there are challenges ahead. Increasingly focusing on domestic demand as the driver of economic growth requires changing the Chinese mentality of 'saving for a rainy day'. Despite increasing consumption, Chinese people generally want to save for retirement, for any health crises and especially for their child (and with a relaxing of the one-child policy, children). Moreover, if they do spend, they view property as a safe purchase. The potential for a housing bubble bursting is always there. Nonetheless, as the government correctly realized, China could not be the world's factory forever. And while cheap labour played a part in the current might of the Chinese economy, it could not take the economy to the next level. In the end, just like every developed country before it, rising labour costs in China were inevitable. For China as a whole, that is not a negative, but a positive.

Note

1 For Su Lan and Valentina.

References

Al-jazeera (2014) 'Is China–Africa cooperation a win–win situation?', 25 September, www.aljazeera.com/indepth/opinion/2014/09/china-africa-cooperation-win-w-2014924202811161705.html.

Angang, H. (2015) 'Embracing China's "new normal"', *Foreign Affairs*, May/June, www.foreignaffairs.com/articles/china/2015-04-20/embracing-chinas-new-normal.

Bloomberg (2014) 'Ethiopia becomes China's China in search for cheap labor', July 22, www.bloomberg.com/news/articles/2014-07-22/ethiopia-becomes-china-s-china-in-search-for-cheap-labor.

Bradsher, K. (2014) 'Even as wages rise, China exports grow', *New York Times*, 9 January, www.nytimes.com/2014/01/10/business/international/chinese-exports-withstand-rising-labor-costs.html?_r=1.

China Daily (2014) 'More Chinese investment boosts China–Vietnam trade ties', 16 January, www.chinadaily.com.cn/business/2014-01/16/content_17240039.htm.

CNBC (2015) 'China's trade figures disappoint ahead of GDP', 12 April, www.cnbc.com/id/102575436.

Devonshire-Ellis, C., Zito, M., Ku, E. and Shira, D. (2014) 'China's rising manufacturing costs: challenges and opportunities', *China Briefing*, 8 July, www.china-briefing.com/news/2014/07/08/chinas-rising-manufacturing-costs-challenges-opportunities.html.

The Economist (2012) 'The end of cheap China', 10 March 10, www.economist.com/node/21549956.

Griffiths, M. and Schiavone, M. (2007) 'Anti-Americanism and anti-globalisation', in O'Connor, B. (ed.), *The History of Anti-Americanism*, Oxford: Greenwood, pp. 19–36.

Hindustan Times (2014) 'China to set up industrial parks in Maharashtra and Gujarat', 17 September, www.hindustantimes.com/asiantigersmeet/china-to-set-up-industrial-parks-in-maharashtra-and-gujarat/article1-1265189.aspx.

Hoplin, H.P. and Hsieh, G.S. (1993) 'Outsourcing/rightsizing for the 1990s'. *Industrial Management + Data Systems*, 93(1), 18–24.

Jennings, R. (2015) 'China's economy is surging 7% but everyone thinks that's too slow', *The Street*, 17 April, www.thestreet.com/story/13116211/1/chinas-economy-is-surging-7-but-everyone-thinks-thats-too-slow.html.

Johnston, L. (2015) 'China's road to growth in Africa', *China Spectator*, 9 February, www.businessspectator.com.au/article/2015/2/9/china/chinas-road-growth-africa.

Kan, M. (2015) 'Apple supplier Foxconn expects robots to take over more factory work', *Computerworld*, 27 February, www.computerworld.com/article/2889287/apple-supplier-foxconn-expects-robots-to-take-over-more-factory-work.html.

Larson, C. (2014) 'The new Chinese factory', *Technology Review*, 16 September, www.technologyreview.com/news/530706/the-new-chinese-factory.

Li, S. (2015) 'HK manufacturers in Guangdong struggle with rising costs of labor', *China Post*, 30 March, www.chinapost.com.tw/china/local-news/hong-kong/2015/03/30/432359/HK-manufacturers.htm.

Minter, A. (2014) 'Say goodbye to "made in China"', *Bloomberg*, 29 December, www.bloombergview.com/articles/2014-12-29/welcome-to-the-era-of-chinese-outsourcing.

Murphy, C. (2015) 'GM embraces retail sales reporting in China', *Wall Street Journal*, 11 May, www.wsj.com/articles/china-car-sales-slowest-since-february-2013-1431337048.

Pomfret, J. (2015) 'China exporters expect more pain as economy sputters: survey', *Reuters*, 16 April, http://uk.reuters.com/article/2015/04/16/us-china-exports-.

Rapoza, K. (2014) 'India: China's new low-cost labor hub?', 8 September, www.forbes.com/sites/kenrapoza/2014/09/08/india-chinas-new-low-cost-labor-hub.

Salt Lake Tribune (2015) 'China auto sales growth decelerates in April', 11 May, www.sltrib.com/home/2499100-155/china-auto-sales-growth-decelerates-in.

Schiavone, M. (2006) 'Social movement unionism and the UE', *Flinders Journal of History and Politics*, 23, 57–82.

Shanghai Daily (2015a) 'Shift in foreign investment in China in line with rebalancing efforts', 4 April, www.shanghaidaily.com/article/article_xinhua.aspx?id=275908.

Shanghai Daily (2015b) 'Factories turn to robots amid labor woes', 14 May.

Sirkin, H.L. (2014) 'China vs. the U.S.: it's just as cheap to make goods in the USA', *Bloomberg*, 25 April, www.bloomberg.com/bw/articles/2014-04-25/china-vs-dot-the-u-dot-s-dot-its-just-as-cheap-to-make-goods-in-the-u-dot-s-dot-a.

Trading Economics (2015a) 'China disposable income per capita 1978–2015', www.tradingeconomics.com/china/disposable-personal-income.

Trading Economics (2015b) 'China retail sales YoY 2010–2015', www.tradingeconomics.com/china/retail-sales-annual.

Vietnam Briefing (2014), 'China and Hong Kong increase investment in Vietnam', June 16, www.vietnam-briefing.com/news/china-hong-kong-increase-investment-vietnam.html.

Wall Street Journal (2014) 'As labor costs rise, China turns more to robot workers', 25 August, http://blogs.wsj.com/chinarealtime/2014/08/25/as-labor-costs-rise-china-turns-more-to-robot-workers.

Want China Times (2015) 'Robots offer answer to China's manufacturing challenges', 14 April, www.wantchinatimes.com/news-subclass-cnt.aspx?id=20150414000023&cid=.

Wassener, B. (2014) 'For China, a shift from exports to consumption', *New York Times*, 20 January, www.nytimes.com/2014/01/21/business/international/for-china-a-shift-from-exports-to-consumption.html?_r=1.

Yini, H. (2015) 'Shanghai tops China's disposable income list, gap remains', *China Daily*, 27 February, http://usa.chinadaily.com.cn/business/2015-02/27/content_19670216.htm.

Yongding, Y. (2015) 'An opportunity for China', *Japan Times*, 12 April, www.japantimes.co.jp/opinion/2015/04/12/commentary/world-commentary/opportunity-china/#.VUB8DZNYQUM.

3 Geographic labour mobility, workers and family in China and Australia

Helen Jaqueline McLaren

Mining and resource exports from Australia to China have increased significantly over the last decade. By 2012–2013 approximately 28 per cent (AUS$84 billion) of Australian exports went to China (DFAT, 2013), making this Australia's largest export market. With Australia's emphasis on mining commodities and resource-based industries, rather than manufacturing, China also became Australia's largest import source of manufactured merchandise. In fact, more than 14 per cent (AUS$46 billion) of all of Australia's imports in 2012–2013 were from China (DFAT, 2013). This change in which China has become Australia's largest bilateral trade partner has had a profound effect on each nation's politics, culture and family life as a result of their increasingly inter-related economies.

Over the last couple of decades Australia's economic growth has been dependent on its mining commodities and resource-based industries, and the supporting services where these activities mostly take place. On the other hand, China's manufacturing power has facilitated its rapid rise to becoming a middle-income nation. With most industry and trade activities geographically located from Central to East China, the benefits of economic development for China's western provinces have not been so forthcoming (Batisse, 2005). The cultural contexts and the geographical landscape of the two nations may differ, but rapid growth has placed enormous demands on the human labour necessary for sustaining productivity and sustainable growth in each nation.

Australia's mining commodities and resource-based industries are mostly located in rural and remote localities that are poorly populated, while manufacturing industry and trade activities in China are unequally distributed within provinces and across the country as a whole (Batisse, 2005). In each case, the population spread, labour demand and distribution of economic activity means that each nation shares the unique challenge of managing large populations that are mobile within their own nations in response to opportunities for earning a living. Of particular interest to this chapter are the issues and responses towards the families left behind in their communities of origin by workers responding to increasing labour demands and associated geographic labour mobility.[1]

While social, environmental and economic implications for the host communities of mass-geographic labour mobility has received considerable attention in research and literature, comparatively less is known about the impact of labour mobility on the families and communities that internal labour migrants and fly-in fly-out (FIFO) workers leave behind; they are often viewed as passive recipients of geographic labour mobility. Less is known about families and host communities as it relates to the Australian context. With particular focus on the families left behind, it is proposed that better understanding of the contexts, issues and responses towards these people may contribute to ensuring more equal access in both nations to the broader benefits of the China–Australia economic and trade relationship.

Following an overview of historical, socio-political and economic contexts as stimulus for geographic labour mobility in China and Australia, a range of issues and concerns for the families left behind are briefly explored. In drawing together dialogue on the social, political and corporate responses towards the families of internal labour migrants and FIFO workers, it may be possible to think of new strategies to contribute to the sustainability of China's and Australia's interrelated economies and future development with a focus on family.

Contexts for geographic labour mobility in China

Rising populations, increased production of goods and services and human consumption are regarded as the major causes of environmental degradation and resource depletion. With fears that population growth in China could reach the carrying capacity of the nation's resources, the one-child-per-couple policy[2] was introduced in 1978 as a measure to prevent overpopulation. This policy is often cited as the main causes of reduction in national fertility rates from 2.91 births per woman in 1978 to 1.6 in 2010 (Hesketh *et al.*, 2005; World Bank, 2013b). Growth as a percentage of population has slowed to an average of approximately 0.5 per cent per year over the last decade (World Bank, 2013a). However, this still represents a population increase of more than six million people each year.

In the same year that the one-child-per-couple policy was introduced, China implemented market-oriented reforms in which economic growth was a priority. Increases in gross domestic product (GDP) was experienced at an average of 10 per cent per year (World Bank, 2013a; Zhang, 2012). Industrial advances have influenced China's demand for natural mineral resources. China accounted for 4 per cent of the world's GDP in 2003, yet its consumption of natural resources exceeded that of all other nations: crude oil consumption was 31 per cent of the world's total; ironstone 30 per cent; steel 27 per cent; alumina 25 per cent; and cement 40 per cent (Wen, Z. and Chen, 2008). Some authors suggest that depletion of natural mineral reserves has given rise to increasing importation of natural resources (Beresford *et al.*, 2011; Schandl and West, 2012). Alternatively, Chinese scholars (Fan *et al.*, 2012; Yuxiang and Chen, 2011) suggest a reluctance of government and foreign investors to develop mining commodities and natural resources industries in provinces in China with resource abundance due to these regions performing poorly in terms of economic and financial development – this is consistent with Auty's (1993) resource curse thesis.[3] Whatever the reasons,

China's rapid industrial growth and demand for natural resources has seen its share of ore and metal imports from Australia more than quadruple since the year 2000 (from 13.3 per cent to 55.1 per cent) (Huang and Wang, 2011).

China's solid waste per unit of industrial output is ten times higher than that of developed nations (Wen, Z. and Chen, 2008). Industrial pollution has impacted on China's groundwater and waterways and human subsistence, which has implicated food security for China's people – more so for those of rural *hukou*[4] who rely on water, air and land for their subsistence agriculture (An *et al.*, 2006; Brown and Halweil, 1998; Vennemo *et al.*, 2009). The impact of population growth, increasing affluence and human consumption, as well as the lag in technological advancements to counter rising industrial pollution, has undoubtedly affected China's environment.[5] With sustainability in question, population controls have aimed to contribute to offsetting environmental degradation and improving human existence, but the extent to which strategies such as the one-child-per-couple policy have helped to equitably improve life remains debatable.

Until the introduction of market-oriented reforms in 1978, China was constituted as two segregated economies. The *hukou* system designated around 80 per cent of the population to rural *hukou*, where they worked in agricultural communes and provided food for the remaining population (Meng, 2012). With the central government being motivated by industry, economic growth and national capital accumulation, non-rural residents were assigned to life-long employment in their designated urban *hukou*. Keeping the majority of the population in rural *hukou* was aimed at supporting urban populations which were deemed more important for industrial development. Food was increasingly imported due to degradation of agricultural land, rising consumption and China's constant food crises (Qiang *et al.*, 2013; Zhu, 2012).

While the vast majority of China's population was involved in labour-intensive, low-productivity agriculture, the introduction of market-oriented reforms prompted higher agricultural productivity and underemployment of rural labour. To manage these populations, China shifted people of rural *hukou* over the first two decades of economic reform to village industries and special economic zones that were in demand of unskilled labour (Zhang, 2012). In urban *hukou*, rising unemployment in the 1980s prompted the Chinese government to encourage self-employment for the first time, and in the 1990s small state-owned enterprises which had been failing due to low productivity were given to the private sector (Mohapatra *et al.*, 2007). There was limited geographic labour mobility for the first two decades outside of the government's controlled movements of people, but once China joined the World Trade Organization in the late 1990s its private enterprise and export-led growth accelerated internal labour migration (Meng, 2012). Migration restrictions were relaxed and unskilled labourers in rural *hukou* have accordingly responded to the rising labour demands of China's growing industrial sector and potential opportunities for private enterprise in urban and other locations experiencing economic growth. As well, agricultural failure, lack of industry in some regions and rural poverty further fuelled labour migration for people seeking to alleviate poverty and achieve prosperity (Hu *et al.*, 2008).

The one-child-per-family policy, while aimed to limit the impact of population growth on food security and the environment, had unintended consequences. These include 'skewed sex ratios' and 'an aging society', with large variations between rural and urban populations (Meng, 2012: 93). China has an increasing population aged 65 and older and a decreasing youth population (World Bank, 2013a). The *hukou* system, which generally restricted individuals to receiving education, health and welfare in their designated regions, means that many rural-to-urban labour migrants who are the 'one-child' are compelled to leave their parents and children behind (Hu *et al.*, 2008). These internal labour migrants represent China's 'highly mobile population of 140 million rural-to-urban migrants' (10 per cent of the total population) (Hu *et al.*, 2008: 1718). It is most often women (the grandmothers) and children from rural and marginalized urban regions that are left behind (Toyota *et al.*, 2007; Wen, M. and Lin, 2012), but the feminization of labour migration across Asia means that numbers of female labour migrants are increasing too.

Urban areas have increasingly become host to populations of middle-aged internal labour migrants that it cannot sustain. Hu *et al.* (2008) reported that rural regions are represented by ageing populations with diminished capacity and declining health. This presents implications for individuals and rural communities to manage agriculture or business, their own health and that of the children left in their care.

Economic influences on geographic labour mobility in Australia

The quadrupling of China's share of ore and metal imports from Australia over the last decade is reflected in the growth of Australia's mining commodities and resource-based industries. In the past, large mining corporations responded to the labour demands of industry growth by building whole townships or at least additional family housing in established communities nearby resource regions. In the last two to three decades few purpose-built townships have been constructed. The dominant model of employment is to use non-resident labourers, rather than relocating workers and their families closer to their place of work (Tonts and Plummer, 2012).

Known as FIFO working arrangements, employees are commuted to work for a fixed number of days on site, followed by a fixed number of rest days back home. This, arguably, allows workers to maintain their family home where they are already established and want to live. FIFO employees typically work 12 hours per day by a roster rotation of 28 days on the mines and seven days off (Parliament of Australia, 2013). The services supporting mining and resource-based operations such as service, hospitality, health and welfare workers often work by drive-in–drive-out (DIDO); they have shorter numbers of days in their shift rotations and receive comparatively less pay.

There are a number of reasons for a growing numbers of FIFO workers in Australia, which has direct and indirect associations with the China–Australia trade relationship and their interrelated economies. The rate of growth of China's demand for mining commodities and natural resources has meant that Australian corporations have been unable to build housing, infrastructure, essential and social services at equivalent rates to industry growth (McKenzie, 2010, 2011). Building and construction costs are generally high in Australia; more so in rural and remote locations where most mining and resource-based operations take place. Relative shortages of skilled local labour, the lack of services to support the development of mining towns and time required to seek building and construction approvals means that using FIFO workers is often unavoidable (Ennis *et al.*, 2013; McKenzie, 2010, 2011; Storey, 2001).

Corporations in the mining commodities and natural resources industry have simply learned that employing FIFO workers is cheaper (Peetz and Murray, 2008). Employment and business strategies aim to operate in rural and remote locations at minimum cost, thus reducing investment in housing and infrastructure that could otherwise translate into regional liveability for workers and their families (Bryant and King, 2007; Cheshire *et al.*, 2011; Windle and Rolfe, 2012). Instead, many employers accommodate their FIFO workforce in low-cost transportable housing and high-density shared accommodation (Peetz and Murray, 2008). For nearby towns that source service, hospitality, community and welfare workers, increased populations create demands for housing. Higher demands translate into housing unaffordability and higher cost of living.

In January 2014, Australia's resident population was little more than 23.3 million (ABS, 2014). When compared to China, the world's most populous country, skilled and unskilled labour for mining commodities and resource-based industries are not in ample supply. There are simply not enough people and, for that reason, high wages and other enticements are usually offered to encourage mining and resource-based industry workers to leave their families behind and enter into FIFO work. While obvious benefits for workers are financial and being able to maintain their existing family home, Bryant and King (2007) found that FIFO arrangements presented a number of difficulties for workers and employers. Many workers experienced difficulty with living apart from their families and this impacted negatively on worker wellbeing and employee retention. In comparison, when families re-settled in mining communities, the mine workers were less likely to leave their employment (Bryant and King, 2007). The sheer quantity of labour required to meet the rising demands of Australia's mining commodities and resource-based industries, the lack of housing and housing unaffordability, means that FIFO families are most often denied the option of living together.

Australian families left behind

In May 2000 there were approximately 74,800 people employed in the Australian mining industry (ABS, 2013). From 2000 to 2012 growth has resulted in almost a tripling of mining industry workers to 276,300 (ABS, 2013). The Australian census data, however, do not include FIFO data. Nor do they provide statistics for mine-site workers providing maintenance and services to mining employees: health and welfare, transport, accommodation, catering, cleaning, security, etc. Therefore, the overall quantity of people employed directly and indirectly in the mining commodities and resource-based industries as FIFO workers or otherwise, and the services supporting them, is not easily ascertainable from existing data. It is not known how many FIFO workers have families, partners and/or children, but demands for family housing suggest that many do. A review of housing rental and sale websites in Australia shows marketing to FIFO families of housing located near the airports servicing FIFO operations. Also, anecdotal evidence from welfare organizations indicate that over the last decade enclaves of FIFO families have developed nearby these airports and some concern for social, health and welfare are noted as specific to these families.

The impact of FIFO work on those employed by mining commodities and resource-based industries in Australia has been of growing interest to researchers and others. While the obvious financial benefits exists from high earnings, McKenzie (2010) studied the FIFO workforce in Western Australia and argued that more money does not necessarily equate with better lifestyles because some people manage their money better than others. While impacting variably on each worker, many Australian studies identify concerns for workers and their families when FIFO workers spending their earnings on drugs, alcohol, gambling and sex workers to alleviate the disruption to normal lifestyle patterns, loneliness, homesickness, depression and feelings of missing out on normal family and social life (Carrington *et al.*, 2011, 2013; Carrington and Pereira, 2011; Kinnear *et al.*, 2013; Watts, 2004). Research reports that growing sex worker industries operating around mining townships, which is not unique to Australia, have brought with them higher rates of sexually transmitted disease (Kwan *et al.*, 2012; Scott, 2013). These researchers argue that the provision of family housing nearby the place of employment rather than FIFO operations can significantly reduce disease transmission to the mine workers' partners.

FIFO employees work long hours for long roster blocks and many do not develop meaningful relationships with their host communities (Carrington *et al.*, 2011). At the same time, spending comparatively little time at home means that FIFO workers are disengaged for long periods from family and social life in their source community. Some researchers express difficulty for FIFO workers adjusting to constant family change (Murray and Peetz, 2007), but more recent Australian literature suggests families have more difficulty adjusting to recurring cycles of partings, reunification and negative emotional engagement than the workers themselves (Taylor and Simmonds, 2009; Voysey, 2012). This may be because negative psycho-emotional responses to FIFO lifestyle patterns spill over from work to family, which impacts on workers' levels of positive emotional engagement with their partners and children (MacBeth *et al.*, 2012). Taylor and Simmonds (2009) examined family issues relevant to FIFO lifestyles and found that families who were better prepared with understanding of the potential impact of FIFO work on their relationships had superior coping mechanisms. When FIFO causes tensions for workers and families, this affects employee retention rates (Bryant and King, 2007), which provides logical reason for focused attention on supporting FIFO workers and their families.

A number of strategies have been implemented by corporations employing FIFO workers in Australia to increase employee retention rates. These include 'family-friendly' incentives such as roster flexibility around family needs, counselling services for employees and family members, family medical benefits insurance and travel subsidies for family to visit FIFO workers – some mining and resource-based corporations offer school holiday or university vacation work for FIFO workers' children (Bryant and King, 2007; Jefferson and Preston, 2008; Shah *et al.*, 2005). However, Voysey (2012) surveyed a sample of 254 FIFO workers and 314 partners of FIFO workers in Western Australia and found that more than half of FIFO workers' partners did not know about employee assistance schemes, nor other supports available to them. Some partners read information from websites about FIFO lifestyles, engaged their own formal supports or sought the informal support of family and friends. The study concluded that the partners of FIFO workers who received any form of support were less likely to perceive ongoing lifestyle and relationship stress. Together with findings from Taylor and Simmonds (2009) it is understood that families cope better with FIFO lifestyles when they have knowledge, understanding and support.

However, corporate and government interests invested in the China–Australia economic and trade relationship have come to realize that regional liveability is important to encourage workers and their families to move to rural locations. Keeping families together and supporting them translates into worker wellbeing and thus staff retention. Where rural living keeps the families together and this has shown to reduce the health implications for workers and their families in mining commodities and resource-based industries, assisting the families of those who choose to engage in FIFO work has obvious economic benefits for both mining commodities and natural resources industries and government.

Despite increasingly interrelated economies, China and Australia have vastly different economic ideologies which inform responses towards workers, families and communities affected by the changing economies variably in each nation. Australia's economy is profit motivated and represented by an individualistic capitalist system where everyone is primarily responsible for the self (Ralston *et al.*, 1997). Becoming popular in the 1960s, and with the spread of global norms, notions of corporate social responsibility became incorporated into the business models of Australian mining commodities and natural resources corporations (Cheshire *et al.*, 2011; Morrison *et al.*, 2012). The business ethic carried with it a belief that corporations needed to take responsibility for their actions on the environment, consumers, employees, their families and communities and all others in the public sphere that may be considered stakeholders. However, the allure of an ethical corporate identity calls into question the authenticity of corporate responsibility of those who are in aggressive pursuit of profit. Where

Australian corporations may variably weigh up opportunity costs of supporting or otherwise 'giving back' to their stakeholders, Baker and Roberts (2011) suggested that being viewed as responsible is often confused with actual responsibility. Corporate responses of Australian FIFO employers in the mining commodities and natural resources industry towards host communities, employees and their families (e.g. investment in host community infrastructure, employee assistance schemes, family medical benefits insurance, etc.) may be more about fulfilling legal requirements and reducing risk associated with negative publicity than ethically responsible acts.

China's economic ideology and the families left behind

In contrast to Australia's capitalist ideology, China's economic system is founded on collectivist views of socialism in which all of the nation's people should be viewed as equally responsible for the wellbeing of the nation, society and their communities. This notion of an equitable society purports that the nation's people should share equally in its rewards (Ralston *et al.*, 1997), which socialist systems aim to achieve through redistributive systems. By operating as two segregated economies (e.g. rural and urban *hukou*) the socialist system had unintended consequences because it created a privileging of one economy over the other, as well as hierarchies that benefited 'redistributors' over 'direct producers' (Szelenyi and Kostello, 1996). Market-oriented reforms of 1978 gave producers more power, opportunity and incentive, and when followed by the relaxing of China's internal migration restrictions this meant that farmers and peasants could venture further geographically to sell produce and seek employment, and for entrepreneurship. China's authorities came to understand that a socialist market economy had the potential to narrow social equity disparities and, according to Tuñón (2006), China actively encouraged internal labour migration as one migrant had the potential to lift whole families out of poverty, develop entrepreneurial skills and bring these back to improve local economies.

However, there have been debates about the cost–benefit balance of internal labour migration. As mentioned earlier, it often deprives rural families of their most productive workers and leaves millions of children in rural areas without one or both of their parents. Particularly for children left behind in China, it is widely reported that the emotional and psychological implications can compounded labour migration hardship, when daily life is upturned and whole household routines require reorganization (Biao, 2007; Gao *et al.*, 2010; Lee, 2011). Although remittances are sent home, which serves to fund education and health care, monies are frequently consumed rather than invested in economic development. Many migrants who return to their *hukou* are largely those who 'failed' and who lack skills for business or entrepreneurship (Tuñón, 2006; Wang and Fan, 2006); alcoholism among these parents has been noted as a concern (Lee, 2011). What all this means is that the families of labour migrants may not necessarily be better off.

More recent strategies in China have focused on encouraging internal labour migrants, mostly of rural origin, to return to their *hukou* to work and care for their families. In recognition that labour migrants do not always return to their rural *hukou* with entrepreneurial and other skills, strategies have been implemented that include village-based development projects and initiatives aimed at redressing economic inequality in China's Central and Western regions (Lai, 2007). While relatively little has been published in the English language on the aims of China's central and provincial governments to equalize rural and urban opportunities for work and prosperity, it is projected that motivations for rural to urban labour mobility will decrease. Strengthening of family and community, and having parents at home with their children, offers obvious benefits.

Conclusion

The China–Australia economic relationship that has become increasingly intertwined though bilateral trade arrangements, development and growth is one that is producing huge benefits for safeguarding both nations' future prosperity. However, in both nations the benefits of development are unevenly spread. In China, the urban areas have benefited from the financial joys of economic development more than have the rural areas. For Australia's mining and natural resource industries, while operations take place in rural and remote localities, equitable economic advantage is not experienced by the communities that play host to these operations. There remain many issues that receive far too little attention as it relates to both economic distribution and human costs associated with development in both nations. Some of the social impact for internal labour migrants in China and FIFO workers in Australia, and their families, have been briefly mentioned here – the brevity is a reflection of the far too little attention to the broader implications for workers, families and their host communities arising from the demands for labour in times of booming development.

Although very different contexts exist, institutional constraints in both China and Australia present obstacles for geographically mobile labourers to bringing their families with them. Some of the many costs of development and the response of geographically mobile labour is the rise in social harms for host and source communities, and implications for workers' families. These are seriously under-researched issues and, despite there being a growing interest in families left behind in China and rural development, there is a comparative paucity of empirical understanding of FIFO families left behind in Australia. Research variably debates the implications for Australian FIFO families, but there seems to be a consistency of thought that these families perceive informal supports as the best support. Anecdotal evidence suggests families have made appropriate informal support possible through co-locating housing and by developing their own geographical communities around the airports servicing FIFO workers. However, had there been greater government and corporate social responsibility aimed to support FIFO families left behind, then their perceptions of the appropriateness of formal supports may be different.

All literature suggests that when labourers and families live together they do better – socially, psychologically and in terms of other health outcomes. It is also known that when FIFO and other geographically mobile workers, and their families, receive appropriate supports, this increases staff retention and improves economic outcomes. Government and corporations, therefore, would benefit from policy and development activities that have a greater focus on the families and host communities of geographically mobile labour migrants. At the very least, families need to be provided with knowledge of the impact they are likely to experience as families left behind and the range of supports available to them.

Notes

1 For the purposes of this chapter, 'geographic labour mobility' includes geographical movements of people away from families and communities and within their own nation to undertake or search for work. This includes short- and longer-term internal labour migration in China and commute work in Australia (e.g. where employers fly-in–fly-out (FIFO) and drive-in–drive-out (DIDO) their employees).
2 China's one-child-per-couple policy applies to mainland China. It has restricted, until recently, urban couples to only one child per couple, while rural couples may have additional children (e.g. if the first born is female, couples who do not have siblings themselves and some ethnic minorities) (Hesketh *et al.*, 2005). Recent changes allow a second child per couple where at least one parent has no siblings.
3 The 'resource curse thesis' suggests that countries rich in mineral and other natural resources are unable to use that wealth to develop their economies, and that they experienced lower economic growth than countries with few mineral and other natural resources.
4 The household registration system in China, known as *hukou*, has historically enabled the government to control geographical labour movement within China by restricting entitlement to employment, health, schooling and other social supports to the regions in which individuals' households were registered, or where individuals were designated to live and work by the government. Special mechanisms to change *hukou* status are outside the scope of this chapter.
5 $I=PAT$ equation: Impact (I) of human activity on the environment equals the product of Population (P), Affluence (A) and Technology (T) (Commoner, 1972; Ehrlich and Holdren, 1971).

References

ABS. 2013, 'Australian social trends: towns of the mining boom', www.abs.gov.au.
ABS. 2014, 'Population clock', www.abs.gov.au/ausstats.
An, S., Wang, Z., Zhou, C., Guan, B., Deng, Z., Zhi, Y., Liu, Y., Xu, C., Fang, S. and Xu, Z. 2006, 'The headwater loss of the western plateau exacerbates China's long thirst', *AMBIO: A Journal of the Human Environment*, vol. 35, no. 5, pp. 271–272.
Auty, R.M. 1993, *Sustaining Development in Mineral Economies: The Resource Curse Thesis*, Routledge, London.
Baker, M. and Roberts, J. 2011, 'All in the mind? Ethical identity and the allure of corporate responsibility', *Journal of Business Ethics*, vol. 101, no. 1, pp. 5–15.
Batisse, C. 2005, 'The location of manufacturing industry and spacial imbalance', *China Perspectives*, vol. 60, http://chinaperspectives.revues.org/502.

Beresford, A., Pettit, S. and Liu, Y. 2011, 'Multimodal supply chains: iron ore from Australia to China', *Supply Chain Management: An International Journal*, vol. 16, no. 1, pp. 32–42.

Biao, X 2007, 'How far are the left-behind left behind? A preliminary study in rural China', *Population, Space and Place*, vol. 13, no. 3, pp. 179–191.

Brown, L.R. and Halweil, B. 1998, 'China's water shortage could shake world food security', *World Watch*, vol. 11, no. 4, pp. 10–21.

Bryant, L. and King, P. 2007. *Recruiting and Retaining Workers in Rural Australia: Case Studies of Mining and Food and Beverage Processing Industries*, Barton and Kingston, Australia: Rural Industries Research and Development Corporation.

Carrington, K. and Pereira, M. 2011, 'Assessing the social impacts of the resources boom on rural communities', *Rural Society*, vol. 21, no. 1, pp. 2–20.

Carrington, K., Hogg, R. and McIntosh, A. 2011, 'The resource boom's underbelly: criminological impacts of mining development', *Australian & New Zealand Journal of Criminology*, vol. 44, no. 3, pp. 335–354.

Carrington, K., McIntosh, A., Hogg, R. and Scott, J. 2013, 'Rural masculinities and the internalisation of violence in agricultural communities'. International Journal of Rural Criminology, vol. 2, no. 1, pp. 3–24.

Cheshire, L., Everingham, J.-A. and Pattenden, C. 2011, 'Examining corporate-sector involvement in the governance of selected mining-intensive regions in Australia', *Australian Geographer*, vol. 42, no. 2, pp. 123–138.

Commoner, B. 1972, 'The environmental costs of economic growth', in R. Dorfman and N.S. Dorfman (eds), *Economics of the Environment: Selected Readings*, Norton, New York, pp. 261–283.

DFAT. 2013, *Composition of Trade of Australia: 2012–2013*, Trade Analysis and Statistics Section, Department of Foreign Affairs & Trade (DFAT), Australian Government, Canberra.

Ehrlich, P.R. and Holdren, J.P. 1971, 'Impact of population growth', *Science*, vol. 171, no. 3977, pp. 1212–1217.

Ennis, G., Finlayson, M. and Speering, G. 2013, 'Expecting a boomtown? Exploring potential housing-related impacts of large scale resource developments in Darwin', *Human Geographies: Journal of Studies and Research in Human Geography*, vol. 7, no. 1, pp. 33–42.

Fan, R., Fang, Y. and Park, S.Y. 2012, 'Resource abundance and economic growth in China', *China Economic Review*, vol. 23, no. 3, pp. 704–719.

Gao, Y., Li, L.P., Kim, J.H., Congdon, N., Lau, J. and Griffiths, S. 2010, 'The impact of parental migration on health status and health behaviours among left behind adolescent school children in China', *BMC Public Health*, vol. 10, no. 1, p. 56.

Hesketh, T., Lu, L. and Xing, Z.W. 2005, 'The effect of China's one-child family policy after 25 years', *New England Journal of Medicine*, vol. 353, no. 11, pp. 1171–1176.

Hu, X., Cook, S. and Salazar, M. 2008, 'Internal migration and health in China', *The Lancet*, vol. 372, no. 9651, pp. 1717–1719.

Huang, Y. and Wang, B. 2011, 'From the Asian Miracle to an Asian century? Economic transformation in the 2000s and prospects for the 2010s'. In Hugo Gerard and Jonathan Kearns (eds), *The Australian Economy in the 2000s*, Reserve Bank of Australia, Sydney.

Jefferson, T. and Preston, A. 2008, 'Western Australia's boom economy: insights from three studies', *Journal of Australian Political Economy*, vol. 61, pp. 181–200.

Kinnear, S., Kabir, Z., Mann, J. and Bricknell, L. 2013, 'The need to measure and manage the cumulative impacts of resource development on public health: an Australian perspective'. www.intechopen.com/books/current-topics-in-public-health/the-need-to-measure-and-manage-the-cumulative-impacts-of-resource-development-on-public-health-an-au

Kwan, K.S., Giele, C.M., Greville, H.S., Reeve, C.A., Lyttle, P.H. and Mak, D.B. 2012, 'Syphilis epidemiology and public health interventions in Western Australia from 1991 to 2009', *Sexual Health*, vol. 9, no. 3, pp. 272–279.

Lai, H. 2007, 'Developing Central China: a new regional programme', *China: An International Journal*, vol. 5, no. 1, pp. 109–128.

Lee, M.-H. 2011, 'Migration and children's welfare in China: the schooling and health of children left behind', *The Journal of Developing Areas*, vol. 44, no. 2, pp. 165–182.

MacBeth, M.M., Kaczmarek, E. and Sibbel, A.M. 2012, 'Fathers, adolescent sons and the fly-in/fly-out lifestyle', *Australian Community Psychologist*, vol. 24, no. 2.

McKenzie, F.H. 2010, 'Fly-in fly-out: the challenges of transient populations in rural landscapes'. In Gary W. Luck, Digby Race and Rosemary Black (eds), *Demographic Change in Australia's Rural Landscapes*, Springer, New York, pp. 353–374.

McKenzie, F.H. 2011, 'Attracting and retaining skilled and professional staff in remote locations of Australia', *The Rangeland Journal*, vol. 33, no. 4, pp. 353–363.

Meng, X. 2012, 'Labor market outcomes and reforms in China', *Journal of Economic Perspectives*, vol. 26, no. 4, pp. 75–101.

Mohapatra, S., Rozelle, S. and Goodhue, R. 2007, 'The rise of self-employment in rural China: development or distress?', *World Development*, vol. 35, no. 1, pp. 163–181.

Morrison, T., Wilson, C. and Bell, M. 2012, 'The role of private corporations in regional planning and development: opportunities and challenges for the governance of housing and land use', *Journal of Rural Studies*. doi:10.1016/j.jrurstud.2012.09.001

Murray, G. and Peetz, D. 2007, 'Coal rushes: progress report on women miners, miner's women and their communities', in AIRAANZ, 21st Conference of the Association of Industrial Relations Academics of Australia and New Zealand, University of Auckland, New Zealand.

Parliament of Australia. 2013, 'Cancer of the bush or salvation for our cities? Fly-in, fly-out and drive-in, drive-out workforce practices in Regional Australia', www.aph.gov.au.

Peetz, D.R. and Murray, G. 2008, 'Black gold, white nights and big girls' toys', *Griffith Review*, vol. 22, pp. 213–226.

Qiang, W., Liu, A., Cheng, S., Kastner, T. and Xie, G. 2013, 'Agricultural trade and virtual land use: the case of China's crop trade', *Land Use Policy*, vol. 33, pp. 141–150.

Ralston, D.A., Holt, D.H., Terpstra, R.H. and Kai-Cheng, Y. 1997, 'The impact of natural culture and economic ideology on managerial work values: a study of the United States, Russia, Japan, and China', *Journal of International Business Studies*, vol. 28, no. 1, pp. 177–207.

RIRaD Corporation. 2007, 'Recruiting and retaining workers in rural Australia: case studies of mining and food and beverage processing industries', Australian Government.

Schandl, H. and West, J. 2012, 'Material flows and material productivity in China, Australia, and Japan', *Journal of Industrial Ecology*, vol. 16, no. 3, pp. 352–364.

Scott, J. 2013, 'Fly-in crime?', *Arena Magazine*, vol. 124, p. 44.

Shah, C., Cooney, R., Long, M. and Burke, G. 2005, 'Availability of skilled labour in selected occupations in Western Australia', Centre for the Economics of Education and Training, Monash University.

Storey, K. 2001, 'Fly-in/fly-out and fly-over: mining and regional development in Western Australia', *Australian Geographer*, vol. 32, no. 2, pp. 133–148.

Szelenyi, I. and Kostello, E. 1996, 'The market transition debate: toward a synthesis?', *American Journal of Sociology*, vol. 101, no. 4, pp. 1082–1096.

Taylor, J. and Simmonds, J 2009, 'Family stress and coping in the fly-in fly-out workforce', *Australian Community Psychologist*, vol. 21, no. 2.

Tonts, M. and Plummer, P. 2012, 'Natural resource exploitation and regional development: a view from the west', *Dialogue*, vol. 31, pp. 19–25.

Toyota, M., Yeoh, B.S. and Nguyen, L. 2007, 'Bringing the "left behind" back into view in Asia: a framework for understanding the "migration–left behind nexus"', *Population, Space and Place*, vol. 13, no. 3, pp. 157–161.

Tuñón, M. 2006, 'Internal labour migration in China: features and responses', Beijing, ILO.

Vennemo, H., Aunan, K., Lindhjem, H. and Seip, H.M. 2009, 'Environmental pollution in China: Status and trends', *Review of Environmental Economics and Policy*, vol. 3, no. 2, pp. 209–230.

Voysey, W. 2012, 'Satisfaction with a fly-in/fly-out (FIFO) lifestyle: Is it related to rosters, children and support resources utilised by Australian employees and partners and does it impact on relationship quality and stress?', Bachelor of Psychology (Hons) thesis, Murdoch University.

Wang, W.W. and Fan, C.C. 2006, 'Success or failure: selectivity and reasons of return migration in Sichuan and Anhui, China', *Environment and Planning A*, vol. 38, no. 5, pp. 939–958.

Watts, J. 2004, 'Best of both worlds: seeking a sustainable regional employment solution to fly in–fly out operations in the Pilbara', Pilbara Regional Council.

Wen, M. and Lin, D. 2012, 'Child development in rural China: children left behind by their migrant parents and children of nonmigrant families', *Child Development*, vol. 83, no. 1, pp. 120–136.

Wen, Z. and Chen, J. 2008, 'A cost–benefit analysis for the economic growth in China', *Ecological Economics*, vol. 65, no. 2, pp. 356–366.

Windle, J. and Rolfe, J. 2012, 'Using discrete choice experiments to assess the preferences of new mining workforce to commute or relocate to the Surat Basin in Australia', *Resources Policy*, vol. 38, no. 2, pp. 169–180.

World Bank. 2013a, 'China overview', www.worldbank.org/en/country/china/overview.

World Bank. 2013b, 'Development data', http://databank.worldbank.org/data/home.aspx.

Yuxiang, K. and Chen, Z. 2011, 'Resource abundance and financial development: evidence from China', *Resources Policy*, vol. 36, no. 1, pp. 72–79.

Zhang, J. 2012, 'Delivering environmentally sustainable economic growth: The case of China', Asia Society, University of California.

Zhu, X. 2012, 'Understanding China's growth: past, present, and future', *Journal of Economic Perspectives*, vol. 26, no. 4, pp. 103–124.

4 The contradictions of developmentalism and the Chinese Party-state's goal of ethnic harmony

The case of Xinjiang

Gerry Groot

Introduction

China's high rates of economic growth since the reform and opening up of the late 1970s are well known; to borrow from Churchill, never have so many become so much better off in such a short time. Yet rising affluence in and of itself doesn't guarantee happiness, and many Chinese are very unhappy. This discontent manifests in many ways, including China being the only country where female suicides outnumber those of males, where attacks against society often involve stabbing children, where doctors are often attacked at work and where mutual trust is often lacking. This declining subjective perception of well-being has been tracked by local researchers (Blumenthal, 2013) and the *United Nations Happiness Report* in which China ranked 93rd for happiness (Helliwell *et al.*, 2013). And if this is the case for the 91.5 per cent who make up the majority Han population, what, then, of the other 8.5 per cent classified as belonging to one of the 56 officially recognized minorities?

China's minority ethnic groups each have their own history and issues, but with a few exceptions they tend to live in rural and remote, often mountainous areas and their standards of living and incomes are general much lower than those of the Han. Only two groups are well known, the mostly Sunni Muslim Uyghurs of Xinjiang in the north-west and the Tibetans. The Uyghurs became part of the People's Republic of China with the Chinese Communist Party's (CCP) defeat of the Nationalist Guomindang in 1949, while Tibet was taken over by the CCP's People's Liberation Army in 1951. Since the 1950s, the Chinese Party-state has spent billions of renminbi (RMB) to develop Xinjiang and Tibet and to integrate the regions into a cohesive modern nation. A key assumption behind this considerable investment and effort was that in developing their economies, bringing modernity and raising living standards, not only would national goals be met, it would also be welcomed by the minorities themselves and hence promote their integration if not eventual assimilation.

The reality, though, has been much more complex. There have been numerous outbreaks of resistance to Chinese rule in both areas as the CCP sought to consolidate control over them. Perhaps most worrying for today's leaders is the spate of these incidents over the last half-decade. In March 2008 there was serious unrest in Tibet's capital, Lhasa, and in July 2009 a major outbreak of violence in Urumqi, the capital of Xinjiang, which escalated into inter-communal clashes in which almost 200 people, both Uyghur and Han, were reported killed. Since then, Tibetan areas of China have also seen a series of self-immolations by Tibetan monks and nuns, which totalled some 129 by early 2014 (RFA, 2014). Early 2014 also saw an attack on the Kunming Railway station in the southern province of Yunnan on 1 March. Eight black-clad men and women reported to be Uyghurs stabbed 29 people to death and injured many dozens more. The latter was particularly disturbing to many Chinese because it was the first time events in Xinjiang had resulted in the apparent targeting of Han Chinese outside the province, and to many it was as shocking as the events of 9/11 were to Americans. In some ways just as shocking was the bombing of Urumqi Railway station on 30 April 2014, in which three people died because it occurred just as Party Chairman Xi Jinping was concluding a special inspection tour of Xinjiang.

It was against this background of rising unrest that earlier in January Xi Jinping chaired a meeting on Xinjiang and announced a major shift in policy, from stressing economic development as the priority in solving its problems, to one that emphasized achieving stability. Xi's shift of emphasis implies that economic development has not addressed the underlying causes of ethnic unrest in either area and more surveillance and force are required instead.

Despite this reliance on coercion, there have been serious debates within China about the best ways to address the increasingly obvious problems of Han-minority relations in many parts of the country. Ethnicity and its related elements, such as religion and language, have been discussed in academic conferences, policy arenas and on public internet forums. Much of this discussion has revolved around the minority policies that treat minorities in a collective way, provide legal recognition as so-called autonomous areas for places where minorities historically dominate and promote preferential treatment in many areas, such as education and which are now increasingly seen by many Han analysts as part of the problem. The strongest voices against the status quo, people like Ma Rong, now assert that these policies have failed to bring minorities into the mainstream and the new emphasis should, for example, be on emphasizing the agency of individuals and boosting this agency by having them learn Mandarin and other skills so they are able to enjoy the benefits of progress. The current system, they believe, encourages a sort of identity politics which is against the national interest. The result is an increasing interest in more explicitly assimilationist policies (Leibold, 2013). Nevertheless, none of the new critics see anything wrong with the CCP's general push for economic development and seem to accept the need for harsh measures against any unrest that might threaten national stability.

Coercion, though, fails to address the underlying problems giving rise to the unrest. These are many and complex, and only need brief treatment here in order to provide the necessary context. Instead, this chapter focuses on the nature of the Party-state's top-down emphasis on promoting rapid economic development to the extent that it effectively became an ideology in itself, hence the notion of developmentalism and how this applies to Xinjiang. This sub-ism of the Communist Party policy stresses rapid economic growth as measured almost solely in terms of gross domestic product (GDP), material progress and the accumulation of state power, while hitherto lacking much concern for the many problems this approach has generated: pollution, environmental degradation, growing social inequality and the like, relegating most to externalities which can be solved later, when China is richer again. It also assumes that, some getting rich before others notwithstanding, almost everybody will ultimately be materially much better-off and be able to take pride and comfort in China having become a strong state. In both cases they will be much happier and better off financially and therefore more supportive of the Party-state which brought about this state of affairs. Behind this version of developmentalism is the tautology that a rich and powerful China will be able to solve all problems, while many problems will be solved merely by becoming rich and powerful.

To help it deal with ethnic minorities and other key groups outside of the CCP's once standard target groups of workers, peasants and soldiers, the Party has its own (non-government) United Front Work Department (*Tongyi Zhanxian Gongzuo Bu or* UFD). The UFD once worked to win over targeted groups to defeat common enemies like the Japanese or Guomindang, or to achieve mutual goals like the transition to socialism of 1949–1956. While the UFD became largely moribund during the last decade of former leader Mao Zedong, who once called it one of the Party's three great secret weapons, it was revived to assist the reform and opening of the Chinese economy after Mao's death in 1976. The UFD continues to liaise with and rally ethnic groups, religious believers, Overseas Chinese and others to achieve Party goals, particularly modernization and development. It is therefore of particular relevance to the happenings in Xinjiang, Tibet and Mongolia and is part of a complex and large bureaucratic mix which includes the State Ethnic Affairs Commission (*Guojia Minzu Shiwu Weiyuanhui* or SEAC), employing an estimated five million people nationwide. The heads of the SEAC, more importantly, usually have senior roles in UFD bodies and in the past many have been UFD heads. Despite the UFD's intimate connections with Uyghurs and Tibetans in particular, they have not been able to forestall the unrest already noted, and a key part of the reason is precisely because its priority is to achieve Party goals like rapid development rather than to advocate from within the Party to change such goals to better suit the interests of minorities.

This chapter examines why the billions of Renminbi invested in the rapid, largely state-driven economic development in Xinjiang have not had the social consequences assumed by the proponents of this developmentalism with Chinese characteristics. There is, though, an alternative form of developmentalism which more explicitly takes into account the interests and concerns of ordinary people rather than privileging state power. This form may be a more successful way for the CCP to achieve its other stated key goals of increased social harmony, prosperity and positive inter-ethnic relations, though its emphases mean that the state-centred nature of the present form is unattractive to Beijing. The nature and origins of this Party-state's developmentalism originate from its Marxist foundations, but the discussion of developmentalism is more recent.

What is developmentalism?

The term developmentalism is not usually associated with China as much as with Latin America, especially Brazil (Loris and Loris, 2013), and other areas of the 'global South', as post-1945 its leaders and intellectuals sought state-centred ways to 'catch up' with the developed West, often using the level of material and institutional development of their former colonial masters as a basis. Instead of being developed by the colonial powers, they would develop themselves using methods such as state mechanisms and policies like import substitution (Wallerstein, 2005).

However, as Wallerstein also pointed out, the Soviet Union called development socialism (Loris and Loris, 2013). When Mao Zedong and the leaders of the CCP promised 'New Democracy' and a long period of transition including the coexistence with capitalism, in order to build the material basis for socialism in 1949, they too were aiming for rapid state-directed industrialization and modernization, as well as eventually catching up with the colonialist and capitalist powers. Chinese socialism was another basic form of developmentalism in the sense that development and modernization were the key goals, but it differed from the post-war developmentalism of surrounding states like Japan and Korea because it was intended to bring about communism and the complete elimination of capitalism and classes, as Marxist teleology foretells.

Understandings of developmentalism are also closely associated with the idea of the developmental state advocated by Chalmers Johnson and reflected in the post-war success of Japan and the other Asian Tiger economies, all strong national governments invoking nationalist goals and using industrial policy to direct capital, capitalists and labour to achieve high growth rates. Their success, Chalmers Johnson showed, resulted from first having articulated a national essence. China had begun the transition from socialist development with its particular form of developmentalism to something akin to the Japanese model in the wake of the success of the post-Mao reforms, and by the 1990s Johnson saw the beginnings of the elements of a Chinese developmental state (Johnson 1999: 40).

Chinese developmentalism predates the emergence of the shoots of what might be a Chinese developmental state, but a brief examination of how it arises in capitalist states is instructive. The idea of the developmental state originated with Chalmers Johnson's 1982 examination of the contribution of the Ministry of International Trade and Industry (MITI) to Japan's successful industrialization and modernization between 1925 and 1975 (Johnson, 1982). The role of the subsequent developmental state and its industrial policy was summed up as 'The plan rational capitalist development' that linked private ownership with state guidance to achieve 'rapid and sustained industrial growth' (Johnson, 1999: 2).

According to Johnson, a state seeking to emulate or match Japan 'should first be a developmental state and only then a regulatory or welfare or equality or whatever sort of state. Such a state prioritises economic development while economic development comes to serve other goals' (Johnson, 1999: 37). One central aspect of such states generally overlooked is that of the legitimacy of the goal and of the state itself. For Johnson, such legitimacy comes from 'devotion to a widely believed in revolutionary project or overarching social projects their societies endorsed and they carried out' (Johnson, 1999: 52). In the case of the Asian Tigers rebuilding themselves in the wake of the Second World War and civil strife, it was the goal of development itself (Johnson, 1999). For the CCP, too, the war with Japan and later the civil war with the American-supported Guomindang were the formative experiences and Mao's 1949 declaration that China had stood up and defeated the forces of feudalism, imperialism and capitalism. That came to include catching up with both America and Japan and today Xi Jinping's 'China Dream' includes China's revival (*fuxing*) as a major world power, enforcing claims of national sovereignty and avenging past national humiliations (Xinhua, 2012). The stability and integration of China's western regions, particularly Xinjiang and Tibet, are crucial to this dream.

Developmentalism in China

The first 25 years of CCP rule were marked by an emphasis on development based on Marxist theory and the Soviet model as interpreted by the Party and particularly by Mao Zedong. It meant moving rapidly to transform a backward agricultural country into a strong, industrialized state. The first stage was the transition towards socialism, the control of capitalist elements and markets, and the building of cooperatives and state-owned enterprises, in that order. Socialism in the form of centralized planning guiding socially owned enterprises would eventually be replaced by communism and the complete elimination of classes. Each stage meanwhile would see enormous increases in productivity, standards of living and material development.

In practice, these steps involved the creation of entire new industries such as steel, petrochemicals, chemicals and other forms of heavy industry to create an enormous military–industrial complex crucial to defending the new autarkic Communist state at the onset of the Cold War and in the wake of China's involvement in the Korean War (1950–1953). It was paid for by exploiting the countryside. In Xinjiang this meant moves to turn the pastoralists into sedentary farmers, establish the Xinjiang Production Construction Military Corporation (*Xinjiang Shengchan Jianshe Bingtuan* or Bingtuan) to promote agriculture and encourage Han immigration as well as step-up resource extraction. Mao's Great Leap Forward (1958–1961), which demanded the rapid collectivization of agriculture and industry to maximize use of China's abundant labour and overcome educational and technological backwardness became intensely politicized, subject to unrealizable production targets and resulted in the deaths of many millions of peasants nationwide. Xinjiang was not exempt with the added complication of an influx of over a million Han youth from eastern provinces and a dramatic reduction in animal herd numbers (Starr, 2004: 93).

Growth subsequently recovered at the national level, but by the time of Mao's death in 1976 living standards had only begun to return to those of 1956, when Mao had arbitrarily declared that the basis for socialism had been laid. This poor outcome was mainly the result of population growth and the redirection of enormous amounts of capital into military defence capacity, notably Mao's Third Front initiative. Not only were the Party's promises of the material advantages of socialism undermined, China had also fallen behind neighbouring Asian Tiger economies which had rebuilt after the war, were industrializing, exporting to the world, and were developing more advanced technologies. The CCP's 'four modernizations' (agriculture, industry, national defence and science and technology) of 1963 (it lapsed with the onset of the Great Proletarian Cultural Revolution between 1966 and 1976) were therefore revived in 1978 at the same time as the policies of reform and opening up meant the relaxation of controls on markets and the selling of private labour, allowing in foreign investment, emphasizing exports and the acquisition of modern technology from abroad. These measures were justified by the claim that China was still in the 'initial stage of socialism', while it should also be remembered that they were still part of deliberate and comprehensive economic planning in the form of Five-Year Plans mapped out by the Party-state bureaucracy, not a plan for a transition to free market capitalism even if it sometimes seems that way at street level.

These reforms have been very successful in promoting economic growth and bringing about the desired modernizations, as well as dramatically improving living standards and raising hundreds of millions out of poverty. Growth rates have hovered at, around or just under 10 per cent per year for the last 30 years (Lin, 2013). The overall economy was already worth more than US$13.5 trillion in 2011 and, based on purchase parity pricing, is set to soon overtake that of the US (Forsythe and Gough, 2014).

The consequences of developmentalism with Chinese characteristics

As already noted, though, with this success has also come unhappiness, including significant demonstrations and protests throughout China. The number of mass incidents (involving more than 100 people) has increased annually, with 180,000 reported in 2010, after which the statistics became state secrets. In 2013 the official *Legal Daily* reported that based on publicly known cases, the causes of unrest were increasing, with the main ones being social disputes (24.2 per cent), forced demolitions of property 22.2 (per cent), conflict with officials (13.3 per cent), defence of environmental rights (8.9 per cent), and ethnic conflict (8.9 per cent). Those involved were residents of towns and cities (51.1 per cent), farmers and rural residents (46.7 per cent), migrants (17.8 per cent), students (11.1 per cent), minorities (4.4 per cent) and foreign nationals (2.2 per cent) (Barmé and Goldkorn, 2013). A 2014 report noted that since 2000 the main sparks have been labour disputes, land acquisitions, forced demolitions, pollution, traffic accidents and incidents involving ethnic groups. Some 79 people have died in 37 clashes. This report noted that such unrest was increasingly common in developed areas, notably Guangdong Province (Hou Liqiang, 2014) where much of the initial reform and opening up began.

At an individual level it is not clear that matters are much better. As Lemos has eloquently demonstrated in *The End of the China Dream*, despite appearances of rising prosperity, young men worry about being able to find a partner and then afford to marry her, parents fret about being able to pay for their child's education in a hypercompetitive environment, the elderly worry about being bankrupted by health care costs, while farmers worry about losing their land and hence any income and security, as well as their low social status (Lemos, 2012). In contrast to the Asian Tigers that saw declining inequality with development, China has seen a dramatic increase in inequality as a result of the reforms, which meant the Gini coefficient stood at 0.474 in 2012, although this was a decline compared to its peak of 0.491 in 2008 (Reuters, 2013). Evidence of unrest from Xinjiang suggests that unhappiness there is even more pronounced.

Xinjiang and China's developmentalism

When the CCP's People's Liberation Army entered Xinjiang in north-west China from the National Guomindang in late 1949, it took control of a sparsely populated desert and semi-desert area inhabited by mostly nomadic pastoralists of many ethnicities and religions, notably the Sunni Islamic Uyghurs. Other groups included Hui, Kazaks and Tajiks (all Islamic) while Han Chinese were a small minority of around 6 per cent (Howell and Fan, 2011: 123). Xinjiang was also a key area of strategic contestation between the great powers, while the Soviet Union had been very active in encouraging communist and nationalist movements and trading with local powers. For a brief period in 1933–1934, Xinjiang had also seen a self-declared Eastern Turkestan Republic, which though it quickly fizzled, is a key nationalistic symbol for many Uyghurs, then the largest dominant ethnic group, and which was later subject to the brutal oversight of warlord and Guomindang governor Sheng Shicai (Millward, 2007: 201)

Xinjiang posed major problems for the CCP as it sought to consolidate power locally and nationally, balance Soviet influence and win over the locals when Han Chinese were few. It also had to develop policies to implement the region's transition to autarkic socialism and eventual industrialization. Xinjiang's religious animal herders and oasis traders were obvious backward elements in this scheme and thus development and progress were clearly needed. Consequently, the CCP implemented policies similar to those of both the Nationalists and the Qing dynasty (1644–1911) rulers before them: importation of Chinese-style administration, increasing immigration, expanding agriculture and promoting education (Millward, 2007: 212).

As in the rest of China, the policies of confiscating land and redistributing it down the social ladder to increase the number of radicalised stakeholders with a vested interest in the new system and socializing industry, trade and commerce also gradually cut off cross-border trade with the Soviet Union and halted other traditional cross-border movements of people, animals and goods. In 1952 Liu Shaoqi launched complementary policies based on Qing precedents, that of resettlement of Han farmers from the East and the creation of military state farms which later became the Bingtuan, which combined developing agricultural production with militia duties. Using both Han migrants and prisoners, the Bingtuan became 'shock troops to tame nature and wrest farmland from nature' by undertaking vast irrigation and reclamation works, which by 1961 had tripled the areas under agriculture to 3.4 million hectares (Millward, 2007: 253–254). As noted, Xinjiang was also not spared Mao's political campaigns, including the Great Leap Forward and the Cultural Revolution, which went as far as raising pigs in mosques.

After Mao's death in 1976 and the beginning of economic reform, Xinjiang and the western area generally were not well placed; Deng Xiaoping famously promised they could benefit later, after eastern China had become much wealthier. In 1985 the Bingtuan was also revived but under increased central control. Though heavily reliant on central government subsidies, it is noticeable that investment, even military investment, in Xinjiang was relatively low. If the USSR invaded, the region could be sacrificed (Millward, 2007: 296). The eventual economic success of Eastern China and the collapse of the Soviet Union in 1990 did result in the promised dramatic shift in Beijing's priorities in Xinjiang and western China, first with the 1992 policy of opening up the north-west and then the 2000 Great Development of the West (*Xibu Da Kaifa*) policy in which the 'Great' was included by Jiang Zemin to emphasize its large-scale nature (Ptackova, 2013: 26).

As Becquelin has pointed out, Beijing is politically much stronger in Xinjiang compared to other provinces as a result of not only its strategic status and potential for ethnic unrest, but also because of its control over the Bingtuan, which answers to the State Council, and the very limited power exercised by the province's minorities over policy (Becquelin, 2004: 363). He might have added the inherent influence exerted by the heavily subsidised state-owned enterprises, which are also major players (Millward, 2007: 302). A key consequence of these features is that Xinjiang's leaders appointed from elsewhere by Beijing enjoy a closer relationship with central leaders than most provincial leaderships elsewhere. This closeness explains in part why Xinjiang has been able to lobby successfully for major projects and infrastructure projects and be granted a 'leading position' in the implementation of the Go West campaigns (Becquelin, 2004: 363). Legislatively, the money was accompanied by revisions to the *Law on National Regional Autonomy* and the combination of these economic, legal and other measures,

> ... although construed as an effort to alleviate poverty and bridge the growing gap of economic disparity between the Eastern and Western regions, is actually an attempt to quell ethic unrest, solidify the nation, and legitimise the current regime by taming the 'wild West'.
>
> (Moneyhon, 2003: 492)

Key to this long-term 'staged' development strategy were huge investments in infrastructure, promoting agriculture (especially cotton) and resource extraction, particularly oil and related infrastructure, such as gas pipelines, railways and roads, and extending to industrial restructuring, international trade, tourism, etc. These plans were subsequently incorporated into the CCP's Tenth and subsequent Five-Year Plans. A 2002 Xinhua report stated that nearly 60 per cent of the necessary investment would come from Beijing and state-owned enterprises (Becquelin, 2004: 364). Another strategy is the use of capital and expertise from Eastern provinces in conjunction with organizations in Xinjiang, notably from Shanghai, Jiangsu and Zhejiang. This is yet another form of state investment, even if not directly from Beijing. Foreign and private investment is also encouraged, but state money is easier to promise and deliver. Speaking in 2000 as the head of SEAC, Li Dezhu had declared:

> ... so the final solution for these problems lies in developing social productivity in areas of minority nationalities. The strategy to promote social and economic development of Western China is a fundamental way to speed up the development of minority nationalities, and a necessary choice to solve China's nationality problems under new historical circumstances.
>
> (Clarke, 2011: 153)

Increased investment was the way to achieve this.

If we examine this situation from the point of view of developmental state features, we can see that even if China as a whole cannot readily be forced to comply with the key features of such a state (as Howell, 2006: 276 has argued), it comes much closer in the case of Xinjiang, which does reflect most closely the features Howell lists. The CCP Politburo, together with the State Council and its ministries, do form the necessary political and policy elite committed to growth. Based on nationalist calls for national security, sovereignty and the like, they do have the legitimacy to bring about the necessary changes and they can call on an increasingly sophisticated, well-trained bureaucratic elite for help and advice. In the case of Xinjiang in particular (and by implication other areas of the north- and south-west), these elites are insulated from local nationalities such as the Uyghurs. Authorities can take advantage of the underdeveloped civil society to push through their policies and programmes. Finally, the post-1990s developmentalism has delivered the rapid growth the model requires.

Xinjiang's development today

Between 2000 and 2008, the most basic measure of growth, GDP, increased in Xinjiang by an average of over 15 per cent (Freeman, 2013: 18). Since then it has continued to grow rapidly at around 10.7 per cent, reaching 12 per cent in 2011, while by 2013 GDP totalled some RMB851 billion (Statistics Bureau of Xinjiang Autonomous Region, 2013), dramatically more than the RMB148.5 billion in 2001. Overall, growth rates have also been higher than the national average.

By 2012 primary industry made up 17.6 per cent of GDP, secondary 46.4 per cent and tertiary 36 per cent, of which industry made up 38 per cent. Reflecting state priorities of previous decades, oil and natural gas extraction now make up 44.1 per cent of value-added industrial output. Electricity production trails in the second spot with 10 per cent while oil processing, nuclear fuel processing (7.8 per cent) and petrochemicals fall away even further. Despite the level of agricultural production including cotton, processing the output only makes up 2.7 per cent (HKTDC, 2014). Xinjiang has also seen the results of infrastructure spending in the forms of dramatic increases in the number of oil and gas pipelines, railway lines, highways and rapid urban growth. It even includes a 1,776 km high-speed rail line from Lanzhou to Urumqi (*The Economist*, 2013) The real-estate construction boom has been both to accommodate the rate of natural increase in population, as well as that from increased immigration of Han Chinese, with the population reaching 21,813,300 by the 2010 census (almost double that of 1978). Significantly, though, the more than 8,746,100 Han Chinese now make up almost 40 per cent of the population. Given the nature and extent of Xinjiang's rapid growth, it is also not surprising that on almost any measure, the people of Xinjiang, whether Han, Uyghur or other minority, are now much better off than they were in the 2000s, let alone the 1990s. Average incomes, for example, have increased from RMB717 per annum in 1978, to RMB2,272 in 1990, RMB8,717 in 2000 to RMB32,361 in 2010 (Jin Jianxin, 2011: 91). A key goal of the CCP's developmentalism should have been realized, but recent events tell us that something has gone wrong.

Unintended consequences

Rapid economic development in eastern China has resulted in unintended problems of pollution, corruption, arbitrary land confiscation, etc., which by their nature are almost certainly going to be replicated in the north-west and which would create problems enough. Unfortunately for some, the likelihood of this occurring has increased since Beijing made the decision to move many polluting industries to areas like Xinjiang, in part because of its size and relatively sparse population (*Bloomberg*, 2014).

It is also now clear that a number of unspoken assumptions behind pronouncements such as those of Li Dezhu about the benefits of economic growth and how these would rally all behind the CCP were, at best, naive. Nor have the other nominally preferential policies for minorities necessarily had the desired results (Sautman, 1998). Perhaps even worse, analysis of the July 2009 riots and subsequent events, notably the calls for the dismissal of then Governor Wang Lequan may be an indication that it is not only Uyghurs who are unhappy but also those Han Chinese who were in Xinjiang before the wave of post-1990s immigrants. Even many Han from the Bingtuan have come to resent these newcomers. The element in common is resentment of the immigration directly linked to Beijing's development and modernization investments (Cliff, 2012). The enormous investments in oil extraction, for example, have not resulted in many jobs in the resultant state-owned enterprises for either Uyghurs or established Han, but have instead gone to new, well-educated recruits from elsewhere in China, who also often have better material conditions and wages. Locals are in some cases literally locked out of the new districts built to house the recent arrivals (Cliff, 2013). A similar tale applies to the massive infrastructure building which employs few locals and even fewer Uyghurs or others.

Development in Xinjiang has resulted in increased average GDP per capita, but by 2007 average income at RMB13,775 was well behind that of Beijing or Shanghai at RMB55,752. There are also major discrepancies within Xinjiang itself, with the wealthier Han in the north dominating oil, gas and mining, with the Uygur-dominated agricultural south being much poorer (Cao in Szadziewski, 2011: 103). In 2010, for example, the official average income in Urumqi was RMB41,529, compared to RMB28,421 for Aksu. Oil industry (Han) employees in Urumqi earned RMB59,512, while locals (mainly Uyghurs) earned RMB21,219. In some poor counties such as Zepu, annual income was only RMB8,333 (Jin Jianxin, 2011: 92–95). Not only is unemployment for Uyghurs double that of Han Chinese, even well-qualified Mandarin speakers have much difficulty finding suitable work as thousands of similarly qualified Han move to Xinjiang to take advantage of the opportunities flowing from its rapid growth (Grose, 2010: 100).

According to one Chinese source responsible for educating the police,

> socio economic development is seen as a source of inequality, contributing to large unemployment rates among non-Han labour in rural areas. They have not experienced rising living standards and the government is not perceived as involved in addressing their grievances.
>
> (Odgaard and Nielsen, 2014: 544)

These problems are then compounded by the difficulty of communicating problems to government. Behind such resentment are deep feelings about inequality and unfairness similar to those animating Chinese elsewhere, but here they carry an added racial element. As a result, not only has there been a major failure to successfully integrate Uyghurs into the new system, these new conditions have actually brought about a heightened sense of Uyghur ethnic consciousness and even resistance, albeit hitherto usually overwhelmingly passive, against the Chinese nation state (Bovingdon, 2010).

An alternative developmentalism?

As noted at the outset, developmentalism comes in many forms; the form chosen by the CCP is not the only one. Szadziewski (2011: 105) makes the point that there is almost no meaningful way local groups such as Uyghurs can have input into the Party-state's planning decisions, which are shaping their lives in the most profound ways. The May 2010 Work Forum on Xinjiang in the wake of the riots and deaths of July 2009 also failed to directly address any of the underlying socio-economic drivers behind the violence. Instead, Hu Jintao promised to step up spending on both development and security, and although concessions were made to increase the amount of oil and gas revenue that could be retained in Xinjiang, no policies were unveiled to increase employment of Uyghurs (Szadziewski, 2011: 105, 109). Current policies have failed to give many locals an effective stake in the nation of which they are a part.

Other forms of developmentalism like those proposed by Midgley put locally oriented social policies, economic development and raising living standards ahead of state interpretations of national interest. These bottom-up developmentalists believe that 'a positive role for the state is combined with a strong belief in people's participation and community involvement in social welfare, reflecting a wider commitment to pluralism' (Midgley, 2003: 8). In this schema, Beijing works to develop policies that are productivist in that they generate employment 'by promoting economic participation and generating positive rates of return to the economy'. This approach stresses 'people's participation and community involvement in social welfare reflecting a wider commitment to pluralism' (Midgley, 2003: 8). Policies along these lines are intended to generate widespread inclusion so that participants would develop a perceived and material stake in the system and hence result in increased legitimacy for the state promoting it.

It is not that the CCP lacks the basic infrastructure to allow for a rapid realignment of existing systems and mechanisms to allow the sort of participation imagined by Midgley and others. The existing United Front system, the State Ethnic Affairs Commission and the political expression of the Party-state's work with China's many ethnic groups and other important constituencies, the Chinese People's Political Consultative Conference (*Zhongguo Renmin Zhengzhi Xieshang Hui*) system, could all be utilized to sound out opinions and to work with ethnic groups such as Uyghurs. A clear two-transmission belt function for this system rather than the largely top-down version currently in-place would greatly strengthen the Party's claims to democracy over the often symbolic representation which dominates. United Front recognition of the problems of inequality between minorities and the Han is certainly clear (Lin and Xiao, 2011: 230).

Conclusion

Just as the China model of development is not necessarily bringing happiness to all Chinese, the even more extreme form of the developmental state transforming Xinjiang is failing to adequately win over the Uyghurs. More and more Uyghurs are now responding by retreating to a form of identity politics, and more are willing to use violence against Beijing's control, with some even resorting to terrorism.

While the Western accounts of Xinjiang generally focus on religion, repression and identity politics as causes, this chapter has sought to demonstrate that underlying these issues is the overriding importance of the CCP's developmental state model and developmentalist mindset that assumed that rapid economic growth would solve most of the area's problems. Although growth has been rapid and all people in Xinjiang are in absolute terms materially better off than two decades ago, the inequalities and inequities generated by this model are creating new problems and exacerbating old ones. As noted, there are alternatives but it is hard to imagine that CCP leaders, particularly Xi Jinping, will be inclined to invoke them. As a result of Xi Jinping's desire to build a strong state that can assert itself with confidence in all areas, the general thrust of development policy is unlikely to change even if the costs in China generally, and in areas such as Xinjiang, Tibet and Mongolia in particular, continue to rise.

Bibliography

Barmé, Geremie and Goldkorn, Jeremy (eds) (2013), *China Story Yearbook 2013: Civilising China*, Australian Centre for China in the World, Australian National University, Canberra.

Becquelin, Nicholas (2004), 'Staged development in Xinjiang', *China Quarterly*, vol. 178, pp. 358–378.

Bloomberg (2014), 'China outsourcing smog to west region stirs protest'. www.bloomberg. com/news/2014-03-06/china-outsourcing-smog-to-west-region-stirs-protest.html.

Blumenthal, Daniel (2013), 'China is unhappy', *Foreign Policy*, 7 May. http://shadow. foreignpolicy.com/posts/2013/05/07/china_is_unhappy.

Bovingdon, Gardner (2010), *The Uyghurs: Strangers in Their Own Land*, Columbia University Press, New York.

China Story Yearbook (2013), 'Mass incidents in 2012'. www.thechinastory.org/ yearbooks/yearbook-2013/chapter-4-under-rule-of-law/mass-incidents-in-2012.

Clarke, Michael E. (2011), *Xinjiang and China's Rise in Central Asia*, Routledge, London.

Cliff, Thomas (2012), 'The partnership of stability in Xinjiang: state–society interactions following the July 2009 unrest', *The China Journal*, vol. 68, pp. 79–105.

Cliff, Tom (2013), 'Peripheral urbanism: making history on China's northwest frontier', *China Perspectives*, vol. 3, pp. 13–23.

The Economist (2013), 'Faster than a speeding bullet', 9 November. www.economist. com/news/china/21589447-chinas-new-rail-network-already-worlds-longest-will-soon-stretch-considerably-farther-faster.

Forsythe, Michael and Gough, Neil (2014), 'By one measure, China set to become largest economy', *New York Times*, 30 April. http://sinosphere.blogs.nytimes.com/2014/04/30/ by-one-measure-china-set-to-become-largest-economy/?_php=true&_type=blogs&_r=0.

Freeman, Carla (2012), 'From "blood transfusion" to "harmonious development": the political economy of fiscal allocations to China's ethnic regions', *Journal of Current Chinese Affairs*, vol. 41, no. 4, pp. 11–44.

Göbel, Christian and Ong, Lynette H. (2012), *Social Unrest in China*, ECRA, London.

Grose, Timothy A. (2010), 'The Xinjiang class: education, integration, and the Uyghurs', *Journal of Muslim Minority Affairs*, vol. 30, no. 1, pp. 77–109.

Helliwell, John, Layard, Richard and Sachs, Jeffrey (eds) (2013), *World Happiness Report*.   http://unsdsn.org/wp-content/uploads/2014/02/WorldHappinessReport2013_ online.pdf.

HKTDC (2014), *Xinjiang Market Profile*, http://china-trade-research.hktdc.com/business-news/article/Fast-Facts/Xinjiang-Market-Profile/ff/en/1/1X000000/1X06BVVK.htm.

Hou, Liqiang (2014), 'China report identifies sources of mass protests', *China Daily*, 9 April.

Howell, Anthony and Fan, Cindy C. (2011), 'Migration and inequality in Xinjiang: a survey of Han and Uyghur migrants in Urumqi', *Eurasian Geography and Economics*, vol. 52, no. 1, pp. 119–139.

Howell, Jude (2006), 'Reflections in the Chinese state', *Development and Change*, vol. 37, no. 2, pp. 273–297.

Jin Jianxin (2011), *Xinjiang Statistical Yearbook*, China Statistics Press, Beijing.

Johnson, Chalmers (1982), *MITI and the Japanese Miracle: The Growth of Industrial Policy 1925–1975*. Stanford University Press, Stanford, CA.

Johnson, Chalmers (1999), 'The developmental state: odyssey of a concept', in Meredith Woo Cummings (ed.), *The Developmental State*, Cornell University Press, Ithaca, NY.

Johnson, Ian (2014), 'China's way to happiness'. www.nybooks.com/blogs/nyrblog/2014/feb/04/chinas-way-happiness.

Leibold, James (2013), *Ethnic Policy in China: Is Reform Inevitable?* East West Center, Honolulu.

Lemos, Gerard (2012), *The End of the Chinese Dream: Why Chinese People Fear the Future*, Yale University Press, New Haven, CT.

Lin Shangli and Xiao Zunliang (2011), *Tongyi zhanxian lilun yu shijian qianyan 2011* (United Front Theory and Practice Forward Position), Fudan Daxue Chubanshe.

Lin, Yifu (2013), 'Long live China's boom', *Project Syndicate*, August. www.project-syndicate.org/commentary/growth-and-the-chinese-economy-s-latecomer-advantage-by-justin-yifu-lin.

Loris, Rafael and Loris, Antonio A.R. (2013), 'The Brazilian developmentalist state in historical perspective: revisiting the 1950s in light of today's challenges', *Journal of Iberian and Latin American Research*, vol. 19, no. 1, pp. 133–148.

Midgley, James (2003), 'Assets in the context of welfare theory: a developmental interpretation', Working Paper No. 03-10, Center for Social Development, Washington University in St. Louis.

Millward, James A. (2007), *Eurasian Cross Roads: A History of Xinjiang*, Hurst & Co., London.

Moneyhon, Matthew D. (2003), 'China's Great Western Development Project in Xinjiang: economic palliative or political Trojan horse', *Denver Journal of International Law and Policy*, vol. 31, no. 3 pp. 491–519.

Odgaard, Liselotte and Nielsen, Thomas Galasz (2014), 'China's counterinsurgency strategy in Tibet and Xinjiang', *Journal of Contemporary China*, vol. 23, no. 87, pp. 535–555.

Ptackova, Jarmila (2013), 'The Great Opening of the West Strategy and its impact on the life and livelihoods of Tibetan pastoralists' (PhD Dissertation, Humboldt University).

Reuters (2013). China lets Gini out of the bottle; wide wealth gap. www.reuters.com/article/2013/01/18/us-china-economy-income-gap-idUSBRE90H06L20130118.

RFA (Radio Free Asia) (2014), 'Two Tibetan monks self-immolate on crackdown anniversary', 16 March. www.rfa.org/english/news/tibet/burning-03162014125839.html.

Sautman, Barry (1998), 'Preferential policies for ethnic minorities in China: the case of Xinjiang', *Nationalism and Ethnic Politics*, vol. 4, no. 1–2, pp. 86–118.

Shan Wei and Weng Cuifen (2010), 'China's new policy in Xinjiang and its challenges', *East Asian Policy*, vol. 2, no. 3. www.eai.nus.edu.sg/Vol. 2No3_ShanWei&Weng Cuifen.pdf.

Starr, S. Frederick (ed.) (2004), *Xinjiang: China's Muslim Borderland*, M.E. Sharpe, Armonk, NY.

Statistics Bureau of Xinjiang Autonomous Region (ed.) (2013) *Xinjiang Statistical Year-book 2013*, China Statistics Press, Beijing.

Szadziewski, Henryk (2011), 'Commanding the economy: the recurring patterns of Chinese central government developmental planning among Uyghurs in Xinjiang', *Inner Asia*, vol. 13, pp. 97–116.

Wallerstein, Immanuel (2005), 'After development and globalization, what?' *Social Forces*, vol. 3, pp. 1263–1278.

Woo-Cumings, M. (ed.) (1999), *The Developmental State*, Cornell University Press, New York, NY.

Wu Zhong (2011), 'Green motives in Inner Mongolian unrest', *Asia Times Online*, 8 June. www.atimes.com/atimes/China/MF08Ad01.html.

Xinhua (2006), 'China publishes its resolution on building a harmonious society'. www.china.org.cn/english/report/189591.htm.

Xinhua (2012), 'Xi pledges great renewal of Chinese nation'. 29 November. http://news.xinhuanet.com/english/china/2012-11/29/c_132008231.htm.

5 Spatial analysis on the contribution of industrial structural adjustment to regional energy efficiency

A case study of 31 provinces across China

Jiajun Liu

Introduction

Energy is an important factor in production. Due to an increase in energy input, human activities have greatly improved labour productivity and promoted economic and social development. However, over-reliance on non-renewable energy and excessive consumption of energy has jeopardized sustainable development and damaged the ecological environment. In China, energy-saving and emission reduction is one of the important goals of current and future economic development; meanwhile, improving energy efficiency is one of the ways to solve energy contradictions. Upgrading industrial structure is closely related to improvements in regional energy efficiency. Industrial structure and energy efficiency together reflect a country's direction of economic development and capacity for sustainable economic development. It has tremendous meaning for correctly understanding the contribution of industrial structure change to energy efficiency in temporal-spatial variation. Acknowledgement of the spatial variation characteristics of regional energy efficiency is important for making economic policies that promote regional energy-saving and efficient and sustainable development.

The impact of structural change on energy efficiency was initially reflected in the structural bonus hypothesis derived from Lewis' (1954) dual economy model. Denison (1967) and Maddison (1987) argued that, due to systematic differences of various industry sectors in terms of productivity level and growth rate, when energy factors transfer from the low-productivity growth sectors to higher productivity, the total energy efficiency of economies in each sector increases. The contribution of structural change to productivity growth is the balance of the weighted sum of total productivity growth that exceeds each sector's productivity growth. In periods of low economic development, industrial energy use is almost negligible; thus, industrial energy intensity is close to zero. When industrial production peaks, industrial energy intensity rises. Due to continuous technological innovation, adoption of new technology and development of emerging sectors, energy intensity begins to rise, then stabilizes, then declines. In the post-industrial era, with the transformation from an industrial-oriented economic structure to a service-oriented one, energy intensity continuously declines (Nakicenovic *et al.* 1998).

To our knowledge, studies have mainly focused on measuring the impact of industrial structural change on the growth of regional energy consumption and its temporal-evolution; there has also been a focus on changes in industrial structure and adjustment of energy efficiency mechanisms. Shi (2002) analysed China's energy efficiency from 1978 to 2000, employing factor decomposition, and found that energy efficiency improved since the process of reform and opening up. Shi argued that since opening up, industrial structure and economic systems have become important factors affecting energy efficiency, and pointed out that economic systems were enhanced to improve energy efficiency. Han *et al.* (2004) used the calculation method of structure and efficiency share to analyse the energy intensity changes in China. They found that the decline in China's energy intensity was primarily driven by improvements in industrial energy efficiency, and that the decline in industrial energy intensity was the main reason for the overall decline in energy intensity. Qi *et al.* (2006, 2007) analysed the reasons for the decline in macro energy intensity from 1980 to 2003 and industrial energy intensity from 1993 to 2003 in China. They argued that technological progress was a decisive factor in China's energy efficiency, while changes in industrial structure had little effect. Generally, change in light and heavy industrial structure influenced industrial energy intensity as well as energy consumption per unit of GDP less than sector-intensity factors. From 2002, increases in the proportion of heavy industry significantly affected industrial energy intensity; 78 per cent of that can be attributed to this factor. In 2003 industrial energy intensity rose abnormally.

He and Zhang (2006) quantitatively analysed the impact of changes in industrial structure on the improvement of energy efficiency in recent years. They argued that the rise in energy efficiency is mainly attributed to increases in the proportion of industry, particularly heavy and chemical industries. However, with strategic adjustment of the industrial structure, upgrading of industrial technology and the application of energy-saving technology, energy consumption intensity will continue to show a steady downward trend.

Zhou and Li (2006) discussed influential factors in domestic energy intensity variation for 1980 to 2003 by adopting weighting Divisia index methods. They found that industrial structure factors and industrial sector energy intensity factors had a significant positive effect on the decline of China's total energy intensity. From 1991 to 2001, the role of the industrial structural factors weakened, while the role of the industrial sector energy intensity further strengthened. From 2002 to 2003, both factors contributed to the rise in total energy intensity.

Wu and Cheng (2006) looked at China's energy intensity and analysed influential factors by adopting the Laspeyres index. They argued that China's energy intensity decline was mainly due to the improvement in energy efficiency in various industries; compared to efficiency, structure had much less impact on energy intensity – adjustment of the industrial structure had a negative effect on reducing energy consumption intensity.

Research on China has been carried out for two periods: before 2000, when energy consumption was declining; and around 2000, when energy consumption was rising. Due to different periods of the process of industrialization, the impact of structural adjustment on variation in overall energy efficiency is also different. Most studies adopt factor decomposition methods; application of different methods would lead to different results. Because studies employ different tools to analyse the characteristics of different subjects, it is not surprising to have inconsistent conclusions. However, it is not that common to spatially explore the contribution of industrial structure changes to improvements in regional energy efficiency. This chapter uses GDP and energy usage in terms of three industry divisions and adopts models and spatial analyses. We use data from mainland China's 31 provinces (municipalities and autonomous regions; due to limited data collection, Hong Kong, Macao and Taiwan are not included) to research the spatial evolution of the contribution of China's industrial structure to regional energy efficiency.

Data sources and model

Data sources

The economic aggregate of each province is divided into three parts. The energy consumption of each province is also divided into three categories according to the three industries. Economic data comes from the provinces and the *National Statistical Yearbook* 1998–2009. Data were converted from the industrial energy consumption based on the 1998–2009 *Statistical Yearbook* for each province and the *China Energy Statistical Yearbook*. The *Statistical Yearbook* of some provinces (municipalities and autonomous regions) contains energy consumption data statistics according to the three industries division. For some provinces that have no separate statistics for energy consumption according to the three industrial divisions, the primary energy consumption in the balance sheet was used and converted to standard coal equivalents according to the average calorific value of this fuel. The model analysis uses each sector's total energy consumption after conversion. The total energy consumption statistic in industry is divided into agricultural, industrial, construction, transportation, storage and postal industry, wholesale, retail trade and accommodation, food and beverage industry in the *China Energy Statistical Yearbook*, *China Statistical Yearbook* and the *Statistical Yearbook* of the provinces. The total industrial energy consumption is translated from the total primary energy consumption according to the three industrial divisions, and then used to calculate the rate of growth of regional energy efficiency.

Model construction

Contribution of regional industrial structure adjustment to improvement of energy efficiency

The World Energy Council defines energy efficiency as a reduction of capital investment for providing the same energy services. A country's comprehensive energy efficiency is the energy demand to increase a unit of GDP, that is, the energy consumption per unit of output value. A distinction is made between two types of energy efficiency: energy economy efficiency and energy technology efficiency. Energy economy efficiency is the ratio of energy input to the final output when considering energy as fuel and power. This is the optimal utilization capacity of existing resources, with maximum output under various input elements or the ability to minimize inputs under a given level of output. Energy technology efficiency is the ratio of energy input to final output when considering energy as another form of energy converted by raw materials after processing. This refers to the ability to optimize the input–output combination under given factor prices. In a complete competition market, the output elasticity of all kinds of elements is equal to the ratio of input elements to total cost, which reaches efficiency allocation. Because a complete competitive market hypothesis does not exist in real life, investigation and estimation of energy efficiency mainly relates to its economic efficiency. To calculate the energy economy efficiency, energy consumption should use final energy consumption and total energy consumption to calculate energy technology efficiency. In this chapter, if not specified, energy efficiency refers to energy economy efficiency. There are two ways to calculate energy efficiency. The first is total factor energy efficiency, which is the energy efficiency considering the interaction of all kinds of input factors. The second is single factor energy efficiency, which is the energy efficiency only comparing energy elements and output. Total factor energy efficiency is closer to reality, but calculation is more complicated and collection of corresponding statistics more difficult. For single factor energy efficiency, although easier to calculate, energy efficiency is exaggerated; moreover, the substitution effect between each factor is neglected. Based on data availability, this chapter uses single factor energy efficiency.

Learning from the model for contribution of regional industrial structure adjustment to economic growth and introducing energy efficiency (Ge *et al.* 2000), we construct a model for the contribution of regional industrial structural adjustment to the improvement of energy efficiency. The relationship between industrial structural variation and energy efficiency is as follows.

If e^t is the regional efficiency at year t, then:

$$e^t = \frac{E}{GDP} = \frac{\sum_i E_i^t}{\sum_i GDP_i^t}, i = 1, 2, 3$$

where GDP_i^t is GDP in industry i at year t. E_i^t is industry energy consumption in industry i at year t.

Furthermore, we decompose e^t into

$$e^t = \frac{\sum_i E_i^t}{\sum_i GDP_i^t} = \frac{\sum_i e_i^t \cdot GDP_i^t}{\sum_i GDP_i^t} = \sum_i e_i^t \cdot \alpha_i^t, i = 1,2,3$$

where e^t is energy efficiency in industry i at year t, $\alpha_i^t = \dfrac{GDP_i^t}{GDP^t}$ is the proportion of industry i for regional GDP in year t.

β_i^t indicates the proportion of energy efficiency of industry i at year t of total energy efficiency in the same year:

$$\beta_i^t = \frac{e_i^t \cdot \alpha_i^t}{e^t}, i = 1,2,3$$

Growth rate of energy efficiency at industry i at year t is calculated as follows:

$$g_i^t = \frac{\Delta e_i^t}{e^t}$$

Then growth rate of total energy efficiency can be represented as g^t,

$$g^t = \frac{1}{e^t} \sum_i \Delta e_i^t \cdot \frac{e_i^t \cdot \alpha_i^t}{e^t} = \frac{1}{e^t} \sum_i \Delta e_i^t \cdot \beta_i^t = \sum_i \frac{\Delta e_i^t}{e^t} \cdot \beta_i^t$$

So we can derive the growth rate of total energy efficiency:

$$g^t = \sum_i g_i^t \cdot \beta_i^t, \quad i = 1,2,3$$

Industrial structure variation is

$$\Delta \alpha_i^t = \alpha_i^t - \alpha_i^{t-1}$$

Furthermore, decompose g^t:

$$g^t = \sum \frac{e_i^t}{e^t}(\alpha_i^{t-1} + \Delta \alpha_i^t) \cdot g_i^t = \sum \frac{e_i^t}{e^t}(\alpha_i^{t-1} \cdot g_i^t + \Delta \alpha_i^t \cdot g_i^t)$$

$$g^t = \sum \frac{e_i^t}{e^t}(g_i^{1t} + g_i^{2t})$$

Growth rate of total energy efficiency g^t can be decomposed to two parts:

- $z_i^{1t} = \alpha_i^{t-1} \cdot g_i^t$ indicates the contribution to improve the regional overall energy efficiency by initial economic structure;

- $z_i^{2t} = \Delta\alpha_i^t \cdot g_i^t$, $i=1,2,3$ indicates the contribution to improve regional energy efficiency by adjustment in industrial structure;
- z_i^{2t} is the contribution of adjustment in industrial structure to improvement of energy efficiency.

Z_n^t is defined as the column vector of contribution of adjustment in industrial structure to the improvement of energy efficiency in n region at t year. In this study the definition of the contribution of energy efficiency by regional industrial structure changes is as follows:

$$Z_n^t = \overline{\Delta\alpha_{ni}^t} \times \overline{g_{ni}^t}, \tag{5.1}$$

where: $\Delta\alpha_{ni}^t = \alpha_{ni}^t - \alpha_{ni}^{t-1}$, $n=1,2,3,\ldots,31$, $i=1,2,3$

Formula (2) is further expanded as a determinant:

$$z_n^t = \begin{bmatrix} \Delta\alpha_{11}^t & \Delta\alpha_{12}^t & \Delta\alpha_{13}^t \\ \Delta\alpha_{21}^t & \Delta\alpha_{22}^t & \Delta\alpha_{23}^t \\ \vdots & \vdots & \vdots \\ \vdots & \vdots & \vdots \\ \Delta\alpha_{n1}^t & \Delta\alpha_{n2}^t & \Delta\alpha_{n3}^t \end{bmatrix} \times \begin{bmatrix} g_{11}^t & g_{21}^t & \cdots & g_{n1}^t \\ g_{12}^t & g_{22}^t & \cdots & g_{n2}^t \\ g_{13}^t & g_{23}^t & \cdots & g_{n3}^t \end{bmatrix}$$

where: Z_n^t is the contribution of adjustment in industrial structure to improvement of energy efficiency in region n ($n=1,2,3\ldots,31$ of year t.

α_{ni}^t is the proportion of *GDP* of sector i, in n region at t year accounting for the region's total GDP_n^t. (In this study, the total regional economic and energy consumption is divided into three parts according to the third industrial, so $i=1,2,3$).

$\Delta\alpha_{ni}^t$ is the adjustment of industrial structure in sector i, in n region at t year.

$\overline{\Delta\alpha_{ni}^t}$ is the horizontal amount of adjustment of industrial structure $\Delta\alpha_{ni}^t$ in sector i, in n region at t year.

g_{ni}^t is the column vector of energy efficiency g_{ni}^t in sector i, in n region at t year.

When Z_n^t is positive it shows that adjustment in regional industrial structure can promote regional energy efficiency improvements. When Z_n^t is negative it shows that adjustment in regional industrial structure can hinder the regional energy efficiency improvements.

Model for the share of industrial structure adjustment in energy efficiency improvements

M_n is defined as the share of industrial structural change in the average energy efficiency in region n for many years, of which the mathematical expression is:

$$M_n = \frac{\overline{Z_n^t}}{g_n^t} \times 100\% \tag{5.2}$$

Among them: $\overline{Z_n^t}$ is the annual average of Z_n^t in region n; $\overline{g_n^t}$ is the annual average increase of energy efficiency in various departments in region n.

The substance of the value of M is to examine the impact of industrial structural adjustment on regional energy efficiency improvement of an area over a long timescale, and depends on many factors, which influences industrial structural adjustment and regional energy efficiency, including industrial structural policy, investment in fixed assets, technology upgrading and the industrial development in the base period. Policy-makers should formulate regional industrial policy according to regional resource endowments, geographic conditions, economic foundation, technical conditions and the provincial and national industry policy, which can adjust regional energy efficiency while directly adjusting regional industrial structure. The industrial development structure level in the base period is the basis of the difference in industrial energy efficiency growth, and the technical level and scale of production of each industry is the basis of industrial energy efficiency, thereby affecting the value of M.

Results and analysis

Analysis of industry structure changes contribution to improvement of energy efficiency (Z value)

Using Equation (5.1), Table 5.1 was generated based on 1997–2008 data for each province. The Z value is the contribution of industry structure adjustment in one year to the improvement of energy efficiency in the next year. The Z value is small generally, and Z is minus in some years. In some years, industry structure adjustment in some provinces could block the improvement in energy efficiency. This further supports Qi and Chen's (2006) conclusion that industrial structural adjustment has little to no effect on improving energy efficiency in the short term. Industry structure adjustment is a long-term process and improvements to energy efficiency in the short term are mainly based on technological progress. To improve energy efficiency with industrial structural adjustment should be a long-term policy target with no expectation of short-term effects.

Z values vary greatly across the 31 provinces of mainland China (Table 5.2). For 1998–1999 and 2002–2005 the variance in the Z value is greater than for other years. The maximum value of the max./min. of the Z value appears in 2008 as 14.28. Generally, Z values vary in greatly during 1997–2008 in different provinces, which means industrial structural adjustment affects the improvement of energy efficiency in different regions differently. Before 2006, potential efficiency has achieved and China gradually entered the middle stage of industrialization, with a more rapid process of urbanization and rapidly developing high energy-consumption industries because of basic the construction of each province. The economic structure factor has an effect on energy efficiency in different provinces. The total amount of resident consumption has accelerated rapidly rather than steadily increasing, and the ratio of speed of increase in heavy and light industry is differentiated.

Table 5.1 The value of Z^t_n of 31 provinces in mainland China from 1997 to 2008

Year/region	The contribution of changes in industrial adjustment to improvement of energy efficiency Z^t_n (%)												$\overline{Z}_n$ (%)
	2008	2007	2006	2005	2004	2003	2002	2001	2000	1999	1998	1997	
Beijing	0.26	0.23	0.19	0.69	0.25	0.20	0.18	0.40	0.04	0.05	0.79	1.32	0.26
Tianjing	1.00	-0.01	0.24	0.60	0.20	0.68	0.08	0.22	0.00	-0.15	0.43	0.27	1.00
Hebei	0.33	0.11	0.17	0.37	0.55	0.09	-0.27	-0.08	0.07	0.03	0.04	0.04	0.33
Shanxi	0.33	0.68	0.13	0.59	0.81	0.62	-0.07	-0.29	0.05	-0.23	0.03	0.19	0.33
Inner Mongolia	0.84	0.84	-0.99	0.27	1.14	0.30	-0.60	-0.08	0.94	-0.04	0.11	0.07	0.84
Liaoning	0.80	0.25	0.08	-0.36	0.28	0.07	0.11	-0.08	-0.03	0.05	0.65	0.40	0.80
Jilin	0.14	0.75	0.13	0.39	-0.53	0.15	0.02	0.01	0.64	-0.07	0.03	0.49	0.14
Heilongjiang	0.13	0.32	0.09	-0.18	0.22	-0.24	-0.01	-0.62	-0.10	-0.84	-0.66	-0.13	0.13
Shanghai	0.02	0.47	0.02	1.00	0.15	0.45	-0.02	-0.02	-0.02	-0.12	0.25	0.33	0.00
Jiangsu	0.11	0.23	0.16	0.18	0.05	0.26	0.11	0.02	0.06	0.02	-0.08	0.08	0.11
Zhejiang	0.17	0.11	0.13	0.15	0.10	0.14	0.22	0.36	0.02	-0.11	-0.06	0.06	0.17
Anhui	0.40	0.42	0.28	0.65	-0.17	-1.35	4.73	0.02	0.25	0.19	-0.55	0.63	0.40
Fujian	0.10	0.19	0.13	0.01	-0.56	0.32	0.03	-0.12	0.02	0.01	-0.08	0.04	0.10
Jiangxi	0.20	0.38	0.46	-0.98	0.88	0.06	0.26	0.10	-0.52	-0.02	-0.19	0.43	0.20
Shandong	0.01	0.11	0.13	-0.64	0.58	0.26	0.08	-0.15	0.31	0.04	0.03	0.07	0.01
Henan	0.69	0.34	0.22	0.15	0.67	0.62	0.04	-0.18	-0.46	-0.44	-0.20	0.01	0.69
Hubei	0.42	0.47	0.24	-0.44	0.20	-0.48	0.20	-0.16	-0.15	-0.22	0.21	0.23	0.42
Hunan	0.38	0.27	0.24	-0.02	0.42	-0.22	-0.35	-0.15	-0.14	-0.04	-0.36	-0.06	0.38
Guangdong	0.06	0.11	0.12	1.88	-0.01	0.19	-0.21	0.02	-0.18	0.06	-0.02	0.05	0.06
Guangxi	0.58	0.45	0.30	0.46	0.86	0.04	-0.39	-0.80	0.01	-0.54	-3.01	0.01	0.58
Hainan	-0.02	0.93	0.46	0.93	0.73	0.76	-1.02	-0.27	0.06	0.00	0.02	-0.08	-0.02
Chongqing	0.51	0.48	-0.17	-2.18	-0.17	0.84	0.09	0.06	0.24	-0.11	-0.80	0.01	0.51
Sichuan	0.64	0.44	-0.06	0.06	0.04	0.02	0.04	0.12	0.08	0.00	-0.67	0.49	0.64
Guizhou	0.14	0.68	-0.08	0.44	0.54	0.16	-0.07	1.63	0.23	1.76	-0.79	-0.12	0.14
Yunnan	0.08	0.25	0.28	0.74	0.12	-0.04	-0.05	0.04	-0.24	0.12	0.21	1.22	0.08
Tibet	0.10	-0.16	0.92	0.75	-0.02	1.41	0.14	0.72	-0.43	0.40	-1.21	-0.43	0.10
Shaanxi	0.71	0.08	1.32	-0.55	-1.03	0.44	0.06	0.38	-0.33	3.98	0.04	0.47	0.71
Gansu	0.20	0.35	0.47	1.58	0.41	0.06	0.04	0.04	0.08	-0.34	-0.01	0.09	0.20
Qinghai	0.30	0.29	0.38	0.50	-1.31	0.45	0.28	0.45	0.45	-1.88	0.11	0.56	0.30
Ningxia	-0.07	0.57	0.28	0.64	0.87	1.28	0.02	0.03	-0.70	-0.67	0.00	-0.44	-0.07
Xinjiang	0.75	0.19	-0.01	0.30	-1.40	3.59	0.59	0.34	1.01	0.62	0.03	0.45	0.75

Table 5.2 The analysis index of the value of Z of 31 provinces in mainland China for the 12 years sampled

Region	Year											
	2008	2007	2006	2005	2004	2003	2002	2001	2000	1999	1998	1997
Variance	0.08	0.06	0.13	0.55	0.37	0.59	0.78	0.17	0.13	0.80	0.44	0.14
[MAX/MIN]	14.28	5.81	1.33	0.86	0.81	2.65	4.63	2.03	1.44	2.11	0.26	3.02

From 2007, because of deterioration of the eco-environment and scarcity of energy resources, energy saving, emission reduction and consumption reduction became much more important. For eastern provinces, action is needed for an industrial structural upgrade and to increase the high-tech industry to improve energy usage efficiency. For central and western provinces with a poor industrial base (mainly resource-intensive industries) and extensive economic development modes, there is little effect on the improvement of energy usage efficiency from improvements in manufacturing technology and resource-intensive industries. In total, regional differences exist in terms of structure adjustment for energy usage efficiency.

For 1997–2008, Beijing, Shanxi, Inner Mongolia, Jilin, Heilongjiang, Anhui, Jiangxi, Henan, Guangdong, Guangxi, Hainan, Chongqing, Guizot, Xizang, Shaanxi, Gansu, Qinghai, Ningxia and Xinjiang have higher *Z* value variances and max./min., which means the effects of industrial structure on energy-use efficiency varies more for these provinces (Table 5.3).

In 1997, *Z* values for the majority of mainland provinces are less than 0.2 per cent – only Beijing, Anhui, Qinghai and Yunnan are greater than 0.5 per cent (Figure 5.1). In 2000, *Z* values of the majority of areas are less than 0.2 per cent – only Xinjiang, Inner Mongolia and Jilin were greater than 0.5 per cent. In 2005, *Z* values were differentiated in different regions; eastern and central provinces were less than 0.2 per cent; Beijing, Gansu, Ningxia, Tianjin, Xizang, Shanxi, Anhui, Shanghai, Guangdong, Yunnan and Hainan were greater than

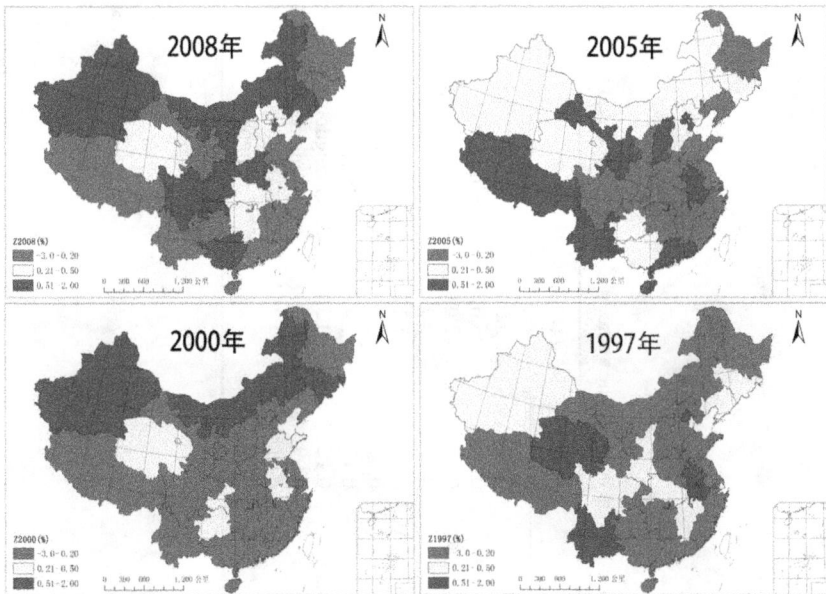

Figure 5.1 Spatial distribution of *Z* value of 31 provinces in mainland China in a representative year.

Table 5.3 Analysis index of the value of Z of 31 provinces in mainland China

Region	Variance	[Max/min]	Region	Variance	[Max/min]	Region	Variance	[Max/min]
Beijing	0.13	33.00	Anhui	1.94	3.50	Sichuan	0.10	0.96
Tianjing	0.10	6.67	Fujian	0.04	0.57	Guizhou	0.48	2.23
Hebei	0.04	2.04	Jiangxi	0.22	0.90	Yunnan	0.14	5.08
Shanxi	0.12	2.79	Shandong	0.08	0.91	Tibet	0.46	1.17
Inner Mongolia	0.37	1.15	Henan	0.15	1.50	Shaanxi	1.46	3.86
Liaoning	0.09	2.22	Hubei	0.09	0.98	Gansu	0.20	4.65
Jilin	0.11	1.42	Hunan	0.07	1.17	Qinghai	0.57	0.30
Heilongjiang	0.12	0.38	Guangdong	0.28	8.95	Ningxia	0.34	1.83
Shanghai	0.09	8.33	Guangxi	0.95	0.29	Xinjiang	1.18	2.56
Jiangsu	0.01	3.25	Hainan	0.30	0.91			
Zhejiang	0.01	3.27	Chongqing	0.55	0.39			

0.5 per cent. The majority of western provinces were greater than 0.2 per cent and less than 0.5 per cent. In 2008, regional differences in *Z* values increased; two provinces of the north, north-east, coastal southeast, southwest and western Gansu province were less than 0.2 per cent; Qinghai, north China plain and the Middle-Lower Yangtze Area were greater than 0.2 per cent and less than 0.5 per cent; only Xinjiang, Inner Mongolia, Tianjin, Henan, Sichuan basin and part of Guangxi were greater than 0.5 per cent.

From 2000 the regional differences in *Z* values increased. Despite some variation, the number of provinces with *Z* values greater than 0.2 per cent increased, which means development of the manufacturing industry is gradually transferred from the east to the centre and the west. In the beginning of the new loop of industry structural adjustment, with upgrades of traditional industry and progress in industrialization, correlation between energy efficiency and industry structural adjustment is enhanced and the contribution of structural adjustment caused by industry policy and gradient transfer of industries emerges. For 2005–2008, except for the Tibetan Plateau, the *Z* values of central and western regions is 0.2 per cent higher in some years, indicating industry structural adjustment contributed to energy efficiency. After 2005 the direct contribution of structural adjustment to regional energy efficiency is clearer, a result of a wide range of policy changes.

Analysis of part of structural adjustment (M value) in yearly average improvement of energy efficiency

From Equation (5.2), the average *M* value can be obtained (Table 5.4; Figure 5.2). For 1997–2008, regions with *M* values greater than 6 per cent were mainly located in the north-west, south-east, Beijing, Tianjin, Shanghai, Guangdong and Hainan. Two southern provinces of the north-east, northern and south-eastern coastal provinces, Sichuan basin and part of Guangxi provinces, were greater than 3 per cent and less than 6 per cent. Heilongjiang, Tibetan Plateau and the Middle-Lower Yangtze Area were less than 3 per cent. At a national scale, developed provinces and western provinces (except the Tibetan Plateau) had

Table 5.4 *M* values for 31 provinces in mainland China from 1997 to 2008

Region	M (%)	Region	M (%)	Region	M (%)
Beijing	7.417	Anhui	2.309	Sichuan	3.202
Tianjing	6.120	Fujian	3.124	Guizhou	6.275
Hebei	3.426	Jiangxi	2.367	Yunnan	6.783
Shanxi	6.829	Shandong	3.122	Tibet	1.037
Inner Mongolia	7.738	Henan	3.496	Shaanxi	6.826
Liaoning	3.246	Hubei	1.113	Gansu	6.701
Jilin	3.995	Hunan	1.048	Qinghai	1.862
Heilongjiang	1.011	Guangdong	6.436	Ningxia	6.189
Shanghai	5.312	Guangxi	5.954	Xinjiang	7.413
Jiangsu	3.184	Hainan	6.971		
Zhejiang	3.056	Chongqing	3.325		

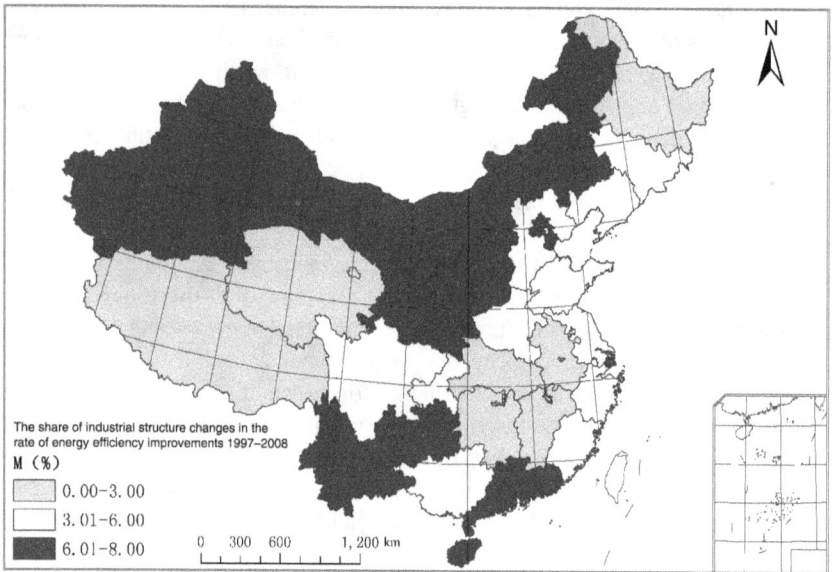

Figure 5.2 Spatial distribution of *M* value of 31 provinces in mainland China from 1997 to 2008.

higher *M* values, while north of the northeast and the Middle-Lower Yangtze Area had lower *M* values.

For 1997–2008, evident variation in the increase in energy usage efficiency could be seen in the provinces (Figure 5.3). Before 2005, increases in energy use efficiency improved gradually for most provinces. During 2000–2005, as for energy usage efficiency, the west and northeast improved rapidly; central areas improved slowly; a lane constituted by Yungui Plateau and Tibetan Plateau improved a little slowly; and eastern area improvements became gradually slower. In 2008, the majority of mainland provinces gained fewer improvements in energy usage efficiency. Due to 2008's international financial crisis, export reduction hindered the development of resources and the material industry, exposing the inability of China's resources-dependent and export-processing economic structure to resist sudden economic crises. Generally, China's regional energy efficiency is gradually improving, and this improvement is spreading to western areas.

From Figure 5.2 we can see that:

1   Beijing, Tianjin, Shanghai and Guangdong, with well-developed economies, have higher *M* values, and energy usage efficiency improves quickly. After 30 years of development, with accumulated capital and technology, these are the main areas where China's high-level industries are located. In these areas, technology-intensive and capital-intensive industries dominate,

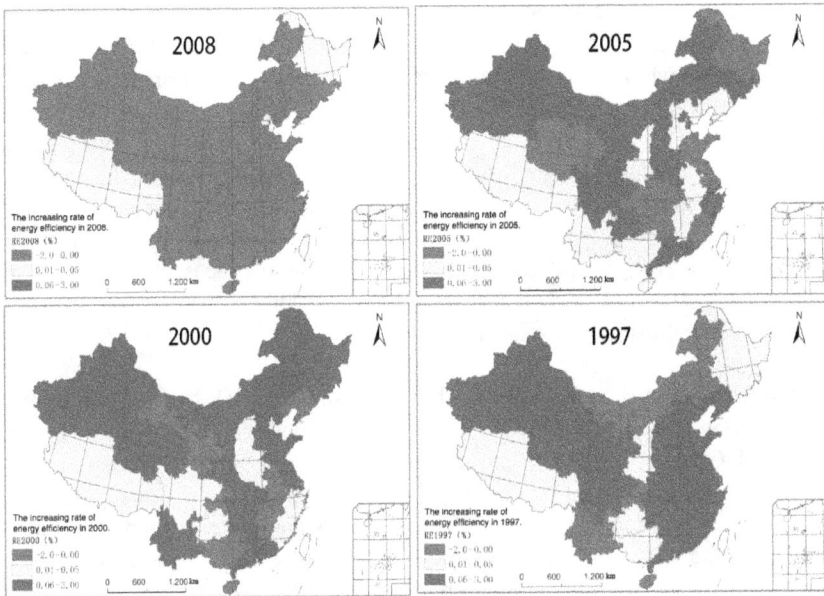

Figure 5.3 Spatial distribution of the increasing rate of energy utilization efficiency for 31 provinces in mainland China in a representative year.

there is greater knowledge and technology accumulation and innovative capability, proper industry structure, rapid upgrading of industry structure and evident reductions in energy consumption per GDP. Because of Hainan's appropriate industry orientation. the contribution of industry structural adjustment to energy efficiency is high.

2　Some eastern coastal regions and the Sichuan basin have average *M* values and energy usage efficiency improvements are falling. For these areas, at the beginning of industrial structural adjustment, lower resource-dependent and labour-intensive industries dominated, there was less knowledge and technology accumulation and innovative capability, and a slow upgrading of the industry structure. Thus, it not evident that industrial structure adjustment led to improvements in energy usage efficiency.

3　Provinces in the Middle-Lower Yangtze Area, such as Hunan, Hubei, Anhui and Jiangxi have lower *M* values and energy usage efficiency improves slowly. For these provinces, there is a mismatch of industry and resources, minus the effects of western resource and inappropriate policies and an improper industry upgrade orientation; it is impossible to see strong effects of regional industry structure adjustment on energy usage efficiency in the short term. However, implementation of the Rising Strategy in the central region will bring policy change to these areas, so it is expected that the effects of industrial structural adjustment on energy efficiency will be enhanced.

4   Most of the western high-energy consumption provinces have higher *M* values and energy efficiency improved quickly. For these regions, upgrading of resources-dependent industry and higher ratios of manufacturing industry within the whole economy dominate power consumption, bringing decreases in energy consumption per GDP, with great potential for improvement in energy efficiency during the early industrialization stage; it is evident that industry structure changes lead to improvement of energy usage efficiency.
5   The Tibetan Plateau has a low *M* value and energy efficiency always improves slowly. This area has a low level of industry structure, and is dominated by primary industry and has an immature processing manufacture industry. It is not evident that there is a contribution from policy industry structure adjustment to energy efficiency.

Different areas show different contributions of industrial structure adjustment to improving energy efficiency. Well-developed regions such as Beijing, Tianjin, Shanghai, Guangdong and the late-starting Hainan show evident effects of industrial structural adjustment on energy efficiency improvements. For regions in a transitional stage, including the north-west and south-west areas, greater contribution of industry structure adjustment to energy efficiency improvement is observed. Regarding eastern coastal regions with low levels of proper industrial structure, it is not clear whether contributions from industry structural adjustment improve energy efficiency. For regions such as the Tibetan Plateau and Middle-Lower Yangtze Area, slow energy efficiency improvements have not obviously stemmed from industrial structural adjustment, and this indicates a need for further industrial structural adjustment.

Discussion and conclusions

Policy direction and adjustment in industrial structure is an important factor in the cyclical growth of regional energy efficiency. When regional development is accompanied by a higher energy efficiency growth rate, which tends to have a more reasonable industrial structure, adjustment in industrial structure tends to be a smaller contribution to energy efficiency. When the growth rate of regional energy efficiency is reduced, irrational industrial structure begins to intensify, which is needed to adjust industrial structure. Then, the contribution of structural adjustment begins to rise and the industrial structure becomes more reasonable, resulting in another increase in energy efficiency.

We are able to conclude that adjustment in industrial structure to improve energy efficiency has been limited along the east coast of China and the Sichuan basin. Industrial restructuring has not offered a great contribution to improvements in energy efficiency in the middle reaches of the Yangtze River region of central China; industrial restructuring contributed significantly to improvement of energy efficiency in north-west and south-west regions of China. Therefore, in the future, the Chinese eastern coastal areas and the Sichuan basin should set Beijing, Shanghai and other developed areas as targets to improve energy efficiency. These areas should promote advanced manufacturing and service-oriented industries to (1) optimize regional industrial structure; (2) improve energy efficiency by the use of high technology and advanced management; and (3) give priority to the development of high-tech industries as the representative of low power consumption, low pollution and technology-intensive industries. Central and north-eastern areas of China are subject to long-term multiple 'low-locked' phenomenon of low-level industrial structure, industrialization, market-orientation, government influence and energy consumption. To approach improvements in energy efficiency, these regions should optimize industrial structure, upgrade levels of industrialization, improve market mechanisms and regulate government behaviour as the preferred paths to improve regional energy resource endowment. North-west and south-west areas of China have more resources, which often results in focus on the immediate resource dividend and ignores regional industrial structure upgrades and crowding-out effects, and fall into the 'resource curse', resulting in low-level industry hindering development of energy efficiency improvements. Approaches to improving energy efficiency for these areas should be based on high technology and advanced applicable technologies to transform and upgrade traditional industries, especially high energy-consuming industries in the future. These areas should improve techno-logical content and added value, reduce energy consumption per unit of product, actively develop a circular economy, improve environmental quality and finally realize the optimization and upgrading of industrial structure, reduce energy con-sumption and harmonize environmental improvements.

This study has revealed the spatial characteristics of the effect of China's regional industrial structural adjustment on improvements in energy efficiency. Because policy factors cannot be directly quantified, we cannot quantitatively illustrate the relationship between the influence of these factors and regional industrial structure on the contribution to regional energy efficiency gains. Indus-trial energy consumption accounts for most of China's energy consumption, and high energy-consuming industries should become a focus of research. However, due to the inability to obtain complete industrial energy consumption index data from all provinces in China, we cannot separate the various industry indicators and examine the relationship between regional industry structure and energy efficiency. This should be the goal of future research.

References

Denison, E.F. 1967. *Why Growth Rates Differ: Postwar Experience in Nine Western Countries*. Washington, DC: Brookings Institution Publishing.

Ge, X.Y., Wang, D.H., Yuan, Q. and Fang, F.K. 2000. A quantitative analysis on the con-tribution of Chinese economic structure change to the economic growth. *Journal of Beijing Normal University (Natural Science)*, 36(1): 43–48. (In Chinese)

Han, Z.Y., Wei, Y.M. and Fan, Y. 2004. Research on change features of Chinese energy intensity and economic structure. *Application of Statistics and Management.* 23(1): 1–6. (In Chinese)

He, J.K. and Zhang, X.L. 2006. Analysis of China's energy consumption intensity reduction tendency during the 11th five-year-plan period. *China Soft Science*, 4: 33–38. (In Chinese)

Lewis, W.A. 1954. *Economic Development with Unlimited Supplies of Labour*. Manchester: Manchester School of Social Science.

Maddison, A. 1987. Growth and slowdown in advanced capitalist economies: techniques of quantitative assessment. *Journal of Economic Literature*, 2: 649–698.

Nakicenovic, N., Alcamo, J., Davis, G., *et al.* 1998. *Special Report on Emissions Scenarios: A Report of Working Group III of the Intergovernmental Panel on Climate Change*. Cambridge: Cambridge University Press.

Qi, Z.X. and Chen, W.Y. 2006. Analysis of china's energy efficiency improvement factors after China's reform and opening up. *Shanghai Economic Review*, 6: 8–16. (In Chinese)

Qi, Z.X., Chen, W.Y. and Wu, Z.X. 2007. Effect of light–heavy industry structure changes on energy consumption. *China Industrial Economy*, 5: 8–14. (In Chinese)

Shi, D. 2002. The improvement of energy consumption efficiency in China's economic growth. *Economic Research Journal*, 9: 49–56. (In Chinese)

Wu, Q.S. and Cheng, J.H. 2006. Change in energy consumption intensity and the main factors during the process of China's industrialization: an empirical analysis based on the decomposition model. *Journal of Finance and Economics*, 32(6): 75–85. (In Chinese)

Zhou, Y. and Li, L.S. 2006. The action of structure and efficiency on Chinese energy intensity: an empirical analysis based on AWD. *Industrial Economics Research*, 4: 47–50. (In Chinese)

6 WTO accession and efficiency gains

Evidence from China's banking sector

Kai Du

Introduction

The almost unregulated shadow-banking sector in China is frequently on the news, which leads to financial hazards mounting in the fragile financial system.[1] For example, *The Economist* reported that a three billion yuan (US$490 million) investment product was almost defaulting on 31 January 2014, when it was due to mature.[2] This financial product was created for Shanxi Zhenfu Energy Group Ltd. (hereafter Zhenfu), a private firm that was borrowing the money to invest in coalmines, which turned to the China Credit Trust after being rejected by the commercial banks.[3] The poor performance of commercial banks is one of the reasons for firms to look for financial support from the shadow-banking sector. In China, firms often struggle to obtain enough financial support from the underdeveloped and inefficient banking sector, but this problem could be partly countered by the increased efficiency of commercial banks. As part of its World Trade Organization (WTO) commitments, China promised to open up its banking sector to foreign banks in a five-year adaptation phase from 2001 to 2006. Schmidt (1997), Berger *et al.* (2009) and Matthews and Zhang (2010) argue that the possibility of going bankrupt will push managers to put in a great deal of effort to save their banks and their jobs when the newcomers enter the market. The question of interest to this chapter is: did the efficiency of the banks in the Chinese banking sector increase after WTO accession? To answer this question, this chapter estimates the evolution of bias-corrected data envelopment analysis (BC-DEA) efficiency of 145 commercial banks in urban areas during the period 2000–2009.

According to the restriction levels in the Chinese banking sector, the transition process following China's accession to the WTO may be separated into three stages: before the WTO accession (pre-2001); during the transition process from 2001 to 2006; and after the adaptation phase (post-2006).[4] The whole process could be treated as an exogenous event to all commercial banks in the market. Immediately upon WTO accession in 2001, foreign banks were allowed to conduct foreign exchange business without any restriction in the already opened areas, such as Shanghai, Shenzhen, Tianjin and Dalian, and these areas were extended gradually in the adapting phase. After 2006, foreign banks were granted right of entry to the whole market without restriction.

The rest of this chapter is structured as follows. The second section reviews relevant literature; the third provides data sources and discussion on selected input and output specification. The fourth section presents methodology and the algorithm of the bootstrapping technique. The fifth reports the empirical results in detail, while the sixth 6 shows the sensitivity analyses. Concluding remarks and suggestions for policy-makers are contained in the final section.

Literature review

Going back to Schumpeter (1911), a long empirical literature has shown that the development of a country's financial system stimulates innovation and helps to increase the growth rate of small and medium enterprises, thereby contributing to economic growth.[5] It is therefore important to examine what practical measures a country may take to promote the efficiency of banks, such as a series of deregulation policies in the Chinese banking sector. Unfortunately, the existing literature focuses only on the first part of the deregulation policies (or before 2006). For example, Li *et al.* (2001) investigate the performance of 15 Chinese commercial banks in 1998 by using financial ratios, and find that the much lower profit margin in four state-owned commercial banks (SOBs) decreases their level of return on asset (ROA) and return on equity (ROE).[6] Consequently, their profitability is lower than 11 joint-stock commercial banks (JSCBs) in the dataset.

Their findings are supported by Lin and Zhang (2009), Garcia-Herrero *et al.* (2009), Berger *et al.* (2009) and Ariff and Can (2008). Lin and Zhang (2009) look at 60 banks over the period 1997–2004, and find that the SOBs are less profitable in ROA and ROE and less efficient in the cost-to-income ratio than JSCBs, city banks and policy banks.[7] Using the same sample period (1997–2004), Garcia-Herrero *et al.* (2009) employ annual data for 87 Chinese banks, and find that the average profitability of the whole dataset decreased by the poor performance of the SOBs. Berger *et al.* (2009) use a panel of 38 Chinese banks over the period 1994–2003, and find that the SOBs are the least efficient type of bank in their sample period. Ariff and Can (2008) use the non-parametric DEA-based technique to investigate the efficiency of four SOBs, nine JSCBs and 15 city banks over the period 1995–2004, and find that the SOBs are the least efficient banks and JSCBs are the most efficient banks. However, this conclusion is far from conclusive. For example, Yao *et al.* (2008) employ the DEA model to create a 'compound' single index to fully evaluate bank performance for the 15 largest Chinese national commercial banks in 2005. Their empirical results show that three large SOBs (or CCB, BOC, ICBC) dominate the market due to their higher technical efficiency and the ratio of pre-tax profit over total assets.

Over a similar sample period (1999–2006), Heffernan and Fu (2010) investigate the bank performance by net interest margin and economic value added in 76 Chinese commercial banks – the four SOBs, 13 national JSCBs, 51 city banks and eight rural commercial banks. They find that efficiency gains from WTO accession are not significant in their analysis. Heffernan and Fu (2010) argue that the benefits from WTO accession are not likely to have materialized yet, since the effect is relatively recent for their sample period 1999–2006.[8] Similar evidence from Matthews and Zhang (2010) implies that the productivity growth was almost neutral over the period 2003–2007, the second part of their whole sample period (1997–2007). They claim that one possible reason to explain their findings is that the foreign banks only command a small share of the banking market until 2007. As a result, the impact from WTO accession is still weak in their sample period. In order to fill the gap in the literature, a more comprehensive and recent dataset is employed in this chapter to capture the efficiency dynamics over the period of 2000–2009.

Another challenge that arises in the literature is how to measure bank efficiency. Berger and Humphrey (1997) survey 130 studies that apply frontier efficiency analysis to financial institutions in 21 countries, and find a common weakness. Most of the analyses do not provide the statistical inference for their results. As a sort of linear programming technique, DEA creates the efficiency frontier by enveloping all observations with a strong assumption that there is no error term in the model and consequently no statistical inference for the estimation results from DEA. In this chapter, the bootstrapping technique conceived by Simar and Wilson (1998; 2000) is employed in order to provide the statistical inference for the results. Matthews and Zhang (2010) utilize the similar bootstrapping technique to estimate the Malmquist index of total factor productivity by the DEA model with the same bootstrapping technique as the proxy of the productivity growth of four SOBs, ten JSCBs and 47 city banks in the Chinese banking sector over the period 1997–2007.[9]

Data

The financial information of commercial banks is obtained from the Bankscope database maintained by Bureau van Dijk.[10] To be consistent with the literature, all data are downloaded in millions of US dollars and adjusted by the consumer price index to eliminate the impact of inflation. The observations are separated into four sub-category groups to catch the reaction of the different types of banks, namely big banks, domestic banks, private banks and foreign banks. The first group is the observations from all banks operating in China (145 banks, which includes 36 foreign banks). The second group is a subset of the first – domestic banks (109 banks) with the foreign banks removed. The private banks are the third group that includes observations from JSCBs and city banks (104 banks). The five biggest banks (or 'Big Five') are removed in this group. The last group is 88 local city banks. These four groups are expected to respond differently to the event of the WTO accession; the number of banks in each group is listed in Table 6.1.[11]

As an event study to assess the impact of removing the trade barriers on the Chinese banking sector, the event window (2000–2009) is selected based on the

Table 6.1 Number of banks in each group

Groups	Foreign banks	Big Five	National JSCBs	City banks	Bank no.
All banks	36	5	16	88	145
Domestic banks		5	16	88	109
Private banks			16	88	104
City banks				88	88

Source: author's calculations.

Notes
1 Hong Kong, Macau and Taiwan are not included due to the different institutional systems in these three regions.
2 Since the focus of this chapter is the commercial banks in the urban area, observations from policy banks and rural commercial banks are removed.
3 The 'Big Five' is ABC, ICBC, BOC, CCB and Bank of Communications.

following two reasons. The financial reform in China is the first reason. City banks were established after 1999 by merging the urban credit unions in local markets. Thus, it is impossible to find their data before 2000. In addition, the Chinese government injected US$4.3 billion (RMB27 billion) of capital into four SOBs to improve their balance sheets in 1998. In 1999 there was US$224.2 billion (RMB1,400 billion) of non-performing loans (NPLs) which were transferred to four asset management companies from these four SOBs.[12] These reform measures would have significantly influenced the performance of the SOBs, but these transfers are not related to the research topic of this chapter. Second, the DEA assume that the technology is constant throughout the entire sample period and this assumption will be challenged if the sample period is too long. Therefore, we do not include the data before 2000 or after 2009.

The specification of input and output variables is another challenge for the DEA, since commercial banks have diverse functions in the economy: to be the intermediation of funding, to be the financial product providers or to maximize the profit as a banking firm. To date, there is no uniformly accepted specification in the literature. Focusing on the Japanese banking sector, Drake *et al.* (2009) argue that the result of DEA depends strongly on the specification of the input and output variables, that is the intermediation, profit/revenue and product specification. This analysis adopts these three specifications, as shown in Table 6.2.

The summary statistics are presented in Table 6.3a for input variables and Table 6.3b for output variables. Two main observations can be made about banks in Table 6.3a. First, a larger size of banking operation does not always result in scale efficiency and could result in huge losses in operating efficiency. An example could be the huge expenses in the 'Big Five' banks. In these five banks, the non-interest operating expenses are US$4,680.23 million, and the other operating expenses are US$3,211.88 million, which is much higher than the average of the other banks, and could be a reason for the relative inef-

Table 6.2 Input and output variables in three specifications

Specification	Input	Output
Intermediation	Total deposits Operating expenses Total provisions	Total loans Total other earning assets Net commission and fees Total other operating income
Profit/revenue	Non-interest operating expenses Other operating expenses Total provisions	Net interest income Net commission and fees Other operating income
Product	Total non-interest expenses Other operating expenses Total provisions	Total loans Total other earning assets Net commission and fees Total other operating income Total deposits

Source: Drake *et al.* (2009).

Notes
1 Since the loan loss provision reflects the capability of banks to withstand risks, Laeven and Majnoni (2003) argue that the loan loss provision should be considered as a kind of cost. Following their suggestion, the variable of total provisions is added to represent the ability of commercial banks to deal with risk. It is like a pool to cover the potential loss from assets, so it could be a negative number if assets have shrunk compared with the previous period.
2 The other operating income is the revenue from the other operating business minus the related expenses (such as gold trading business); the commission and fees are mainly from the charges minus the related costs which are mainly associated with investment banking, corporate financial management, and asset custody and cash management. These two variables could be negative if the expenses are greater than the income.

ficiency of big banks in existing analyses. Second, the mean value of loan size (US$1,793.40 million) and loan loss provisions (US$3.89 million) in 36 foreign banks is significantly lower than other banks. The policy restriction from the government could be the possible reason for the low value, which impedes the development of foreign banks and thereby their loan size.

The most notable feature of the output variables in Table 6.3b is the average value of the net interest income. Its value is much greater than the rest of the income variables and indicates that conventional lending business is the main profit source for the Chinese banks, even in the group of foreign banks. The average value of the net interest income in foreign banks (US$53.77 million) is more than three times the mean value of the commission and fees (US$16.99 million). Second, the asset variables (such as net loans and other earning assets) are shown to be a great deal larger than the revenue variables (such as commission and fees, net interest income and other operating income). The mean value of loans is US$22,569.92 million in domestic banks, but the value of other operating income is US$6.98 million.

Table 6.3c presents the summary statistics of total assets, which are used as a weight to balance the effect of bank size. The mean value of the 'Big Five' (US$440,805.30 million) is more than ten times as much as for the rest of the

Table 6.3a Summary statistics of input variables (US$ million)

Groups	All banks	Domestic banks	Private banks	City banks	Foreign banks	Big Five
Deposits						
Mean	31,730.66	38,973.96	15,423.58	5,363.59	2,693.91	399,799.48
S.D.	106,165.80	117,565.40	30,250.03	8,336.63	4,000.61	274,038.53
Min.	17.88	164.84	164.84	164.84	17.88	42,942.70
Max.	1,075,395	1,075,395	213,525	62,602	18,243	1,075,394
Non-interest operating expenses						
Mean	366.86	447.20	170.92	55.53	44.77	4,680.23
S.D.	1,277.82	1,416.77	343.46	70.61	74.74	3,497.86
Min.	0.54	3.01	3.01	3.01	0.54	780.88
Max.	12,560	12,560	2,581	488	409	12,560
Other operating expenses						
Mean	248.94	303.82	114.01	42.94	28.95	3,211.88
S.D.	821.32	909.75	203.59	48.33	42.45	1,994.64
Min.	0.32	3.01	3.01	3.01	0.32	780.88
Max.	8,092	8,092	1,735	421	203	8,092
Loan loss provisions						
Mean	126.44	157.01	65.13	24.62	3.89	1,564.77
S.D.	456.01	505.19	125.39	34.89	10.11	1,368.14
Min.	−34.24	−14.95	−14.95	−8.87	−34.24	31.21
Max.	5,805	5,805	906	250	42	5,805

Source: author's calculations.

Table 6.3b Summary statistics of output variables (US$ million)

Groups	All banks	Domestic banks	Private banks	City banks	Foreign banks	Big Five
	Net loans					
Mean	18,421.90	22,569.92	9,198.82	2,913.64	1,793.40	227,434.30
S.D.	58,985.86	65,278.88	18,607.91	4,386.40	2,429.23	141,830.40
Min.	17.20	81.74	81.74	81.74	17.20	36,763.81
Max.	563,376	563,376	137,699	35,057	11,095	563,376
	Other earning assets					
Mean	14,662.92	18,003.42	6,849.61	2,623.87	1,271.61	188,895.60
S.D.	52,653.72	58,382.19	13,498.82	4,545.80	2,031.13	149,714.70
Min.	5.50	60.74	60.74	60.74	5.50	28,409.95
Max.	605,943	605,943	91,604	33,812	10,432	605,943
	Net interest income					
Mean	722.84	889.74	387.08	134.60	53.77	8,591.22
S.D.	2,476.22	2,742.84	795.74	205.48	80.24	7,176.08
Min.	0.41	3.87	3.87	3.87	0.41	1,069.46
Max.	25,207	25,207	6,055	1,442	408	25,207
	Other operating income					
Mean	7.57	6.98	5.71	1.51	9.96	26.44
S.D.	187.40	209.04	13.94	3.18	28.41	857.03
Min.	−3,337.52	−3,337.52	−7.17	−7.17	−50.39	−3,337.52
Max.	896	896	149	16	142	896
	Commission and fees					
Mean	130.63	158.98	39.98	15.12	16.99	1,982.17
S.D.	644.07	717.03	102.84	20.62	38.19	2,200.75
Min.	−497.90	−497.90	−10.75	−9.76	−4.43	−497.90
Max.	8,629	8,629	962	145	265	8,629

Source: author's calculations.

Table 6.3c Summary statistics of total assets (US$ million)

Groups	All banks	Domestic banks	Private banks	City banks	Foreign banks	Big Five
	Total assets					
Mean	34,925.43	42,825.01	16,849.60	5,879.69	3,257.84	440,805.30
S.D.	115,654.20	128,067.90	33,260.50	9,120.10	4,605.14	290,671.00
Min.	46.09	178.79	178.79	178.79	46.09	69,677.94
Max.	1,164,349	1,164,349	232,838	69,928	21,242	1,164,349

Source: author's calculations.

domestic banks (US$42,825.01 million) and the mean value from the private banks is only half the value of other domestic banks.

Methodology

The meaning of technical efficiency (*TE*) in this chapter is borrowed from the concept of Debreu (1951) and Farrell (1957), which is defined as 'one minus the maximum equi-proportionate reduction in all inputs that still allows continued production of given outputs'. Based on their concept and the convexity assumption, Charnes *et al.* (1978; 1979), Deprins *et al.* (1984) and Färe *et al.* (1985) develop the DEA model to measure efficiency relative to a non-parametric, maximum likelihood estimate of an unobserved but true frontier. In this model, the first fundamental assumption is that all banks have the same possibility to access the production set (ψ). This production set ψ of physically attainable points (x, y) is given by:

$$\psi = \{(x, y) \in R_+^{p+q} \mid x \text{ can produce } y\} \tag{6.1}$$

In other words, this production set includes any possible input and output combination from the observations, which can be described by the corresponding output set.[13]

$$Y(x) = \{y \in R_+^q \mid (x, y) \in \psi \text{ defined } \forall x \in \psi \tag{6.2}$$

This set means all possible output y can be found in the production set ψ if any input x ($x \in \psi$) is given. Inputs x in any bank can be freely obtained in the long run. Given this duality, we adopt the output approach to estimate bank efficiency.[14]

The following requirement set is calculated by the linear programming technique to evaluate the parameter ($\hat{\psi}$) of the model:

$$\hat{\Psi} = \{(x, y) \in R^{p+q} \mid y \leq \sum_{i=1}^{n} \gamma_i y_i, x \geq \sum_{i=1}^{n} \gamma_i x_i, \tag{6.3}$$

$$\sum_{i=1}^{n} \gamma_i = 1, \gamma_i \geq 0, \ i = 1, 2, \dots n\}$$

In this estimated set ($\hat{\psi}$), the best practice participants in the dataset are on the boundary and the rest of the observations are enveloped by the boundary. The idea of DEA is to estimate the attainable set ψ by its subset $\hat{\psi}$ ($\hat{\psi} \in \psi$) that envelops all observations, so $\hat{\psi}$ is the smallest convex free-disposal hull that fits all observed data. Its upper boundary is a piece-wise linear estimate of the theoretical frontier. The projected point (x, y) is a linear combination of other observations on the frontier, and the efficiency score is estimated by the following linear programming algorithm:

$$\left(\hat{\delta}_{Output}\left(x,y\right)\right)^{-1} = \max\left\{\beta|\beta y \le \sum_{i=1}^{n}\gamma_i y_i,\right.$$

$$x \ge \sum_{i=1}^{n}\gamma_i x_i,$$

$$\sum_{i=1}^{n}\gamma_i = 1,$$

$$\left.\gamma_i \ge 0,\ \beta > 0, i = 1,\ldots n\right\} \tag{6.4}$$

γ_i is an $n \times 1$ vector of radial constants of the input and output vector and the constraint of varied returns to scale is adopted by adding $\sum_{i=1}^{n}\gamma_i = 1$. Finally, the output direction efficiency $\hat{\delta}_{Output}(x, y)$ is evaluated for each observation k and it is employed as the proxy of bank efficiency ($\widehat{TE}_k$). In order to handle the huge difference in variables from different financial statements,[15] all input and output variables are standardized before the frontier evaluation by the following formula:

$$x_{k,j} = \frac{x_{k,j} - \min\limits_{1 \le i \le n} x_{i,j}}{\max\limits_{1 \le i \le n} x_{i,j} - \min\limits_{1 \le i \le n} x_{i,j}}$$

$$k = 1, 2, \ldots, n; j = 1, 2, \ldots, p \text{ in input or } j = 1, 2, \ldots, q \text{ in output} \tag{6.5}$$

$\max\limits_{1 \le i \le n} x_{i,j}$ or $\min\limits_{1 \le i \le n} x_{i,j}$ is the maximum or minimum value of that variable. $x_{k,j}$ is the observations in variable j from bank k and their values resulting from this formula are standardized to the value range from 0 to 1.

Following the suggestions from Berger and Humphrey (1997), the statistical foundation of DEA estimation (standard deviation and confidence intervals) is provided by adopting the bootstrapping technique proposed by Simar and Wilson (1998; 2000). The intuition is that the observation point is fixed, but it faces many random frontiers created in the bootstrapping process. The number of bootstrapping frontiers is huge and it is enough to form an empirical distribution of the estimated frontier for statistical inference and tolerate the possible measurement errors, and finally to provide conservative estimates of bank efficiency. Borrowing the mathematic expression from Simar and Zelenyuk (2007), the dataset is generated from a true but unobservable data generating process, where $\wp = \wp(y, g(TE, \eta, x))$. $g(.)$ is the production process, which is based on the parameter of technology (TE) and other parameters η. The limited observations (N) from the real world are used as the population in the bootstrapping world. In each loop of bootstrapping, some of the observations are randomly chosen from the so-called population (N) with replacement, and these observations make up the 'pseudo' subsample for one of the bootstrapping frontiers.[16] If the bootstrapping is consistent, the relationship between the bootstrapping estimate $(\widehat{TE}{}^*)$ and the original estimate $(\widehat{TE})$ mimic the relationship between the original estimate $(\widehat{TE})$ and the true but unobserved efficiency score (TE), so that:

$$\widehat{TE}{}^* - \widehat{TE} \mid \wp \; asy. \; \widehat{TE} - TE \mid \wp$$

The bootstrapping process is briefly summarized as follows:

Step 1. Apply DEA to the original sample $S_n = \{(x_k, y_k): k = 1, 2, \ldots N\}$ to obtain the estimate $\widehat{TE}_k: k = 1, 2, \ldots N$ of the true (but observable efficiency scores $\{TE \, (x_k, y_k): k = 1, 2, \ldots N\}$. Separate the original sample into l groups for each year ($l \in \{1,2 \ldots, 10\}$), $S_n^l = \{(x_k, y_k): k = 1, 2, \ldots n\}$, and estimates $\{\widehat{TE}_k^l: 1, 2, \ldots n\}$ representing the efficiency score in each specific year (l). Obtain estimates of the aggregate efficiency scores $\widehat{TE}{}^l$).

Step 2. Generate bth bootstrapping samples by drawing s_k^l out of S_n^l observations randomly and independently ($k < n$) and S_n^l is part of original sample set S_n in the specific year (l). Denote these samples as $S_b^{*,l} = \{(x_{b,k}^{*,l}, y_{b,k}^{*,l}): k = 1, 2, \ldots s\}$ and denote the pooled sample as $S_b^* = \{(x_{b,k}^*, y_{b,k}^*): k = 1, 2, \ldots s\}, s = s^1 + \ldots + s^{10}$.

Step 3. Use DEA for the pooled bootstrapping sample $S_b^* = \{(x_{b,k}^*, y_{b,k}^*): k = 1, 2, \ldots s\}$ to obtain the bootstrapping-estimated frontier and compute efficiency scores to this frontier, denote them as $\{\widehat{TE}_{b,k}^*: k \in \{1, 2, \ldots s\}$, which is used to obtain bootstrapping estimates of the aggregate score, denoting them as $\widehat{TE}_b^{*,l}$.

Step 4. Repeat steps 2–3 B times to obtain and save $\widehat{TE}_b^{*,l}$ from all bootstrapping iteration to infer about the relationship $\widehat{TE}^{(*,l)} - (\widehat{TE})^l \mid < \wp$ and $(\widehat{TE})^l - (TE^l) \mid \wp$ and to calculate the relative parameters, such as the expected value of

$$\widehat{\overline{TE}}{}^{*,l} = \frac{1}{B} \sum_{b=1}^{B} \widehat{TE}_b^{*,l} \text{ or the standard deviation, } \frac{1}{B-1} \left[\sum_{b=1}^{B} \left(\widehat{TE}_b^{*,l} - \frac{1}{B} \sum_{b=1}^{B} \widehat{TE}_b^{*,l} \right)^2 \right]^{1/2}.^{17}$$

Empirical results

Figure 6.1 shows the estimated trend of four sub-category groups (all banks, domestic banks, private banks and city banks). The x-axis (or the value of 1) is the frontier, which means that a bank is fully efficient. The dot is the conventional DEA score without bootstrapping for each group in each year.

The BC-DEA score is the line in the middle, which is surrounded by its corresponding 95 per cent upper bound and lower bound confidence interval.[18] For example, the score of 1.089 in 2009 for the group of all banks shows that inputs used could produce 1.089 times the output that they are actually producing.

The value of BC-DEA scores is greater than the original scores, since the observations on the original frontier are due to the fact that they are the relative 'best practice' in the dataset. It is still possible for them to be more efficient than themselves. Another reason for the difference between the conventional DEA scores and BC-DEA scores could be the measurement errors in the dataset. The outliers or observations with measurement errors have less possibility of being selected in the bootstrapping process.

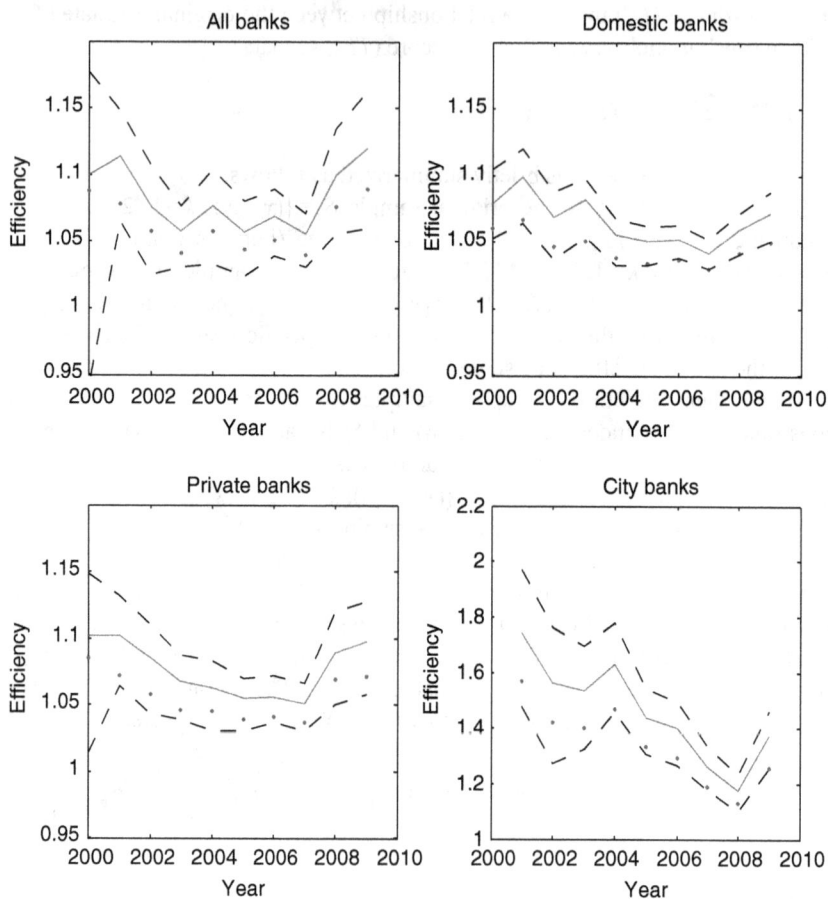

Figure 6.1 Efficiency evolution in profit/revenue specification (2000–2009) (source: author's calculations).

Notes
1 The conventional DEA scores are represented by the dots which are, together with the 95 per cent confidence interval, around the bias-corrected efficiency scores.
2 Since most of the city banks were established in 2000, the efficiency estimation for this group is from 2001 to 2009.

From 2001 onwards, the Chinese banking sector opened up gradually to the foreign banks by removing the geographical and product restrictions. Figure 6.1 shows that the efficiency trends in the groups of domestic banks and private banks increased until 2007, and the aggregated efficiency line for the city banks went up until 2008. These results reveal that the efficiency of the domestic banks increased in the adapting phase of the WTO accession (2001–2006), but these trends blurred when the data from the foreign banks were added (i.e. the group of all banks in the top left corner of Figure 6.1).

The city banks are the most inefficient banks in four sub-category groups. Efficiency in 2000 is around 1.742, which is the worst performance in all four groups. This result is partially supported by the findings from Ariff and Can (2008), who show that city banks were inefficient compared to JSCBs over the period 1995–2004, due to the limited operating area (city banks are not permitted to operate in other geographic regions) which restricts their profit sources. However, the efficiency of city banks increased very rapidly until 2008, from 1.742 in 2000 to 1.176 in 2008. One of the possible explanations could be the 'quiet life' hypothesis of Hicks (1935).[19]

As a potential consequence of the Global Financial Crisis (GFC) in 2007, the figures show that the efficiency of the Chinese commercial banks decreased in 2008 and 2009. Yu (2010) states that the losses of the Chinese commercial banks were significantly larger from early 2008, because their huge amount of investments in mortgage-backed securities and collateralized debt obligations in global capital markets were turning bad due to the 2007 GFC. Consequently, the losses would deteriorate their annual financial reports.

Sensitivity analyses

Since the DEA results are strongly influenced by the input and output specifications adopted, the same four sub-category groups are estimated in two other specifications – the intermediation (in Figure 6.2) and product specification (in Figure 6.3).[20] Since the intermediation and product specifications use different input and output variables to create the efficiency frontier, the least efficient group varies in these two specifications. The group of domestic banks has the higher DEA scores in the intermediation specification at the upper right corner of Figure 6.2. The inclusion of the 'Big Five' commercial banks in the domestic bank group is the distinction between the groups of the domestic banks and private banks, so the 'Big Five' are the reason to decrease the efficiency of the group of domestic banks and the least efficient banks in the intermediation specification. This result is consistent with findings from Lin and Zhang (2009) and Berger *et al.* (2009), which find that large bank size does not always result in a more efficient bank.

The upper left corner of Figure 6.3 shows that the least efficient group in the product specification is the group of all banks. The inclusion of foreign banks is the main distinction between the groups of all banks and domestic banks. Thus, foreign banks are the least efficient banks in product specification. During the adapting phase, the restrictions are removed gradually, which could be the reason for the lower efficiency of foreign banks in the product specification, since the restrictions limit their performance in providing financial products or services.

Generally speaking, the efficiency of domestic banks decreased from 2007 onwards in the profit/revenue and product specification, but it decreased from 2008 in the intermediation specification. Furthermore, the efficiency of city banks decreased from 2008 onwards in the profit/revenue specification, but decreased from 2007 in the intermediation and product specifications.

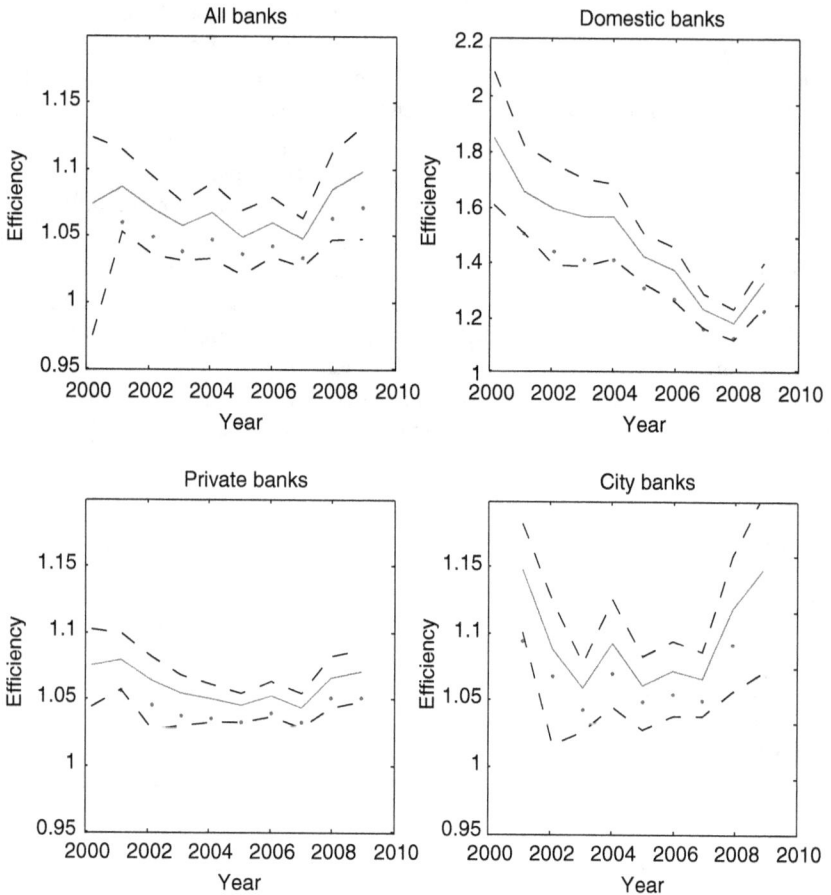

Figure 6.2 Efficiency evolution in intermediation specification (2000–2009) (source: author's calculations).

Notes
1 The conventional DEA scores are represented by the dots which are, together with the 95 per cent confidence interval, around the bias-corrected efficiency scores.
2 Since most of the city banks were established in 2000, the efficiency estimation for this group is from 2001 to 2009.

The most common methodology is to simply average the score in each year. The results of the simple average are presented above. However, Simar and Zelenyuk (2007) offer an example, which shows that the simple average might ignore the importance of the observations in the group. In order to overcome this weakness, the Färe–Zelenyuk weighting method (2003) is employed to aggregate the efficiency score of each year. Since the general trend is almost the same using these two methods, the results of the Färe–Zelenyuk weighting method are presented in the Appendix (see Tables 6.A6, 6.A7 and 6.A8). The

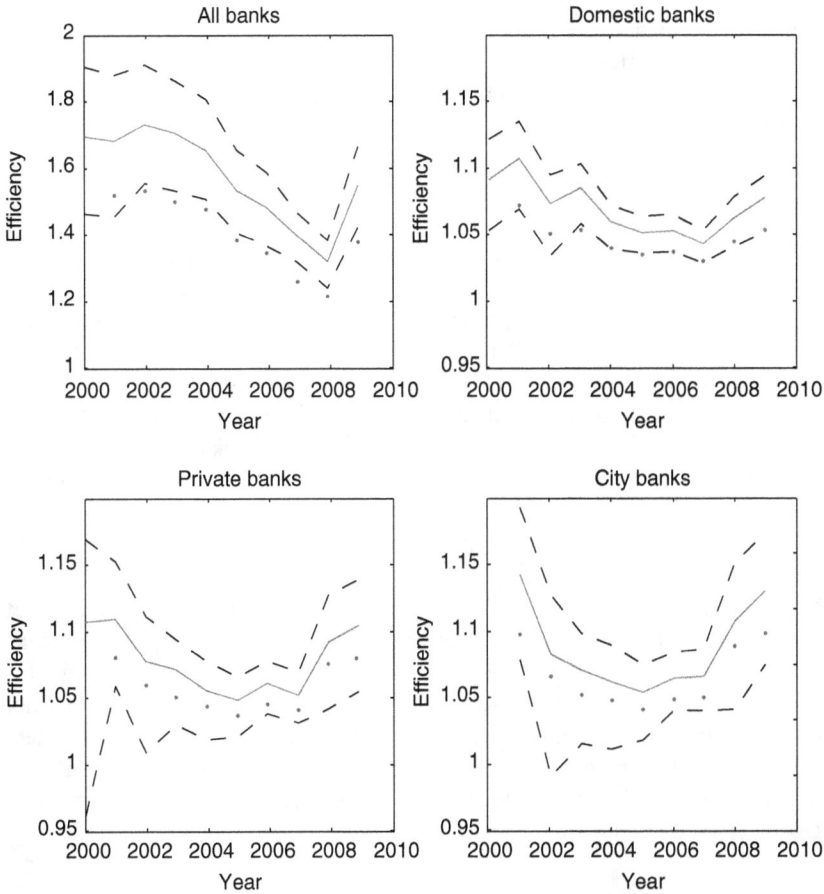

Figure 6.3 Evolution of efficiency in product specification (2000–2009) (source: author's calculations).

Notes
1 The conventional DEA scores are represented by the dots which are, together with the 95 per cent confidence interval, around the bias-corrected efficiency scores.
2 Since most of the city banks were established in 2000, the efficiency estimation for this group is from 2001 to 2009.

only difference is that the aggregated score based on the simple averaging method is slightly lower than the score from the Färe–Zelenyuk weighting method. However, these differences do not challenge the main results and the efficiency of the banks increased after WTO accession, especially between 2001 and 2007.

Concluding remarks

In the adapting phase of the WTO accession, the gradual removal of restrictions on foreign banks offers a unique setting for exploring the relationship between foreign bank entry and bank efficiency. By considering the WTO accession as an exogenous event, this chapter calculates the annual change of bank efficiency using the observations of 145 Chinese commercial banks in the period from 2000 (from 2001 for city banks) to 2009. It is well known that the DEA is sensitive to the specification of input and output variables, so three different input and output specifications (profit/revenue, product and intermediation specifications) are selected to evaluate bank efficiency and they cover almost all bank functions. In terms of profit maximizing, city banks tend to be the least efficient among all banks, but not the SOBs as is suggested previously in the literature. The SOBs could have benefited from earlier financial reforms before 2000 that include the setting up of asset management companies to take over the NPLs and the moving of policy-oriented businesses to policy banks. Nonetheless, the catch-up effect is strong among city banks, since their efficiency as a group has increased dramatically compared to other banks.

When these crises occur, it reminds how important the banking sector is to the functioning of the economy as a whole. The empirical evidence in this chapter speaks of a positive association between deregulation in the form of removing restrictions on foreign banks and bank efficiency, which could merit further investigation on the effect of specific deregulation policies on bank efficiency. According to the news from *The Economist*, the Zhenfu incident is not the first trouble for the Chinese financial system and is only the largest incident in the record. It should trigger alarms for the Chinese government and even around the world. If bank efficiency does not increase, the probability of a banking crisis will increase.

Appendix

Table 6.A1 lists the detail of the deregulation policies in the Chinese banking sector from 2000 to 2006. Immediately upon WTO accession in 2001, foreign banks were allowed to conduct foreign exchange business without any restrictions in the already opened areas, such as Shanghai, Shenzhen, Tianjin and Dalian, and these areas were extended gradually in the adapting phase. After 2006, foreign banks were granted right of entry to the whole Chinese market without any restriction.

Table 6.A1 Deregulation of foreign banks from 2001 to 2006

	The opened area	*Renminbi (RMB) business in the area (local currency business)*
2001 (before WTO)	Shanghai; Shenzhen; Tianjin; Dalian	Before 2001, no RMB business
2002	Guangzhou; Zhuhai; Qingdao; Nanjing; Wuhan	After 2003, RMB business to local enterprises
2003	Jinan; Fuzhou; Chengdu; Chongqing	
2004	Kunming; Beijing; Xiamen	After 2006, RMB business to any customer
2005	Shantou; Ningbo; Shenyang; Xi'an	
2006	No restrictions	

Source: summarized by author based on the information from the website of the WTO.

Table 6.A2 Distribution of observation number by groups

Groups	*2000*	*2001*	*2002*	*2003*	*2004*	*2005*	*2006*	*2007*	*2008*	*2009*
All banks	258	291	251	275	221	234	170	170	87	74
Domestic banks	211	228	206	215	180	181	136	126	62	51
Private banks	200	218	196	206	173	175	132	122	60	49
City banks		166	148	159	132	135	102	95	45	37

Source: author's calculations.

Table 6.A3 DEA scores in profit/revenue specification

Year	2000	2001	2002	2003	2004	2005	2006	2007	2008	2009
All banks										
Original	1.088	1.078	1.058	1.041	1.058	1.044	1.051	1.040	1.076	1.089
Corr.	1.100	1.114	1.076	1.058	1.077	1.057	1.069	1.056	1.100	1.120
S.D.	0.060	0.020	0.021	0.012	0.019	0.014	0.012	0.010	0.020	0.026
Lower	0.940	1.065	1.025	1.031	1.033	1.024	1.039	1.031	1.056	1.060
Upper	1.177	1.148	1.107	1.077	1.104	1.080	1.089	1.071	1.135	1.163
Domestic banks										
Original	1.061	1.067	1.047	1.051	1.038	1.034	1.037	1.030	1.042	1.050
Corr.	1.079	1.099	1.069	1.082	1.056	1.051	1.052	1.042	1.060	1.072
S.D.	0.012	0.014	0.014	0.011	0.008	0.007	0.006	0.005	0.007	0.009
Lower	1.053	1.064	1.037	1.054	1.033	1.033	1.038	1.030	1.041	1.051
Upper	1.105	1.120	1.088	1.098	1.068	1.062	1.063	1.052	1.072	1.088
Private banks										
Original	1.085	1.072	1.058	1.046	1.045	1.039	1.041	1.037	1.069	1.071
Corr.	1.102	1.102	1.085	1.068	1.063	1.055	1.056	1.051	1.089	1.098
S.D.	0.035	0.017	0.017	0.013	0.013	0.010	0.009	0.008	0.018	0.018
Lower	1.014	1.064	1.043	1.039	1.031	1.031	1.037	1.031	1.050	1.058
Upper	1.149	1.132	1.110	1.087	1.083	1.070	1.072	1.066	1.120	1.128
City banks										
Original		1.569	1.421	1.402	1.466	1.332	1.294	1.191	1.129	1.258
Corr.		1.742	1.562	1.533	1.629	1.436	1.401	1.264	1.176	1.373
S.D.		0.121	0.125	0.097	0.082	0.060	0.054	0.040	0.035	0.051
Lower		1.479	1.274	1.323	1.459	1.307	1.267	1.178	1.098	1.258
Upper		1.971	1.763	1.697	1.778	1.543	1.496	1.336	1.234	1.462

Source: author's calculations.

Notes
1 The 95 per cent confidence interval (lower and upper bound) is provided for the bias-corrected DEA score (corr.) based on 1,000 replications in the stage of bootstrapping.
2 Original means the DEA score without bootstrapping.
3 S.D. means the standard deviation of the bias-corrected DEA score.

Table 6.A4 DEA scores in intermediation specification

Year	2000	2001	2002	2003	2004	2005	2006	2007	2008	2009
All banks										
Original	1.066	1.066	1.055	1.044	1.053	1.042	1.048	1.039	1.070	1.078
Corr.	1.081	1.094	1.077	1.064	1.074	1.055	1.066	1.054	1.092	1.106
S.D.	0.041	0.016	0.015	0.011	0.015	0.012	0.011	0.009	0.017	0.022
Lower	0.979	1.059	1.041	1.037	1.038	1.026	1.040	1.032	1.053	1.054
Upper	1.132	1.123	1.102	1.082	1.097	1.076	1.086	1.070	1.121	1.141
Domestic banks										
Original	1.644	1.524	1.459	1.429	1.428	1.325	1.284	1.174	1.139	1.239
Corr.	1.879	1.682	1.619	1.587	1.588	1.442	1.389	1.246	1.197	1.347
S.D.	0.124	0.083	0.099	0.084	0.070	0.048	0.049	0.032	0.029	0.041
Lower	1.633	1.527	1.406	1.403	1.432	1.340	1.275	1.177	1.131	1.256
Upper	2.124	1.853	1.784	1.729	1.710	1.526	1.475	1.303	1.246	1.418
Private banks										
Original	1.055	1.052	1.041	1.033	1.031	1.028	1.035	1.028	1.047	1.047
Corr.	1.072	1.076	1.060	1.050	1.046	1.041	1.048	1.039	1.062	1.067
S.D.	0.015	0.012	0.014	0.009	0.007	0.005	0.007	0.006	0.010	0.010
Lower	1.040	1.053	1.022	1.025	1.028	1.028	1.032	1.024	1.039	1.044
Upper	1.100	1.097	1.078	1.064	1.057	1.050	1.059	1.050	1.079	1.084
City banks										
Original		1.092	1.065	1.039	1.067	1.045	1.051	1.046	1.089	1.111
Corr.		1.147	1.086	1.056	1.091	1.058	1.069	1.063	1.117	1.147
S.D.		0.022	0.029	0.013	0.022	0.014	0.015	0.013	0.027	0.036
Lower		1.099	1.012	1.022	1.041	1.024	1.034	1.034	1.053	1.068
Upper		1.183	1.123	1.075	1.124	1.080	1.092	1.084	1.158	1.205

Source: author's calculations.

Notes
1 The 95 per cent confidence interval (lower and upper bound) is provided for the bias-corrected DEA score (corr.) based on 1,000 replications in the stage of bootstrapping.
2 Original means the DEA score without bootstrapping.
3 S.D. means the standard deviation of the bias-corrected DEA score.

Table 6.A5 DEA scores in product specification

Year	2000	2001	2002	2003	2004	2005	2006	2007	2008	2009
All banks										
Original	1.535	1.530	1.542	1.509	1.488	1.392	1.353	1.267	1.223	1.387
Corr.	1.708	1.693	1.744	1.718	1.666	1.543	1.493	1.406	1.327	1.559
S.D.	0.118	0.111	0.095	0.087	0.081	0.066	0.058	0.039	0.037	0.062
Lower	1.473	1.466	1.565	1.544	1.519	1.414	1.377	1.326	1.248	1.435
Upper	1.919	1.896	1.925	1.878	1.823	1.665	1.600	1.477	1.393	1.678
Domestic banks										
Original	1.072	1.075	1.053	1.056	1.042	1.037	1.039	1.032	1.047	1.056
Corr.	1.094	1.110	1.076	1.088	1.062	1.054	1.055	1.045	1.065	1.080
S.D.	0.017	0.016	0.016	0.012	0.009	0.007	0.007	0.006	0.009	0.010
Lower	1.056	1.072	1.036	1.061	1.041	1.038	1.039	1.031	1.043	1.054
Upper	1.125	1.138	1.098	1.106	1.075	1.066	1.068	1.056	1.081	1.097
Private banks										
Original	1.094	1.079	1.058	1.049	1.042	1.035	1.043	1.039	1.074	1.078
Corr.	1.106	1.108	1.076	1.070	1.054	1.047	1.059	1.050	1.091	1.103
S.D.	0.056	0.023	0.028	0.017	0.015	0.011	0.010	0.009	0.021	0.022
Lower	0.958	1.057	1.007	1.028	1.017	1.019	1.036	1.029	1.040	1.053
Upper	1.169	1.152	1.110	1.093	1.076	1.064	1.076	1.068	1.126	1.138
City banks										
Original		1.096	1.064	1.050	1.046	1.039	1.047	1.048	1.087	1.097
Corr.		1.142	1.081	1.069	1.060	1.052	1.063	1.064	1.106	1.129
S.D.		0.030	0.039	0.021	0.020	0.014	0.011	0.012	0.028	0.026
Lower		1.077	0.989	1.013	1.009	1.016	1.038	1.038	1.039	1.073
Upper		1.193	1.126	1.097	1.088	1.073	1.082	1.085	1.150	1.173

Source: author's calculations.

Notes
1 The 95 per cent confidence interval (lower and upper bound) is provided for the bias-corrected DEA score (corr.) based on 1,000 replications in the stage of bootstrapping.
2 Original means the DEA score without bootstrapping.
3 S.D. means the standard deviation of the bias-corrected DEA score.

Table 6.A6 DEA scores in profit specification (Färe–Zelenyuk weighting method)

Year	2000	2001	2002	2003	2004	2005	2006	2007	2008	2009
All banks										
Original	1.080	1.060	1.043	1.062	1.049	1.056	1.043	1.088	1.097	1.139
Corr.	1.116	1.078	1.060	1.082	1.062	1.075	1.060	1.117	1.132	1.239
S.D.	0.021	0.021	0.013	0.021	0.016	0.015	0.012	0.023	0.028	0.006
Lower	1.067	1.027	1.030	1.032	1.025	1.038	1.031	1.066	1.066	1.224
Upper	1.152	1.110	1.080	1.111	1.088	1.097	1.077	1.157	1.179	1.251
Domestic banks										
Original	1.065	1.052	1.054	1.039	1.035	1.038	1.031	1.046	1.052	1.116
Corr.	1.096	1.074	1.085	1.058	1.053	1.054	1.044	1.064	1.075	1.209
S.D.	0.014	0.016	0.012	0.009	0.007	0.006	0.005	0.008	0.009	0.004
Lower	1.061	1.037	1.055	1.032	1.034	1.039	1.031	1.043	1.053	1.199
Upper	1.117	1.096	1.103	1.071	1.064	1.065	1.054	1.078	1.091	1.216
Private banks										
Original	1.073	1.066	1.050	1.048	1.041	1.043	1.039	1.079	1.076	1.134
Corr.	1.103	1.097	1.073	1.067	1.059	1.058	1.053	1.101	1.106	1.236
S.D.	0.018	0.021	0.016	0.016	0.011	0.009	0.009	0.020	0.019	0.005
Lower	1.064	1.043	1.038	1.028	1.034	1.037	1.031	1.057	1.063	1.224
Upper	1.135	1.125	1.095	1.090	1.075	1.075	1.069	1.137	1.137	1.246
City banks										
Original		1.505	1.496	1.503	1.385	1.326	1.206	1.150	1.271	1.396
Corr.		1.686	1.662	1.677	1.503	1.442	1.283	1.204	1.392	1.605
S.D.		0.124	0.106	0.087	0.067	0.059	0.045	0.040	0.054	0.027
Lower		1.420	1.446	1.494	1.359	1.302	1.190	1.116	1.279	1.547
Upper		1.909	1.855	1.832	1.620	1.550	1.363	1.269	1.489	1.661

Source: author's calculations.

Notes
1 The 95 per cent confidence interval (lower and upper bound) is provided for the bias-corrected DEA score (corr.) based on 1,000 replications in the stage of bootstrapping.
2 Original means the DEA score without bootstrapping.
3 S.D. means the standard deviation of the bias-corrected DEA score.

Table 6.A7 DEA scores in intermediation specification (Färe–Zelenyuk weighting method)

Year	2000	2001	2002	2003	2004	2005	2006	2007	2008	2009
All banks										
Original	1.068	1.057	1.044	1.057	1.046	1.052	1.042	1.080	1.084	1.136
Corr.	1.097	1.080	1.063	1.079	1.060	1.071	1.058	1.106	1.116	1.239
S.D.	0.017	0.015	0.012	0.016	0.014	0.013	0.011	0.020	0.023	0.006
Lower	1.060	1.042	1.035	1.038	1.026	1.041	1.033	1.061	1.060	1.227
Upper	1.127	1.105	1.083	1.104	1.083	1.093	1.075	1.139	1.154	1.249
Domestic banks										
Original	1.535	1.501	1.474	1.446	1.352	1.314	1.186	1.155	1.247	1.386
Corr.	1.698	1.680	1.649	1.613	1.478	1.425	1.261	1.219	1.358	1.589
S.D.	0.081	0.096	0.086	0.071	0.053	0.058	0.035	0.031	0.043	0.031
Lower	1.547	1.470	1.472	1.455	1.367	1.289	1.187	1.147	1.266	1.524
Upper	1.875	1.848	1.806	1.736	1.570	1.523	1.323	1.273	1.432	1.652
Private banks										
Original	1.051	1.045	1.036	1.033	1.030	1.036	1.029	1.050	1.049	1.114
Corr.	1.075	1.065	1.054	1.049	1.044	1.050	1.040	1.067	1.070	1.206
S.D.	0.012	0.017	0.011	0.009	0.006	0.007	0.007	0.011	0.010	0.004
Lower	1.050	1.020	1.023	1.027	1.029	1.033	1.024	1.041	1.046	1.197
Upper	1.096	1.086	1.068	1.061	1.053	1.062	1.052	1.085	1.088	1.213
City banks										
Original		1.069	1.044	1.073	1.051	1.058	1.051	1.106	1.120	1.151
Corr.		1.090	1.060	1.098	1.065	1.076	1.070	1.142	1.161	1.261
S.D.		0.029	0.015	0.025	0.016	0.020	0.015	0.031	0.038	0.008
Lower		1.017	1.023	1.040	1.030	1.029	1.034	1.066	1.078	1.244
Upper		1.128	1.083	1.136	1.091	1.105	1.093	1.190	1.222	1.275

Source: author's calculations.

Notes
1 The 95 per cent confidence interval (lower and upper bound) is provided for the bias-corrected DEA score (corr.) based on 1,000 replications in the stage of bootstrapping.
2 Original means the DEA score without bootstrapping.
3 S.D. means the standard deviation of the bias-corrected DEA score.

Table 6.A8 DEA scores in product specification (Färe–Zelenyuk weighting method)

Year	2000	2001	2002	2003	2004	2005	2006	2007	2008	2009
All banks										
Original	1.569	1.569	1.534	1.508	1.409	1.376	1.290	1.260	1.408	1.462
Corr.	1.750	1.777	1.750	1.691	1.565	1.522	1.442	1.378	1.592	1.705
S.D.	0.106	0.097	0.090	0.084	0.069	0.063	0.043	0.044	0.065	0.048
Lower	1.539	1.600	1.574	1.539	1.433	1.398	1.352	1.285	1.459	1.630
Upper	1.945	1.961	1.914	1.855	1.693	1.638	1.520	1.458	1.716	1.803
Domestic banks										
Original	1.076	1.058	1.060	1.044	1.038	1.041	1.033	1.051	1.059	1.124
Corr.	1.110	1.082	1.093	1.064	1.056	1.057	1.046	1.070	1.083	1.222
S.D.	0.016	0.019	0.014	0.010	0.007	0.007	0.006	0.010	0.011	0.004
Lower	1.071	1.034	1.061	1.040	1.039	1.039	1.031	1.046	1.056	1.211
Upper	1.138	1.107	1.113	1.079	1.068	1.070	1.058	1.088	1.102	1.229
Private banks										
Original	1.081	1.069	1.056	1.046	1.038	1.046	1.041	1.085	1.085	1.134
Corr.	1.111	1.090	1.079	1.058	1.050	1.061	1.053	1.105	1.112	1.232
S.D.	0.024	0.036	0.023	0.019	0.012	0.011	0.010	0.026	0.024	0.006
Lower	1.059	0.995	1.021	1.015	1.021	1.035	1.031	1.042	1.058	1.219
Upper	1.156	1.131	1.108	1.084	1.069	1.080	1.072	1.146	1.152	1.244
City banks										
Original		1.084	1.063	1.053	1.044	1.050	1.051	1.103	1.104	1.147
Corr.		1.108	1.086	1.068	1.057	1.066	1.067	1.124	1.140	1.254
S.D.		0.052	0.031	0.026	0.015	0.012	0.013	0.036	0.028	0.007
Lower		0.975	1.005	1.002	1.020	1.039	1.038	1.041	1.080	1.238
Upper		1.164	1.123	1.101	1.081	1.087	1.090	1.178	1.186	1.269

Source: author's calculations.

Notes
1 The 95 per cent confidence interval (lower and upper bound) is provided for the bias-corrected DEA score (corr.) based on 1,000 replications in the stage of bootstrapping.
2 Original means the DEA score without bootstrapping.
3 S.D. means the standard deviation of the bias-corrected DEA score.

Notes

1 The shadow banking sector means the collection of non-bank financial intermediaries that provide services similar to conventional commercial banks, such as trust and investment companies or asset management companies. Because they do not take deposits, they are not subject to the laws and regulations for commercial banks and lack access to central bank funding or safety nets, such as deposit insurance. However, their functions are almost the same as the commercial banks – to provide credit and increase the liquidity of the financial system.
2 www.economist.com/news/finance-and-economics/21595483-big-default-averted-credit-paroled.
3 The three billion-yuan investment product was issued by China Credit Trust (CCT) in 2011 by advertising annual returns of about 10 per cent, and distributed by Industrial and Commercial Bank of China (ICBC). The CCT is one of the biggest trust and investment companies and ICBC was the biggest bank in the Chinese financial system.

4 The deregulation policies of geographical and product restrictions is summarized in the Appendix (see Table 6.A1).

5 Recent research on the relationship between the economic growth and financial development are from Rajan and Zingales (1998) and Beck *et al.* (2007, 2008).

6 Four SOBs are Agriculture Bank of China (ABC), Industrial and Commercial Bank of China (ICBC), Bank of China (BOC) and China Construction Bank (CCB).

7 The three policy banks in China implemented the policy-related business, taking the place of SOBs who performed these roles prior to this. Since they are not commercial banks, the policy banks are not included in this analysis.

8 Their argument is supported by the findings from the Indian banking sector over the period 1988–2004. Gormley (2010) investigates the effect of foreign bank entry on domestic credit access of domestic firms following India's 1994 commitment to the WTO, and finds the observed effect of foreign bank entry occurs after one to two years and appears to persist for the duration of the following time period.

9 Matthews and Zhang (2010) finds that the average productivity growth has been positive for the city banks, but neutral for the SOBs and JSCBs over the period 2003–2007, which is the second part of their sample period.

10 The Bankscope database provides two kinds of financial statement – consolidated and unconsolidated. The consolidated statement aggregates the information from all branches of the bank (e.g. financial leasing company or insurance company established by the bank) which are not related to the bank's main business. Hence, the unconsolidated statement is selected unless the consolidated statement is the only option available. Ultimately, it is only necessary to rely on consolidated statements for nine banks.

11 The distribution of the observations is in the Appendix (Table 6.A2).

12 www.forbes.com/2009/03/30/loans-banks-china-business-oxford.html.

13 The DEA efficiency score can be estimated in the input or output direction. The input direction measures the proportional reduction in input quantities without changing the output quantities produced. Alternatively, the output direction measures the proportional increase in the output quantities produced without altering the input quantities employed. The DEA model is illustrated in the output direction.

14 One reason for choosing the output approach is that the inputs of banks are usually fixed in the real world. For example, there are regulations for the minimum number of staff (such as four people at least) in each branch in order to avoid moral hazards. Because the bank may not be able to minimize inputs such as manpower, it has to seek to maximize output.

15 For example, the total loans and total deposits are the variables from the balance sheet at a given point in time, but the net commissions and fees as well as total other operating income are revenue variables from the statement of comprehensive income.

16 The observations are chosen with replacement, which means that the observations in the dataset could be chosen more than once in the bootstrapping iteration. After each loop, the selected observations are put back into the dataset before the next loop. Follow the suggestion from Simar and Zelenyuk (2007), 70 per cent of observations in each year (subsample size) are randomly chosen in each iteration, which they consider to be a reasonable percentage for precision purposes. That 'pseudo' subsample is calculated by the DEA method and aggregated to get the efficiency score for each year.

17 The efficiency frontier is estimated 1,000 times ($B = 1,000$) in order to get a consistent estimate in the bootstrapping stage.

18 The results of the profit/revenue specification are presented in the Appendix (see Table 6.A3).

19 This hypothesis states that the managers of the least competitive banks in the market have the greatest pressure on them to increase efficiency.

20 The results of the intermediation and product specifications are presented in the Appendix (see Tables 6.A4 and 6.A5).

References

Ariff, M. and Can, L. (2008). Cost and profit efficiency of Chinese banks: A non-parametric analysis. *China Economic Review*, 19, 260–273.

Beck, T., Demirguc-Kun, A. and Levine, R. (2007). Finance, inequality and the poor. *Journal of Economic Growth*, 12(1), 27–49.

Beck, T., Demirguc-kunt, A., Leaven, L. and Levine, R. (2008). Finance, firm size, and growth. *Journal of Money, Credit & Banking*, 40(7), 1379–1405.

Berger, A.N. and Humphrey, D.B. (1997). Efficiency of financial institutions: International survey and directions for future research. *European Journal of Operational Research*, 98, 175–212.

Berger, A.N., Hasan, I. and Zhou, M. (2009). Bank ownership and efficiency in China: What will happen in the world's largest nation? *Journal of Banking & Finance*, 33, 113–130.

Charnes, A., Cooper, W.W. and Rhodes, E. (1978). Measuring the efficiency of decision-making units. *European Journal of Operational Research*, 2(6), 429–444.

Charnes, A., Cooper, W.W. and Rhodes, E. (1979). Short communication: Measuring efficiency of decision-making units. *European Journal of Operational Research*, 3(4), 339.

Debreu, G. (1951). The coefficient of resource utilization. *Econometrica*, 19(3), 273–292.

Deprins, D., Simar, L. and Tulkens, H. (1984). *Measuring Labor-Efficiency in Post Offices: The Performance of Public Enterprises – Concepts and Measurement*. Amsterdam: North-Holland.

Drake, L., Hall, M.J.B. and Simper, R. (2009). Bank modelling methodologies: A comparative non-parametric analysis of efficiency in the Japanese banking sector. *Journal of International Financial Markets, Institutions & Money*, 19(1), 1–15.

Färe, R. and Zelenyuk, V. (2003). On aggregate Farrell efficiencies. *European Journal of Operational Research*, 146(3), 615–620.

Färe, R., Grosskopf, S. and Lovell, C.A.K. (1985). *The Measurement of Efficiency of Production*, Boston, MA: Kluwer-Nijhoff Publishing.

Farrell, M.J. (1957). The measurement of productive efficiency. *Journal of the Royal Statistical Society*, Series A (General), 120(3), 253–290.

Garcia-Herrero, A., Gavila, S. and Santabarbara, D. (2009). What explains the low profitability of Chinese banks? *Journal of Banking & Finance*, 33, 2080–2092.

Gormley, T.A. (2010). The impact of foreign bank entry in emerging markets: Evidence from India. *Journal of Financial Intermediation*, 19, 26–51.

Heffernan, S.A. and Fu, X. (2010). Determinants of financial performance in Chinese banking. *Applied Financial Economics*, 20, 1585–1600.

Hicks, J. (1935). Annual survey of economic theory: The theory of monopoly. *Econometrica*, 3, 1–20.

Laeven, L. and Majnoni, G. (2003). Loan loss provisioning and economic slowdowns: Too much, too late? *Journal of Financial Intermediation*, 12(2), 178–197.

Li, S., Liu, F., Liu, F. and Whitmore, G.A. (2001). Comparative performance of Chinese commercial banks: Analysis, findings and policy implications. *Review of Quantitative Finance & Accounting*, 16, 149–170.

Lin, X. and Zhang, Y. (2009). Bank ownership reform and bank performance in China. *Journal of Banking & Finance*, 33, 20–29.

Matthews, K. and Zhang, N. (2010). Bank productivity in China 1997–2007: Measurement and convergence. *China Economic Review*, 21(4), 617–628.

Rajan, R.G. and Zingales, L. (1998). Financial dependence and growth. *American Economic Review*, 88(3), 559–586.

Schmidt, K.M. (1997). Managerial incentives and product market competition. *Review of Economic Studies*, 64, 191–213.

Schumpeter, J.A. (1911). The theory of economic development. *Harvard Economics Studies*, 46.

Simar, L. and Wilson, P. (1998). Sensitivity analysis of efficiency scores: how to bootstrap in nonparametric frontier models. *Management Science*, 44(1), 49–61.

Simar, L. and Wilson, P. (2000). A general methodology for bootstrapping in nonparametric frontier models. *Journal of Applied Statistics*, 27(6), 779–802.

Simar, L. and Zelenyuk, V. (2007). Statistical inference for aggregates of Farrell-type efficiencies. *Journal of Applied Econometrics*, 22(7), 1367–1394.

Yao, S., Han, Z. and Feng, G. (2008). Ownership reform, foreign competition and efficiency of Chinese commercial banks: A non-parametric approach. *The World Economy*, 31, 1310–1326.

Yu, Y. (2010). *The Impact of the Global Financial Crisis on the Chinese Economy and China's Policy Responses*. Penang: Third World Network.

7 The faster things change, the more they stay the same

The influence of cultural norms, customs and traditions on venture capital in China

Zhiqiang Xia, Noel Lindsay, Pi-Shen Seet and Steve Goodman

Introduction

Venture capital commonly refers to equity financing of unquoted ventures ranging from the seed stage to the late stage of pre-initial public offering (IPO) (Haemmig, 2003). Venture capital is important for entrepreneurship development (Arthurs and Busenitz, 2003). It plays a catalytic role in the entrepreneurial process, with significant contribution to job creation, innovative products and services, competitive vibrancy and the dissemination of the entrepreneurial spirit (Bygrave and Timmons, 1992).

The availability of venture capital to new high-potential businesses has been viewed as critical in supporting a vibrant modern information economy (Kortum and Lerner, 2000). The scale and sophistication of the venture capital industry in the US has made significant contribution to the US economy's exceptional ability to propel innovation and technology commercialization (Maula *et al.*, 2005). However, the peak of the venture capital investment boom in North America was reached in 2000, and it has not recovered since the bursting of the so-called 'dot-com' bubble (see Figure 7.1).

While there was a partial rebound in venture capital activity in Australia in 2005–2007, the market has undergone a significant reversal since the collapse of Lehman Brothers and the Global Financial Crisis (GFC) (see Figure 7.2).

In contrast, China's rise to be the second largest economy in the world has seen a concomitant growth in its venture capital industry, a form of finance that has largely been adopted from Western developed economies. It is now the fastest-growing market for venture capital investment. In the ten-year period from 2002 to 2011, capital raised by venture capital funds in China increased from US$1.30 billion to US$26.46 billion, with the amount growing by 162.0 per cent in 2010–2011 alone (Zero2IPO, 2011). The number of new funds and the amount raised each year in China from 2002 to 2011 are presented in Figure 7.3, which shows a clear trend of growth in the last ten years.

Despite this rapid change, venture capitalists (VCs) operating in China have shown some distinctive behavioural characteristics, which are partly reflected in

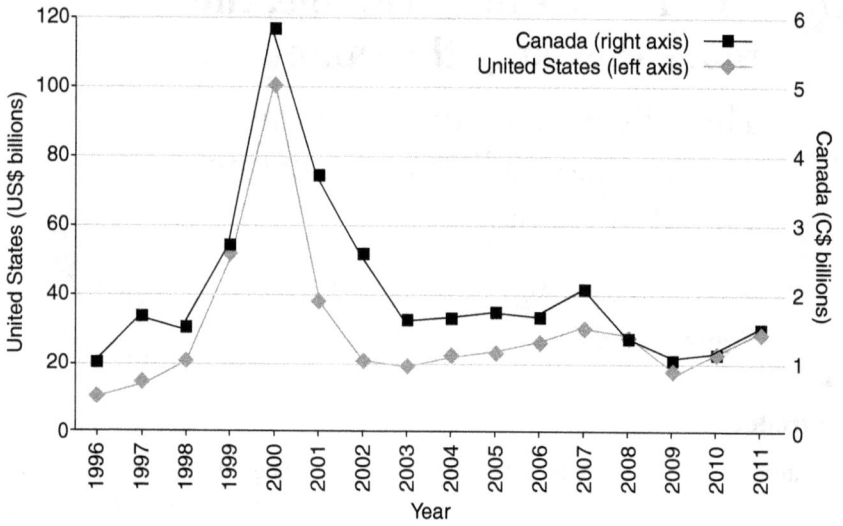

Figure 7.1 Venture capital trends in the US (source: Science Technology and Innovation Council, 2013).

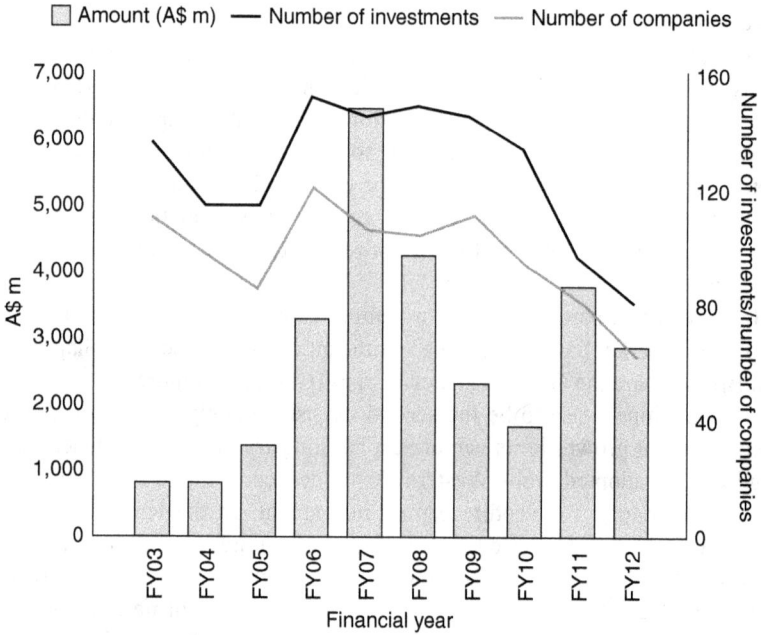

Figure 7.2 Venture capital trends in Australia (source: AVCAL, 2013).

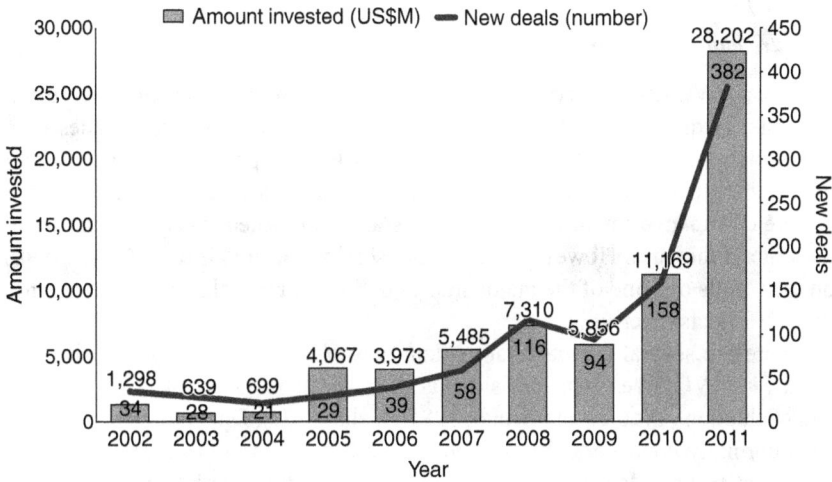

Figure 7.3 Venture capital trends in China (source: adapted from Zero2IPO, 2011).

their investment decision preferences. This chapter argues that institutions which include cultural norms, customs and traditions have a significant impact on VCs' decision preferences in China. China has an institutional environment substantially different from that of the rest of the world. Chinese cultural norms, customs and traditions are pervasive and permeate decision-making at all levels and facets of Chinese life, including the shaping of entrepreneurial behaviour and investment in entrepreneurial ventures.

With a key objective of achieving superior financial returns on their investment, VCs are expected to possess strong domain knowledge for operating in uncertain and complex business environments. They need to rely on their professional knowledge and experience to make judgements and investment decisions.

To explore this, the study surveyed 50 individual senior VCs operating in China. Results show that there are indeed differences between Chinese VC decision preferences and those in other countries. Specifically, some of the criteria (entrepreneur's track record, proprietary protection and market competition) endorsed by existing research were not considered to be of much importance by the Chinese VCs. However, some additional criteria such as the entrepreneur's commitment and integrity, user benefits, meeting crucial user needs and customer focused strategy were highly regarded by Chinese VCs. Surprisingly social network is not deemed particularly important.

Our findings suggest that institutions and cultural norms, customs and traditions, in particular, affect not only how VCs use information but also what information they use. Therefore, in spite of the rapid growth of the venture capital industry and the global nature of this form of finance, our study finds that there are significant differences in decision preferences between Chinese venture capitalists and their counterparts in Western developed economies.

Literature review

Venture capitalist decision-making

The area of VC decision criteria and preferences has attracted extensive research interests, leading to a series of studies conducted in the last two decades (e.g. Macmillan *et al.*, 1985, 1987; Muzyka *et al.*, 1996; Shepherd *et al.*, 2000; Zacharakis and Meyer, 1998). Founded upon common professional practices, a shared culture of VC investment implies that VCs are homogeneous across countries in the criteria they use. However, the comparison by Zacharakis and Meyer (1998) on the results of some of the major studies in this area reveals strong heterogeneity in VC decision criteria.

There are several reasons that explain why VCs hold different decision criteria. First, VC investment decisions go through at least two stages: screening and evaluation (Tyebjee and Bruno, 1984; Wells, 1974). Due to time constraints, VCs normally concentrate on a selected number of criteria to screen out deals perceived to have low potential for success. They then apply a wide range of preferred and compensatory criteria (Tyebjee and Bruno, 1984) to evaluate the more valued ones. Second, criteria may differ when VCs assess ventures at different lifecycle points. Smart (1999) finds that VC emphasis may switch from entrepreneur dynamic capabilities in reacting to different challenges for early-stage ventures, to entrepreneur performance track record within the firm for later-stage ventures. Third, criteria may differ based upon venture types (Zacharakis and Shepherd, 2007). The approach to evaluating high-tech ventures is most likely different from that of evaluating service-based businesses as the revenue models and risk profiles vary significantly.

Besides the above reasons, the heterogeneity shown in past studies can be partially attributed to the limitations of the research methods applied (Muzyka *et al.*, 1996; Riquelme and Rickards, 1992; Shepherd, 1999; Shepherd and Zacharakis, 1999; Zacharakis and Meyer, 1998). In response to this, Muzyka *et al.* (1996) adopted conjoint analysis and found consistently important criteria in VCs' decision-making. Applying conjoint analysis, Zacharakis *et al.* (2007) find that VCs in the US, Korea and China use the same eight criteria in making investment decisions due to the shared culture of the VC profession. The eight criteria are leadership, market size, market growth, industrial expertise, start-up record, number of competitors, competitor strength and proprietary protection. They claim that economic institutions primarily influence the importance weight attributed to the criteria, but not what criteria are used.

Institutional theory, however, argues that institutions in general, and culture in particular, shape the actions of firms and individuals in a number of subtle but substantive ways. Wright *et al.* (2002) show that US VC companies modified their working approaches according to the local market conditions when entering India. Moreover, the local regulatory and cognitive institutions further shaped the behaviour of VC managers. As one of the most dynamic and fastest growing economies in the world, China has an institutional environment substantially different from that of the rest of the world, as shown in several empirical studies (e.g. Bruton and Ahlstrom, 2003; Cornelius, 2005; Zacharakis *et al.*, 2007). VCs in China are faced with challenges that are significantly different from those in other countries. Some evidence shows that the operation of venture capital in emerging markets shares some similar features as well as substantial differences with those in the more developed Western economies (e.g. Bruton and Ahlstrom, 2003; Bruton *et al.*, 2002, 2004). Even though various external factors including VC decision stage, venture growth phase and venture type are controlled, VC decision preferences in China may still differ from those in other countries in both the criteria used and the importance and weight attributed to the criteria, due to institutional influence. In other words, institutions have a larger impact than has been reported in the literature as far as China is concerned.

Institutional theory and Chinese institutions

Institutions are conceptualized as 'the rules of the game in a society' (North, 1990). Institutional forces are subtle but pervasive, and strongly influence the goals and beliefs of individuals, groups and organizations (Dacin *et al.*, 2002; North, 1990). Social and cultural elements are incorporated in institutional theory to provide a more socialized illustration of the impact of institutional forces (Dacin *et al.*, 2002).

As we begin to examine VCs' decision preferences, a more finely grained set of institutions needs to be considered. Institutions can be categorized into regulatory, normative and cognitive groupings (Scott, 1995), which have been widely used effectively for analytical purposes. Regulatory institutions are the most formal, representing standards provided by laws and other sanctions. Normative institutions are less formal and define the roles or actions that are expected of individuals. Finally, cognitive institutions help individuals construct beliefs and taken-for-granted rules (Scott, 1995), though in the most informal forms.

Although Zacharakis *et al.* (2007) report that Chinese VCs use the same eight criteria for decision-making as their counterparts in the US and Korea, we do not fully agree with this. Asia in general, and China in particular, has an environment that is substantially different from the US or Europe (Boisot and Child, 1996; Peng, 2000). It remains to be seen how institutions actually impact the investment decision preferences of venture capitalists in China.

Hypothesis 1: *Not all of the eight criteria reported in the VC literature based on conjoint analysis will be considered important by Chinese VCs.*

Though useful, conjoint analysis also has its limitations. It is constrained by the number of attributes to be examined. If relevant factors are excluded from this type of discrete choice experiment, choice variability will decrease naturally, whereby respondents will tend to choose more consistently and choose more familiar alternatives (Kardes *et al.*, 2004). Some researchers point out that limiting the number of variables could leave out important evaluation criteria (Csaszar *et al.*, 2006). Possible bias in conclusions about mean attribute effects resulting from such issues have been highlighted (Islam *et al.*, 2007). Even in the context of mature and developed economies, there have been studies that highlight the diversity of VC decision criteria. In an attempt to identify criteria that influence high-tech venture performance, Kakati (2003) found 21 criteria that differentiated successful from unsuccessful ventures. China has an institutional environment that is less developed, has more diverse and complex social and cultural dimensions, and is still in the early stages of institutional isomorphism.

Hypothesis 2: *Besides the eight criteria reported by literature using conjoint analysis, there will be other important criteria used by Chinese VCs in making investment decisions.*

Legal protection for investors and legal enforcement are two important aspects of regulatory institutions. An important dimension for VC investors is the level of legal protection they can expect as minority shareholders in the investee company. Differences in the level of investor protection and legal enforcement could impact the way the individual VC behaves (Bruton *et al.*, 2003). A stable institutional regime with predictable legal enforcement helps VCs safeguard and achieve their investment returns. Trust is an important factor in generating deals. VCs in any country will want to deal with entrepreneurs they trust to provide accurate information and behave in a non-opportunistic manner. The weak legal enforcement and strong unpredictability, typifying many emerging economies like China (Meyer, 2001; Peng, 2000), require the entrepreneur's commitment and trustworthiness to be more salient.

Hypothesis 2a: *When making investment decisions, most Chinese VCs will place greater weight on both commitment and integrity of the entrepreneur than other factors.*

Based on institutional theory and given the low predictability and weak legal enforcement in the Chinese institutional context, it is hypothesized that:

Hypothesis 1a: *Chinese VCs will not rely heavily on intellectual property and proprietary protection when making investment decisions.*

Institutions are typically situation-specific. Institutional characteristics of a country should be evaluated with regard to a specific phenomenon rather than general arrangements (Busenitz *et al.*, 2000). Entrepreneurial track record is considered essential by Western VCs. However, due to the short history of the private sector in China as a transition economy (Bliss, 1999), the emphasis on entrepreneurs' track record seems unreasonable to entrepreneurs.

Hypothesis 1b: *Chinese VCs will not emphasize the entrepreneur's track record when making investment decisions.*

Cognitive institutions build from the culture of the society. Social network not only provides benefits to its members, but also imposes obligations on them (Tsang and Walls, 1998). In Western economies, social network is important, but economic performance may be more critical to businesses. In Asia, the need to be part of a social network could be vital. Biggart and Hamilton (1992) argue that 'Asian economies espouse different institutional logics from Western economies, ones rooted in connectedness and relationships', or 'guanxi' as it is known in China. Personal trust embedded in the networks initially functions in response to the weak legal framework to enforce contracts or sanction violators (Perkins, 2000). Previous empirical evidence has shown the importance of networks in East Asia for entrepreneurship as a whole (Butler *et al.*, 2003). There is also research on venture capital that considers, among other things, the function of networks in emerging economies in East Asia (Bruton *et al.*, 2002, 2004; Lockett *et al.*, 2002). To seek VC financing in China, social capital is found to be critical (Batjargal and Liu, 2004).

Hypothesis 2b: *Chinese VCs will place greater weight on the entrepreneur's social network when making investment decisions.*

China is a large and rapidly growing market with abundant opportunities that are still expanding. The tastes of Chinese customers are continuously evolving, though they may not be as sophisticated as their counterparts in developed economies. In such a unique business environment, whether and how products can reach customers effectively and efficiently is one of the most prominent considerations, and the market competition factor is relatively indirect and less predictable for assessing business attractiveness.

Hypothesis 1c: *Compared with other important factors, Chinese VCs are not particularly concerned with market competition when making investment decisions.*

Kakati (2003) shows that entrepreneur quality, resource-based capability and competitive strategy are critical determinants of firm viability and achievement.

According to this study, major differences between successful and unsuccessful ventures are in the resource-based capabilities and business strategies. Particularly, it is the firm's ability to meet the unique requirements of customers that brings success. However, criteria pertaining to these two dimensions were either ignored or given less attention by previous research in VC decision criteria and/or new venture success criteria.

Hypothesis 2c: *Criteria directly addressing customer benefits will be considered important by Chinese VCs in making investment decisions.*

Method

We identified 25 criteria based on the literature and further discussion with five VCs outside the sample of the study. The 25 criteria and the descriptions are shown in Table 7.1.

The literature was predominantly sourced from US and European scholarly journals, since there is no systematic research focused on Chinese VC decision criteria to date. These 25 criteria include the eight criteria studied by Zacharakis *et al.* (2007). Within these eight, two criteria (the number of competitors and competitor strength) are merged into one – market competition – in the current study. The other criteria fall into five broad categories: trustworthiness (full commitment and personal integrity), product feature (user benefits, user acceptance and cruciality of user needs), business strategy (customer focus strategy, innovation-driven strategy, low-cost-driven strategy), resource (VC resource fit, intellectual property, product portfolio, resource flexibility, capital intensity, exclusive rights, strategic alliance and social network) and market (market entry barriers and supply chain constraints).

We developed the Likert-scale survey questions based on these 25 criteria. We controlled for a number of factors in our survey, including VC decision stage, venture growth phase and venture type. The respondents were asked to indicate their perception of the importance of each criterion in affecting the survivability or profitability of technology-based new ventures in China (refer to Table 7.1 for an illustration). In view of the nature of this exploratory study, we purposely set the response in three categories: 'unimportant', 'neutral' and 'important'. Each scale allowed the respondent to provide distinct indications of the perceived importance of the criteria. By so doing, we aimed to reduce the tendency of some respondents' bias on the importance of the listed criteria. We did not adopt conjoint analysis for this task as it is constrained by the number of testing factors and may be too complicated for the current study owing to its exploratory nature. At this stage, encouraging the participation of the Chinese VC respondents was also one of the key considerations for us. However, we are aware of the limitations of respondent introspection (Fischhoff, 1988) in using the Likert-scaling. To overcome this problem, we limited our survey sample to

Table 7.1 The 25 major VC investment criteria identified in the literature

The objective of this survey is to find out from venture capitalists' perspective the importance of various attributes in affecting the survivability or profitability of technology-based new ventures in China. In the last three columns of the following table, please key in 'U' to denote the attribute as 'Unimportant', 'N' as Neutral, and 'I' as 'Important'.

S/N	Attribute	Description	Unimportant U	Neutral N	Important I
1	Leadership	Do the core entrepreneurial team members have strong leadership?			
2	Personal integrity	Is the integrity of the core team members strong or questionable?			
3	Start-up experience	Do the core team members have substantial start-up experience?			
4	Industry expertise	Does the team possess strong industry expertise?			
5	Full commitment	Are the core team members fully committed to the venture?			
6	Market entry barrier	Is the market entry barrier high or low?			
7	Market competition	Does the venture face intense or mild market competition?			
8	Market size	Is the target market big or small?			
9	Market growth	Is the target market growing fast?			
10	User benefits	Does the product provide significant user benefits?			
11	Cruciality of user needs	Is the user need addressed by the product crucial?			
12	User acceptance	Can the product be easily accepted by the users?			
13	Intellectual property	Does the venture have IP protection for its key technologies?			
14	Proprietary technology	Are the key technologies of the venture proprietary?			
15	Capital intensity	Is the product development or marketing capital-intensive?			
16	Resource flexibility	Does the venture have flexibility to commit and un-commit resources?			
17	Supply chain constraint	Does the upstream or downstream of the supply chain set constraints on the venture development?			
18	Exclusive rights	Does the venture possess strong exclusive rights?			
19	Strategic alliance	Can the venture form strategic alliance with external parties?			
20	Social network	Does the venture possess a strong social network?			
21	Customer focus	Does the venture have a strong customer focus as its business policy?			
22	Innovation driven	Is the venture development driven by innovation?			
23	Low-cost driven	Does the venture strive to achieve low-cost as its winning strategy?			
24	Product portfolio	Is the venture able to develop a series of products or a portfolio?			
25	VC resource fit	Is there a strategic fit between the venture mix and the VC resources?			

only experienced VCs practicing in China, because preferences consolidate over time with knowledge accumulation (Hoeffler and Ariely, 1999). The marketing literature informs that preferences stabilize when customers possess deep domain knowledge. The expert VCs are expected to have stable preferences and the consistency between their 'espoused theory' and 'theory-in-use' will be high.

The instrument has two language versions. The original English version was translated into Chinese and then translated back into English to ensure accuracy. The instrument was then presented in the VC's native language. Data were collected in two rounds, through emails and during the Ninth China Venture Capital & Private Equity Annual Forum in Shanghai in December 2009. Of the 78 senior VCs contacted, 50 senior VCs provided useable insightful responses. The 50 practising VCs comprised 33 from Shanghai, 11 from Beijing and six from Shenzhen, which represents three major cities for venture capital in China. Participants were senior members holding designations of investment director or partner and above in domestic and foreign-owned VC firms operating in China. Each participant had extensive VC experience and some had worked in Western VC investment environments. Twenty out of the 36 firms represented by these senior VC respondents were ranked among the top 50 VC firms operating in China.

We received 35 responses in the first round of data collection and a further 15 responses in the second round. In analysing the data, we found the additional 15 responses did not have a significant impact on the results. Therefore, we contend that the 50 responses are a fair representation of the Chinese VC population.

Results

Table 7.2 provides the results of the responses pertaining to each criterion. Means are computed by assigning the scores 1, 0 and -1 to 'unimportant', 'neutral' and 'important', respectively. Standard deviations and the percentage of the respondents reporting a criterion as important are also presented in the table. In addition, we conducted χ^2 tests for the criteria. In computing χ^2 statistics, the number of 'unimportant' and 'neutral' indications are combined and compared with the number of 'important' indications for each criterion.

From a review of these statistics, the following observations were made. Eleven (out of the 25) criteria were acknowledged as 'important' by more than 60 per cent of the Chinese VC respondents. They are full commitment, leadership, personal integrity, market size, user benefits, market growth, cruciality of user needs, user acceptance, industry expertise, customer focus strategy and innovation-driven strategy. Among the 11 more important criteria, innovation-driven strategy had the lowest mean score of 0.56 and full commitment had the highest mean score of 0.98. The χ^2 tests helped to verify whether the importance attribution by the survey sample to the 11 criteria was significantly different to the rest. The only one not supported by the χ^2 statistics was innovation-driven strategy. Therefore, this study identifies the top ten criteria as important criteria.

Compared with the other 15 criteria, these ten important criteria had relatively lower standard deviation, which means a higher consensus on the importance

Table 7.2 Results

		Mean	SD	%	χ^2
Leadership	Do the core entrepreneurial team members have strong leadership?	0.94	0.24	94	1E-08
Proprietary technology	Are the key technologies of the venture proprietary?	0.36	0.63	44	0.1735
Industry expertise	Does the team possess strong industry expertise?	0.72	0.45	72	0.0091
Start-up experience	Do the core team members have substantial start-up experience?	0.2	0.53	26	9E-05
Market size	Is the target market big or small?	0.8	0.40	80	0.0002
Market growth	Is the target market growing fast?	0.76	0.48	78	0.0005
Market competition	Does the venture face intense or mild market competition?	0.22	0.62	32	0.0022
Personal integrity	Is the integrity of the core team members strong or questionable?	0.96	0.20	96	2E-09
Full commitment	Are the core team members fully committed to the venture?	0.98	0.14	98	3E-10
User benefits	Does the product provide significant user benefits?	0.88	0.33	88	1E-06
User acceptance	Can the product be easily accepted by the users?	0.68	0.51	70	0.0201
Cruciality of user needs	Is the customer need addressed by the product crucial?	0.62	0.57	66	0.0787
Customer focus	Does the venture have a strong customer focus as its business policy?	0.66	0.52	68	0.0412
Innovation driven	Is the venture development driven by innovation?	0.56	0.58	60	0.3642
Low-cost driven	Does the venture strive to achieve low-cost as its winning strategy?	-0.2	0.64	12	4E-09
VC resource fit	Is there a strategic fit between the venture mix and the VC resources?	0.44	0.61	50	0.6097
Intellectual property	Does the venture have IP protection for its key technologies?	0.34	0.69	46	0.2812
Product portfolio	Is the venture able to develop a series of products or a portfolio?	0.28	0.67	40	0.0538
Resource flexibility	Does the venture have flexibility to commit and un-commit resources?	0.14	0.67	30	0.0008
Capital intensity	Is the product development or marketing capital-intensive?	0.12	0.66	28	0.0003
Exclusive rights	Does the venture possess strong exclusive rights?	-0.02	0.74	26	9E-05
Strategic alliance	Can the venture form strategic alliance with external parties?	0.04	0.64	22	7E-06
Social network	Does the venture possess a strong social network?	0	0.57	16	1E-07
Market entry barrier	Is the market entry barrier high or low?	0.44	0.61	50	0.6097
Supply chain constraint	Does the upstream or downstream of the supply chain set constraints on the venture development?	0.4	0.64	48	0.4272

perception of these criteria among the respondents. Full commitment and personal integrity had the highest means and lowest standard deviations, providing strong support for *hypothesis 2a*. Strong support was also shown for all three criteria relating to product feature (user benefits, user acceptance and cruciality of user needs) and one of the business strategy criteria (customer focus), although they were not included in the previous conjoint analysis studies.

To address the potential multi-collinearity concern, the next step was to check the correlation among these ten important criteria. A correlation matrix was therefore generated, as shown in Table 7.3.

Four pairs of criteria were found to correlate to each other relatively highly: (1) leadership and market growth (0.4072); (2) leadership and full commitment (0.5654); (3) personal integrity and user acceptance (0.4746); (4) user acceptance and cruciality of user needs (0.4854). As the integrity of the core team members and the easy acceptance of the product by the users are two largely different criteria in nature, the reason for the high correlation between these two remains to be examined. However, user acceptance was also highly correlated with cruciality of user needs. It suggests that this criterion may be excluded in later studies. If full commitment and user acceptance are removed from the list due to high correlation with other criteria, four criteria (personal integrity, user benefits, cruciality of user needs and customer focus) which are new and have not shown to be important in previous conjoint analysis still remain significant. Therefore, *hypothesis 2* and *hypothesis 2c* are supported.

It is worth noting that social network (or 'guanxi') received a mean value of zero, while only 16 per cent of the respondents reported this criterion as important. This is contradictory to the belief that social network is one of the distinctive sources of competitive advantage. The survey results show that Chinese VCs are not concerned with this factor. Therefore, *hypothesis 2b* is not supported.

While four of the conjoint analysis criteria appear again in the important criteria list, the others (start-up record, number of competitors, competitor strength and proprietary protection) do not. Only 44 per cent of the respondents indicated proprietary technology was important, largely resulting in the low mean of 0.36. In addition, less than one-third of the respondents indicated start-up experience and market competition were important. *Hypothesis 1a*, *1b* and *1c* are all supported. These results confirm *hypothesis 1*.

Discussion, conclusion and future research

Given the importance of venture capital as a source of external financing for growth-oriented entrepreneurial ventures, understanding how venture capitalists make investment decisions is important for start-ups (Gupta and Sapienza, 1992). Entrepreneurs are keen to have insights into VC decision preferences to gain an advantage when seeking VC funding. However, knowledge about the VC decision preferences in China is limited. This study fills this gap by exploring the institutional impact on the VCs' decision preferences in China.

Table 7.3 Correlation matrix

	Leadership	Industry expertise	Market size	Market growth	Personal integrity	Full commitment	User benefits	User acceptance	Cruciality of user needs	Customer focus
Leadership	1.0000									
Industry expertise	0.0300	1.0000								
Market size	0.0842	0.2450	1.0000							
Market growth	0.4072	-0.0340	0.2757	1.0000						
Personal integrity	-0.0516	0.3273	-0.1021	-0.1039	1.0000					
Full commitment	0.5654	-0.0891	0.2857	0.2302	-0.0292	1.0000				
User benefits	-0.0933	0.1809	-0.1846	-0.0574	-0.0754	-0.0528	1.0000			
User acceptance	-0.1593	0.2212	-0.0197	-0.1537	0.4746	-0.0901	0.2522	1.0000		
Cruciality of user needs	-0.1709	0.1332	-0.0712	-0.1933	0.2253	-0.0966	0.2980	0.4854	1.0000	
Customer focus	-0.1671	-0.0658	-0.0389	0.0759	-0.1350	-0.0945	0.2346	-0.1104	0.1066	1.0000

Specifically, research into early-stage investors has shown that investment decision-making can have significant country-specific characteristics (Zacharakis *et al.*, 2007) and, as such, we believe that this study makes the following contributions: (1) there are indeed differences between Chinese VC sets of investment criteria and those identified in other countries; and (2) cultural norms, customs and traditions affect not only how VCs use information but also what information they use. The research extends Zacharakis *et al.*'s (2007) findings that VCs from different countries (US, Korea, China) use the same information factors in their screening decisions and the institutions primarily influence the 'importance weights' attributed to the information.

While conjoint analysis as a method may be limited, especially in the context of substantive complexities in the social, economic and cultural aspects of a diverse transition economy such as China, where there is significant heterogeneity in VC decision criteria, our findings confirm that besides the eight criteria reported by the literature using conjoint analysis, there are other important criteria such as personal integrity, user benefits, cruciality of user needs and customer focus strategy that are highly valued by Chinese VCs in making investment decisions. The research also shows that both normative and cognitive institutions are important to the formulation of VC decision preferences in China. Due to the unique institutional environment of China as an emerging economy with special cultural norms and traditions, less weight is placed on start-up record, proprietary protection and market competition compared to more developed economies. There are indeed differences between Chinese VCs' sets of decision preferences and those identified in developed economies. It means the incorporation of limited criteria in the VC research in China may cause important aspects of a venture to be overlooked while at the same time cause some criteria to be over-emphasized and given undue weight.

The findings provide practical insights for other countries. For example, with the introduction of the Business Innovation and Investment (Provisional) visa (subclass 188) in Australia, as part of the Business Innovation and Investment Program introduced by the former Federal Labour government to attract both foreign talent and investment into Australia (Department of Immigration and Border Protection, 2013), this research will assist the Australian venture capital and entrepreneurial sectors as they prepare for an influx of largely Chinese venture capital by understanding the decision-making characteristics of Chinese early-stage investors. Among the three streams of business innovation, investor and significant investor, it is expected that the significant investor stream will have the greatest impact on early-stage ventures in Australia as it allows potential international investors who have a minimum of AUS$5 million to invest in Australia to qualify for specially created 188 Business Innovation and Investment (Temporary) visas. A number of venture capitalists and financial institutions are putting together managed funds by pooling strategic investor stream applicants' funds so that by the first quarter of 2014 it is estimated that there will be up to AUS$1.5 billion of investments available arriving in Australia, much of it available as potential venture capital for the Australian start-up sector (Riley, 2013).

While the focus of the study has been on Chinese VCs, given the diversity of the VC industry, one major area of future inquiry is to examine the differences in decision preferences across different types of VCs (e.g. foreign vs domestic, expert vs novice) and the implication for entrepreneurs in China. Another possibility is to examine a collective group of resource attributes through the lens of the resource-based view. If we pay close attention to the resource-related criteria examined in the current study, we can see the 'importance weights' placed on them by Chinese VCs differ to a large extent. From the resource perspective, a start-up's main resources are human and social capital. Social capital includes social network and a variety of entrepreneurship literature has informed that social network positively contributes to venture performance. Surprisingly, the hypothesized importance of social network was not supported in the current study, which contradicts with the extensive social network literature related to China. Further research into this could make important contributions to the literature.

References

Arthurs, J.D. and Busenitz, L.W. 2003. The boundaries and limitations of agency theory and stewardship theory in the venture capitalist/entrepreneur relationship. *Entrepreneurship: Theory & Practice*, 28(2): 145–162.

AVCAL. 2013. *2013 Yearbook*. Sydney: Australian Private Equity & Venture Capital Association.

Batjargal, B. and Liu, M. 2004. Entrepreneurs' access to private equity in China: the role of social capital. *Organization Science*, 15(2): 159–172.

Biggart, N.W. and Hamilton, G.G. 1992. On the limits of a firm based theory to explain business networks: the Western bias of neoclassical economics. In N.N.G.G. Eccles (ed.), *Networks and Organizations*, pp. 471–490. Boston, MA: Harvard Business School Press.

Bliss, R.T. 1999. A venture capital model for transitioning economies: the case of Poland. *Venture Capital: An International Journal of Entrepreneurial Finance*, 1: 241–257.

Boisot, M. and Child, J. 1996. From fiefs to clans and network capitalism: explaining China's emerging economic order. *Administrative Science Quarterly*, 41: 600–628.

Bruton, G.D. and Ahlstrom, D. 2003. An institutional view of China's venture capital industry: explaining the differences between China and the West. *Journal of Business Venturing*, 18(2): 233–259.

Bruton, G.D., Ahlstrom, D. and Singh, K. 2002. The impact of the institutional environment on the venture capital industry in Singapore. *Venture Capital*, 4: 197–218.

Bruton, G.D., Ahlstrom, D. and Wan, J.C.C. 2003. Turnaround in Southeast Asian firms: evidence from ethnic Chinese communities. *Strategic Management Journal*, 24: 519–540.

Bruton, G.D., Ahlstrom, D. and Yeh, K.S. 2004. Understanding venture capital in East Asia: the impact of institutions on the industry today and tomorrow. *Journal of World Business*, 39: 72–88.

Busenitz, L.W., Gomez, C. and Spencer, J.W. 2000. Country institutional profiles: interlocking entrepreneurial phenomena. *Academy of Management Journal*, 43: 994–1003.

Butler, J.E., Brown, B. and Chamornmarn, W. 2003. Informational networks, entrepreneurial action and performance. *Asia Pacific Journal of Management*, 20: 151–174.

Bygrave, W.D. and Timmons, J.A. 1992. *Venture Capital at the Crossroads*. Boston, MA: Harvard Business School Press.

Cornelius, B. 2005. The institutionalisation of venture capital. *Technovation*, 25(6): 599–608.

Csaszar, F., Nussbaum, M. and Sepulveda, M. 2006. Strategic and cognitive criteria for the selection of startups. *Technovation*, 26(2): 151–161.

Dacin, M.T., Goodstein, J. and Scott, W.R. 2002. Institutional theory and institutional change: introduction to the special research forum. *Academy of Management Journal*, 45(1): 45–56.

Department of Immigration and Border Protection. 2013. Business Innovation and Investment (Provisional) visa (subclass 188). Commonwealth of Australia.

Fischhoff, B. 1988. Judgment and decision-making. In R. Sternberg and E. Smith (ed.), *The Psychology of Human Thought*, pp. 155–187. Cambridge: Cambridge University Press.

Gupta, A.K. and Sapienza, H.J. 1992. Determinants of venture capital firms' preferences regarding the industry diversity and geographic scope of their investment. *Journal of Business Venturing*, 7: 347–362.

Haemmig, M. 2003. *The Globalization of Venture Capital: A Management Study of International Venture Capital Firms*. Zurich: Swiss Private Equity and Corporate Finance Association.

Hoeffler, S. and Ariely, D. 1999. Constructing stable preferences: a look into dimensions of experience and their impact on preference stability. *Journal of Consumer Psychology*, 8(2): 113–139.

Islam, T., Louviere, J.J. and Burke, P.F. 2007. Modeling the effects of including/excluding attributes in choice experiments on systematic and random component. *International Journal of Research in Marketing*, 24: 289–300.

Kakati, M. 2003. Success criteria in high-tech new ventures. *Technovation*, 23(5): 447–457.

Kardes, F.R., Posavac, S.S. and Cronley, M.L. 2004. Consumer inference: a review of processes, bases and judgment context. *Journal of Consumer Psychology*, 14: 230–256.

Kortum, S. and Lerner, J. 2000. Assessing the contribution of venture capital to innovation. *Rand Journal of Economics*, 31(4): 673–692.

Lockett, A., Wright, M., Sapienza, H. and Pruthi, S. 2002. Venture capital investors, valuation and information: A comparative study of the U.S., Hong Kong, India and Singapore. *Venture Capital*, 4(3): 237–252.

Macmillan, I.C., Siegel, R. and Narasimha, P.N.S. 1985. Criteria used by venture capitalists to evaluate new venture proposals. *Journal of Business Venturing*, 1(1): 119–128.

Macmillan, I.C., Zemann, L., and Subbanarasimha, P.N. 1987. Criteria distinguishing successful from unsuccessful ventures in the venture screening process. *Journal of Business Venturing*, 2(2): 123–137.

Maula, M.V.J., Autio, E. and Murray, G.C. 2005. Corporate venture capitalists and independent venture capitalists: what do they know, who do they know, and should entrepreneurs care? *Venture Capital: An International Journal of Entrepreneurial Finance*, 7(1): 3–19.

Meyer, K.E. 2001. Institutions, transaction costs, and entry mode choice in Eastern Europe. *Journal of International Business Studies*, 32(2): 357–367.

Muzyka, D., Birley, S. and Leleux, B. 1996. Trade-offs in the investment decisions of European venture capitalists. *Journal of Business Venturing*, 11(4): 273–287.

North, D. 1990. *Institutions, Institutional Change and Economic Performance*. Cambridge: Cambridge University Press.

Peng, M.W. 2000. *Business Strategies in Transition Economies*. Thousand Oaks, CA: Sage.

Perkins, D.H. 2000. Law, family ties and the East Asian way of business. In S.H.L. Harrison (ed.), *Culture Matters: How Values Shape Human Progress*, pp. 232–243. New York: Basic Books.

Riley, J. 2013. Preparing for the Chinese venture capital boom, *Business Spectator*, Australia.

Riquelme, H. and Rickards, T. 1992. Hybrid conjoint analysis: an estimation probe in new venture decisions. *Journal of Business Venturing*, 7: 505–518.

Science Technology and Innovation Council. 2013. *State of the Nation 2012: Canada's Science, Technology and Innovation System – Aspiring to Global Leadership*. Ottawa, Canada: Science, Technology and Innovation Council Secretariat.

Scott, W.R. 1995. *Institutions and Organizations*. Thousand Oaks, CA: Sage Publications.

Shepherd, D.A. 1999. Venture capitalists' introspection: a comparison of 'in use' and 'espoused' decision policies. *Journal of Small Business Management*, 37(2): 76–87.

Shepherd, D.A. and Zacharakis, A. 1999. Conjoint analysis: a new methodological approach for researching the decision policies of venture capitalists. *Venture Capital*, 1(3): 197–217.

Shepherd, D.A., Ettenson, R. and Crouch, A. 2000. New venture strategy and profitability: a venture capitalist's assessment. *Journal of Business Venturing*, 15(5/6): 449.

Smart, G.H. 1999. Management assessment methods in venture capital: an empirical analysis of human capital valuation. *Venture Capital*, 1(1): 59–82.

Tsang, E. and Walls, W. 1998. Can Guanxi be a source of competitive advantage for doing business in China. *Academy of Management Executive*, 2(2): 64–73.

Tyebjee, T.T. and Bruno, A.V. 1984. A model of venture capitalist investment activity. *Management Science*, 30(9): 1051–1066.

Wells, W.A. 1974. Venture capital decision making, thesis, Carnegie Mellon University.

Wright, M., Lockett, A. and Pruthi, S. 2002. Internationalization of Western venture capitalists into emerging markets: risk assessment and information in India. *Small Business Economics*, 19(1): 13–29.

Zacharakis, A.L. and Meyer, G.D. 1998. A lack of insight: do venture capitalists really understand their own decision process? *Journal of Business Venturing*, 13(1): 57–76.

Zacharakis, A.L. and Shepherd, D.A. 2007. The pre-investment process: venture capitalists' decision policies. In H. Landström (ed.), *Handbook of Research on Venture Capital*, pp. 3–65. Cheltenham: Edward Elgar.

Zacharakis, A.L., McMullen, J.S. and Shepherd, D.A. 2007. Venture capitalists' decision policies across three countries: an institutional theory perspective. *Journal of International Business Studies*, 38(5): 691–708.

Zero2IPO. 2011. *China Venture Capital Annual Report*. Beijing: Zero2IPO Research Centre, Jan.–Nov. Data.

8 Inter-generational transitions of family businesses using private equity

Lessons for China and Australia from Chinese family-owned enterprises in Singapore

Pi-Shen Seet, Christopher Graves and Wee-Liang Tan

Introduction

Chinese family businesses have played a major role in the development of Singapore's economy since the early nineteenth century. Some of them have grown to be large, established businesses that form a significant part of the Stock Exchanges of Singapore and Kuala Lumpur (Lee and Chan, 1998). With the prominence given by media, society and the establishment to the large, successful, multi-generational Chinese family businesses in both countries (Pan, 1990), the bulk of the research in this area has also focused on these large firms. For example, some research has been conducted on intergenerational transitions of large Chinese family businesses in Singapore (Tan and Fock, 2001). However, the majority of family businesses in Singapore, and the rest of the world, are small or medium-sized, and an estimated 80 per cent of all small-to-medium-sized enterprises (SMEs) in Singapore are Chinese family businesses (Carey *et al.*, 2005).

In addition, most existing research has focused largely on the success factors behind Chinese family businesses in various parts of the world, with studies alluding to the network effects, immigrant culture and business savvy characteristics to explain their success (Gambe, 2000; Lee and Loh, 1998; Menkhoff and Gerke, 2002; Saxenian, 1999; Zapalska and Edwards, 2001). However, there is little research focusing on how they secure resources and financing in the context of inter-generational change.

This chapter aims to address some of these research gaps by looking at family-owned SMEs (SMFEs). In particular, it examines the considerations of Chinese SMFES in Singapore when they engage with the private equity (PE) sector as part of the overall capital-raising and harvest strategy. This is relevant as there is a crisis in family business succession, with the majority of Asian SMFE owners unable to hand over their business to the next generation and many hoping to sell out in the near future (Yeung, 2000). Following recent trends of PE involvement in family businesses in Europe and North America, which have more rapidly ageing populations (Maherault, 2004; Reier, 2006), the rapid growth of Asian PE since the 1997 Asian Financial Crisis (Lockett and Wright, 2002) has led to options to restructure business ownership using PE firms (e.g. via management buy-outs (MBOs), management buy-ins (MBIs) or buy-in management buy-outs (BIMBOs) (BVCA, 1999). However, most SMFE owners are unprepared or ill-equipped to engage with such organizations.

Building on previous work by Poutziouris *et al.* (2000), this chapter presents findings from research based on in-depth interviews with five Chinese SMFE owners in Singapore as to what fears and issues are preventing these family business owners from currently seeking such funding. In doing so, the study finds knowledge and perception gaps among Chinese SMFE owners in Singapore vis-à-vis the PE community and proposes several measures for how financial and economic development agencies, as well as trade and professional services associations, can help bridge the gaps. Overcoming these gaps can assist in helping Asian economies achieve a smooth transition for SMFEs and build on the value that they have created in the past.

The chapter is structured as follows. We begin by outlining the context of Chinese SMFEs and PE in Singapore. We explore issues surrounding empathy and knowledge gaps between family firms and PE to develop a model of barriers to the use of PE in family firms which forms the foundation for this study. This is followed by an examination of the model through a qualitative study of Chinese SMFEs in Singapore. The chapter argues that there are similar trends among family businesses in China as well as Australia, with their rapidly ageing populations creating succession difficulties, and concludes that there are significant opportunities for PE investment in both countries, particularly in China, given the rapid development of the PE sector in China.

The context

Family business and SMFEs in Singapore

SMEs form 99 per cent of all firms in the Singapore economy and employ 70 per cent of workers, as well as contribute to over 50 per cent of national GDP (Department of Statistics Singapore, 2013). Family businesses form the bulk of these SMEs, and while on average they employ between 10 and 100 people and have an average turnover of less than S$10 million, as a group they make up 80–90 per cent of industrial companies, thereby forming a significant component of the Singapore economy (Lee, 2006). In spite of this, most of the research in the Singapore family business sector has focused on larger firms and not on SMEs (Lee and Chan, 1998; Tan and Fock, 2001).

Chinese family businesses in Singapore

Among the SMEs in Singapore, it is estimated that 80 per cent of all SMEs in Singapore are founded and operated by the ethnic Chinese community as family businesses (Carey *et al.*, 2005). These ethnic Chinese form part of the overseas Chinese diaspora that have become a fascination for many researchers and policy makers in the past century or so, with studies alluding to the network effects, immigrant culture and business-savvy characteristics to explain the success of overseas Chinese firms (Gambe, 2000; Lee and Loh, 1998; Menkhoff and Gerke, 2002; Saxenian, 1999; Zapalska and Edwards, 2001). They differ from mainland Chinese entrepreneurs as they are born and bred and have worked in overseas Chinese communities for generations. They may have been descendants of the Chinese diasporas over the last few hundred years, with most leaving China during the Opium Wars, World Wars and Civil War between the Communists and the Kuo Min Tang (Pan, 1990).

While many of the Chinese SMFEs in Singapore have thrived in the last few decades and many have grown to be large firms (Lee and Loh, 1998), they face a unique set of challenges in the coming years. Among the issues is that with the decline in birth rates among the Singapore Chinese population, which was accelerated by a highly effective population planning policy in the 1970s and 1980s following the baby boom (Cheng, 1989), there have been fewer members of the next generation to succeed the Singapore Chinese SMFE owners when they retire. Research by the Economist Intelligence Unit and Citibank in Singapore has shown that 40 per cent of these SMFEs have given up on finding a suitable family successor and are prepared to handover to professional managers, with only 22 per cent of them confident of passing on the business to the next generation and 17 per cent wishing to sell out altogether (Economist Intelligence Unit and Citibank, 2006). This is in line with the trend of the majority of Asian SMFE owners unable to hand over their business to the next generation and many hoping to sell out in the near future (Yeung, 2000). The problem seems to have grown in recent years, with one-third of family businesses in Singapore now considering selling out altogether (KPMG, 2012). As the recent KPMG study comments:

> Our view is that business owners usually want to pass the business to their own family member. They will not plan to employ someone from outside the family unless they have no option.... The younger generation sometimes do not want to take over the business as they have other career plans.
>
> (KPMG, 2012)

PE in Singapore

In the last 20 years or so, in order to move up the value chain and develop innovative firms, the government of Singapore has had a policy of promoting the development of the PE industry in general and early-stage venture capital in particular, in an attempt to imitate the Silicon Valley model (Koh and Koh, 2002). In line with this, research into venture capital in Singapore has been subject to quite a large number of studies (Bruton *et al.*, 2002; Hindle and Lee, 2002; Ray, 1991; Wang and Sim, 2001; Zutshi *et al.*, 1999). To that end, it is now acknowledged that the venture capital market in Singapore is 'well-established' (Wright *et al.*, 2005).

The studies point to four main trends that have a significant impact on SMFEs. First, the government has a significantly high participation rate in the venture capital industry. In 2000, government-originated funding provided for at least 19 per cent of the US$7.4 billion invested (Guide to Venture Capital in Asia, 2001). Second, while the aim of the government is to support the development of innovative local firms, the bulk of the investments in the Singapore venture capital industry is not invested in local firms, with more than 85 per cent of funds invested overseas, mainly in the surrounding region, as there are insufficient opportunities in Singapore (Bruton *et al.*, 2002). Third, 40 per cent of funds are invested in the early-stage firms, largely due to venture firms needing to meet the criteria for preferential tax treatment for investment gains (Koh and Koh, 2002). This is significantly higher than in other Asian countries (e.g. 25 per cent in Taiwan (*European Venture Capital Journal*, 1999)), and reflects the government's attempts to support the early-stage technology firms. However, fourth, of the funds that are invested in Singapore firms, about 60 per cent are in 'low-technology' firms (Zutshi *et al.*, 1999).

The net result of these trends for SMFEs in Singapore is that unless the firm is an early-stage firm operating in a sector considered 'strategic' by the Singapore government, it is less likely that the venture firms would consider investing in them. While Asian, venture capital and PE have historically focused more on late-stage expansion financing and investment in mature companies, rather than early-stage financing in start-ups (Chu and Hisrich, 2001), the government incentives have shifted the focus to early-stage firms. The lack of interest in later-stage PE investments is also reflected in that there are almost no research studies on private-equity funded management buy-outs in Singapore.

Literature review

PE and family firms

PE investment, especially through buy-outs, has been found to be attractive in the private family firm sector (Wright and Burrows, 2008). It has been found to offer an alternative exit route for family firms that have not been able to find appropriate successors to assume ownership and/or management responsibilities (Bachkaniwala *et al.*, 2001; EVCA, 2005; Wright *et al.*, 1992). Even if there are potential successors, families may not have the entrepreneurial commitment or the requisite resources and capabilities for continued growth and survival in an increasingly competitive and dynamic global marketplace. However, there may be professional managers who possess sufficient interest and knowledge to take on the challenge of making innovative and entrepreneurial changes and thereby ensuring business growth and survival (Howorth *et al.*, 2004). Although a trade sale or an initial public offering (IPO) may be alternative options, these may be unattractive as the family may no longer be involved in the business (Scholes *et al.*, 2008) or it may require technical and financial resources beyond the capabilities of the family (Poutziouris, 2002). In such cases, an MBO may be appropriate as it

> may be a means of effecting succession and be acceptable to the founder as the best way to preserve their psychic income (non-monetary satisfaction) through maintaining the company's independent identity and culture, as well as continuing to be involved in the business.
>
> (Wright, 2007: 296)

If internal professional managers do not possess sufficient interest or skills to be owner-managers, but external parties can identify potential opportunities in the family business, then an MBI may be more appropriate (Robbie and Wright, 1996).

A survey of family firms involved in PE-backed buy-out deals in Europe by the EVCA found that 33 per cent would have ceased to exist had it not been for a buy-out/buy-in involving PE (EVCA, 2001). In Europe, PE-backed deals involving family firms have been increasing as a proportion to other deals (Figure 8.1) so that in the decade leading up to 2007, the combined value of European buy-outs/buy-ins involving family firms rose from €11.2 billion to €18.3 billion and a majority of them (62 per cent) were PE-backed (Wright *et al.*, 2008).

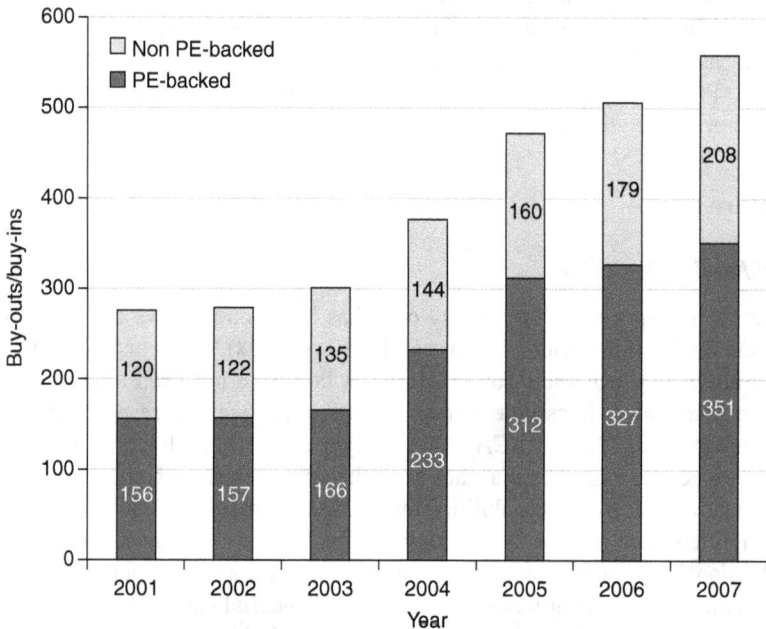

Figure 8.1 Number of PE and non-PE-backed buy-outs/buy-ins of family firms (€ million) (source: Wright *et al.* 2008).

While there is currently little evidence of active engagement by SMFEs with PE, there has been, in general, little research into how SMFEs and/or their advisers engage with the PE sector (Romano *et al.*, 2001), let alone in the Asian and particularly Chinese family business context. In some studies, a dislike for institutional finance, particularly external PE, has been identified (Gallo and Vilaseca, 1996; Upton and Petty, 2000). This 'empathy gap' may be due to asymmetries between family business sources of capital and their personal, business and familial objectives (Gasson, 1999). Poutziouris *et al.* (2000), in exploratory work, show that some family businesses are open to external capital for long-term investment to develop new technologies and markets. However, this may not be significant as the evidence indicates that when there is PE involvement, most of the deals are on restructuring ownership (e.g. MBOs) instead of facilitating entrepreneurs to grow new ventures (Joseph, 1999).

Moreover, Poutziouris (2001: 289) remarks that the 'empathy gap' may not be as significant as a knowledge gap as 'family companies (may be) antithetic to venture capital options simply because they feel less knowledgeable and comfortable about deal structures' in particular and the PE industry in general. Harvey and Evans (1995: 164) agree, noting that:

> The cost of capital from venture capital firms normally goes well beyond the financial parameters of the loan arrangement. They frequently expect ... a host of other requirements. Many of these requests would seem foreign in the privacy of the family business.

Poutziouris (2001) also notes that his comments above, which reflect the state of existing research, are based on anecdotal evidence and calls for more rigorous examination of the relationships between PE and family businesses, which this study aims to partly address.

One way to close the empathy or knowledge gap between business owners and PE may be through the use of professional advisers, because when the SMFE grows, such advisers are engaged to advise the owners on the increasing complexities of business transactions as part of the professionalization process (Gersick, 1997; Gurd and Thomas, 2006; Hofer and Charan, 1984). This is shown in the model in Figure 8.2. However, there is little research or evidence that the professional adviser may have experience in PE deals or appropriate knowledge of the sector and therefore the capability to help bridge any empathy or knowledge gaps that the business owners have.

Methodology: multiple-case study design, in-depth interviews and content analysis

The research is exploratory in nature, and given the lack of in-depth literature and empirical studies conducted in the past, a multiple-case study design was adopted (Holstein and Gubrium, 1997). As it was important in this exploratory research to gather 'rich' data (Steyaert and Bouwen, 1997), the data were

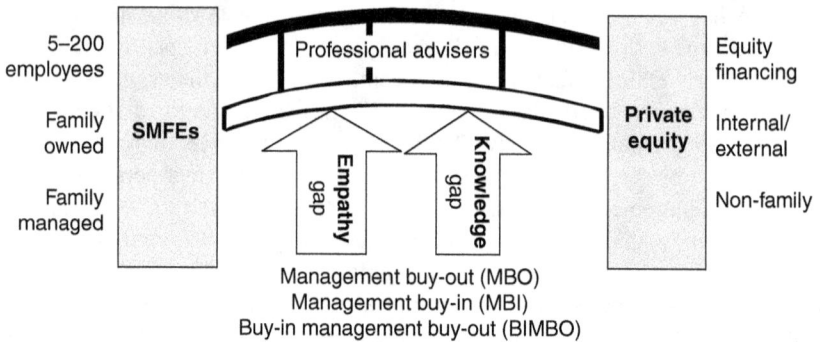

Figure 8.2 Model 'barriers to using PE in family firms'.

collected primarily via in-depth guided interviews with five Chinese SMFE owners in Singapore as there were few media and other research reports and the contexts were important and could not be discounted (Patton, 1990). The interview guide was adapted from a similar study conducted in Australia (Seet and Graves, 2010b).

As we did not have access to an official register or database of the population, a non-probability convenience sampling process based on snowballing was used as this offered a better solution to the problem of data collection among hidden groups (Van Meter, 1990).

For triangulation purposes and also to investigate their role in the PE engagement process, interviews were also conducted with various professional advisers to the Singapore Chinese SMFEs. A content analysis of the interview data revealed themes associated with the engagement of PE by the Singapore Chinese SMFEs.

Respondent profile

A profile of the Singapore Chinese SMFEs is shown in Table 8.1.

Findings

The interviews support the earlier theories that there are major empathy and knowledge gaps among SMFE owners when it comes to engaging with the PE community.

Empathy gaps

Finding out the attitudes towards PE among SMFE owners was an important part of the interviews. These questions were generally more open-ended than the ones on knowledge of PE. An example of an empathy-related question is: 'How do you feel about PE involvement in family businesses?'

Table 8.1 Overview of the five SMFEs

Item	SMFE 1	SMFE 2	SMFE 3	SMFE 4	SMFE 5
Industries	Infrastructure and electrical supply	Publishing	Construction	Commodities trading	Lifestyle
Gender of SMFE owner	M	M	F	M	F
Age of firm (years)	25	37	10	57	19
No. employees	50	9	10	30	5
Generation	First	First /second	First	Third	First
Succession plan in place	No	Yes	Yes	Yes	No
Annual turnover (SGD)	SGD 20–50M	SGD 1–5M	SGD 1–5M	SGD 20–50M	SGD <1M

In terms of empathy, three sub-themes emerge. First, there is a fear of losing control among SMFE owners. This is illustrated in the extracts of some of the interviews below.

> I would prefer not to include outsiders in my family business ... (the main) risks (are) losing control to these firms as well as releasing proprietary information to outsiders.
>
> (SMFE 3)

> I have seen how my friends' companies lose their freedom and control and they are slogging to keep up with the management team. It also means they have lost freedom to do whatever they like at their own time, like going out for coffee time, even breakfast at 11 a.m.
>
> (SMFE 4)

> I am open to the idea of venture capitalists and private equity but (they) must be prepared to give (me) management control ... (the main) risk (is to) lose control over my business.
>
> (SMFE 4)

This focus on retaining control is a common theme among family businesses (Adler and Gunderson, 2008; Tanewski and Carey, 2007). In our discussions with the SMFE owners, it became apparent that most of them were not aware that PE firms often take control of the firms they invest in.

Second, there is the issue of trust. Of the five SMFE owners interviewed, only one seemed to have a positive opinion of PE. This is illustrated in the extracts of some of the interviews below.

I feel that top management should comprise family members, as they know the business the best, having been in the line for so long (the more senior members) and having grown up learning about the business (the younger ones). The key is trust; the trust that a family has cannot be underestimated. I feel that when you have a family that works together effectively, and puts the good of the family above the interest of self, a family business beats a professionally run one any time.

(SMFE 2)

It is a matter of trust. I trust my family members that they will perform in the best interest of the company. Like I mentioned before, it would be very hard to give control of my business to outsiders and also to trust them in what they are doing without my questioning which may then lead to conflicts. In the long run, it may not be healthy to the business.

(SMFE 1)

The importance of trust is also a common finding among family businesses, especially small family businesses (EVCA, 2005; Wu *et al.*, 2007). While non-family members may be seen as less trustworthy than family ones, despite material that indicate the positive influence of PE (Wang and Ahmed, 2007), it is likely that the largely negative image of the PE world as portrayed in mainstream media has reinforced the distrust (Davidsson, 2004; Schoenberger, 2002).

Third, reinforcing the lack of trust is the lack of commitment to understanding the nature and potential advantages of PE, an issue which is explored in greater detail in the next section. The Singapore Chinese SMFE owners do not seem to be open to devoting time, energy and resources in engaging with PE. Some comments are as follows:

I have not gone for any courses. There is no time in our business to attend talks or courses as we are very hands on in the business.

(SMFE 3)

I have not read any books or materials (on private equity). Reason is lack of time. The business is moving every day and I am involved overseeing the business so there is hardly time to be involved in reading up. I would rather use the time to source for useful suppliers or customers or to expand my business plans.

(SMFE 1)

To me, it sounds like they engage in deals that amount in millions which I think my company has not reached. So, it's the bigger companies that are involved more in this sector.

(SMFE 5)

It is understandable that SMFE owners have other, more pressing business-related concerns than to devote resources and effort to learning more about and engaging with the PE community (Helfat, 2007; Kaplan, 2000). It is also not unexpected as the five Singapore Chinese SMFEs that were studied currently do not have any upcoming succession concerns and three of them have succession plans that involve handing over the business to the next generation. However, of the two SMFEs that indicated they did not have succession plans, at least one of them noted that the likely end-state will be to sell the business. It is of concern here that if they do not make the effort to explore PE options, their means for exiting the business will be limited.

Knowledge gaps

The study found evidence of two areas whereby the Singapore Chinese SMFE owners were found to be lacking in knowledge of the PE sector. First, the SMFE owners did not fully understand basic concepts of PE. The semi-structured interviews asked them three questions based on common actions among PE firms when engaging with family businesses (Table 8.2):

1 Can you describe what you understand by a management buy-out (MBO)?
2 Can you describe what you understand by a management buy-in (MBI)?
3 Can you describe what you understand by a buy-in management buy-out (BIMBO)?

None of the SMFE owners answered all three questions correctly. In two of the cases they simply responded that 'I am not sure what these mean.' There also seems to be confusion on other fundamental concepts e.g. the difference between debt and equity. For example, one respondent saw PE as a provider of loans as follows:

> I understand all the offers and proposals put forward. I do not have any concerns. I know what they are talking or offering to me as I have gone for business talks, seminars and through peer sharing derived sufficient knowledge to handle these propositions … private equity always comes up with new systems structuring new funding/structure loans.
>
> (SMFE 4)

Reinforcing the findings of lack of enthusiasm above is the view that attempting to understand these basic concepts in dealing with PE is too difficult. As one respondent put it:

Table 8.2 Correct/incorrect responses to MBO, MBI and BIMBO question

Item	SMFE 1	SMFE 2	SMFE 3	SMFE 4	SMFE 5
MBO	✓	✗	✓	✗	✗
MBI	✗	✗	✓	✓	✗
BIMBO	✗	✗	✗	✗	✗

I do not have very high education levels and have not heard such terms. I think education plays a part in knowing such financial terms and tools. For me, it is running a simple business and through experience, to run it in the most profitable way and not based on theories.

(SMFE 5)

This finding is unsurprising as this knowledge-gap is not limited to family firms and is quite representative of all small businesses and start-ups (De Clercq *et al.*, 2006; Zider, 1998).

Second, although the majority of the Singapore Chinese SMFE owners acknowledged that they needed to learn more, they did not fully buy into the idea that they would engage professional advisers or get their trade associations to help bridge their knowledge gaps. We asked them three questions:

1   Have your professional advisers suggested private equity options for your business? Why and why not?
2   Have you discussed private equity options with your trade association and/ or family business association?
3   Describe what other sources of information and education on the private sector that you have looked at?

Some responses were:

No, we do not employ professional advisers ... we feel that we are able to cope sufficiently well on our own.

(SMFE 2)

Never brought it up. They may feel that our profits are not big enough.

(SMFE 5)

My professional adviser concentrates on getting their jobs done, which is auditing and accounting for our company. Unless we are on very close terms, if not, I do not think it would be the place of my auditors to suggest private equity options for my company unless I ask about it.

(SMFE 3)

While some of them attended talks organized by government agencies, e.g. SPRING Singapore, none of them mentioned any specific educational initiatives by their respective trade associations. This finding may be more significant among family firms as there have been initiatives over the last decade or so to encourage start-ups to capitalize on networks, alliances and other intangible resources available to build up their entrepreneurial capabilities (Alvarez and Barney, 2000, 2002).

Summary of findings from Singapore Chinese SMFEs

In general, given the effectiveness of the population control policies with other factors on reducing the fertility rate over the years, family businesses in Singapore are facing issues of succession. We set out to establish whether there were any empathy and knowledge gaps among Singapore Chinese SMFE owners in terms of dealing with PE. We found evidence of three main empathy gaps: (1) the fear of losing control; (2) the lack of trust of outsiders; and (3) the lack of enthusiasm to engage with the PE sector. We also found that there are two main knowledge gaps among Singapore Chinese SMFE owners: (1) the lack of understanding of basic concepts of PE; and (2) an indifferent attitude towards using professional advisers, trade associations and/or government resources to bridge that gap. In the next section we extend our findings to show why they may be applicable beyond Singapore, especially in China and Australia, which face similar contexts of rapidly ageing populations that may be having an impact on family businesses.

Lessons for China

Socio-economic drivers for inter-generational transition issues for SMFEs in China

The phenomenon of ageing does not only apply to more developed Asian economies like Singapore (*The Economist*, 2009). The United Nations, in 2009, conducted research on ageing and found that it was a global issue, with the older population growing faster than the total population in almost all regions of the world (United Nations, 2009). The UN estimated that 737 million people were aged 60 years or over and constituted the 'older population' of the world, nearly two-thirds of whom lived in developing countries. Their number is projected to increase to two billion in 2050, by which time older persons will outnumber children (persons aged 0–14 years). Because of the one-child policy, which has been in place for about 30 years, China's population is ageing faster than those of developed countries (Guo and Marinova, 2006). Figure 8.3 shows the population pyramids of Singapore as compared to China, while Figure 8.4 shows the relative population size trends.

From the diagrams, China has a population that is ageing rapidly; given that the one-child policy started a few years after Singapore's population planning initiative in the early 1970s, there is about 5–10 years of lag in terms of China feeling similar effects to that of Singapore. More critically, given that the birth and fertility rates have slowed down in China significantly, the mainland Chinese population will not only slow down but reverse from about 2030 onwards, much earlier than Singapore.

While much of the present research on the impact of ageing in China focuses on the social and economic implications (Guo and Marinova, 2006; Zuo and Yang, 2009), we believe that this will also affect the upcoming inter-generational

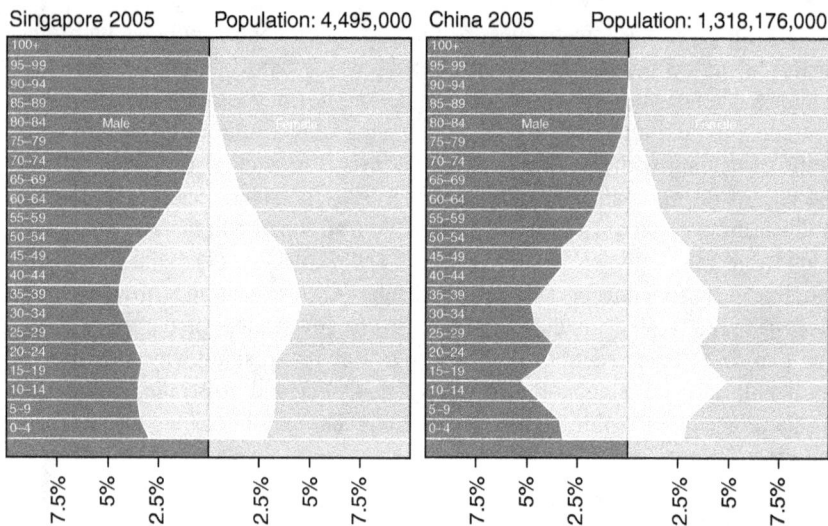

Figure 8.3 Population pyramids of Singapore (left) and China (right) as at 2005 (source: United Nations, 2009).

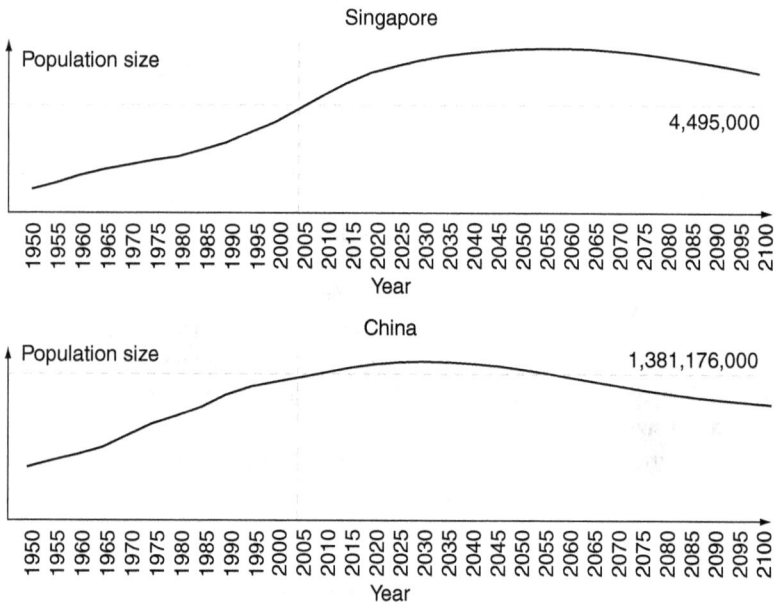

Figure 8.4 Population trends of Singapore (top) and China (bottom) (source: United Nations, 2009).

transition for mainland Chinese family businesses, especially the many that were started since the beginning of the economic reforms from 1978 onwards. This means that in the next 10–20 years, it is expected that some of the founders who started businesses in China following economic reforms that began in the late 1970s will want to hand-over to the next generation, but that there will be limited successor options. If, as suggested earlier for Singapore, the scale of these problems suggests that not all family business owners in China can look forward to alternative traditional exit options such as trade sales, then exits via PE, e.g. through MBOs, should be explored.

Inter-generational transition issues for SMFEs in China

In a recent study on children of family business owners in China, it was found that only a small portion of offspring (36 per cent of the survey respondents) intended to join their parents' businesses, let alone take over the family business (Wang and Jia, 2009). The study found that among potential successors, the most important factor influencing their intentions to succeed their parent(s) in the family business was whether there was an opportunity in the business to allow them to 'aspire to reach high professional position in [their] career'. Given that the parents of these offspring operated family businesses that employed between 21 and 500 people, the authors note that this would be difficult:

> 'Therefore, it would be a great challenge for the Chinese family business owners who intend to transfer their enterprises to the heir. Based on the findings, we can predict that only a small portion of family businesses could carry out an inside succession smoothly, while the others have to decide when and how to sell the company shares, or employ outsiders to manage the firm.
>
> (Wang and Jia, 2009: 4)

Compounding this is the widening generation gap between parents and children born after the implementation of the one-child policy (Fowler *et al.*, 2010).

Potential of PE investment in family firms in China

China's rapid economic growth has led to an equally rapid development of the alternative investment market that has started to invest in the many growth opportunities in the country. While the first domestic venture capital/PE firm was only set up in 1986, the PE industry grew rapidly after 1998 following the introduction of specific policies to promote such investments by the Chinese government (Batjargal and Liu, 2004). The result is that the Chinese PE market is now the largest in the Asian region with almost one-third of investments or US$122 billion out of US$376 billion of all capital under management in Asia (AVCJ Research, 2012). This compares with only US$32 billion for Singapore (SVCA, 2013), which suggests that the Chinese market for venture capital and PE is at least ten times larger than the size of the Singapore market.

Furthermore, research by KPMG in the PE sector in China has found that while growth capital will continue to be the predominant form of investment in Chinese targets in the near future, PE investors have expressed a rising interest in buy-out activity (KPMG, 2009). This may reflect growing confidence of investors in company management, more realistic valuations and maturity in China's mergers and acquisitions sector (Figure 8.5).

This is reinforced by the potential growth of SMFEs in the various industries in China. As noted above, PE investors generally look to invest in firms in growth industries. Due to the huge domestic market in mainland China, family businesses in China have much more growth potential when compared to family businesses set up by Chinese overseas (Zhang and Ma, 2009). As recent research shows, it is highly likely that the Chinese PE sector will rapidly catch up with more mature economies like Singapore and Australia in terms of investments in family businesses over the coming years (EYGM, 2014) (Figure 8.6).

Furthermore, recent media reports note that Chinese cities are now engaged in fierce competition to lure PE firms to set up operations in their locations (Chen and Zheng, 2010). Big cities like Shanghai, Chongqing and Beijing have been doing deals with big PE firms like Blackstone, Carlyle and TPG. The belief is that luring a PE firm to set up in the city would bring not only prestige and access to foreign investment funds for domestic projects, but also jobs. According to the mayor of Chongqing, PE 'is the crown jewel of the investment industry' (Chen and Zheng, 2010). PE firms have been offered 'dowries' which may include waiver of set-up fees, financial subsidies and pro-investment policies.

In spite of these trends, there has been little research conducted on how SMFEs in China perceive PE and vice versa.

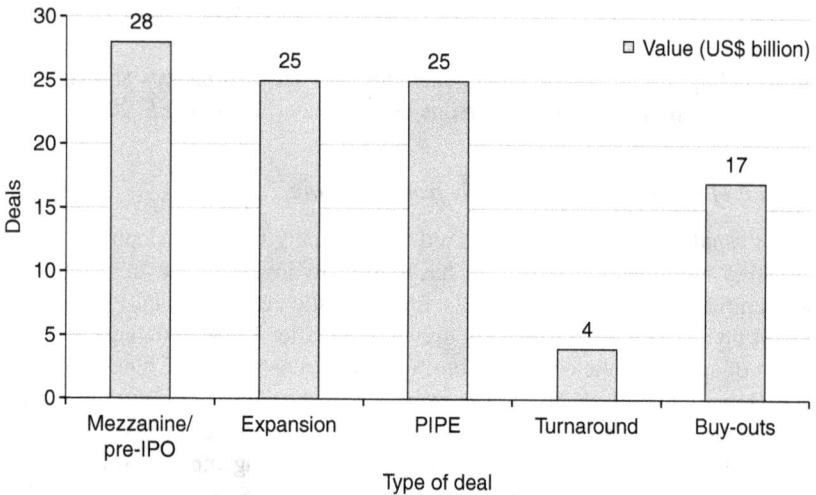

Figure 8.5 Types of deals done by private equity firms in China (2005–2010) (adapted from Ahn *et al.*, 2011).

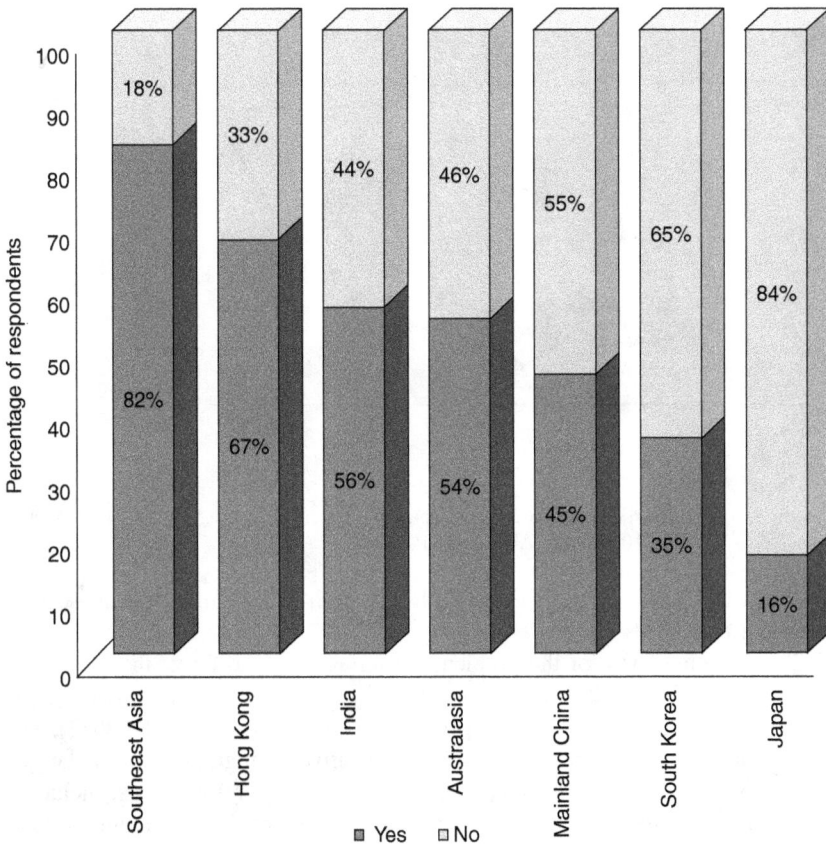

Figure 8.6 Perceptions among PE investors of investment activity growth among family-owned businesses in 2014 (source: EYGM, 2014).

Lessons for Australia

Socio-economic drivers for inter-generational transition issues for Australian SMFEs

Although Australia has not had a deliberate population control policy, there are similar demographic trends, and the main reasons for the upcoming succession problem for Australian SMFEs are the socio-economic trends of an ageing population combined with a lower birth and fertility rate.

As shown in Figure 8.7, the Australian population and workforce is ageing and has been doing so since the early 1990s.

This trend has resulted in people working for longer and rising retirement ages. There are many causes for this (e.g. people are healthier, a shift from manufacturing to services in the economy), but the most notable long-term trend

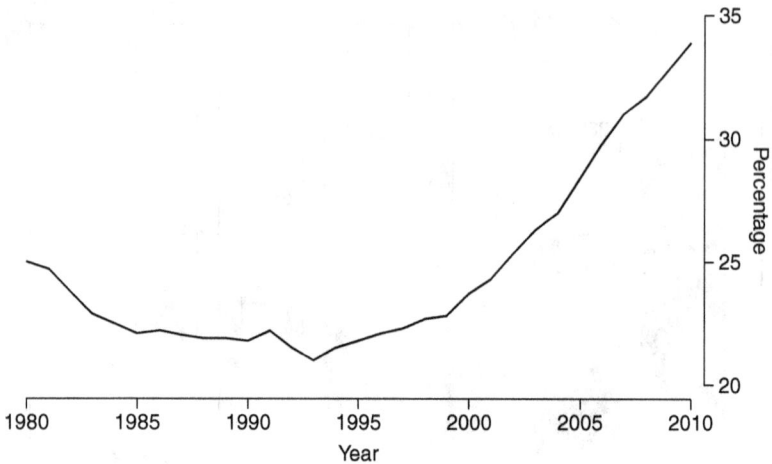

Figure 8.7 Australian labour force participation of people aged 55 years and over – 1980–2010 (source: ABS, 2010a).

has been the stabilization and decline in the birth and fertility rates as seen in Figures 8.8 and 8.9.

To overcome some of the problems of an ageing workforce, the Australian government has undertaken policy reform, such as gradually increasing the qualifying age for the government pension (to be 67 years of age by 2023). The Australian government has kept up a very positive immigration policy, largely driven by growth in the Temporary Business (Long Stay) migrants, including full fee paying international students and higher levels of skilled temporary long-term migration (see Figure 8.10) (ABS, 2009).

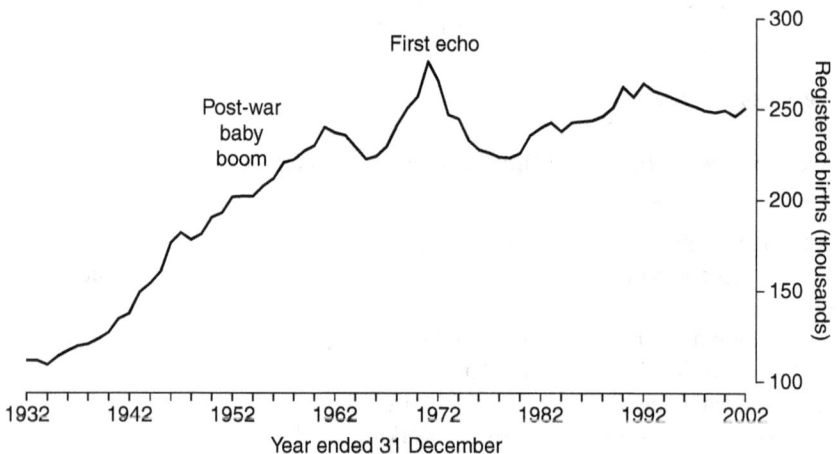

Figure 8.8 Number of registered births in Australia (source: ABS, 2010a).

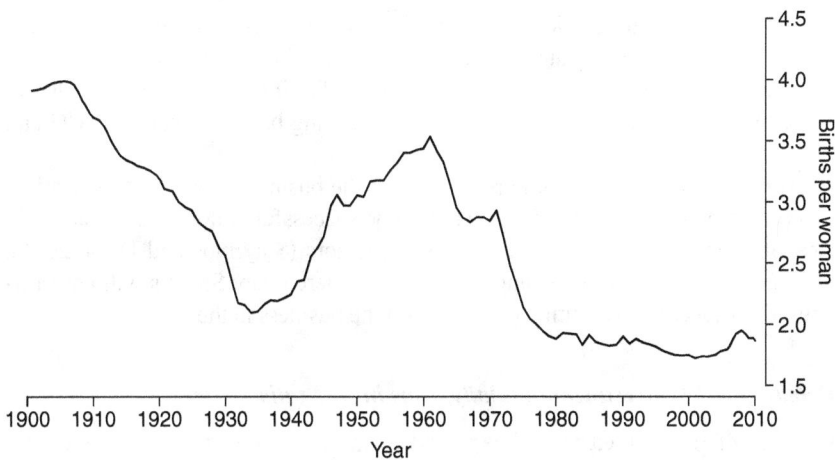

Figure 8.9 Total fertility rate in Australia: 1900–2012 (source: ABS, 2012).

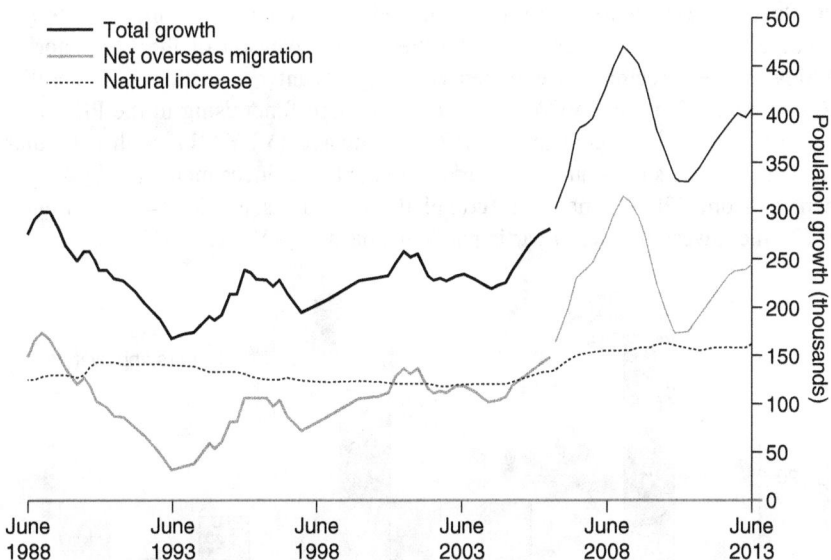

Figure 8.10 Components of population growth in Australia (source: ABS, 2013).

Notes
Annual components calculated over each quarter.
Estimates for June quarter 2002 onwards and preliminary.
NOM estimates have been calculated using a range of methods over the period, and include a break in series at September quarter 2006.
Estimates for September quarter 2012 onwards are preliminary.

Inter-generational transition issues for SMFEs in Australia

However, using immigration is not really a viable option for family business owners, and given that many of the founder-owners are from the baby-boomer generation (Figure 8.11), around 60 per cent of family business owners plan to retire by 2016 as part of the general trend of retiring baby boomers (KPMG and FBA, 2007).

Although over 55 per cent hope to pass on the business to the next generation, it is estimated that only 25–35 per cent will be successful in doing so because of a lack of interested and/or suitable family successors (Smyrnios and Dana, 2006). This suggests that there is an impending crisis where many SMFEs will have difficulties in successfully exiting or passing on the business in the near future.

Potential of PE investment in family firms in Australia

Because PE has increasingly been used in the ownership transition of family firms in developed countries, especially in Europe and North America, there is growing interest in whether PE investors can provide a practical solution to the upcoming succession crisis among SMFEs in Australia (Seet and Graves, 2010a). However, while there was sustained interest among PE investors to get involved in the SMFE sector, unlike the rapid expansion of the PE sector in China, the PE sector has experienced a significant contraction in Australia. Recent research from AVCAL show that although fundraising in the PE sector has grown by 54 per cent in FY2012 as compared to FY2011, with particular resilience in the small- and mid-market segments, PE investments fell by 25 per cent and only 28 PE managers completed new deals in FY2012 (see Figure 8.12), the lowest number of participants in a decade (AVCAL, 2012).

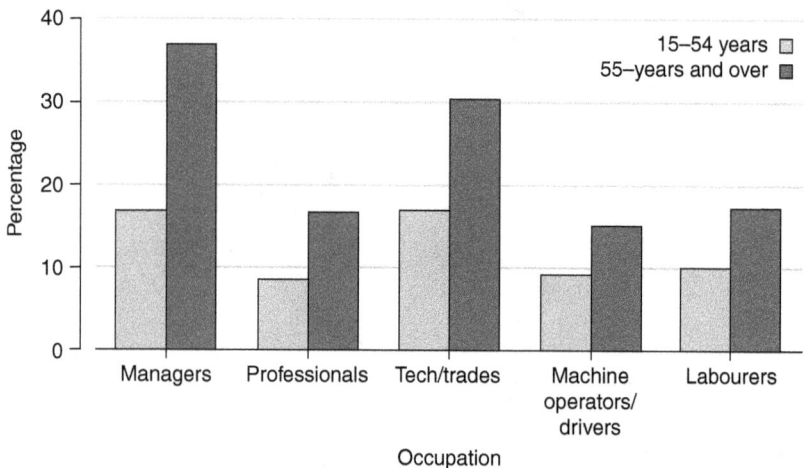

Figure 8.11 Proportion of Australian owner managers and selected occupations (2010) (source: ABS, 2010b).

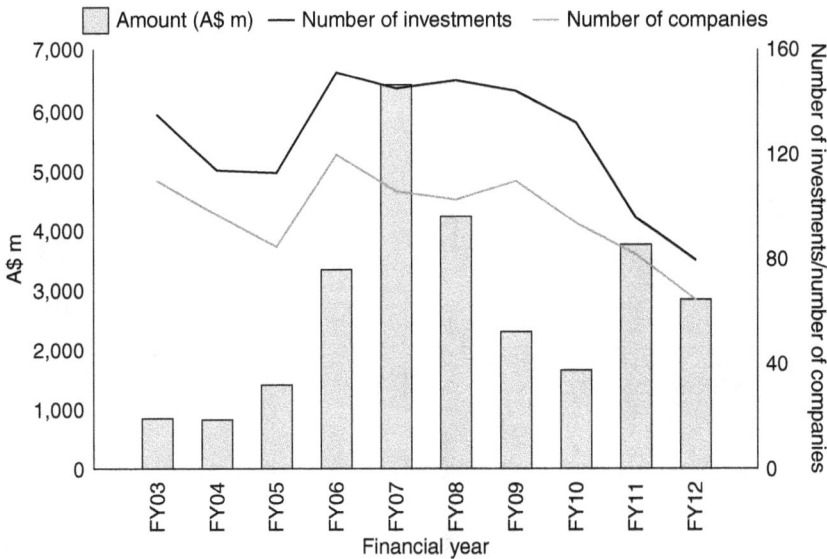

Figure 8.12 Australian PE funds raised by fiscal year (in A$ millions) (source: AVCAL, 2012).

In terms of interest among family business owners for using PE, Pricewater-houseCoopers (PwC), in collaboration with AVCAL, has recently conducted similar research and found

> that private equity (PE) may have something of an image problem. With a significant proportion of companies surveyed either planning investments or ownership succession (or both), there appear to be widespread misconceptions about what private equity is and the role it can play for owners considering investments and/or succession.
>
> (PwC, 2012b: 3)

In this research, only 5 per cent of respondents were considering PE as a source of investment (see Figure 8.13). This is very similar to the 4 per cent of family firms considering PE as a source of investment that PwC found in a much more detailed study of a small group of 50 selected firms (PwC, 2012a).

PwC's survey focused on firms with revenues of approximately A$10 million to A$100 million per year. Of these, only 10 per cent of respondents had any experience with PE, with 22 per cent admitting that they did not know enough about PE as an option (PwC, 2012b). This mirrors findings from earlier exploratory research in Australia that focused on even smaller firms, namely SMFEs, which found that for these firms, many would look for advice on engaging with PE through their business advisers and especially through their accountants, their preferred advisers (Seet and Graves, 2010b).

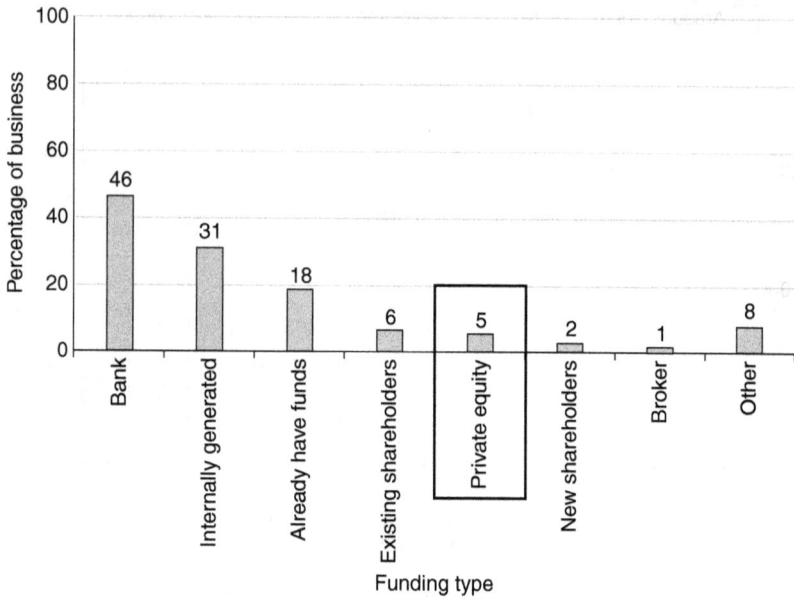

Figure 8.13 Percentage of businesses considering different types of funding (source: PwC, 2012b).

Note
Base: planning investment (*n*=342).

Conclusion, further research and policy implications

Regardless of the potential opportunities for PE to provide solutions to the upcoming succession crisis among SMFEs in Singapore, our exploratory research suggests that SMFE owners are ill-prepared or unwilling to explore such opportunities. There appears to be significant gaps in knowledge with regard to the PE sector in general, and specifically how PE can provide owners with alternative options to exit as owners. It is also evident that even if owners develop a greater understanding of PE, they are unlikely to engage with this type of financing largely because of their overriding desire to preserve family control. Given the fact we are interested in the use of PE when owners may be willing to forgo family control (i.e. exit as owners), efforts should be directed to educating owners looking to exit on how the PE sector can provide alternatives to traditional exit routes such as a trade sale.

The findings of the research on Chinese SMFEs in Singapore correlates with exploratory research in Australia that indicates there are significant barriers that exist between family business owners and PE providers which create not only knowledge and empathy gaps, but also finance gaps between the two parties, i.e. PE investment in SMFEs may be a theoretical possibility but not necessarily a practical reality in the Australian context (Seet and Graves, 2010b). As there is little research in mainland China about the barriers to and opportunities for SMFEs to access PE, further research needs to be conducted to understand whether these empathy and knowledge gaps exist; specifically, are there any aspects that are peculiar to the mainland Chinese context.

In terms of policy, given that the research findings indicate that if policy-makers and the PE community want to assist SMFEs by giving them alternative exit and harvest options, they will have to work hard to address these empathy and knowledge gaps. Some suggestions for initial action that may assist in bridging these identified empathy and knowledge gaps between SMFE business owners and the PE sector, which are applicable not only in Singapore but also in China and Australia, are:

- Target accountants and professional advisers to family businesses as part of the ongoing professional upgrading of skills and knowledge of the PE sector.
- The PE community must market itself differently when it comes to dealing with family businesses as they have different concerns to the traditional high-technology start-up firms.
- Besides conducting educational activities, government agencies, trade associations and family business associations should actively promote interaction and confidence-building activities between the SMFE owners and the PE.
- Government agencies, trade associations and family business associations should actively develop innovative ways to educate SMFE owners on the expectations of the PE community and vice-versa.

References

ABS. 2009. *Australian Demographic Statistics*. Canberra: Australian Bureau of Statistics.
ABS. 2010a. *1980–2010 Labour Force Survey*. Canberra: Australian Bureau of Statistics.
ABS. 2010b. *Australian Social Trends September 2010*. Canberra: Australian Bureau of Statistics.
ABS. 2012. *Year Book Australia 2012*. Canberra: Australian Bureau of Statistics.
ABS. 2013. *Australian Demographic Statistics, June Quarter 2013*. Canberra: Australian Bureau of Statistics.
Adler, N.J. and Gunderson, A. 2008. *International Dimensions of Organizational behaviour* (5th edn). Eagan, MN: Thomson/South-Western.
Ahn J., Bhagat, C., Honda, K., Kwan, I., Lind, F., Pandit, V., Poullet, J.-M., Roy B. and Ye T. 2011. Private equity Asia-Pacific: rebounds, glocalization, and other tales. In *Private Equity & Principal Investing*. McKinsey & Company, Inc.
Alvarez, S.A. and Barney, J.B. 2000. Entrepreneurial capabilities: a resource-based view. In G.D. Meyer and K.A. Heppard (eds), *Entrepreneurship as Strategy: Competing on the Entrepreneurial Edge*, pp. 63–81. London: Sage.
Alvarez, S.A. and Barney, J.B. 2002. Resource-based theory and the entrepreneurial firm. In M.A. Hitt, R.D. Ireland, S.M. Camp and D.L. Sexton (eds), *Strategic Entrepreneurship: Creating A New Mindset*, pp. 89–105. Oxford: Blackwell.

AVCAL. 2012. *2012 Yearbook*. Sydney: Australian Private Equity & Venture Capital Association.

AVCJ. 2001. *The 2001 Guide to Venture Capital in Asia*. Hong Kong: AVCJ Group Limited.

AVCJ Research. 2012. *Asian Private Equity and Venture Capital Report 2012*. Hong Kong: AVCJ Group.

Bachkaniwala, D., Wright, M. and Ram, M. 2001. Succession in South Asian family businesses in the UK. *International Small Business Journal*, 19(4): 15–27.

Batjargal, B. and Liu, M. 2004. Entrepreneurs' access to private equity in China: the role of social capital. *Organization Science*, 15: 159–172.

Bruton, G.D., Ahlstrom, D. and Singh, K. 2002. The impact of the institutional environment on the venture capital industry in Singapore. *Venture Capital: An International Journal of Entrepreneurial Finance*, 4(3): 197–218.

BVCA. 1999. *Report on Investment Activity*. London: British Venture Capital Association.

Carey, P., Simnett, R. and Tanewski, G. 2005. Providing business advice for small to medium enterprises. In *CPA Australia Business Management Reports*. Melbourne: CPA Australia.

Chen, H. and Zheng, H. 2010. China's high-stakes race for PE 'crown jewel'. *Caixin Online*, 2 September 2010.

Cheng, L.-K. 1989. Post-independence population planning and social development in Singapore. *GeoJournal*, 18(2): 163–174.

Chu, P. and Hisrich, R.D. 2001. Venture capital in an economy in transition. *Venture Capital: An International Journal of Entrepreneurial Finance*, 3(2): 169–182.

Davidsson, P. 2004. *Researching Entrepreneurship*. New York. Springer.

De Clercq, D., Fried, V.H., Lehtonen, O. and Sapienza, H.J. 2006. An entrepreneur's guide to the venture capital galaxy. *Academy of Management Perspectives*, 20(3): 90–112.

Department of Statistics Singapore. 2013. *The Singapore Economy*. Singapore: Government of Singapore.

The Economist. 2009. A survey of ageing.

Economist Intelligence Unit and Citibank. 2006. Not keeping it in the family: Most small businesses want professional managers to run firms in the long run – survey. *Today*.

European Venture Capital Journal. 1999. Singapore venture capitalists pile into hi-tech sector. *European Venture Capital Journal*, 64: 15.

EVCA. 2001. *Survey of the Economic and Social Impact of Management Buyouts & Buyins in Europe*. Zaventem, Belgium: European Private Equity & Venture Capital Association.

EVCA. 2005. *The Contribution of Private Equity to the Succession of Family Business in Europe*. Zaventem, Belgium: European Private Equity & Venture Capital Association.

EYGM. 2014. *Asia Pacific Private Equity Outlook 2014*. Singapore: EYGM.

Fowler, A.R., Jie Gao and Carlson, L. 2010. Public policy and the changing Chinese family in contemporary China: the past and present as prologue for the future. *Journal of Macromarketing*, 30(4): 342–353.

Gallo, M.A. and Vilaseca, A. 1996. Finance in family business. *Family Business Review*, 9: 387–401.

Gambe, A. 2000. *Overseas Chinese Entrepreneurship and Capitalist Development in Southeast Asia*. Basingstoke: Palgrave Macmillan.

Gasson, C. 1999. The private equity market. In C. Gasson and A. Jolly (eds), *Corporate Finance Handbook*. London: Kogan Page.

Gersick, K.E. 1997. *Generation to Generation: Life Cycles of the Family Business.* Boston, MA: Harvard Business School Press.

Guo, X. and Marinova, D. 2006. Population ageing and sustainability in China: comparisons with Australia. *ACESA 2006 International Conference*, Melbourne, Victoria University.

Gurd, B. and Thomas, J. 2006. Finance managers in family-owned small-to-medium enterprises. In *CPA Australia Business Management Reports*. Melbourne: CPA Australia.

Harvey, M. and Evans, R. 1995. Forgotten sources of capital for the family-owned business. *Family Business Review*, 8(3): 159–176.

Helfat, C.E. 2007. *Dynamic Capabilities: Understanding Strategic Change in Organizations*. London: Blackwell Publishing.

Hindle, K. and Lee, L. 2002. An exploratory investigation of informal venture capitalists in Singapore. *Venture Capital: An International Journal of Entrepreneurial Finance*, 4(2): 169–177.

Hofer, C.W. and Charan, R. 1984. The transition to professional management: mission impossible? *American Journal of Small Business*, 9(1): 1–11.

Holstein, J.A. and Gubrium, J.F. 1997. Active interviewing. In D. Silverman (ed.), *Qualitative Research: Theory, Method and Practice*. London: Sage.

Howorth, C., Westhead, P. and Wright, M. 2004. Buyouts, information asymmetry and the family management dyad. *Journal of Business Venturing*, 19(4): 509–534.

Joseph, M. 1999. Trends in private equity. In C. Gasson and A. Jolly (eds), *Corporate Finance Handbook*, pp. 69–76. London: Kogan Page.

Kaplan, D. 2000. *Structural Equation Modeling: Foundations and Extensions*. London: Sage Publications.

Koh, W.T. and Koh, F. 2002. Venture capital and economic growth: an industry overview and Singapore's experience. http://papers.ssrn.com/sol3/papers.cfm?abstract_id=355920.

KPMG. 2009. Private equity in China. In *Market Sentiment Survey*. Hong Kong: KPMG.

KPMG. 2012. *Family Business in Singapore*. Singapore: CPA Australia.

KPMG and FBA. 2007. *KPMG and Family Business Australia Survey of Family Businesses 2007*. Geelong: Deakin University.

Lee, J. 2006. Impact of family relationships on attitudes of the second generation in family business. *Family Business Review*, 19(3): 175–191.

Lee, J. and Chan, J. 1998. Chinese entrepreneurship: a study in Singapore. *Development*, 17(2): 131–141.

Lee, S.-Y. and Loh, G. 1998. *Beyond Silken Robes: Profiles of Selected Chinese Entrepreneurs in Singapore*. Singapore: Times Academic Press.

Lockett, A. and Wright, M. 2002. Venture capital in Asia and the Pacific Rim. *Venture Capital: An International Journal of Entrepreneurial Finance*, 4(3): 183–195.

Maherault, L. 2004. Is there any specific equity route for small and medium-sized family businesses? The French experience. *Family Business Review*, 17(3): 221–235.

Menkhoff, T. and Gerke, S. (eds). 2002. *Chinese Entrepreneurship and Asian Business Networks*. London: RoutledgeCurzon.

Pan, L. 1990. *Sons of the Yellow Emperor: The Story of the Overseas Chinese*. London: Secker & Warburg.

Patton, M.Q. 1990. *Qualitative Evaluation and Research Methods* (2nd edn). London: Sage.

Poutziouris, P. 2001. The views of family companies on venture capital: empirical evidence from the UK small to medium-size enterprising economy. *Family Business Review*, 14(3): 277–291.

Poutziouris, P. 2002. The financial affairs of smaller family companies. In D.E. Fletcher (ed.), *Understanding the Small Family Business*, pp. 111–126. London: Routledge.

Poutziouris, P., Michaelas, N., Chittenden, F. and Sitorious, S. 2000. The financial structure, behaviour and performance of SMEs: family and private companies. Paper presented at the Small Business and Enterprise Development Conference, Manchester.

PwC. 2012a. *Growing the Future of Australia's Family Businesses*. Sydney: PricewaterhouseCoopers.

PwC. 2012b. *Private Business Barometer: Private Equity Supplement*. Sydney: PricewaterhouseCoopers.

Ray, D.M. 1991. Venture capital and entrepreneurial development in Singapore. *International Small Business Journal*, 10(1): 11–26.

Reier, S. 2006. When blood is thicker than money: family-run firms gain favor with investors seeking long-term values. *International Herald Tribune*: 14.

Robbie, K. and Wright, M. 1996. *Management Buy-Ins: Entrepreneurship, Active Investors, and Corporate Restructuring*. Manchester: Manchester University Press.

Romano, C.A., Tanewski, G.A. and Smyrnios, K.X. 2001. Capital structure decision making: a model for family business. *Journal of Business Venturing*, 16(3): 285–310.

Saxenian, A. 1999. *Silicon Valley's New Immigrant Entrepreneurs*. San Francisco, CA: Public Policy Institute of California.

Schoenberger, C.R. 2002. Vulture capital scavengers pick through investment portfolios. *FORBES*, 169(1): 38–39.

Scholes, L., Westhead, P. and Burrows, A. 2008. Family firm succession: the management buy-out and buy-in routes. *Journal of Small Business and Enterprise Development*, 15(1): 8–30.

Seet, P.-S. and Graves, C. 2010a. Submission to the Commonwealth Government's Senate Economics Committee's Inquiry into Access of Small Business to Finance. In *Australian Commonwealth Government Senate Standing Committee on Economics Inquiry into Access of Small Business to Finance*. Canberra: Parliament of Australia.

Seet, P.-S. and Graves, C. 2010b. *Understanding the Barriers to and Opportunities for Access to Private Equity for Small-to-Medium-sized Family-owned Enterprises (SMFEs)*. Melbourne: CPA Australia.

Smyrnios, K. and Dana, L.E. 2006. *MGI Australia Family & Private Business Survey*. Melbourne: RMIT.

Steyaert, C. and Bouwen, R. 1997. Telling stories of entrepreneurship: towards a contextual epistemology for entrepreneurial studies. In R. Donckels and A. Mietten (eds), *Entrepreneurship and SME Research: On Its Way to the Next Millennium*, pp. 3–19. Aldershot: Ashgate.

SVCA. 2013. SVCA Awards 2013. Press release, Singapore SVCA.

Tan, W.-L. and Fock, S.-T. 2001. Coping with growth transitions: the case of Chinese family businesses in Singapore. *Family Business Review*, 14(2): 123–140.

Tanewski, G. and Carey, P. 2007. *Determinants of Value Adding Business Advice Provided By External Accountants to SME Clients*. Paper presented at the 52nd International Council for Small Business World Conference, Turku, Finland.

United Nations. 2009. *Population Ageing and Development*. New York: United Nations.

Upton, N. and Petty, W. 2000. Venture capital investment and US family business. *Venture Capital*, 2(1): 39.

Van Meter, K.M. 1990. Methodological and design issues: techniques for assessing the representatives of snowball samples. In Elizabeth Lambert (ed.), *The Collection and*

Interpretation of Data from Hidden Populations, pp. 31–33. Rockville, MD: US Department of Health and Human Services.

Wang, C.K. and Sim, V.Y.L. 2001. Exit strategies of venture capital-backed companies in Singapore. *Venture Capital: An International Journal of Entrepreneurial Finance*, 3(4): 337–358.

Wang, C.L. and Ahmed, P.K. 2007. Dynamic capabilities: A review and research agenda. *International Journal of Management Reviews*, 9(1): 31–51.

Wang, X. and Jia, S. 2009. Factors that influence offspring intentions to join the family businesses: evidence from Zhejiang, China. Paper presented at the 6th International Conference on Service Systems and Service Management.

Wright, M. 2007. Private equity and management buyouts. In H. Landstrom (ed.), *Handbook of Research on Venture Capital*, pp. 281–312. Cheltenham: Edward Elgar.

Wright, M. and Burrows, A. 2008. Entrepreneurship and management buy-outs. In M. Casson (ed.), *The Oxford Handbook of Entrepreneurship*, pp. 484–507. Oxford: Oxford University Press.

Wright, M., Thompson, S. and Robbie, K. 1992. Venture capital and management-led, leveraged buy-outs: a European perspective. *Journal of Business Venturing*, 7(1): 47–71.

Wright, M., Pruthi, S. and Lockett, A. 2005. International venture capital research: from cross-country comparisons to crossing borders. *International Journal of Management Reviews*, 7(3): 135–165.

Wright, M., Scholes, L., Ball, R., Howorth, C., Kloeckner, O., Westhead, P. and Burrows, A. 2008. A report on private equity investments in family firms across Europe. Nottingham: CMBOR.

Wu, Z., Chua, J.H. and Chrisman, J.J. 2007. Effects of family ownership and management on small business equity financing. *Journal of Business Venturing*, 22(6): 875–895.

Yeung, H. 2000. Limits to the growth of family-owned business? The case of Chinese transnational corporations from Hong Kong. *Family Business Review*, 13(1): 55–70.

Zapalska, A. and Edwards, W. 2001. Chinese entrepreneurship in a cultural and economic perspective. *Journal of Small Business Management*, 39(3): 286–292.

Zhang, J. and Ma, H. 2009. Adoption of professional management in Chinese family business: a multilevel analysis of impetuses and impediments. *Asia Pacific Journal of Management*, 26(1): 119–139.

Zider, B. 1998. How venture capital works. *Harvard Business Review*, 76(6): 131–139.

Zuo, X. and Yang, X. 2009. The long-term impact on the Chinese economy of an aging population. *Social Sciences in China*, 30(1): 197–208.

Zutshi, R.K., Tan, W.L., Allampalli, D.G. and Gibbons, P.G. 1999. Singapore venture capitalists (VCs) investment evaluation criteria: a re-examination. *Small Business Economics*, 13(1): 9–26.

9 Confucian principles to enhance China's environmental governance

Han Lin and Jeffrey Gil

Introduction

China's modernization has brought environmental issues into sharp focus. It is now widely acknowledged that the environmental damage associated with the rapid development that has occurred since the beginning of the reform era represents a significant threat to economic sustainability. A report from the Chinese Academy of Environmental Planning, for example, stated that the annual cost of environmental damage reached 1.54 trillion yuan (US$230 billion) or 3.5 per cent of gross domestic product (GDP) in the year 2010 (*New York Times*, 2013). It is therefore urgent that China improve its environmental governance in such a way as to protect the environment while at the same time ensuring modernization can continue. In this chapter we argue that Confucian principles offer sound guidelines for reforming China's environmental governance to achieve this outcome. While the potential contributions of Confucianism (as well as other Asian philosophical and religious traditions such as Daoism and Buddhism) to the enhancement of environmental governance have been discussed over a number of years (Callicott and Ames, 1989; Snyder, 2006), previous proposals have failed to acknowledge the challenges of environmental governance in the contemporary Chinese context (for example, Ivanhoe, 1998; Kalton, 1998, 2010; Kassiola, 2010; Tucker, 1991, 1994; Tu, 1989, 1998, 2001); made no concrete, practical suggestions for the implementation of Confucian principles (for example, Ivanhoe, 1998; Kalton, 2010; Kassiola, 2010; Li, 2003; Tucker, 1991, 1994; Tu, 1989, 1998, 2001; Weller and Bol, 1998); and sometimes amounted to little more than a collection of quotes from Confucius and/or Confucian scholars (for example, Kassiola, 2010; Li, 2003).

We aim to address these shortcomings by providing an analysis of the development and current state of environmental governance in China and the challenges it faces before proceeding to outline Confucian principles for its enhancement. In the first section of this chapter we therefore give a brief historical overview of China's environmental governance apparatus, while in the second and third sections we analyse the challenges of enforcing environmental laws and the limitations of environmental non-governmental organizations (ENGOs), respectively. Our analysis reveals that prompt and effective reversal of China's environmental outcome has to rely on top-down directives in the short to medium term, and we argue that Confucian principles are a means of achieving this. The fourth and final section of this chapter discusses the manner in which we believe the key Confucian principles of higher virtue, universal education, moderation and systematic approach to truth can overcome these issues. Primary and secondary literature comprise our main sources in the first section of the chapter, and these are supplemented with interviews that Han Lin conducted with 50 Chinese people from a range of backgrounds (see H. Lin, 2009 for further details of the interviews) in the second through to fourth sections.

Development of China's environmental protection sector: progress and challenges

For many years, environmental protection had a lower status than economic development, reflecting the government's pro-development policy direction, and this contributed to rapid environmental deterioration with potentially very serious consequences for public health and long-term environmental and economic sustainability (Li *et al.*, 2007; Mol and Carter, 2006).

Since attending the 1972 United Nations Stockholm Conference on Human Environment, the rank of China's environmental sector has been raised six times. In 1974 the National Environmental Protection Office was set up. The Office did not, however, have the right to issue orders to lower levels of government due to its low rank. After the promulgation of China's first environmental protection law in 1979, local Environmental Protection Bureaus (EPBs) were established. They had direct access to local government leaders and the power to organize meetings as well as the right to establish specific sub-units. The functioning of China's environmental sector improved as a result. However, during the 1982–1983 bureaucratic restructuring, which aimed to reduce the size and expenditure of the government, the Environmental Protection Office at the central level was positioned under the newly created Ministry of Urban and Rural Construction and Environmental Protection. This arrangement seriously restricted the independence of the environmental protection sector's administration and created obvious conflicts between development and environmental protection within the one ministry (Jahiel, 1998).

After receiving numerous complaints from those in academia, an inter-organizational body, the Environmental Protection Commission, was created by the State Council in 1984. This did improve the coordination between the environmental protection sector and the industrial ministries to some extent, and gave relative independence to the environmental protection sector. In the same year, the Environmental Protection Office was upgraded to the National Environmental Protection Bureau, with a higher rank than other second-tier organizations (Jahiel, 1998). The concept of environmental protection was at this time set as a basic national policy and a national regulatory framework was established (Mol and Carter, 2006).

The National Environmental Protection Bureau gained complete independence from the Ministry of Urban and Rural Construction and Environmental Protection in 1988, and was re-named the National Environmental Protection Agency. Unfortunately, however, during the 1993–1994 government administrative reform, the local- and county-level EPBs were largely reduced, resulting in the flourishing of heavy polluting town and village enterprises (TVEs) and leaving pollution at local levels unchecked (Jahiel, 1998).

In March 2008, the full cabinet-ranked Ministry of Environmental Protection (MEP) was established, giving China's environmental protection sector the same ranking as its major economic development sector for the first time – the MEP was now level with the leading economic and planning ministry, namely the National Development and Reform Commission (NDRC), and was part of the important State Council.

Nevertheless, the power distribution within the government is extremely complex, fragmented and uneven. Lieberthal (2004: 186) describes China's multi-level bureaucratic system as a 'matrix muddle', which vividly reflects the power fragmentation between central, provincial and local governments, and among different departments at each level. At the central level, different ministries have different rankings. The ministries with higher rankings at the central level guarantee their provincial and local branches a higher ranking over those with lower-ranking parents at the central level. Therefore, government offices with lower rankings do not have authority over those with a higher ranking, and those of the same rank cannot manage each other (Ma and Ortolano, 2000).

The environmental protection sector, as explained above, has been in a lower position in the central government for many decades. This lower position not only decided the lower ranking of its sub-branches within provincial and local governments, but also prevented it from being involved in any major policy development at the central level (Jahiel, 1998). The recent elevation of the MEP, while a positive move, is likely to have only a limited effect on China's overall environmental outcome due to the fact that the provincial EPBs need not only respond to the central MEP, but also need to report to the provincial governments in their own locations (Jahiel, 1998; Mol and Carter, 2006; Shi and L. Zhang, 2006). As a result of the provincial government's provision of funding and selection of personnel, the provincial EPBs often listen to the provincial government more than to their parent ministry in the central government (Jahiel, 1998; Zhang, 2007). Driven by tax revenue and possible future promotion – one of the most important criteria used to judge Chinese officials' performance is economic growth and significant constructions in his or her governing area – the majority of the provincial governments give priority to economic development rather than environmental protection. Therefore, when polluting projects are proposed, environmental protection officers are often forced to disobey and violate relevant environmental laws because they know when the large polluting industries are gone, the provincial government will lose tax revenue and the consequence will be that they will lose their jobs. Even worse, for some local EPBs who rely on pollution fines to cover their operation expenditure and staff salaries, polluting industries are welcome, because in effect they live on pollution – the more pollution there is, the more money they can collect (van Rooij, 2004; Xue *et al.*, 2006). Such circumstances appear to be even more severe among the township- and village-level EPBs, who are supervised by provincial and local EPBs and do not have direct contact with the central MEP.

While the overall trend of China's environmental protection sector has been an increase in importance and prominence, there have also been occasional setbacks, and many unsolved issues remain. We turn our attention to these in the next section.

The enforcement of environmental laws

The actual implementation of environmental policies relies on provincial and local bureaucracies, and these are where the greatest problems happen in China's current environmental governance system (Mol and Carter, 2006).

Since the approval of the People's Republic of China Law on Environmental Protection (Trial) on 13 September 1979, China had, by the late 2000s, developed

> six environmental protection laws, nine resource management laws, seven related enforcement regulations, eleven laws related to sustainable development, nearly thirty environmental administrative regulations, more than seventy departmental regulations and more than four hundred national environmental standards.
>
> (Li *et al.*, 2007: 40)

This is to say China has already established a relatively comprehensive environmental law system. However, due to light penalties for pollution; the public's lack of knowledge of environmental laws; official corruption; and weak ENGOs and civil society, the enforcement of environmental laws in China faces great obstacles.

Light penalties

The penalties contained in many environmental laws and regulations are too light, which makes it cheaper to violate the law than to obey the law. As then deputy minister of the Ministry of Environmental Protection Wang Jirong (*People's Daily Online*, 2009) pointed out, light penalties and caps on pollution fines have severely weakened the deterrent effect of many environmental laws.

The *Environmental Protection Law* set pollution fine caps for average polluting activity at 100,000 yuan (US$16,499.20), while according to the *Water Pollution Prevention Law*, the fine for big pollution accidents can be as high as 30 per cent of the direct financial loss caused by the accident, but cannot exceed the cap of one million yuan (US$164,992). The caps on pollution fines have led to many big industries purposely not operating their pollution control equipment.

According to Wang's 2009 report, for example, one company installed a set of 200 million yuan (US$32,998,400) waste-water treatment equipment, and was therefore definitely capable of limiting its pollution level to the required standard. However, because the operating cost of the equipment was about 100,000 yuan (US$16,499.20) per day, which was similar to the cap of the pollution fine, the company decided not to use the equipment because the EPB officers could not come to check every day; therefore, it was cheaper to pay fines occasionally than to operate the pollution treatment equipment on a daily basis. Atmospheric pollution control faces the same problem. The pollution fine for each kilogram of sulphur dioxide (SO_2) is 0.2 yuan (US$0.03); however, if coal-fired power plants treat SO_2 they need to spend 1 yuan (US$0.16) on each kilogram of SO_2, which is five times as expensive as paying fines (*People's Daily Online*, 2009).

The public's lack of knowledge of environmental laws

Furthermore, the public's knowledge of environmental laws is limited, and when their environmental rights are threatened, few make use of legal action. As Ho (2001) noted, most Chinese choose to visit the government in person (*shang fang*) rather than go to court when facing environmental conflicts. According to the interviews conducted for this chapter, 11 of the 50 interviewees said they did not know much about China's environmental laws; 29 said they had heard of environmental laws but did not have detailed knowledge of them; nine said they knew something about China's environmental laws through tertiary education; while only one claimed he knew how to use environmental law as a tool to protect his rights as one of his relatives had such an experience. He explained:

> My uncle was a farmer who grew garlic chives on the outskirts of the city. Once, his farm was flooded by the waste water from the nearby chemical factory. He sued the factory and got a lot of compensation. It was great to use a legal tool. The compensation he got was much more than he could get from selling one season's worth of garlic chives. When the water drained he cut down the dirty bits [of the garlic chives], and he could still sell the new growth.

While the garlic chive farmer's legal action against the polluter is encouraging, selling contaminated vegetables to unaware consumers is worrying. Clearly there is a need for broader legal and environmental education for China's citizens.

Corruption

Corruption involving environmental affairs appears to be a particularly insidious obstacle for effective enforcement of environmental laws. It is large-scale, widespread and commonly despised by the general public. Although there is limited literature on this issue, it was the most frequently mentioned topic by interviewees who participated in this study. When asked 'What do you think is the cause of atmospheric pollution in your city?', one participant, a retired engineer of a state-owned company, answered:

> Because factories emit large amounts of pollutants and the government does not manage them well. Especially now, many state owned companies have been privatised and belong to individuals. In order to make the maximum amount of profit, they [the new owners of the companies] will do whatever they want. If the government [EPB officials] comes to check, they would hand in some *ming bai fei* [understanding fee, a euphemism for bribery] and it's all fixed. This money actually cannot reach the country [the government revenue]; it all ends up in individual's [official's] pockets.

For the same question, a middle-aged couple who did not want to be identified by their occupations, answered as follows:

> Why is the air polluted? There are many reasons. Take the residential area where we live for example, very nice tiled footpaths were built earlier this year; a few weeks later it was all dug up because they [the local government] wanted to repair the water pipe. Why didn't they repair it before the tiles were laid! There was dust everywhere! I couldn't even go out for a walk because the dust made me cough. This was not the only case; it's always been like this. Dig it up today, fill it in tomorrow, dig it up again next week and fill it in the week after. They just couldn't repair all the pipes in one go! You know why they don't repair all the things together? Because to dig it up one time, it counts as one project, and they get one load of funding from above [higher level of government]; dig it up ten times, it counts as ten projects, and they get ten loads of money. There is oil to be pressed [meaning the local government officials can corrupt money from the funding]. There is knowledge behind where they buy those things [tiles, turf, pipes and other construction materials]; they all eat commissions [meaning suppliers have special relations with local government and pay commissions to relevant officials for purchases].

When asked 'Do you think rapid economic development brings harm to the environment?', a community leader for local welfare responded with strong emotion and ironic tones:

> You know why we have developed so fast? We have to thank those corrupted officials! Without them how can we achieve today's development! Do you think they would have worked so hard – building railways today, highways tomorrow – if they were not allowed to taste the *tian tou* [sweet bits, meaning money corrupted from big government constructions]? Hell, they wouldn't be bothered! They were born bone lazy!

From the above responses we can observe that EPBs are not necessarily com-pletely innocent. Although most previous studies have blamed EPBs' ineffec-tiveness on objective conditions such as their lower rank, institutional conflicts and lack of funding, in reality individual EPB officers sometimes also act unethi-cally. Local governments' numerous repetitive 'projects' carried out on the same plot were not only a waste of resources but also created environmental hazards and inconvenience for local residents. These 'projects' were not aimed at improving the quality of people's lives, but were instead an excuse for local gov-ernment officials to act corruptly. For large-scale constructions, the *tian tou* appears to be even bigger and sweeter. Although the scale of these cases is hard to identify, it is believed to be common among provincial and local govern-ments. Corruption has no doubt built up a great barrier for the enforcement of China's environmental laws, and it must be tackled for any fundamental improvement of China's environment outcome.

Weak ENGOs and civil society

The lack of public accountability of the government imposes the greatest obs-tacle for the enforcement of environmental laws (Ho, 2001; Lo *et al.*, 2000). Based on international experiences, ENGOs play an important role in fighting for environmental justice and against pollution, influencing governments' decision-making on environmental affairs and conserving biodiversity and the balance of ecological systems in general (Xue *et al.*, 2006). Governments of most developed countries have gradually embraced the full capacity of ENGOs and have removed many legal, political and financial restrictions on their operation.

In China, however, the communist political system provides very limited institutional channels for ordinary people to participate in and influence environ-mental policy development, and ENGOs also have much less freedom (Alper-mann, 2010; Lo *et al.*, 2000; Xie, 2009). As a result, although the emergence and development of ENGOs has achieved some important results since the mid-1990s through engagement in environmental education, ecological conservation and assisting the public in environmental disputes (Fu, 2007; Xie, 2009; Yang, 2005), the strength of Chinese ENGOs is considerably weaker than ENGOs in developed countries, and the spread of Chinese ENGOs is not wide enough when considering the size and scale of China's population.

According to Ho (2001), there were no genuine ENGOs in China prior to the mid-1990s. Many of the indigenous ENGOs were initially set up by the govern-ment, and are therefore not completely independent. These government-organized NGOs (GONGOs) are said by Fu (2007: 299) to 'lack innovation and flexibility', and be 'separated from the needs of people and communities'. Some of the well-known and highly professional ones, such as the China Society of Environmental Sciences, the China Energy Conservation Association and the Chinese Society for Sustainable Development, are academically oriented and provide advice to the government in the fields of environmental planning, technical decision-making, environmental protection, etc. (Fu, 2007). Therefore, as the name indicates, these GONGOs work more in the role of government advisory bodies than ENGOs. Consequently, they do not have much to say when policy enforcement goes wrong in practice.

Students have set up a large number of environmental organizations. These young people are very enthusiastic, but the members, especially the leadership, change very frequently. Fewer organizations have been set up by communities, and while they are active, most of them lack serious structure and management. Most important of all, ENGOs of the above two types are seriously lacking funding. Branches of international environmental organizations make up only a small portion of ENGOs in China, and although they have good funding and management, many of them are not legally registered (Yang, 2005).

Statistics on the conditions and activities of ENGOs in China are difficult to find, and the most comprehensive ones remain those contained in the *Report on the Development of China's Environmental Organisations* by the All-China Environment Federation, released in 2006. According to this report, up until the end of 2005 there were a total of 2,768 ENGOs in China; 1,382 of these were initially set up by the government, making up nearly 50 per cent of the total; 202 were set up by communities (7.3 per cent); 1,116 were set up by students (40.3 per cent); and 68 were branches of international ENGOs (2.5 per cent). These organizations employ 69,000 full-time staff and 155,000 casual staff. Over 50 per cent of these employees have undergraduate or higher qualifications. There were 76.1 per cent of community ENGOs without stable funding, while 45.5 per cent of international ENGOs' Chinese branches and 22.5 per cent of GONGOs have comparatively stable funding. In 2005 the total funding for all ENGOs in China was 2.977 billion yuan (US$491,181,184). There was no funding for 22.5 per cent, and 81.5 per cent of those who received funding received under 50,000 yuan (US$8,249.60). Ninety-six per cent of the environmental workers believed their salaries were lower than the median income in their local regions (All-China Environment Federation, 2006).

In the same year, 90.8 per cent of student, 75 per cent of community, 63.6 per cent of international and 55.2 per cent of GONGOs had organized volunteer activities at least once. However, when dealing with the relationship with the government, over 95 per cent of these organizations obeyed the rule of 'help but not add trouble, be involved but not intervene, supervise but not replace, carry out the work but not break the law'. Of these organizations, 64.6 per cent prefer to cooperate with the government; 32.1 per cent of them neither cooperate nor oppose; and 3.3 per cent oppose the government. When dealing with industries on pollution issues, 68.8 per cent of the issues were reported to the government; 40 per cent were solved by negotiating with business; and very few were resolved through legal action or protest (All-China Environment Federation, 2006). We explore further the reasons for the limited role of ENGOs in China in the next section.

Reasons for lack of participation in ENGOs

The government intervention, lower income of the majority of ENGO staff and the infrequent and less enthusiastic public participation impose great difficulties for the development of Chinese ENGOs. As the government has recently paid more attention to environmental protection and loosened some control of ENGOs' activities, the lack of enthusiasm from the public appears to be the biggest challenge for ENGO activities. Such a lack of enthusiasm is due to five major reasons: prioritizing economic wellbeing over environmental wellbeing; lack of environmental knowledge and awareness; employment by polluting industries; the absence of a democratic tradition; and the belief that treating pollution is the government's responsibility.

Prioritizing economic wellbeing over environmental wellbeing

Under the current economic conditions it appears more important for ordinary Chinese people to secure a job and put dinner on the table than to worry about the environment. While there have been some quite large-scale and forceful public protests over environmental issues in recent years (Lampton, 2008; Shirk, 2008), generally speaking, an individual would not carry out any serious actions towards the government's poor environmental management unless his or her direct interests or rights are harmed (Martens, 2006). This is a common phenomenon according to Maslow's Human Motivation Theory, which states that people will only start to be concerned with their higher needs such as ecological consciousness once their basic needs – including food, shelter and security – have been met (Nordhaus and Shellenberger, 2007). China's per capita gross national income was only US$6,560 in 2013, and there were still over 84 million people, or 6.3 per cent of the population, living on less than US$1.25 per day as of 2011 (World Bank n.d. a, b). Therefore, there is still a long way to go before the majority of Chinese are likely to voluntarily pursue their higher environmental needs and actively participate in environmental affairs.

Lack of environmental knowledge and awareness

Indeed, the Chinese public's environmental awareness is lower on average than that of publics in developed countries (Martens, 2006). In the past, environmental education was not included in China's public education. Students could only obtain a small amount of environmental knowledge from biology and geography classes. Since the release of *The Syllabus for Environmental Education in Primary and Secondary Schools* in 1993, and the formal implementation of environmental education in China's education system in 1994, the situation of environmental education for the younger generation improved significantly (Wang, 2007). However, the older generations who did not receive this education remain largely unaware of many environmental issues. Our interviews indicate that the majority of members of the older generations are only aware of visible, obvious, immediate and close-by environmental problems, such as litter on the street, smog from factories and lack of green areas (trees, lawns, parks) in residential areas.

ENGOs have contributed to China's environmental education in recent years. For example, Friends of Nature's Environmental Education Van travels between Chinese cities and rural areas and delivers environmental education to the public, while the Sunflower Action Project carried out in 2005 by Shanxi Volunteer Mothers Association and Friends of the Earth encouraged women to take the lead in community environmental education and promoted an eco-household model and eco-friendly usage of energy in rural areas (Wang, 2007). However, due to China's large population and geographical size, these initiatives cannot reach everyone, and therefore have limited impact, again highlighting the need for broader environmental education.

Employment by polluting industries

A significant proportion of the Chinese population are employed by polluting industries, many of them state owned. As a result, employees are very unlikely to protest against their polluting employers even though they understand that pollution is bad, because they do not wish to lose their jobs. Among all 50 interviewees, 18 of them were from state-owned polluting industries, including the mining, defence, oil refinery, paper mill and cement industries. When asked if they would participate in a protest against a local polluter's illegal waste discharge or a severe environmental accident, only one of them expressed willingness to participate in a potential ENGO-organized protest against local pollution. He said: 'When the environment becomes good, it is beneficial for everyone. So I will attend.' However, when asked if he would consider becoming the organizer and leader of the protest, the answer was no.

The absence of a democratic tradition

Following on from the above point, the public's unenthusiastic attitude towards organized protest, the most commonly used method by Western ENGOs, is fundamentally related to the absence of a democratic tradition throughout Chinese history (since the Xia Dynasty, 2070–1600 BC). Although some scholars such as Yang (2005) see ENGOs as an agent of force for China's future democratic social change, we are not able to agree with such a statement. When the majority of urban citizens are not yet used to democratic concepts and activities such as voting for their own leaders and having their say in political polls, it is very unlikely that they will voluntarily participate in ENGO-organized activities. The interview data support this argument. For example, in regards to participation in ENGO protests, only four of the interviewees expressed that they would participate. Ten of the interviewees said they would see what others would do first and only participate if most people in the community also participated. Another 25 of the interviewees believed that it was not necessary to carry out protests; instead, they believed the best course of action was to report the pollution to the government or to elect a few representatives to negotiate with the industries. The remaining interviewees firmly expressed their negative attitudes towards any forms of protest.

In the 2006 meeting between representatives of the US Brookings Institution and then Premier Wen Jiaobao, which covered the issue of democracy in China, Wen stated that if the current direct elections at village level are successful they will gradually move upwards to towns, counties and even provinces. However, he also stated that in order to accomplish this, China needed three things: 'peace, friends and time' (cited in Mahbubani, 2008: 144). This indicates that the development of democracy in China is going to be a long process, which is to say that Chinese ENGOs will not become the major force pushing forward China's environmental governance for a long time.

Treating pollution is the government's responsibility

Not surprisingly, therefore, many Chinese people consider it the government's responsibility to deal with environmental issues, a perception vividly reflected in the interviews. For the questions 'Is it the government's responsibility or the ordinary people's responsibility to tackle pollution?', and 'If you believe both should hold responsibilities, whose responsibility is bigger?', many interviewees believed it was the government's responsibility, with the following being a typical answer: 'Of course it's the government's responsibility! If the government doesn't treat pollution, what can we ordinary people do about it!' Some interviewees said that the government and ordinary people both hold responsibilities, but the government holds a bigger responsibility. A common response was: 'The major responsibility should be from the government. If they have good management and do not give approval to polluting industries, the pollution won't be so severe.' One interviewee, who owns a car, gave an interesting answer:

> I know driving pollutes the air, and we all know every individual should contribute to protecting the environment, but it is very hard to do so in reality. It is very convenient to have my own car although traffic jams sometimes give me headaches. Petrol is getting expensive too. But nowadays most people want to own a car if their financial situation allows; this is something the government cannot control. The government can control pollution but cannot control what people buy. Therefore, I think the government should quickly develop clean cars.

Only a small number of interviewees believed it was the people's responsibility, with a typical answer being: 'The government has good environmental policies and plans, but the people don't follow them. No matter how good the plan is, it won't work. Therefore, individuals' behaviour is very important.'

Our interview data support Shapiro's (2012: 91–92) contention that among the Chinese people there is an entrenched assumption, perhaps a legacy of the days when the government controlled all aspects of life, that even public-spirited activities as cleaning trash from a river or from an apartment stairwell should be the job of the authorities.

To summarize, pursuing a better environmental outcome through a bottom-up approach in China currently appears to be very challenging. It is important to note that this challenge should not be simplified as resulting from communist control or lack of ENGOs, as the fundamental challenge stems from the 'quiet' and 'obedient' public. Chinese people's attitude towards the government and the law significantly differ from the publics of Western democracies, not just as a consequence of over 60 years of communist rule, but also over 2,000 years of authoritarian tradition (Guo, 2013; Jacques, 2009; Xie, 2009). It appears that, as a result, people expect the government to implement the best environmental policy and administration automatically, without being asked. Therefore, prompt and effective reversal of China's environmental situation has to rely on top-down directives in the short to medium term.

Confucian principles and environmental governance

We argue that in order to do this China should draw on its own indigenous philosophical resources, as reforms to environmental governance are more likely to be accepted and achieve positive outcomes if they are based in a country's own traditions. In other words, policies and practices which resonate with the cultural, intellectual and philosophical traditions of government policy-makers and the general population are more likely to be long-lasting and successful (Bell, 2000, 2006; Bell and Hahm, 2003; Jacques, 2009; Shapiro, 2012).

After enduring many years of criticism, including being blamed for both China's failure to resist the encroachment of the West and lack of development, and being deemed feudal and reactionary, Confucianism has undergone a major revival in recent times and is widely seen as offering a way forward for environmental thinking (Adler, 2002; Bell, 2008; He and Miller, 2006; Shapiro, 2012). Indeed, the Chinese leadership's concepts of Harmonious Society and Harmonious World are borrowed from Confucian philosophy. They stress sustainable development at the domestic level and cooperation between countries to solve environmental issues at the international level, respectively (Blanchard and Guo, 2008). However, the environmental application of Confucianism has not been spelled out in detail.

Confucianism can be seen as a broad philosophical tradition which encompasses the work of Confucius, Mencius, neo-Confucians and modern-day Confucian scholars (Bell and Hahm, 2003; Goldin, 2011; Miller, 2006; Tucker and Berthrong, 1998). Not all aspects of this tradition, however, will be equally useful or applicable to environmental governance in contemporary China. Given the challenges discussed above, we argue that the most useful and applicable aspect is classical Confucianism, focused on the practical issues of effective management of human behaviour and relationships and effective government administration. As Adler (2002: 31) summarizes, classical Confucianism was primarily concerned with the questions:

> How are we to restore social and political order and harmony? What is the proper role of government in human life, and how should society and government be organized? How can rulers discharge their moral responsibilities to their people? How can they maintain their legitimacy in the light of the Mandate of Heaven?

In applying this approach to environmental governance, we view Confucianism as a means of managing people's behaviour towards the environment through morals, principles, education and examples. As such, the main sources we rely upon are the work of Confucius himself, with some use of the work of Mencius and modern-day Confucian scholars where they fit this approach.

Here, it is important to distinguish between Confucian principles and their manifestations (W. Zhang, 1999). As W. Zhang (1999) points out, many of the social practices, institutions and customs that were developed from Confucian principles in imperial China are not relevant or suitable for the modern world. More specifically, Kalton (2010) points out that the founders of Confucianism could not have considered the possibility of a large-scale environmental crisis and did not deal with environmental issues as we perceive them today. This does not mean, however, that the principles themselves are not relevant or suitable, as they still provide a framework or guidelines for responding to current issues and challenges (Kalton, 2010; W. Zhang, 1999). What is required is the development of new social practices, institutions and customs based on these principles. In the remainder of this chapter, we seek to identify Confucian principles which could contribute to environmental governance in contemporary China and make suggestions as to how they could be appropriately manifested. In particular, we argue that the key Confucian principles of governance through virtue and example, universal education, moderation and systematic approach to truth offer sound foundations for the conduct of environmental governance and can be manifested in ways to increase the chances of positive environmental outcomes.

Environmental governance through virtue and example

According to an important Confucian principle, the government should be composed of talented people, and only the knowledgeable can develop and implement good policies for the nation (Bell, 2008; Creel, 1954). However, as Mol and Carter (2006) have pointed out, many of China's environmental protection personnel lack comprehensive environmental and legal knowledge, and as a result they cannot apply correct judgements and appropriate mitigation procedures to many environmental problems. Therefore, we suggest that environmental protection personnel should be strictly selected through a specially designed examination rather than personal connections or party loyalty. Bell (2000, 2006) explains that civil service examinations currently exist in many East Asia countries – including China – but should be improved so they select higher-quality personnel. He argues that examinations should assess economic and political knowledge of the world; problem-solving ability; knowledge of influential works of philosophy and literature; and ethics.[1] To adapt this idea for our purposes, we argue that an examination for the selection of environmental protection personnel should assess potential employees' knowledge of how the ecosystem functions and important contemporary environmental issues; knowledge and understanding of China's environmental laws; the ability to propose reasonable solutions to the kind of environmental problems they are likely to encounter in their work; and ethical behaviour. The first three of these areas could be assessed through multiple choice questions, while the last two could be assessed through essay questions, with anonymous marking done by a panel of experts (Bell, 2000, 2006). Of course, such an examination cannot completely solve all of the issues we have discussed in this chapter, but it would at least improve the quality of work the environmental protection sector carries out by ensuring high-quality personnel.

Our interview data suggest many people would be comfortable with assigning responsibility for environmental protection to government officials, probably even more so if their quality was improved. Selection of environmental protection personnel through such means may also have a knock-on effect for the rest of the population. If environmental protection personnel are indeed talented, knowledgeable and ethical people, they can change the environmental attitudes of the population through the example they set. This concept is explained in Confucius' advice on governing: 'If you desire what is good, the people will be good. The moral power of the gentleman is wind, the moral power of the common man is grass. Under the wind, the grass must bend' (*Analects*, 12.19; translated by Leys, 1997: 58).[2]

Universal environmental education for the Chinese public

Universal education is also an important principle of Confucianism, as shown when Confucius said: 'My teaching is addressed to all indifferently' (*Analects*, 15.39, translated by Leys, 1997: 79). This should be applied to China's environmental education, especially for the older generation who did not receive environmental education during their schooling. Although many ENGOs have carried out environmental education in recent years in the form of seminars, advertisements, documentaries, news, etc., the impact is still limited, as demonstrated by our interviews. In response to the questions 'Do you know about global warming?' and 'Do you know what has contributed to this problem?', most interviewees responded that they had heard of global warming but were not sure about its cause. One interviewee believed that global warming was caused by the use of air-conditioners in summer:

> I think it's caused by air-conditioners. When we use air-conditioners in summer, it gets cooler inside, but it blows all the hot air outside. Therefore,

it's getting hotter and hotter outside. As a result, we have to turn up the air-conditioner which puts more hot air into the atmosphere. This becomes a bad cycle, and the earth is getting warmer.

In another example of people's lack of environmental knowledge, nearly 40 (close to 80 per cent) of the interviewees said they had never heard of carbon emissions trading. Among the interviewees who had heard of carbon emissions trading, one interviewee discussed in detail its purpose, how it works and the benefits China can obtain from it, but this was because his work involved the environmental management system – certification ISO 14001:2004 – which aims to design strategies for industries' energy intensity reduction.

In line with Confucian principles, it is clear that much more far-reaching environmental education is required in China. Broad and effective environmental education for the entire population, however, requires various approaches. For the older generation, environmental education should adopt an alternative strategy, as Confucius advocated that teaching should be carried out with different methodologies according to students' different characteristics. This can be seen in his responses to his disciples' questions in the following exchange from the *Analects* (Goldin, 2011):

> Zilu asked, 'Should I practise at once what I've just learned?' The Master said, 'Your father and elder brothers are still alive, how can you practice what you have just learned?' When Ranyou asked the same question, the Master said, 'Yes, you should'. [Commenting on this] Gongxi Hua said, 'I'm puzzled. They asked the same question, but got two different answers.' Confucius said, 'Ranyou usually holds himself back, so I urged him on. Zilu is too bold, so I tried to hold him back.'
>
> (*Analects*, 11.22; translated by W. Lin, 2010: 193)

China's current formal environmental education cannot reach this section of the population while environmental education carried out by ENGOs is either limited or unattractive to them. Therefore, to carry out environmental education for this section of the population using standard methods appears to be difficult. However, this group does enjoy watching television, especially soap operas (Rofel, 2007), and we therefore suggest environmental education for this group should take the form of quality soap operas that weave environmental topics into their storylines. Much research shows that people learn more successfully and retain what they learn more thoroughly when learning is interesting, engaging, relevant to their lives and links new information to their existing experience and knowledge (Brown, 2007). Soap operas certainly fulfil these requirements and have the additional advantage that large numbers of people can be reached through television. Universal environmental education for the whole population is the precondition and first step in the development of a strong environmental consciousness among the Chinese people, which can contribute to positive environmental outcomes.

Moderation as the standard for sustainable development

The concept of sustainable development was proposed by the World Commission on Environment and Development in 1987. The core principle of sustainable development is that economic development should be carried out in a fashion that 'development meets the needs of the present without compromising the ability of the future generations to meet their own needs' (World Commission on Environment and Development, 1987: 43).

China formally adopted the concept of sustainable development in 1992 (Lo and Chung, 2003), however, since then much of the development carried out in China appears to be highly unsustainable. The failure to stick with the concept is largely due to the unchecked speed and scale of economic development in practice, but also partly because sustainability is hard to measure in reality (Ekins, 2000). Therefore, we propose to use the Confucian concept of moderation as the standard for sustainability.

Inspiration for moderate development and consumption can be drawn from the passage of the *Analects* which describes Confucius' fishing and hunting habits: 'The Master fished with a line but never with a net. He used corded arrows to shoot birds but never a roosting one' (*Analects*, 7.27; translated by W. Lin, 2010: 127). Giving animals a fair chance of survival in this way rather than catching and consuming everything available contributes to the future sustainability of natural resources.

Mencius (372–289 BC) discussed these issues of production and natural resource conservation at length and also regarded the proper management of natural resources as the foundation of successful governance. When being asked how to exercise royal authority, Mencius said:

> Do not interfere with the seasons of husbandry, nor allow close-meshed nets in the ponds: then the grain and fish and turtles will be more than can be consumed. Have the axes and bills enter the mountain woods only in due season: then the wealth of timber will be more than can be used. This will enable the people to nourish the living and bury the dead without ill will against any man; and that is the first step to royal authority.
>
> (*Mencius*, 1A3.3; translated by Hughes, 1942: 108)

Clearly, from the above statement, Mencius had no intention of stopping people from fishing and logging; what he advocated was to use natural resources in a sustainable manner so the resource could be regenerated and prolonged. Mencius also expressed this idea in his detailed advice on farming practices:

> If each household with a five-acre plot of land is planted with mulberry trees to raise silkworms, fifty-year-olds can wear silk. If the care of chickens, pigs, dogs, and sows does not miss its season, seventy-year-olds can eat meat. If one does not steal the labor during the farming seasons of each hundred-acre field, a clan with many mouths can go without hunger. If one is careful about providing instruction in the village schools, emphasizing the

righteousness of filiality and brotherliness, those whose hair has turned grey will not carry loads on the roadways. It has never happened that someone fails to become King when, among his subjects, seventy-year-olds are wearing silk and eating meat, and the black-hair people are neither hungry nor cold.

(Mencius, 1A3.4; translated by Van Norden, 2008: 4–5)

It is clear that, to eat meat, to dress in silk and to let elderly people have a better standard of living are not contradictory to production according to Mencius; instead, these are the reasons why people should manage the environment sustainably.

In modern China, the majority of the urban population is no longer involved in agriculture; rather, they are employed by industries. Therefore, the strategy of 'sustainable development' mentioned by Confucius and Mencius should be modified to suit modern conditions. First, the government should not issue approvals to heavy polluting industries that may cause irreversible environmental damage in the first place, regardless of how significant the short-term economic benefit is. Essential polluting industries must be equipped with proper mitigation measures before gaining approval, and environmental impact assessment is essential (Xiong, 2007). Second, ongoing monitoring and frequent reviews on the environmental and social impacts of existing industries should be carried out in order to assess and guarantee long-term sustainability. Finally, switching from a quantity-oriented to quality-oriented economic development model will effectively enhance long-term environmental and economic sustainability.

A systematic approach to truth through observation and evaluation

Confucianism offers a systematic approach to truth. Confucius, as Creel (1954: 51) explains, 'made no claim to the possession of the ultimate truth. He was groping toward the truth, by the method of observation and analysis.' This is demonstrated in Confucius' advice that a person should

> hear much, leave to one side that which is doubtful, and speak with due caution concerning the remainder.... See much, but leave to one side that of which the meaning is not clear, and act carefully with regard to the rest.
> *(Analects*, 2.18, translated by Creel, 1954: 51)

And 'to hear much, select what is good, and follow it; to see much and remember it; these are the steps by which understanding is attained' *(Analects*, 7.28, translated by Creel, 1954: 52).

Thus, we can summarize Confucius' approach as to observe, analyse and learn in the process of uncovering the truth. This approach should be adapted in the investigation and mitigation of complex environmental issues as it possesses the exact ingredients required for the study of modern environmental problems – especially complex issues such as atmospheric pollution and global warming – the consequences associated with them and the mitigation procedures needed. Therefore, the Confucian approach to truth should be applied in China's environmental affairs analysis and environmental policy development, which will lead to more informed policy development and outcomes.

Conclusion

In this chapter we have traced the development of environmental governance in China and analysed the challenges it faces in terms of the enforcement of environmental law and the limitations of ENGOs. We argued that such challenges mean improving China's environmental outcome must rely on a top-down approach for the foreseeable future, and that the Confucian principles of higher virtue, universal education, moderation and systematic approach to truth are an appropriate means of achieving this. Confucian philosophy offers a sound framework and guidelines for addressing deficiencies in China's existing environmental governance, and can bring hope to China's environmental future and Chinese society as a whole.

Notes

1 Bell's (2000, 2006) proposal is actually much broader than ours. He argues that in the medium- to long-term future the government system of China should consist of a Lower House of Parliament made up of directly elected members and an Upper House of Parliament made up of members selected on the basis of such examinations. As our proposals are intended for the short to medium term, we have adopted a more limited role for the selection of government personnel through examinations.
2 For Confucius, a gentleman is someone who is 'benevolent, wise, and reverent' (Van Norden, 2011: 20). Some scholars use the term exemplary person instead of gentleman (see, for example, Bell, 2000, 2006).

References

Adler, J.A. 2002, *Chinese Religious Traditions*, Prentice Hall, Upper Saddle River, NJ.

All-China Environment Federation. 2006, *Zhongguo huanbao minjian zuzhi fazhan zhuang kuang baogao* (*Report on the Development of CHINA'S Environmental Organizations*), http://news.sina.com.cn/c/2006-04-28/10128811801s.shtml.

Alpermann, B. 2010, 'State and society in China's environmental politics', in J.J. Kassiola and S. Guo (eds), *China's Environmental Crisis: Domestic and Global Political Impacts and Responses*, Palgrave Macmillan, New York, pp. 123–151.

Bell, D.A. 2000, *East Meets West: Human Rights and Democracy in East Asia*, Princeton University Press, Princeton, NJ.

Bell, D.A. 2006, *Beyond Liberal Democracy: Political Thinking for an East Asian Context*, Princeton University Press, Princeton, NJ.

Bell, D.A. 2008, *China's New Confucianism: Politics and Everyday Life in a Changing Society*, Princeton University Press, Princeton, NJ.

Bell, D.A. and Hahm, C. 2003, 'Introduction: the contemporary relevance of Confucianism', in D.A. Bell and C. Hahm (eds), *Confucianism for the Modern World*, Cambridge University Press, Cambridge, pp. 1–28.

Blanchard, J.M.F. and Guo, S. 2008, 'Introduction: "Harmonious World" and China's new foreign policy', in J.M.F. Blanchard and S. Guo (eds), *Harmonious World' and China's New Foreign Policy*, Lexington Books, Lanham, MD, pp. 1–19.

Brown, H.D. 2007, *Teaching by Principles: An Interactive Approach to Language Pedagogy*, 3rd edn, Pearson Education, White Plains, NY.

Callicott, J.B. and Ames, R.T. 1989, 'Introduction: the Asian traditions as a conceptual resource for environmental philosophy', in J.B. Callicott and R.T. Ames (eds), *Nature in Asian Traditions of Thought: Essays in Environmental Philosophy*, State University of New York Press, Albany, NY, pp. 1–21.

Creel, H.G. 1954, *Chinese Thought from Confucius to Mao Tse-tung*, Eyre & Spottiswoode, London.

Ekins, P. 2000, *Economic Growth and Environmental Sustainability: The Prospects for Green Growth*, Routledge, London.

Fu, T. 2007, 'Development of environmental NGOs in China', in C.J. Liang and D.P. Yang (eds), *The China Environmental Yearbook (2005): Crisis and Breakthrough of China's Environment*, Social Science Academic Press and Brill, Beijing and Leiden, pp. 291–310.

Goldin, P.R. 2011, *Confucianism*, Acumen, Durham.

Guo, S. 2013, *Chinese Politics and Government: Power, Ideology and Organization*, Routledge, New York.

He, X. and Miller, J. 2006, 'Confucian spirituality in an ecological age', in J. Miller (ed.), *Chinese Religions in Contemporary Societies*, ABC-CLIO, Santa Barbara, CA, pp. 281–299.

Ho, J. 2001, 'Greening without conflict? Environmentalism, NGOs and civil society in China', *Development and Change*, vol. 32, no. 5, pp. 893–921.

Hughes, E.R. (ed.). 1942, *Chinese Philosophy in Classical Times.* Dent, London.

Ivanhoe, P.J. 1998, 'Early Confucianism and environmental ethics', in M.E. Tucker and J. Berthrong (eds), *Confucianism and Ecology: The Interrelation of Heaven, Earth, and Humans*, Harvard University Press, Cambridge, MA, pp. 59–76.

Jacques, M. 2009, *When China Rules the World: The Rise of the Middle Kingdom and the End of the Western World*, Allen Lane, London.

Jahiel, A. 1998, 'The organization of environmental protection in China', *China Quarterly*, vol. 156, pp. 757–787.

Kalton, M.C. 1998, 'Extending the Neo-Confucian tradition: questions and reconceptualization for the twenty-first century', in M.E. Tucker and J. Berthrong (eds), *Confucianism and Ecology: The Interrelation of Heaven, Earth, and Humans*, Harvard University Press, Cambridge, pp. 77–101.

Kalton, M.C. 2010, 'Confucian trajectories on environmental understanding', in W. Chang and L. Kalmanson (eds), *Confucianism in Context: Classic Philosophy and Contemporary Issues, East Asia and Beyond*, State University of New York Press, Albany, NY, pp. 191–210.

Kassiola, J.J. 2010, 'Confucianizing modernity and "modernizing" Confucianism: environmentalism and the need for a Confucian positive argument for social change', in J.J. Kassiola and S. Guo (eds), *China's Environmental Crisis: Domestic and Global Political Impacts and Responses*, Palgrave Macmillan, New York, pp. 195–218.

Lampton, D.M. 2008, *The Three Faces of Chinese Power: Might, Money, and Minds*, University of California Press, Berkeley, CA.

Leys, S. 1997, *The Analects of Confucius*, W.W. Norton & Company, New York.

Li, T. 2003, 'Confucian ethics and the environment', *Cultural Mandala: The Bulletin of the Centre for East–West Cultural and Economic Studies*, vol. 6, no. 1, http://epublications.bond.edu.au/cgi/viewcontent.cgi?article=1075&context=cm.

Li, X.W., Ning, C. and Liu, X. 2007, 'Hard-won progress in protecting environmental rights', in C.J. Liang and D.P. Yang (eds), *The China Environmental Yearbook (2005): Crisis and Breakthrough of China's Environment*, Social Science Academic Press and Brill, Beijing and Leiden, pp. 37–50.

Lieberthal, K. 2004, *Governing China: From Revolution through Reform*, 2nd edn, W.W. Norton & Company, New York.

Lin, H. 2009, 'A Confucian approach to China's environmental governance: a case study of China's atmospheric pollution problem', Master's thesis, Flinders University, Adelaide, Australia.

Lin, W. 2010, *Getting to Know Confucius: A New Translation of the Analects*. Foreign Languages Press, Beijing.

Lo, C.W. and Chung, S.S. 2003, 'China's green challenges in the twenty-first century', in J.Y.S. Cheng (ed.), *China's Challenges in the Twenty-first Century*, City University of Hong Kong Press, Hong Kong, pp. 719–760.

Lo, C.W., Yip, P.K. and Cheung, K. 2000, 'The regulatory style of environmental governance in China: the case of EIA regulation in Shanghai', *Public Administration and Development*, vol. 20, no. 4, pp. 305–318.

Ma, X. and Ortolano, L. 2000, *Environmental Regulation in China: Institutions, Enforcement and Compliance*, Rowman and Littlefield, Lanham, MD.

Mahbubani, K. 2008, *The New Asian Hemisphere: The Irresistible Shift of Global Power to the East*, Public Affairs, New York.

Martens, S. 2006, 'Public participation with Chinese characteristics: citizen consumers in China's environmental management', *Environmental Politics*, vol. 15, no. 2, pp. 211–230.

Miller, J. 2006, 'The historical legacy of China's religious traditions', in J. Miller (ed.), *Chinese Religions in Contemporary Societies*, ABC-CLIO, Santa Barbara, CA, pp. 9–30.

Mol, A.P.J. and Carter, N.T. 2006, 'China's environmental governance in transition', *Environmental Politics*, vol. 15, no. 2, pp. 149–170.

New York Times. 2013, 'Cost of environmental damage in China growing rapidly amid industrialization', www.nytimes.com/2013/03/30/world/asia/cost-of-environmental-degradation-in-china-is-growing.html.

Nordhaus, T. and Shellenberger, M. 2007, *Break Through: From the Death of Environmentalism to the Politics of Possibility*, Houghton Mifflin Company, Boston, MA.

People's Daily Online. 2009, '*Huanbao juzhang tong shuo zhi fa nan*' (Minister of Environmental Protection expressed the difficulties in environmental law enforcement), www.people.com.cn/GB/34948/34951/34953/222739.html.

Rofel, L. 2007, *Desiring China: Experiments in Neoliberalism, Sexuality, and Public Culture*, Duke University Press, Durham, NC.

Shapiro, J. 2012, *China's Environmental Challenges*, Polity Press, Cambridge.

Shi, H. and Zhang, L. 2006 'China's environmental governance of rapid industrialisation', *Environmental Politics*, vol. 15, no. 20, pp. 271–292.

Shirk, S.L. 2008, *China: Fragile Superpower*, Oxford University Press, Oxford.

Snyder, S. 2006, 'Chinese traditions and ecology: survey article', *Worldviews: Global Religions, Culture and Ecology*, vol. 10, no. 1, pp. 100–134.

Tu, W. 1989, 'The continuity of being: Chinese visions of nature', in J.B. Callicott and R.T. Ames (eds), *Nature in Asian Traditions of Thought: Essays in Environmental Philosophy*, State University of New York Press, Albany, NY, pp. 67–78.

Tu, W. 1998, 'Beyond the Enlightenment mentality', in M.E. Tucker and J. Berthrong (eds), *Confucianism and Ecology: The Interrelation of Heaven, Earth, and Humans*, Harvard University Press, Cambridge, MA, pp. 3–21.

Tu, W. 2001, 'The ecological turn in New Confucian humanism: implications for China and the world', *Daedalus*, vol. 130, no. 4, pp. 243–264.

Tucker, M.E. 1991, 'The relevance of Chinese neo-Confucianism for the reverence of nature', *Environmental History Review*, vol. 15, no. 2, pp. 55–69.

Tucker, M.E. 1994, 'Ecological themes in Taoism and Confucianism', in M.E. Tucker and J. Grim (eds), *Worldviews and Ecology: Religion, Philosophy, and the Environment*, Orbis Books, Maryknoll, NY, pp. 150–160.

Tucker, M.E. and Berthrong, J. 1998, 'Introduction: setting the context', in M.E. Tucker and J. Berthrong (eds), *Confucianism and Ecology: The Interrelation of Heaven, Earth, and Humans*, Harvard University Press, Cambridge, MA, pp. xxxiii–xlv.

Van Norden, B.W. 2008, *Mengzi: With Selections from Traditional Commentaries*, Hackett Publishing Company, Indianapolis, IN.

Van Norden, B.W. 2011, *Introduction to Classical Chinese Philosophy*, Hackett Publishing Company, Indianapolis, IN.

van Rooij, B. 2004, 'Towards compliance: recommendations for Chinese environmental law enforcement', *Van Vollenhoven Research Report*, vol. 4, no. 6, pp. 1–39.

Wang, P. 2007, 'Diverse approaches to environmental education by Chinese NGOs', in C.J. Liang and D.P. Yang (eds), *The China Environmental Yearbook (2005): Crisis and Breakthrough of China's Environment*, Social Science Academic Press and Brill, Beijing and Leiden, pp. 311–330.

Weller, R.P. and Bol, P.K. 1998, 'From heaven-and-earth to nature: Chinese concepts of the environment and their influence on policy implementation', in M.E. Tucker and J. Berthrong (eds), *Confucianism and Ecology: The Interrelation of Heaven, Earth, and Humans*, Harvard University Press, Cambridge, MA, pp. 313–341.

World Bank, n.d. a. 'GNI per capita, Atlas method (current US$)', http://data.worldbank.org/indicator/NY.GNP.PCAP.CD/countries/CN-4E-XT?display=graph.

World Bank n.d. b. 'Poverty headcount ratio at $1.25 a day (PPP) (% of population)', http://data.worldbank.org/indicator/SI.POV.DDAY/countries/CN?display=graph.

World Commission on Environment and Development. 1987, *Our Common Future: Report of the World Commission on Environment and Development*, Oxford University Press, Oxford.

Xie, L. 2009, *Environmental Activism in China*, Routledge, London.

Xiong, Z.H. 2007, 'Environmental impact assessment: a storm stirs in 2005', in C.J. Liang and D.P. Yang (eds), *The China Environmental Yearbook (2005): Crisis and Breakthrough of China's Environment*, Social Science Academic Press and Brill, Beijing and Leiden, pp. 3–18.

Xue, L., Simonis, U.E., Dubek, D.J., *et al.* 2006, *Environmental Governance in China: Report of the Task Force on Environmental Governance to the China Council for International Cooperation on Environment and Development (CCICED)*, Wissenschaftszentrum fur Sozialforschung, Berlin.

Yang, G.B. 2005, 'Environmental NGOs and institutional dynamics in China', *The China Quarterly*, vol. 181, pp. 46–66.

Zhang, K.J. 2007, 'The shadow of environmental pollution in China', in C.J. Liang and D.P. Yang (eds), *The China Environmental Yearbook (2005): Crisis and Breakthrough of China's Environment*, Social Science Academic Press and Brill, Beijing and Leiden, pp. 179–196.

Zhang, W. 1999, *Confucianism and Modernization: Industrialization and Democratization of the Confucian Regions*, Palgrave Macmillan, Basingstoke.

10 The contribution of the Clean Development Mechanism (CDM) towards China's climate change mitigation and sustainable development

Han Lin

Introduction

Climate change mitigation and adaptation is one common and urgent task that all nations and peoples on this planet face today and into the foreseeable future. On top of this common task, developing countries face another, equally important, task: to continue development in an ecologically sustainable manner. In order to fulfil these two tasks, the United Nations Framework Convention on Climate Change (UNFCCC) proposed the concepts of cost-effective emission mitigation and flexible cross-region cooperation (Dutschke and Michaelowa, 1998: 7). The Clean Development Mechanism (CDM) is one such flexible market mechanism tailored for the above concepts under the Kyoto Protocol. It aims to reduce emission reductions cost in Annex I developed countries and to promote sustainable development in non-Annex I developing countries. CDM allows an Annex I country to invest in low-cost emission reduction projects in developing countries which do not have quantified emission targets under the Kyoto Protocol, through which it can obtain Certified Emission Reductions (CERs) (1 CER = 1 metric ton of CO_2 or CO_2-equivalent) to count towards its total emission reduction obligation. Meanwhile, the projects should also be shown to be beneficial for the host country's sustainable development (Article 12, Kyoto Protocol).

Sustainable development is China's long-term national strategy. A range of national policies aiming to enhance sustainable development have been introduced over the years. Policies on energy conservation, environmental protection and reforestation, for example, have all contributed to sustainable development and simultaneously brought positive impacts in combating climate change. The ratification of the Kyoto Protocol in 2002 gained China eligibility to participate in the CDM, and China gradually became a key player in this scheme (World Bank *et al,*. 2004: xix–xx). So far, China has hosted the largest number of CDM projects among all developing nations. Up until 5 May 2015, 5,073 CDM projects have been approved nationally. By 15 June 2015, 1,450 Chinese-hosted CDM projects have been issued CERs by the CDM Executive Board (CDM EB), which accounts for over 60 per cent of global total CERs and an annual average reduction of 344 million tons of CO_2-equivalents (Department of Climate

Change, National Development and Reform Commission (NDRC) of China, 2015).

This chapter aims to evaluate the impact of CDM on China's climate change mitigation and sustainable development. It argues that Chinese CDM projects do not contribute to China's overall emission reduction. This is because the associated CERs are purchased by buyers from Annex I countries, and are therefore counted as emission reduction for the buyer's country. Instead, the benefits CDM brings to China are more of a practical nature. Among all such practical benefits, the most important is that CDM raises the Chinese public's awareness of climate change, as the improvement of awareness of a relatively new phenomena for a large population is not an easy task. The next most important practical benefit CDM brings is the promotion of renewable energy development. Renewable energy development has avoided the establishment of traditional fossil fuel-based power-generation plants in various locations nationwide, which has a positive impact on local air quality and employment. Finally, CDM sets up a model that can simultaneously deal with emission reduction and sustainable development, and provides inspiration for China's future domestic carbon market. All these practical benefits will encourage China to take further steps in fighting global climate change and to carry out sustainable development in an innovative manner, which is a positive outcome for both China and the world.

Methodology

In this chapter, interviews and qualitative analysis were applied to the evaluation of the CDM's impacts on China's climate change mitigation and sustainable development. Interviews, as a broad term, include a wide range of interactions between interviewer and interviewee(s). It can be casual conversations or highly structured formal interviews (Wolcott, 1999: 52–58). For this chapter, the elite interviewing technique was adopted extensively throughout the evaluation. This is because elite interviewing, when used effectively, can broaden and deepen our understanding of a specific policy area – in this case, China's CDM (Burnham *et al.*, 2008: 231). Semi-structured interviews with set open-ended questions were carried out with a government official from the Centre for Energy, Environment and Climate Change, Energy Research Institute, NDRC; an academic from the Centre for Rural Environmental and Social Research, Chinese Academy of Social Sciences (CASS); and an officer from a CDM-related NGO, Quanlian New Energy Commerce. The reason why these interviewees were selected is that the chosen government officials and academics have high levels of knowledge in terms of China's climate change and sustainable development affairs, and have the experience of participating in relevant policy development processes. The staff member from the CDM-related NGO has good connections with important stakeholders, who have first-hand experience with China's CDM programmes. Although the three interviewees are from different sectors, they nevertheless share a common focus on sustainability. Such information is unlikely to be obtained from other sources, and therefore interviews play an important part in gaining a deep understanding of the phenomena studied in this chapter.

Climate sustainability is the fundamental base of all other forms of sustainability. What people think about climate change and its relation with sustainability plays an important role in how they deal with this issue. Therefore, the CDM's impact on the Chinese public's awareness on climate change will be discussed first. Following this, attention is given to China's energy sector, with wind power being the focal point. This is because carbon emission reduction can only be realistically planned and implemented when the status of energy structure and production is well researched (Darmstadter, 2001: 24). China's further CDM potential will also be discussed, and a range of potential cheap abatement options are proposed. Finally, the possibility of CDM as a domestic market mechanism in China after 2012 will be explored from the initial utilization of the China Certified Emission Reduction (CCER) in the China carbon trade pilot programme to the possibility of establishing a CDM-like co-mechanism for a national carbon market. Through the evaluation of China's existing CDM programme, its strengths and weaknesses will be pointed out, and recommendations for improvement will be proposed. The recommendations will incorporate the findings of the analysis with China's existing CDM planning and operation system in order to seek an updated post-Kyoto flexible market mechanism that suits China's domestic situation.

Climate change and China's participation in CDM

China is one of the most vulnerable countries to the potential damage caused by climate change. In 2011 alone, direct economic loss from natural disasters reached 309.6 billion yuan (approximately US$50 billion) and 430 million Chinese people's livelihoods were affected (NDRC, 2012: 2). In response, the Chinese government has been utilizing a range of resources to control its greenhouse gas emissions. Domestically, energy conservation and energy structure optimization have been the ongoing missions. During China's 11th Five Year Plan (2006–2010), China's energy intensity (energy consumption per unit of GDP) dropped by 19.06 per cent, which resulted in a reduction of 1.5 billion tons of carbon emission, compared with the business-as-usual scenario (Xue and Zhao, 2012). On the global scale, CDM is so far the only major international cooperation on climate change mitigation that China has participated in.

The development of CDM in China began slowly. By the end of 2005 there were only three registered CDM projects nationwide (Maraseni and Gao, 2011: 340). This was partly because of the complexity of the CDM legal framework and administrative system, but it was also backed-up by an argument that CDM might exhaust China's cheap climate change abatement options, the so-called 'low-hanging fruit', and leave future abatement harder and more expensive (Castro, 2012: 199). However, after the initial hesitation, China gradually fully embraced CDM.

This shift in attitude towards CDM is due to a range of reasons. First, CDM is a market mechanism, and the high demand for CERs is no doubt the biggest drive for China's attitude shift. After late 2005, CDM experienced a gold-rush-style boom. This boom was primarily driven by the rising price of EU allowances (the primary carbon credits in the EU Emission Trading Scheme), which reached a high of €30 (~US$36) in July 2005. The prices of CERs were below that of the EU allowance, which made CDM projects feasible and attractive to investors (Michaelowa and Buen, 2012: 5). On top of this, the industrial gas projects, such as HFC-23 and N_2O, have further spurred on the boom due to their highly profitable nature. The technologies for reducing such gases are relatively cheap, while the warming effect of HFC-23, for example, is 11,700 times that of CO_2. This also means that CERs from industrial gas projects are among the cheapest types of all CDM projects (Michaelowa, 2012: 19).

The majority of China's industrial gas projects were registered in the early stage of China's CDM involvement. According to Maraseni and Gao (2011: 342), up to 2010, HFC-related projects were only 0.5 per cent of China's total CDM projects, but accounted for over 14 per cent of expected CDM annual emission reduction. N_2O-related projects were not far behind, generating about 4 per cent of total CDM emission reductions while only taking up 1 per cent in proportion of total CDM projects.

Although industrial gas projects account for a proportionally large percentage of greenhouse gas emissions reductions (CO_2-equivalent), they do not significantly contribute to local sustainable development. First, industrial gas projects do not assist energy structure optimization in host countries, which is to say they do not tackle the most dominant and long-lasting greenhouse gas – CO_2. Therefore, they have a weak impact on the fundamental problem when tackling climate change – how to rehabilitate China's fossil fuel addiction and how to switch to a mix of low-carbon renewable energy sources (Pearson, 2007: 247). Second, the majority of industrial gas projects happened on the sites of existing facilities, and have little contribution to the improvement of local air quality, infrastructure and employment. As a result, the integrity of industrial gas projects on sustainability has been questioned by many (Pearson, 2007; Schneider 2007; Schwank, 2004). Furthermore, the EU has banned CERs generated from industrial gas projects after January 2013 (Gtowacki Law Firm, 2013). For these reasons, this chapter will only focus on CDM projects targeting CO_2 emission and which have positive and long-term impacts on China's energy structure and sustainable development.

The carbon emission reduction capacity of China's energy-related CDM projects is significant. Among all EB-registered projects, renewable energy, energy saving and efficiency improvement and fuels substitute projects make up about 91 per cent of all types projects and have a combined annual reduction of 0.22 billion tons of CO_2 (NDRC, 2014). This is a significant amount compared with China's annual domestic effort in carbon emission reduction. During the 11th Five-Year Plan (2005–2010), China's energy intensity dropped by 19.06 per cent from its 2005 level. This resulted in a total reduction of 1.5 billion tons of CO_2 (approximately 0.3 billion tons per year). It is not difficult to see that the predicted annual combined CO_2 emission from the above-mentioned three types of energy-related CDM projects (0.22 billion tons) is lower, but not far from China's average annual domestic target (0.3 billion tons).

The carbon emission reduction capacity of these CDM projects is undeniably high, but their associated emission reduction achievements do not count as China's effort. This is because CERs from China's CDM projects are sold to Annex I entities and are therefore counted as the buyers' emission reduction. China as a host country solely enjoys the benefits that CDM projects bring in terms of enhancing sustainable development, such as better local air quality and more efficient and advanced local infrastructures. It is important to make clear the right of attribution of emission reduction achievements of CDM projects so that double counting in total global carbon emission reduction can be avoided. Thus, if the discussion is only oriented at the contribution of CDM towards China's total emission reduction target, the conclusion is clear that CDM does not boost China's emission reduction portfolio. However, CDM did bring China a range of other practical benefits, including raising the Chinese public's awareness of climate change; promoting development of renewable energies; and providing inspiration for China's future domestic market mechanism. Each of these benefits will be discussed below.

Raising awareness of climate change

The biggest benefit that CDM has brought to China is the improvement of people's awareness of climate change and how to deal with it in a scientific manner. According to Interviewee 1 from the Energy Research Institute, NDRC:

> The greatest benefit of CDM is to let Chinese people, and especially the Chinese companies, know about climate change, and they can get benefit from emission reduction. It contributes greatly to the improvement of public awareness on climate change. Take the 11th Five Year Plan for example, we have achieved a lot in energy saving and pollution reduction, and public awareness in energy conservation has improved a lot. This is because we gave publicity to environmental protection and energy conservation for the last 30 years, and people's awareness improved gradually. But climate change is an urgent issue, we don't have another 30 years to build up the awareness, and CDM did the work. It is also undeniable that CDM has brought China many good climate change mitigation projects which are very beneficial for energy conservation and long-term sustainable development.

In fact, signs of the positive impact of CDM on public awareness can already be seen in the business sector. For example, Chinese corporations which participated in CDM have adopted a set of more standardized operational systems. Interviewee 2 from the CDM NGO Quanlian New Energy Chamber of Commerce stated:

> The operation process of CDM itself is a systematic operation process for a company, just like the ISO9000.[1] Many small enterprises in China do not

have a standardized operation system, but if they have operated under CDM, their operation such as data monitoring and shifts and other procedures will be more standardized. This is very helpful for the company.

From this we can see that the ongoing implementation of CDM has a positive impact on lifting the public's awareness on climate change; at least the impact is currently obvious at the industrial level by providing learning opportunities to Chinese companies for more advanced and standardized operational procedures when dealing with climate change.

A recent national telephone survey of 4,169 Chinese adults, conducted from July to August 2012 by the China Center for Climate Change Communication, echoed the statements of the above interviewees. The survey focused on investigating Chinese people's awareness, beliefs, attitudes, policy support, and environmental behaviours towards climate change. The results show that a majority of the Chinese public are aware of climate change, believe human behaviour contributes to climate change and wish the government to pay more attention to climate change (see Table 10.1 for detailed information).

Table 10.1 National survey of the Chinese public's awareness on climate change

Factor	Main results
Awareness	93 per cent of respondents say they know at least a little about climate change. 11 per cent say they know a lot; 54 per cent know something; and 28 per cent know just a little about it. 7 per cent have never heard of climate change.
Belief	55 per cent say that climate change is caused mostly by human activities, while 38 per cent say that climate change is caused mostly by natural changes in the environment.
Attitude	78 per cent of respondents say they are either very (23 per cent) or somewhat worried (55 per cent) about climate change. 14 per cent are not very worried and 8 per cent are not at all worried.
Experience	69 per cent say that people in China are already being harmed by climate change, while another 8 per cent say they will be harmed within ten years.
Responsibility	89 per cent of respondents agree and 9 per cent somewhat agree with the statement: 'The government should pay great attention to the issue of climate change.'
Source of information	Majorities of respondents trust scientific institutes (89 per cent), the government (86 per cent), the news media (82 per cent) and their own friends and family members (64 per cent) as sources of information about climate change. Fewer trust NGOs (41 per cent) or corporations (38 per cent).

Source: China Center for Climate Change Communication (2012) Public climate change awareness and climate change communication in China, viewed 10 February 2014, http://environment.yale.edu/climate-communication/files/2sided-highlights-China-e.pdf.

This is a very positive outcome regarding the Chinese public's climate change awareness, given China's traditional reluctant attitude towards climate change mitigation. It is also a significant improvement compared with the survey conducted on the same issue by Lin and Gil in 2009 (refer to Chapter 9 of this volume for details). This improvement in people's climate change awareness will increase public understanding and facilitate China's future climate change mitigation plans.

Promoting China's renewable energy development

The ability of CDM in promoting sustainable development attracts broad attention among scholars, and a range of criteria have been proposed. Pearson (2007: 247) boldly stated that 'The question of whether the CDM is promoting sustainable development can be framed primarily in terms of whether it is promoting renewables in developing countries and thus assisting in the transition away from fossil fuel.' Boyd *et al.* (2009) judged this matter through an in-depth analysis of ten CDM projects' sustainability benefits. They concluded that CDM only enhances sustainability to a high extent by installing small-scale renewable energy in remote regions of developing countries to cover the newly emerged or growing energy demands. Regardless of the different criteria for defining sustainable development, it is most commonly agreed that the development of renewable energy in appropriate regions with a purpose of replacing or avoiding traditional fossil fuel-based energy has a positive impact on sustainable development.

New and renewable energy-related CDM projects account for 73.64 per cent of China's total approved CDM projects. Up until 5 May 2015, among all 5,073 NDRC-approved CDM projects, 3,736 are in the category of new and renewable energy projects (NDRC, 2015). Within this category, wind power is a newborn star after China's traditional hydro power, and attracts much attention.

Wind power in China experienced a slow development. The early wind power projects in China were often very small in scale, located in remote areas and were not connected to the grid. Since the mid-1990s, the wind power and related manufacturing industries emerged following the initial identification of domestic regulations detailing wind power installation targets and the availability of some funding. However, the wind turbines installed were mainly imported as a result of foreign manufacturers' internationalization plans. Even though foreign manufacturers could provide grants or loans for setting up wind power plants in China, the enthusiasm on the Chinese side was still low. This was due to a combination of reasons, including lack of a unified pricing mechanism, unwillingness to lend by banks, high transaction costs and investment risk, and fear of unpopularity of high electricity prices among the public (Buen and Castro, 2012: 64–66). The development of China's wind power has been underestimated by the authorities for quite a long period. For instance, the Research Team of China Climate Change Country Study (RTCCCCS) (1999) has predicted that China's wind power installation capacity would be 2 GW by 2020; in 2010 China's wind power capacity had already reached 44.7 GW (Global Wind Energy Council, 2011: 30). The sudden boom in China's wind power and related manufacturing industry after 2003 was led by a range of supportive domestic policies and triggered by the introduction of CDM (Buen and Castro, 2012: 73).

The first step that the Chinese government took towards a successful wind power industry was to establish a market for wind power products and to protect domestic wind turbine manufacturers and wind power developers from competition. Specifically, it provided concessions for development of large-scale wind farms; provided loans and tax benefits; required developers to purchase 50–70 per cent of equipment from the domestic manufacturing industry; made sure that energy generated from wind farms was purchased at an optimal price and issued long-term power purchasing agreements of 25 years (Buen and Castro, 2012: 70). All these measures set up a solid foundation for the prompt development of China's wind power industry. In 2009, the revised version of the Renewable Energy Law further confirmed the obligation of utilities who absorbed renewable energy into grids that renewable energy must be purchased continually throughout the power plant's life time. The additional cost of renewable energy would be shared among all consumers nationwide instead of by local consumers where renewable energy was generated. Furthermore, the national grid would accept renewable energy generated from regional areas where power could not be completely consumed locally (Buen, 2010). Such guarantees from the revised Renewable Energy Law have further enhanced the robustness of the wind power industry.

Among all renewable energy CDM projects, the Chinese government has given high priority to wind power projects. This is a strategic plan for China's relatively dry northern regions, where wind resources are rich but water resources are scarce, which limits the development of energies that require large amounts of water for production. Also, wind power is one of the cheapest options among renewable energies (Wang and Chen, 2010: 1993). So far, 80 per cent of China's wind power programmes have applied for CDM with EB. For large wind projects that have been approved by EB, their CDM revenue is estimated at about 10 per cent of their total revenue, which appears attractive to investors (Castro *et al.*, 2011).

Nonetheless, the road for wind power in China is not completely smooth. As a market mechanism, CDM was unavoidably affected by the 2008 Global Financial Crisis and CER price dropped consistently afterwards. Although it received both domestic and international support, China's renewable energy industry was not trouble-free under this circumstance. When asked about the impact of the CER price tumble on China's renewable energy CDM projects, Interviewee 2, from Quanlian New Energy Commerce, stated:

At the early stage, CDM did attract some investors in renewable energy industries. Renewable energy required high investment but the return was low, therefore there were few investors. But with CDM, the CERs will compensate some of its investment cost and become relatively more profitable.

This is CDM's advantage in attracting investment. However, CDM has also misled China's renewable industries to a certain extent. The later investments are more or less like this [over-estimated CER revenue]. If they don't find buyers of their CERs, their operation will be under pressure. This is because only at the very start, some foreign investors would provide upfront finance for establishment and obtain CERs according to their investment. But later projects are not like this. They were established by domestic resources and loans were sourced from domestic banks. Only after operation of the project can they get CER revenue. If market demand for CER is lower than predicted, their profit will definitely shrink. Another thing is that the [renewable energy] related manufacturing industries expand blindly because of the stimulation of CERs. Now the market has shrunk, leaving wind turbines and solar panels piled up in the warehouse finding no buyers.

But the good thing is that I haven't heard of any bankruptcy [of CDM renewable energy projects]. It [the financial difficulty] also depends on the type of project though. For example, small hydro-power, the investment requirement is small, even personal/private entities do not face the danger of bankruptcy.

It can be seen from this response that although the Global Financial Crisis brought certain inconvenience to China's renewable energy CDM projects, the negative impact is not severe enough to deny the true benefits CDM has brought to China. This is probably why Michaelowa and Buen (2012: 1) describe the popularity change of CDM in China as a transformation from 'Cinderella to fairy princess'. The 'fairy princess' has certainly shown resilience even under the negative impacts of the Global Financial Crisis in 2008 and failure of the Copenhagen conference in 2009. There was even a last-minute rush for the registration of CDM projects due to the policy that the EU will only accept CERs generated from the least developing countries after 2012 (Michaelowa and Buen, 2012: 30).

Interviewee 1 responded to the same question this way:

I think it [the price drop of CERs] does not matter, because from the point of view of the government, what CDM brings to China has little to do with money. Firstly, through CDM the concept of climate change is already delivered to the Chinese public, and secondly, the projects that are beneficial to climate change mitigation and sustainable development are done. These are both good things. So what we are now discussing is whether we should domestically absorb the Chinese CERs that have not been bought by foreign countries; this includes CERs that EB does not recognize or the CERs EB recognizes but cannot find buyers. This is what NDRC is considering recognizing and bringing these CERs to the domestic carbon market after 2012. We will name this kind of CER 'CCER' – China Certified Emission Reduction, which was defined in The Trading and Management Methods China Voluntary Emission Reduction published last year. As long as the procedure is according to CDM methodology and is approved by

NDRC, even though it is not approved by EB or approved by EB but cannot find buyers, these CERs can be traded in the domestic carbon market. And I think it is a very promising aspect. Although the detailed method for operation, such as where it can be used among the seven [carbon trading] pilot programmes and how it can be used in future national carbon market, are not decided yet, the government will definitely recognize and accept these CERs. This is because you [the investors] have done good things for the environment and the country and the government won't make your effort in vain.

As the Chinese government embraces the concept of CDM more and more and intends to explore domestic markets for CCERs, another issue in regards to China's future low-cost abatement options emerges and will be discussed in the following section.

Future low-cost abatement potential

CDM introduced a great concept of pursuing climate change mitigation and sustainable development at the same pace. Its positive impact on Chinese society is obvious. There may be some concerns that CDM has exhausted China's cheap climate change abatement opportunities, but compared with the overall benefit CDM has brought to China, it is very minor and can be overcome.

According to Castro (2012: 212), China has already used up 32 per cent of its cheapest abatement options available through CDM, which is a significantly high proportion compared with other CDM host countries. This may potentially put pressure on China's future emission abatement. However, one thing which needs to be pointed out here is that the 32 per cent is only of the identified theoretical abatement potential for CDM projects. Looking beyond the pre-identified categories including the above-mentioned industrial gas, new and renewable energy, energy efficiency and fuel substitute projects, there are still plentiful low-cost abatement opportunities. According to Jiang and Tovey (2010), the building sector, which accounts for 25 per cent of China's total emissions, leaves China plenty of opportunities for future emission abatement, as it is almost untouched by the CDM. Other abatement options, such as contracted energy consumption reduction or efficiency improvement for households and companies, localized land-use change and small-scale revegetation based on family and community units in rural areas, can also open up new opportunities for China's future emission reduction activities. Even within the renewable energy sector, abatement opportunities still exist and may upscale as long as the demand for CERs exists and the CER price is high enough to cover the gap between renewable energy and fossil fuels. And as technologies advance, the cost of abatement will drop simultaneously and more low-cost abatement will emerge (Michaelowa and Buen, 2012: 26).

Moreover, abatement cost reduction can also be achieved from simplified administrative measures such as reduction in transaction cost. The high transaction cost associated with CDM projects is often considered as a weakness of CDM. Transaction cost of CDM refers to total expenditures on completing a transaction of CERs between buyers and sellers. It includes project search costs, project document development cost, negotiation cost, validation cost, registration cost, monitoring cost, verification and certification cost and share of proceeds (World Bank *et al,.* 2004: xxxii). Due to the high transaction costs, the majority of Chinese CDM projects, and especially the ones that are popular with CER buyers, are often large in scale, with high CER returns. The transaction cost imposes a great difficulty for many small-scale projects and makes them uneconomical and ineligible for CDM. According to the analysis of Michaelowa and Jotzo (2005) on early CDM projects, small projects with annual CER production under 10,000 would have difficulty covering the transaction cost from the sales of CERs. In this sense, many small-scale projects have been left out by the current CDM programme and reserved for the future. For example, Interviewee 3 from the Centre for Rural Environmental and Social Research, Chinese Academy of Social Sciences (CASS) mentioned that partial reforestation and the return to traditional patterns of land use in certain rural regions of China would bring great benefits to local environments and at the same time would be beneficial to carbon emission reduction.

> Yunnan [Province] has been dry for quite a while. How can this place be dry? This is the last place nationwide which should be dry. This region undoubtedly has a very complex ecology. According to our research, we found that everywhere else is dry apart from the traditional terraced fields with forests on top of the mountains. This is because the forest on top of the mountains has a great ability in conserving water resources. But in many cases, vegetation has been completely cleared. So we are now hoping to relieve the drought through converting farmland on mountain tops into forests. The forests will not only absorb water and hold on to the soil but can also absorb CO_2 and contribute to carbon emission reduction, so I think this will be a very good project for the local communities.

The reforestation project mentioned by the above interviewee is a typical example of small-scale abatement options that can bring solid benefit to local communities. But according to NDRC statistics, among all approved CDM projects there are only five projects within the afforestation and reforestation category, leaving vast potential for the future (NDRC, 2014). This type of small-scale reforestation project can be delivered through the unilateral type of CDM project. Unilateral CDM projects involve solely the host party throughout the planning and implementation process, and therefore impose a lower transaction cost (Maraseni and Gao, 2011: 340; Michaelowa, 2007). If further government support is given, such as giving priority to CERs of small-scale unilateral CDM projects to be traded on domestic carbon trading pilot programmes, more low-cost community-based abatement opportunities will be unearthed in the future. Therefore, currently CDM has not drained China's low-cost abatement opportunities, but only provided inspiration for China's future carbon market.

Potential for CDM and carbon market in post-2012 China

CDM has experienced ups and downs during the years. As a market mechanism, it cannot avoid the influence of the global economy. However, China's attitude towards CDM has stayed positive even though post-2012 CDM projects will mainly focus on the least developed countries. China has gradually recognized the strengths of this form of project-based mechanism and intends to adopt it as a co-programme for its domestic carbon trading. The Chinese government has given out positive political and economic signals on tackling climate change. Politically, it has been actively seeking policy solutions. In 2012, the State Council issued the Work Plan for Controlling Greenhouse Gas Emissions during the 12th Five-Year Plan Period (2011–2015), within which all provinces and autonomous regions have been appointed individual carbon intensity (carbon emission per unit of GDP) reduction tasks. Nationally, carbon intensity is set to reduce by 17 per cent; the new and renewable energy proportion is set to reach 11.4 per cent of the total primary energy mix (NDRC, 2012: 9). The central government has also published the Action Plan for Addressing Climate Change in Industry (2012–2020), the National Plan for the Development of Science and Technology on Climate Change during the 12th Five-Year Plan Period, the Interim Measures on Low-carbon Products Certification Management, the Plans for Energy Development during the 12th Five-Year Plan Period, the Plans for the Development of Energy-Efficient and Environmental-Protection Industries during the 12th Five-Year Plan Period, the Suggestions on Speeding up the Development of Energy-Efficient and Environmental Protection Industries, the Industrial Energy Efficiency during the 12th Five-Year Plan Period, the 2013 Implementation Plans for Industrial Energy Efficiency and Green Development, the Action Plan for Green Architecture, as well as the National Eco-system protection during the 12th Five-Year Plan (NDRC, 2013: 10). Economically, seven cap-and-trade pilot programmes have been implemented across the country. When asked if the Chinese government would invest more in mitigating climate change and to provide feedback on carbon trading pilot programmes, Interviewee 1 from the Energy Research Institute, NDRC answered:

> Certainly we will, but the amount of investment I cannot project. The direction is certain, as it [climate change mitigation] points in the same direction as the concept of ecological civilization and the transition of the social economy, and they complement each other.... I think the more important thing is that we give out two signals, one is a political signal, and the other is a price signal. Price signals such as environmental tax, carbon tax and cap and trade that we are now discussing will give industries a clear signal. The price signal will have an impact on industries' decision-making and they will decide if they will convert to low-carbon production. At the moment,

the political signal is being given out, such as building ecological civilization and transition to a low-carbon economy. But the price signal is not given out yet. That's why we are having pilot programmes, you know the seven cap and trade pilot programmes. We are also doing research on tax, such as resource tax, environmental tax and even carbon tax and they will form a complete system. This is what we are discussing at the moment. We are also learning from the experience of developed countries such as the EU cap and trade and Australia's carbon tax.... We'll certainly have a bigger move towards emission reduction and the signals will be more and more obvious.

Strictly speaking, China's involvement in carbon trading started with CDM, but CERs from CDM are bought by overseas investors. That is the primary market. The secondary market, such as domestic carbon trading, took many years to establish. From 2008 to 2011, the voluntary trading was not in good shape. This is something we were distressed about as there were no buyers apart from a couple of companies that aimed to shape company image for the Olympics. Now we have seven pilot programmes and things are getting serious. The seven pilots are four municipalities [Beijing, Tianjin, Shanghai and Chongqing] plus Guangdong Province, Hubei Province and Shenzhen City. They are doing their own programme under the coordination of NDRC. They may cover different types and numbers of industries because there are such big differences between different areas. Therefore, the types and numbers of industries and even some methodologies are different. This is why NDRC chose seven rather than one pilot. It aims to explore more detailed options and ways that are more suitable for China's situation in front of the big background. As far as I know, only the Shenzhen cap and trade is under operation at the moment. They started on the 18th of June [2013]. The remaining six are in the designing and planning process. But they must be in operation before the end of the year [2013] according to NDRC's deadline as they don't have much time left [to compete the pilot programme], only next year and the year after. The core purpose of cap and trade is to give out the appropriate carbon price signal, and the appropriate carbon price signal depends upon emission reduction cost and the cap you set. The EU's experience is that the cap is too high and the price of carbon dropped significantly. It is difficult to say what kind of cap is appropriate, as it is all according to calculations and assumptions. I've heard that the Shenzhen pilot was very strict, but recently some entities are selling their allowance. This means that they received relatively more allowance than they needed. But we don't know how much more in total. This is really a difficult issue to handle. It is even a difficult issue for the EU because it also cannot calculate how much more allowance they have handed out in total than needed. Therefore, we'll keep on monitoring and modifying the system.

According to this interviewee, the Chinese government regards CDM as a useful medium through which the concepts of climate change mitigation and the carbon market can be successfully delivered to the Chinese public. As China gradually pursues more sophisticated emission reduction policies, there will be a greater utilization of market mechanisms. A combination of domestic CDM and a national cap and trade system may potentially become China's major climate change mitigation model in the future. Although at the current stage only pilot programmes are in operation, it is a positive sign, indicating China holds a more proactive attitude towards climate change mitigation.

Conclusion and recommendations

Overall, CDM is more beneficial than detrimental for China. Although CDM does not directly contribute to China's emission reduction, it brings China a range of practical benefits. The most significant of these is that CDM has introduced the concepts of climate change mitigation and carbon market, which has raised awareness among the Chinese government and public of the threats and consequences of climate change, and encouraged the government to actively seek ways to deal with such issues. Second, a variety of CDM projects have been established, with many of them having contributed greatly to China's sustainable development. Finally, CDM is an inspirational mechanism that combines the goals of both cost-effective emission reduction and sustainable development. It may potentially be carried onto China's future national carbon market by allowing industries to identify low-cost CDM projects domestically and the trade of CCER on the national carbon market.

Nonetheless, a few weaknesses of CDM have been identified through this review. Blindly 'following the fashion' styles of investment have been identified by one of the interviewees. This has resulted in economic loss in many manufacturing industries related to renewable energies. Another issue is the 'large-scale obsession' of many Chinese CDM projects. This may be due to the set-up of CDM as an international mechanism which requires high transaction costs, and therefore large-scale projects appear more economical. However, many small-scale projects are in fact more effective for sustainable development and bring more practical benefits to the local community and environment. Addressing these issues will require more prompt and flexible policies from the government. For example, to better guide investment and to avoid over-production, the government should incorporate more frequent market observations into policy development, and the updating of such policies should be regular and prompt. In order to include small projects that are more beneficial to local sustainable development into the national CDM, the government can incorporate a range of flexible measures to simplify project qualifying criteria and to reduce transaction fees. In sum, the use of CDM as a policy response to climate change mitigation in China leaves significant scope for discussion and future exploration of the issues highlighted in this chapter.

Note

1 This refers to a series of standards developed and published by the International Organization for Standardization (ISO), which define, establish and maintain an effective quality assurance system for manufacturing and service industries.

References

Boyd, E., Hultman, N., Roberts, J.T., Corbera, E., Cole, J., Bozmoski, A., Ebeling, J., Tippman, R., Mann, P., Brown, K. and Liverman, D.M. 2009, 'Reforming the CDM for sustainable development: lessons learned and policy futures', *Environmental Science & Policy*, vol. 12, no. 7, pp. 820–831.

Buen, J. 2010, 'Amendments to China's Renewable Energy Law: increased certainty for CDM developers?' *Analyst Update*, 11 January, Point Carbon.

Buen, J. and Castro, P. 2012, 'How Brazil and China have financed industry development and energy security initiatives that support mitigation objectives', in A. Michaelowa (ed.), *Carbon Markets or Climate Finance?* Routledge, Abingdon, pp. 53–91.

Burnham, P., Lutz, K.G., Grant, W. and Zig, L.H. 2008, *Research Methods in Politics*, 2nd edn, Palgrave Macmillan, Basingstoke.

Castro, P. 2012, Does the CDM discourage emission reduction targets in advanced developing countries?, *Climate Policy*, vol. 12, pp. 198–218.

Castro, P., Hayashi, D., Kristiansen, K.O., Michaelowa, A. and Stadelmann, M. 2011, 'Scoping study: linking RE promotion policies with international carbon trade', International Energy Agency – Renewable Energy Technology Deployment.

Darmstadter, J. 2001, 'The energy–CO_2 connection: a review of trends and challenges', in M.A. Toman (ed.), *Climate Change Economics and Policy*, Resources for the Future, Washington, DC, pp. 24–34.

Department of Climate Change, National Development and Reform Commission of China. 2015, 'Clean Development Mechanism in China'. http://cdm-en.ccchina.gov.cn/list.aspx?clmId=38.

Dutschke, M. and Michaelowa, A. 1998, 'Creation and sharing of credits through the Clean Development Mechanism under the Kyoto Protocol', HWWA Discussion Paper 62. Institut Für Wirtschaftsforschung, Hamburg.

Global Wind Energy Council. 2011, *Global Wind Report*. http://gwec.net/wp-content/uploads/2012/06/GWEC_annual_market_update_2010_-_2nd_edition_April_2011.pdf.

Gtowacki Law Firm. 2013, 'CERs and ERUs market as from 2013'. www.emissions-euets.com/cers-erus-market-as-from-2013.

Jiang, P. and Tovey, K. 2010, 'Overcoming barriers to implementation of carbon reduction strategies in large commercial buildings in China', *Building and Environment*, vol. 45, pp. 856–864.

Maraseni, T.N. and Gao X.Q. 2011, 'An analysis of Chinese perceptions on unilateral Clean Development Mechanism (uCDM) projects', *Environmental Science & Policy*, vol. 14, pp. 339–346.

Michaelowa, A. 2007, 'Unilateral CDM: can developing countries finance generation of greenhouse gas emission credits on their own?', *International Environmental Agreements*, vol. 7, pp. 17–34.

Michaelowa, A. 2012, 'Strengths and weaknesses of the CDM in comparison with new and emerging market mechanisms', Paper No. 2 for the CDM Policy Dialogue. www.

perspectives.cc/typo3home/groups/15/Publications/2012/2012_Strengths-and-weaknesses-of-the-CDM-in-comparison-with-new-and-emerging-market-mechanisms.pdf.

Michaelowa, A. and Buen, J. 2012, 'The Clean Development Mechanism gold rush', in A. Michaelowa (ed.), *Carbon Markets or Climate Finance?* Routledge, Abingdon, pp. 1–38.

Michaelowa, A. and Jotzo, F. 2005, 'Transaction costs, institutional rigidities and the size of the clean development mechanism', *Energy Policy*, vol. 33, pp. 511–523.

NDRC. 2012, *China's Policies and Actions for Addressing Climate Change (2012)*, NDRC, Beijing.

NDRC. 2013, *China's Policies and Actions for Addressing Climate Change (2013)*, NDRC, Beijing.

NDRC. 2015, 'Expected average annual CERs by scope', http://cdm-en.ccchina.gov.cn/NewItemTable10.aspx.

Pearson, P. 2007, 'Market failure: why the Clean Development Mechanism won't promote clean development', *Journal of Cleaner Production*, vol. 15, pp. 247–252.

Research Team of China Climate Change Country Study. 1999, *China Climate Change Country Study*, Tsinghua University Press, Beijing.

Schneider, L. 2007, 'Is the CDM fulfilling its environmental and sustainable development objectives? An evaluation of the CDM and options for improvement.' *Öko-Institut for Applied Ecology, Berlin*, vol. 248, pp. 1685–1703.

Schwartz, J. 2004, 'Environmental NGOs in China: roles and limits', *Pacific Affairs*, vol. 77, no. 1, pp. 28–49.

Wang, Q. and Chen, Y. 2010, 'Barriers and opportunities of using the clean development mechanism to advance renewable energy development in China', *Renewable and Sustainable Energy Reviews*, vol. 14, pp. 1989–1998.

Wolcott, H.F. 1999, *Ethnography: A Way of Seeing*, AltaMira Press, Walnut Creek, CA.

World Bank, Ministry of Science and Technology, P.R. China, Deutsche Gesellschaft für Technische Zusammenarbeit, German Technical Cooperation Unit (GTZ), Federal Ministry of Economic Cooperation and Development Swiss State Secretariat for Economic Affairs. 2004, *Clean Development Mechanism in China: Taking a Proactive and Sustainable Approach*, 2nd edn, World Bank, Washington, DC.

Xue, J.J. and Zhao, Z.X. 2012, *Annual Report on China's Low Carbon Economic Development*, Social Sciences Academic Press, Beijing.

Interviewees

Interviewee 1, Energy Research Institute, NDRC, interview conducted 16 October 2013.
Interviewee 2, Quanlian New Energy Commerce, interview conducted 14 October 2013.
Interviewee 3, the Centre for Rural Environmental and Social Research, Chinese Academy of Social Sciences (CASS), interview conducted 16 October 2013.

11 Changing economies for a more sustainable future

The influence of stakeholders and environmental reporting developments in transforming Chinese corporate practices

Hui Situ, Carol Tilt and Pi-Shen Seet

Introduction

Today, in the face of a range of global environmental problems such as climate change, there is widespread agreement that changes must be made to combat or alleviate the ongoing unsustainable pressures on the global environment (Deegan, 2009b). It is also generally accepted that business organizations should change the way they do business and change the traditional business goals and principles of pursuing maximum profit (Deegan, 2009b). With concern for the environment increasingly becoming a mainstream expectation among communities, there are increasing pressures on corporate entities to provide more information about how they are performing in terms of measures to protect the environment, and therefore, corporations are increasingly keen on disclosing voluntary environmental information to show their concern about the environment. So much so that, according to KPMG (2008a), environmental disclosure is now a common activity of corporations in developed countries. However, the evidence of environmental disclosure in emerging economies is much more limited and this chapter addresses this gap by presenting findings about CER in one such emerging economy – China.

In China, despite the seriousness of the impact of business operations on the environment (Zissis and Bajoria, 2008), corporate environmental reporting (CER) lags far behind other countries. There is currently no evidence of Chinese corporate entities disclosing social and environmental information prior to 2005 (KPMG, 2008a, 2008b). This situation is rapidly changing, with CER in China increasing significantly in recent years (KPMG, 2011; Situ and Tilt, 2012). Since 2005, in order to change the Chinese economy to one that has a more environmentally sustainable model of development, the government has put energy saving and being environmental friendly as a priority in the nation's development policy. To support this, 'Green Reporting' is one of the major programmes introduced (Wang, 2011). In particular, China's Measures for the Disclosure of

Environmental Information (MDEI), which was adopted by the Chinese Ministry of Environmental Protection (MEP) in 2007, has been seen as a new milestone of the Chinese government's environmental governance, with initiatives on transparency, disclosure and participation (Bina, 2010; van den Burg, 2008). The state-driven initiatives are evidence that the Chinese government is likely a major driver behind the increasing trend of Chinese CER. At a deeper level, we also note that, unlike other countries, especially more developed countries, the Chinese government influences corporate environmental reporting in China through its various roles, such as regulator (political power), shareholder (voting power) and creditor/customer/supplier (economic power). However, despite the rise in CER, the Chinese government has raised concerns that environmental problems are still damaging the country's economic development and may potentially threaten the nation's stability. This raises questions as to what the motivations are for Chinese corporations when they engage in environmental reporting and, in particular, what role does the government play in influencing those motivations.

Therefore, in this chapter we aim to understand Chinese governmental influence on Chinese CER based on the following two research questions:

Q1 Has the MDEI had an effect on CER in China?
Q2 Do state-owned enterprises (SOEs) disclose more CER than non-SOEs?

The remainder of the chapter is organized as follows. We begin by reviewing the Chinese government's Green Policy and the MDEI, as well as the research on CER with a focus on state capitalism theory. This is followed by an outline of the research method, the results and a discussion of the findings, including implications for future research. Overall, we find that while CER among major Chinese firms increased dramatically in 2008 in line with the introduction of the MDEI, SOEs performed much better than non-SOEs, both before and after the MDEI was introduced. We therefore argue that CER in China is more top-down and centrally driven by the state as compared to the experience of developed countries, and that legislation like the MDEI has had an impact on CER.

Chinese government's Green Policy and MDEI

Green Policy

Since 2005, the Chinese central government has been trying to shift China's economy to become more sustainable. A new political commitment of building a 'Harmonious Society' was introduced by China's Chairman Hu Jintao at a Provincial Officer Symposium held in 2005. It states that the environment is a key element of a 'Harmonious Society'. Without sufficient protection of the natural environment, sustainable development will not be realized; also, there may be accompanying environmental issues that will also result in serious social problems (Hu, 2005). This commitment was translated into targets of the 11th

Five-year Plan (2006–2010), which maps strategies for the country's development. These targets required, by 2010, the reduction of energy consumption per unit of gross domestic product (GDP) by 20 per cent, and reduced sulphur dioxide (SO_2) and chemical oxygen demand (COD) emissions by 10 per cent from 2005 levels (Chinese Central Government, 2006). Later, at the Sixth National Environmental Protection Meeting (April 2006), Premier Wen Jiabao also announced three new policies: (1) integrating environmental protection and economic decision-making on an equal footing; (2) further decoupling pollutant emissions from economic growth; and (3) applying a mix of instruments to resolve environmental problems (Bina, 2010). These policies reflect the Chinese central government's determination to transform the Chinese economy into one that embraces sustainable development. The commitment of building up a 'Harmonious Society' was re-stated at the 17th National Communist Party of China (CPC) Congress, and was further developed as a 'scientific view point of development'. Hu (2007) pointed out that China's economic growth should incorporate energy saving and environmental protection. He also defined sustainable development in China as an approach to synchronize economic development with population, resources and environmental needs, to harmonize humans and nature, to develop a circular economy and to build an energy-saving and environment-friendly country (Hu, 2007).

In order to translate the nation's drive to clean up the environment into policy risks for many listed polluters and for retail investors in those companies, the Chinese MEP has put into effect a 'green securities' plan aimed at making it harder for polluters to raise capital and encouraging listed companies to disclose more information about their environmental practices. Pan Yue, deputy head of the Chinese MEP, said greater disclosure would not only push companies to meet their environmental responsibilities, but also help to protect investor interests (China.com.cn, 2008). Consequently, the MEP released the MDEI (enacted in May 2008) in 2007. Details of the MDEI are discussed in the next section. This has been further strengthened by a series of guidelines (see Table 11.1).

Table 11.1 List of the guidelines

Name	Date of issue
Guidelines of state-owned enterprises performing social responsibilities	29 December 2007
Guidelines about enhancing supervision of listed companies' social responsibilities	25 February 2008
Guidelines about China's industrial enterprises and industrial associations' social responsibilities	2 April 2008
Guidelines on environmental information disclosure by companies listed on the Shanghai Stock Exchange	14 May 2008
Guidelines on preparation of corporate report on performance of social responsibilities	8 January 2009

MDEI

In 2007, the MDEI was issued by the Chinese MEP. This symbolized the Chinese government's acceptance of environmental disclosure as a new environmental governance mechanism. The MDEI has two environmental disclosing requirements; namely, government environmental disclosure and corporate environmental disclosure. A more detailed analysis of the provisions of the MDEI shows that the mandatory disclosure requirements only apply to government environmental disclosure (see Article 11). For corporations, disclosure is not mandatory and enterprises are 'encouraged' to 'voluntarily disclose' the following environmental information (see Article 19):

1   their environmental protection guidelines, annual environmental protection objectives and achievements;
2   their total annual resource consumption;
3   information on their environmental protection investment and environmental technology development;
4   type, volume and content of pollutants discharged by them and where the pollutants are discharged into;
5   information on the construction and operation of their environmental protection facilities;
6   information on the handling and disposal of waste generated from their production, information on recycling and comprehensive use of waste products;
7   voluntary agreements entered into with environmental protection departments for environment improvement behaviour;
8   information on their performance of social responsibilities; and
9   other environmental information voluntarily disclosed by them.

However, according to Article 20, there are instances whereby environmental disclosure is needed. For example, if an enterprise is included on the list of enterprises with severe pollution and whose emission of pollutants is greater than the national or local emission standard or whose total emission of pollutants is greater than the quota of total controlled emissions determined by the local people's government, it 'shall' disclose to the public the following information:

1   their name, address and legal representative;
2   the names of major pollutants, method, content and total volume of emission, information on emissions that have surpassed the standards or total emissions that have surpassed the prescribed limits;
3   information on the construction and operation of their environmental protection facilities; and
4   emergency plans for sudden environmental pollution accidents.

It can be seen from these actions that the Chinese central government is aware of the importance of public supervision, and has made the decision to govern environmental protection in a more democratic way. China is now 'on the road towards environmental information governance' (van den Burg, 2008).

In spite of these provisions, it needs to be emphasized that the MDEI does not require corporations to disclose environmental information mandatorily. CER is still voluntary in China. However, in a highly centralized country, the Chinese government has significant influence on CER practices even without any mandatory requirements (Situ and Tilt, 2012). Therefore, it is expected that there have been significantly more CERs after the MDEI was enacted.

Literature review

'Around the world, corporate responsibility reporting has become a fundamental imperative for businesses' (KPMG, 2011: 6), with 95 per cent of the top 250 global firms (G250) now reporting their corporate social and environmental activities (KPMG, 2011). Interestingly, this is despite studies that have found that CER in developed countries is predominantly voluntary (Deegan, 2002; Dobbs and Van Standen, 2011), which is different from traditional financial accounting, which is highly regulated.

Previous studies done on developed countries show that the motivations of disclosing CER are varied (Deegan, 2002). Some authors believe that accountability is the reason why companies report voluntary environmental information (Hasnas, 1998), while others argue that there might be some economic advantages in pushing companies towards engaging in CER (Friedman, 1962).

Some find evidence that, in order to reduce the threat of further development of regulations, companies sign up to particular codes of conduct and disclose voluntary environmental information (Deegan and Blomquist, 2001). Others argue that companies put effort into winning environmental, social and sustainable reporting awards, which might reflect positively on the reputation of the company (Deegan and Carroll, 1993). Research also suggests that CER may only be a device that companies use to manage their particular stakeholder groups (Deegan, 2008). For example, as environmental management becomes part of lending institutions' risk management policy, companies are willing to disclose environmental performance information to meet lending institutions' borrowing requirements. Also, as ethical investments increase in the capital market, companies may provide environmental information to attract ethical investment funds.

Other studies show that companies disclose voluntary environmental information to legitimize their environmental activities or to deflect attention away from environmental concerns, rather than take on real accountability. For example, Deegan *et al.* (2000) examined the reaction of Australian companies to five major social and environmental incidents. They found that, following a major incident related to a social and environmental event, sample firms operating in the affected industries provided more environmental information in their annual reports than they did prior to the incident. Recent research by Dobbs and Van

Staden (2011) on 122 New Zealand listed companies confirms this finding. In the research, survey questionnaires were sent to the selected companies, and the results indicate that firms rate 'to satisfy community concerns with operations' as the most important factor in their decision to report.

From the above discussion, we can see that, in developed countries which have a more liberal and developed capital market and where environmental awareness is relatively high, the government's intervention on CER is relatively low. The forces on companies to voluntary disclose environmental information are pluralistic. Most obviously, CER in developed countries has a societal focus.

However, a number of scholars claim that the unique characteristics of each country may result in differences in the corporate environmental disclosure activities seen in different countries (Gao, 2011; Mohammad *et al.*, 2009). In particular, developing countries are at a different stage of economic development from developed countries. For example, China is the largest developing country in the world, and it has a totally different institutional context (e.g. different cultural, political and economic systems), which is driven largely by state capitalism, as compared to places which have more liberal and developed capital markets. It is therefore expected that there will be more governmental influence on Chinese CER.

There have been few CER studies in China since the early 1990s (Song and Li, 1992; Xiao and Mi, 2004; Zhang, 1993). In recent years, along with the increase of CER in China, the study of Chinese CER has attracted a growing number of Chinese scholars.

Some of the previous studies (Guo, 2005; Situ and Tilt, 2012) show that, compared to developed countries, there is more governmental influence on Chinese CER. For example, Situ and Tilt (2012) found that whether or not a firm is state-owned is a major determinant of Chinese CER – being a state-owned company increases the amount of environmental disclosure significantly. However, their study on the top 20 Chinese companies shows only very preliminary evidence. The aim of this study, therefore, is to further explore whether the government significantly influences Chinese CER.

Theoretical framework

Previous studies on developed countries (mainly under free-market capitalism) have often used legitimacy theory, stakeholder theory and institutional theory, which are derived from bourgeois political economy theory, to explain CER. Bourgeois political economy theory assumes that the world is pluralistic (Deegan, 2009a). Meanwhile, the core assumption of free-market capitalism is that the private sector, not the state, must be the primary engine of economic expansion if growth is to be strong and sustainable (Ian, 2010). Therefore, bourgeois political economy theory is appropriate in explaining CER under free-market capitalism. However, to the extent that the state is bureaucratic and uses the market to achieve its political goals, bourgeois political economy theory is limited, as the state is likely the most important stakeholder the company perceives as being legitimate. Therefore, this study borrows from an economic theory, namely state capitalism, to explain how the Chinese government uses a combination of its political power and capitalist power to affect CER in China. The term state capitalism is used in a non-pejorative sense, in that it is not meant as a criticism but rather as a term to describe the nature of political influence in China. This influence can be in a positive, negative or neutral sense.

According to Ian (2010: 250), state capitalism is 'a form of bureaucratically engineered capitalism particular to each government that practices it. It's a system in which the state dominates markets primarily for political gain'. State capitalism tries to meld the power of the state with the power of capitalism. It depends on government to pick winners and promote economic growth. It also uses capitalist tools such as listing state-owned companies on the stock market and embracing globalization (*The Economist*, 2012). Instead of eliminating markets, governments try to harness them for their own purposes. Although a state capitalist economy is different from a command economy where the government directly exerts day-to-day control on the economy, the government still has considerable direct influence over the economy and companies' strategies (Ian, 2010).

It is argued that a number of governments, particularly in the emerging world, are learning to use the market to promote political ends, and that China is one of the world's most influential practitioners of state capitalism (Ian, 2010). As the special report of *The Economist* (2012: 2) notes:

> The Chinese state is the biggest shareholder in the country's 150 biggest companies and guides and goads thousands more. It shapes the overall market by managing its currency, directing money to favoured industries and working closely with Chinese companies abroad.

The special report of *The Economist* further argues that the Chinese Communist Party exercises a degree of control over the economy. It states that:

> The party has cells in most big companies – in the private as well as the state-owned sector – complete with their own offices and files on employees. It controls the appointment of captains of industry and, in the SOEs, even corporate dogsbodies. It holds meetings that shadow formal board meetings and often trump their decisions, particularly on staff appointments. It often gets involved in business planning and works with management to control workers' pay.... There are currently 17 prominent Chinese political leaders who have held senior positions in large SOEs. Conversely, 27 prominent business leaders are serving on the party's Central Committee.

> (*The Economist*, 2012: 6)

As the government has cells in companies, it can influence the companies' decision-making, and therefore is able to shape companies without regulation.

More recently, Ten Brink provides an extended concept of state capitalism that better applies to China. He argues 'the Chinese political economy can be understood as a variegated form of state-permeated capitalism that is at the same time deeply integrated into world economic processes' (Ten Brink, 2013: 18).

In recent years, significant efforts have been made for economic liberalization in China – for example, strengthening the regulatory powers of the central state, local–central fiscal reforms and recouping dividend income from the largest state concerns for the Ministry of Finance (World Bank and Development Research Center of the State Council, 2012). However, economic development policies are continuously shaped by central state and Party bodies, with the Five-Year Plan which maps the medium-term economic development of the country being a particular example. Therefore, McNally *et al.* (2013) argue that, fundamentally, the leadership seeks to continuously restructure and improve central state control over economic decision-making.

In this study we argue that, even though China's economy is now moving towards being more market oriented, decision-making in corporations is still largely driven by the Chinese government. As a part of corporate governance strategy, CER is therefore affected by the Chinese government.

This is consistent with the view of state capitalism that, in a state capitalist economy, the government leads the market, and tries to use capitalist tools to achieve their political aims. China is one of the largest state capitalist countries in the world. Therefore, in this study state capitalism will be drawn upon to examine the role of the state in China, and its influence on CER.

Research method

Sampling

This chapter focuses on firms listed on the Shanghai Stock Exchange, as all listed firms' reports are publicly accessible. Previous studies (Situ and Tilt, 2012) found that size is one of the determinants of CER in China. So to mitigate the size effect, this chapter uses the SSE 180 as the sampling frame, as 'it selects constituents with best representation through scientific and objective method. It is a benchmark index reflecting [the] Shanghai market and serving as a performance benchmark for investment and a basis for financial innovation' and 'it selects top ranking stocks within each industry based on number of constituents allocated' (China Securities Index Co., 2012b).

This study used longitudinal data to test the first research question, i.e. the Chinese government's influences on Chinese CER. The term longitudinal data in this study refers to the same companies for the period 2007–2009. In particular, this will help us understand if the MDEI has had any effect on CER among Chinese listed firms.

For research question 2, in order to examine whether SOEs carry out better CER than non-SOEs, the SSE 180 companies were divided into two groups: SOE and non-SOE. In this study, SOE refers to central SOEs only. According to the CSI (Central SOEs Index), a central SOE is a company that is realistically controlled by the Stated-owned Assets Supervision and Administration Commission of State Council (SASAC) and the Ministry of Finance (China Securities Index Co., 2012a). All SSE 180 companies that are also in the list of CSI were grouped into SOEs, and the rest composed the group of non-SOEs. A total of 50 companies were randomly selected from SSE 180 by using stratified proportional random sampling.

Content analysis

Content analysis is defined as 'an approach to the analysis of documents and texts that seeks to quantify content in terms of predetermined categories and in a systematic and replicable manner' (Bryman and Bell, 2007: 304). Royse (2008: 256) summarizes the advantages of content analysis as follows:

- It is unobtrusive. The most important advantage for content analysis is that it can be virtually unobtrusive (Weber, 1985). Content analysis can be used reactively and non-reactively (Berg, 2004).
- It is generally inexpensive to conduct. Generally, the materials necessary for conducting content analysis are easily and inexpensively accessible (Berg, 2004).
- It allows the investigator to mine existing agency documents and databases.
- It can deal with large amounts of data.

As we were studying publicly listed SOEs, which were engaged in reporting of various kinds, content analysis was used in this study.

Both annual reports and stand-alone social responsibility reports of the observed companies are the data source for conducting content analysis, since Situ and Tilt (2012) found that more Chinese companies have started to use stand-alone social responsibility reports as the medium to report environmental information. Moreover, to avoid any ambiguities in translation, only Chinese reports were read.

The basic categories used in this study were obtained from the Global Reporting Initiative guideline 3.1 (G3.1) and the MDEI, but the content that has been disclosed by companies listed on the Shanghai Stock Exchange was also considered. The definitions of each theme are presented in Appendix A.

Coding rules were developed primarily based on prior studies, such as Situ and Tilt (2012) and Hossain *et al.* (2006). The final coding rules are presented in Appendix B.

Measurement of variables

The unit of analysis in this study is words. Krippendorff (1980) argues that recording units and context units should be separated. Recording units refer to the units that are to be counted in specific categories, while context units refer to those that are of concern to the process of describing the recording units. Therefore, in this study, sentences are used as context units to capture the environmental disclosure information, and number of words is chosen as the recording units to count the amount of environmental disclosures in given categories.

Previous studies on CER have used a score or index to measure disclosure; however, Nurhayati *et al.* (2006) state that 'volume' is more appropriate in developing countries as the extent of disclosure is low. Therefore, the number of words related to the environment found in the annual report and stand-alone social responsibility report provides the dependent variable in this study.

Results and discussion

Trends over time

The results show that the number of companies that disclose environmental information and the number of companies that have a stand-alone social and environmental report both increased dramatically in 2008 (Figure 11.1).

Table 11.2 shows that the number of companies that disclose environmental information increased from 28 (56 per cent) in 2007 to 46 (92 per cent) in 2008. In 2007, only half of the investigated companies have CER; however, there are only four companies that have no CER at all in 2008. In 2009, compared to 2008, there is just one more company that has CER, so the major increase occurred in 2008, after the introduction of the MDEI.

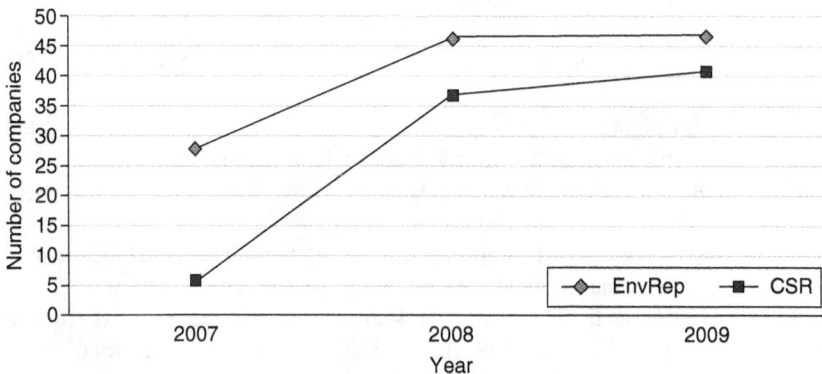

Figure 11.1 Trends of occurrence.

Notes
1 EnvRep: the number of companies that disclose environmental information.
2 CSR: the number of companies that have a stand-alone social and environmental report.

Table 11.2 The occurrence of CER

Year			Frequency	Percentage	Cumulative percentage
2007	Valid	N	22	44.0	44.0
		Y	28	56.0	100.0
		Total	50	100.0	
2008	Valid	N	4	8.0	8.0
		Y	46	92.0	100.0
		Total	50	100.0	
2009	Valid	N	3	6.0	6.0
		Y	47	94.0	100.0
		Total	50	100.0	

Table 11.3 The occurrence of stand-alone CSR reports

Year			Frequency	Percentage	Cumulative percentage
2007	Valid	N	44	88.0	88.0
		Y	6	12.0	100.0
		Total	50	100.0	
2008	Valid	N	13	26.0	26.0
		Y	37	74.0	100.0
		Total	50	100.0	
2009	Valid	N	9	18.0	18.0
		Y	41	82.0	100.0
		Total	50	100.0	

Table 11.3 shows a more dramatic change between 2007 and 2008. While there are six companies that have stand-alone CSR reports in 2007, there are 37 companies in 2008, an increase of 517 per cent. However, from 2008 to 2009, the increase rate is only 11 per cent.

As shown in Figure 11.2, we can also see that in 2008 there was a significant increase in the volume of disclosing words in total (CSR reports plus annual reports) and in the volume of disclosing words in CSR reports only. However, the volume of disclosing words in annual reports decreased slightly from 2007 to 2008, which suggests that more Chinese listed companies are using their CSR report as the medium to communicate environmental information to their stakeholders.

The descriptive analysis in Table 11.4 shows that the volume of disclosing words increased suddenly in 2008. Before 2008, the mean value of total words on environmental information in both CSR reports plus annual reports is 467.6, and increased to 1,579.74 in 2008 and 2,014.4 in 2009. We can also see that the major contribution of the disclosing words is from the CSR reports, as disclosing words in CSR reports increased from 291.12 in 2007 to 1,434.1 and 1,853.22 in 2008 and 2009, respectively.

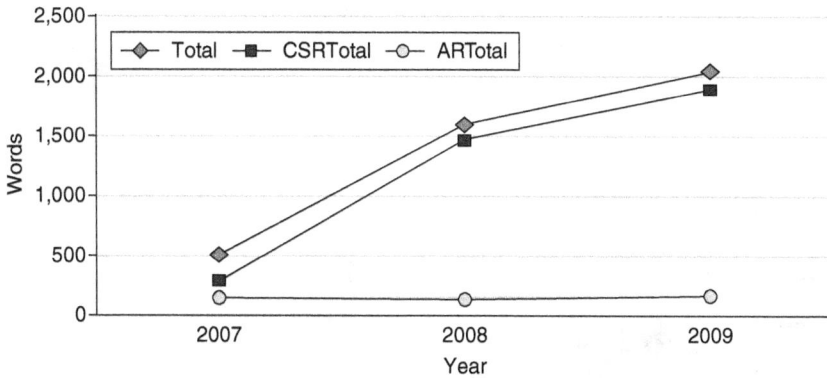

Figure 11.2 Trends of volume.

Notes
1 Total: the volume of disclosing words in CSR reports and annual reports.
2 CSRTotal: the volume of disclosing words in CSR reports only.
3 ARTotal: the volume of disclosing words in annual reports only.

Table 11.4 The volume of environmental disclosing words

Year		N	Minimum	Maximum	Sum	Mean	Std. Deviation
2007	Total	50	0.00	5,396.00	23,380.00	467.60	1,153.97
	CSRTotal	50	0.00	4,552.00	14,556.00	291.12	974.36
	ARTotal	50	0.00	1,313.00	8,824.00	176.48	264.83
2008	Total	50	0.00	7,737.00	78,987.00	1,579.74	1,797.81
	CSRTotal	50	0.00	7,338.00	71,705.00	1,434.10	1,737.54
	ARTotal	50	0.00	7,48.00	7,282.00	145.64	177.53
2009	Total	50	0.00	10,356.00	100,720.00	2,014.40	1,924.59
	CSRTotal	50	0.00	9,682.00	92,661.00	1,853.22	1,830.51
	ARTotal	50	0.00	685.00	8,059.00	161.18	189.22

Notes
1 Total: the volume of disclosing words in CSR reports and annual reports.
2 CSRTotal: the volume of disclosing words in CSR reports only.
3 ARTotal: the volume of disclosing words in annual reports only.

The above results show that both the number of disclosing companies and the volume of disclosing words is increasing. The year 2008 is a benchmark as there is a significant rise in CER. This suggests that the MDEI did significantly influence CER in China.

Descriptive analysis by theme

The volume of words and the number of companies that disclose environmental information with specific themes is also examined, and the result is represented in Figure 11.3 and Table 11.5.

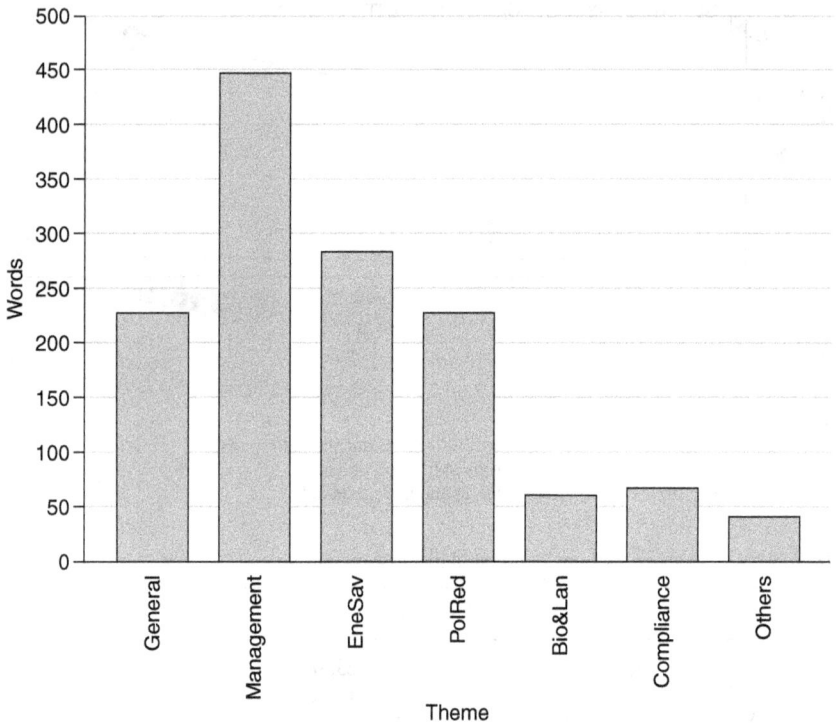

Figure 11.3 Disclosing words by themes.

Not surprisingly, the volume of disclosing words on their 'environmental management approach' ranks at the top, with a mean value of 447.81 (33 per cent). According to the MDEI, Article 19, it encourages companies to voluntarily disclose 'information on their environmental protection investment and environmental technology development' and 'information on the construction and operation of their environmental protection facilities'. Moreover, when reading the reports, it is noted that banks disclose a large amount of information on how they set up criteria for 'Green Credit' and implement it to mitigate the environmental impact of their services and match the government's 'Green Policy'; thus, this contributes most to the theme of 'environmental management approach'.

The mean value of disclosing words for the 'General Statement' theme is 228.54, which is also high (ranked third). This is in line with previous studies (Gao, 2011; Situ and Tilt, 2012) which have claimed that the practice of CER in China is at an emerging stage, whereby companies disclose information about their commitments, goals and policies relevant to the environmental aspects and the environmental risks and opportunities they face rather than disclose specific information about their environmental performance.

Table 11.5 Descriptive statistics (n=150)

Theme	Frequency		Volume of disclosing words					
	N	%	Minimum	Maximum	Sum	Mean	%	Std. Deviation
Environmental management	86	57	0.00	3,775.00	67,171.00	447.80	33	735.93
General statement	105	70	0.00	1,686.00	34,281.00	228.54	17	300.04
Energy saving	87	58	0.00	2,958.00	42,495.00	283.30	21	461.67
Pollution reduction	60	40	0.00	3,975.00	33,935	226.23	17	514.14
Compliance	65	43	0.00	502.00	10,140.00	67.60	5	106.62
Bio-diversity and land rehabilitation	27	18	0.00	1,201.00	8,903.00	59.35	4	172.94
Others	44	29	0.00	963.00	6,162.00	41.08	3	111.95

188   *Hui Situ* et al.

'Resources and energy saving' (ranked second) and 'pollution and emission reduction' (ranked fourth) are the other significant themes that appear in the reports. The mean value of the themes are 283.3 and 226.23, respectively, and combined they contribute 38 per cent of the words in total. In addition, 58 per cent and 40 per cent of the sample companies disclose some information on 'resources and energy saving' and 'pollution and emission reduction', respectively. This result reflects the voluntary requirement of the MDEI, which encourages companies to voluntarily disclose 'their total annual resource consumption', 'type, volume and content of pollutants discharged by them and where the pollutants are discharged into', 'information on the handling and disposal of waste generated from their production' and 'information on recycling and comprehensive use of waste products'.

Although the mean value of disclosing words of 'compliance' is low (ranked fifth), only 67.6, the number of companies that mention this theme in their reports is over 40 per cent. Most of the companies use one sentence to state that they comply with the nation's policy, and fulfil the energy-saving quota that has been allocated to them.

The volume of disclosing words by the theme 'biodiversity and land rehabilitation' is very low (ranked sixth). It contributes only 4 per cent to the total words, and only 27 companies disclosed in this theme, which accounts for 17 per cent of the sample companies. Unsurprisingly, most of the companies ignored this theme as it is not the theme explicitly encouraged by the MDEI.

In general, the disclosure complies with the Chinese government's emphasis – energy saving and pollutant emission reduction are the major themes that are disclosed by Chinese companies, while biodiversity and land rehabilitation have been neglected.

Comparative analysis

Before conducting comparative analysis, the normality of the data was tested by using SPSS. Table 11.6 presents the results from two well-known tests of normality, namely the Kolmogorov–Smirnov and the Shapiro–Wilk tests. The results show that both significance levels of the Kolmogorov–Smirnov and Shapiro–Wilk tests are lower than the 0.01 level, which indicates that the data are not normally distributed. Therefore, to test whether a significant difference

Table 11.6 Tests of normality

| | Kolmogorov–Smirnov[a] | | | Shapiro–Wilk | | |
	Statistic	df	Sig.	Statistic	df	Sig.
Total	0.223	150	0.000	0.757	150	0.000

Note
a Lilliefors significance correction.

Table 11.7 Mann–Whitney U-tests

Null hypothesis	Test	Sig.	Decision
Hypothesis test summary			
1 The distribution of total is the same across categories of SOE	Independent samples Mann–Whitney U-test	0.019	Reject the null hypothesis

Note
Asymptotic significances are displayed. The significance level is 0.05.

appears in the volume of total disclosing words between SOE and non-SOE, non-parametric Mann–Whitney U-tests were applied to the data (Table 11.7).

The results of the Mann–Whitney U-tests suggests that the null hypothesis should be rejected, which is to say that the distribution of total disclosing words is different between SOE and non-SOE. This indicates that state ownership has significant impact on the volume of CER of sampled companies.

Table 11.8 confirms the results of the Mann–Whitney U-tests. The mean value of total disclosing words by SOE is 1,722.36; compared to those by non-SOE it is 69.89 per cent more.

This study examined annual reports and CSR reports of 50 companies that are listed on the SSE from 2007 to 2009. The results show that the trend of CER in China is increasing, both in terms of the number of disclosing companies and the volume of disclosing words. There is evidence of a significant increase in occurrence in 2008, when the MDEI was enacted. Energy saving and pollutant emission reduction, which are the main themes of Chinese government's Green Policy, appear to be the main theme that is disclosed by the examined companies. The comparative analysis shows that SOEs perform better CER than non-SOEs, as the results of Mann–Whitney U-tests indicate that the distribution of total disclosing words by SOE is significantly different from those by non-SOE. Finally, the descriptive analysis by state-ownership shows SOEs disclose much more environmental information than non-SOEs. The findings of the study provide evidence that the Chinese government influences Chinese CER considerably.

Implications

In contrast to free-market capitalism, where it is believed that the 'invisible hand' is sufficient to regulate the market, the power of government under state capitalism on the economy is much stronger. However, state capitalism suggests

Table 11.8 Total disclosing words by state ownership

SOE	N		Minimum	Maximum	Sum	Mean	Std. Deviation
N	Total	78	0.00	5,482.00	79,077.00	1,013.80	1,306.52
Y	Total	72	0.00	10,356.00	124,010.00	1,722.36	2,118.09

that instead of using heavy regulation, the government tries to meld its political power with capitalist power. With regards to Chinese CER, the results of this study show that a dramatic increase took place in 2008, the year the MDEI was enacted. The MDEI encourages companies to disclose a list of environment-related information and, although it is not a mandatory requirement, companies are willing to follow. As discussed previously, state capitalism depends on the government to pick the winner, and the Chinese communist party has cells in most big companies – in the private as well as the state-owned sector. This enables them to be involved in business planning and to influence the board's decisions. As the Green Policy becomes one of the important factors of the government officers' promotion system, these officers will influence the companies' decisions in disclosing environmental information, in order to obtain a promotion. Therefore, it can be seen that the Chinese government can influence CER without needing to mandate or regulate firm practices.

Our results show that resource and energy saving and pollutant emission reduction are the themes which have been disclosed most by Chinese listed companies. This finding also indicates that the Chinese government's impact on Chinese CER is significant. Within the theory of state capitalism, although the government does not direct supplies of scarce resources and attach values to goods and services, it has considerable direct influence over companies. For example, the Chinese government can shape the overall market by managing its currency, directing money to favoured industries and working closely with Chinese companies abroad. With the Chinese government being a major customer, it has sufficient buying power to be essential to Chinese companies' survival. In order to gain support and approval from the Chinese government, Chinese companies disclose environmental information that is desired by the Chinese government.

State capitalism also argues that state ownership can represent a special form of control in the exercise of economic and political power under capitalism. The Mann–Whitney U-tests suggest the distribution of total disclosing words is significantly different between SOE and non-SOE companies, and the comparative analysis suggests that SOEs disclose more environmental information than non-SOEs. The Chinese government is the actual controller of SOEs and has stronger influence on SOEs' decision-making than that on non-SOEs. As green reporting is one of the nation's green policies, SOEs would perform better in CER than non-SOEs. Again, our results indicate that, in a state capitalist country, even without mandatory regulation, government can influence listed companies' CER performance.

Conclusion

As discussed above, we conclude that in a state capitalist economy where public environmental awareness is low, the government's emphasis on environmental issues can encourage companies to pay more attention to their environmental activities which are at an emergent stage. However, it is also noted that, even though companies' environmental disclosure keeps increasing, they mainly disclose information that is desired by the Chinese government. Therefore, it also raises the possibility that the excessive power of the state on CER may diminish the reliability of CER, as companies are ultimately responsible to the government and not to a variety of stakeholders. As such, the government's effort to change the economy to include a more environmentally sustainable approach may be hard to achieve.

There are some limitations in this study. As discussed above, a series of guidelines and regulations came out around 2008, and the increase of Chinese CER is possibly owing to the combination of such guidelines and regulations. However, given the lack of research in this area and the different context of the Chinese economy, it has still been meaningful to study the effect of the MDEI on Chinese CER, as the MDEI is the first regulation released by the Chinese government that mentions environmental reporting, and it has been viewed as a milestone of the Chinese government's environmental governance. Also, we only conducted a descriptive analysis and examined the difference between SOEs and non-SOEs. However, there are other variables, such as industry, size and whether the firms are listed in other exchanges, that may influence the results. To address these limitations, further research is needed by conducting more sophisticated panel data analysis and using a larger sample (including more sample companies and their reports over a longer period). Moreover, research methods other than content analysis could be used to further confirm or refute the results of this study.

The major contribution of this study is the evidence that the development of CER in a state capitalist country, such as China, does not follow the same course of events as in the West. CER in China is largely driven by the government. In a state capitalist economy, the state's political power on CER is far stronger than it is in a country under liberal capitalism.

Appendix A: definition of themes

General statement

- Information about overall performance
- An overview of the company's philosophy and the background to all of their activities that affect the environment.
- Organization-wide goals regarding performance relevant to the environment aspects.
- Brief, organization-wide policy (or policies) that define the organization's overall commitment related to the environment.
- Any information on the company's commitments on future environmental undertakings or improvements.
- Major organizational environmental risks and opportunities.

Environmental management approach

- Existence of department and/or committee for pollution control and/or management positions for environment management.
- Any statement about formal management systems regarding environmental risk and performance.
- Any strategies and procedures for implementing policies or achieving goals.
- Training and/or education in relation to raising environmental awareness.
- Initiatives to mitigate environmental impacts of products and services, and extent of impact mitigation.
- Existence of mechanism in case of environmental accidents.
- Green purchase.
- Environmental evaluation of new projects.
- Research, development and application of environmental technology and/or equipment.
- Total investment in environmental protection.

Resources and energy saving

- Direct/indirect energy consumption.
- Energy saved due to conservation and efficiency improvement.
- Any information about renewable energy used.
- Reuse rate of energy resources.
- Initiatives to reduce indirect energy consumption and reductions achieved.
- Water consumption and water conserved.
- Percentage and total volume of water recycled and reused.
- Materials used by weight or volume.
- Percentage of materials used that are recycled input materials.

Pollution and emission reduction

- Total direct/indirect emission of greenhouse gases.
- Initiatives to reduce greenhouse gas emissions and reductions achieved.
- Other air emissions.
- Total water discharge by quality and destination.
- Total weight of waste by type and disposal method.
- Total number and volume of significant spills.
- Control of production noise.
- Initiatives and technology used to reduce waste gas emissions, waste water emissions and waste residue emissions.

Biodiversity, land conservation and land rehabilitation

- Any activities and improvements done for the purpose of sustaining biodiversity.

- Description of significant impacts of activities, products, and services on biodiversity.
- Habitats protected or restored.
- Prevention or repair of damage to the land resulting from processing natural resources.
- Any information on land care (such as forest reserves and recovery, preventing desertification).

Compliance

- Fines and sanctions for non-compliance with environmental laws and regulations.
- Any information on stewardships, benchmarking and compliance of various environmental acts, regulations, policies or guidelines.
- Any information about memberships or relationships with 'green' groups including government bodies, NGOs and others.
- Any voluntary agreement signed for the purpose of environmental protection.
- Is there any environmental accidents for the year?
- Any information about environmental assessment.

Others

- Environmental award.
- Environmental donation.
- Impacts on third parties.

Appendix B: coding rules

- Headings are not counted.
- Graphs, charts, tables and pictures are excluded.
- Financial statements and notes below financial statements are not counted.
- Repeated disclosures are counted each time they appear.
- The entire sentence is included in the word count if the sentence is relevant to environmental disclosure.
- Only the statements that specifically describe a company's environmental activities will be recorded into the category 'environment protection'. General information such as a company's commitment to save energy and reduce emissions is recorded into the category 'general statements'.
- Any information that refers to increasing loans to green industries and decreasing loans to non-green industries is counted as 'environmental management approach'.

References

Berg, B.L. (2004), *Qualitative Research Methods for the Social Sciences*, 5th edition, Toronto, Pearson.

Bina, O. (2010), 'Environmental governance in China: weakness and potential from an environmental policy integration perspective', *China Review*, Vol. 10, No. 1, pp. 207.

Bryman, A. and Bell, E. (2007), 'Content analysis'. In *Business Research Methods*, New York, Oxford University Press.

China Securities Index Co. (2012a), 'CSI Central State-Owned Enterprises Composite Index and CSI Central State-Owned Enterprises 100 Index'. www.csindex.com.cn/sse-portal_en/csiportal/xzzx/file/CSI Central State-owned Enterprises 100 Index Handbook.pdf.

China Securities Index Co. (2012b), 'SSE180 and SSE50 index methodology'. www.sse.com.cn/sseportal/cs/zhs/xxfw/flgz/temp/Index_Methodology_EN_000010n16.pdf.

China.com.cn (2008), 'Chinese Ministry of Environmental Protection resorted to the 'green securities' sword: 13 categories of industries by strict control (环保总局祭出' 绿色证券'利剑 13类行业受严管)'. www.china.com.cn/news/txt/2008-02/26/content_10767368.htm.

Chinese Central Government (2006), 'The 11th Five-Year Plans of People's Republic of China (中华人民共和国国民经济和社会发展第十一个五年规划纲要)'. http://news.xinhuanet.com/misc/2006-03/16/content_4309517_1.htm.

Deegan, C. (2002), 'Introduction: the legitimizing effect of social and environmental disclosures – a theoretical foundation', *Accounting, Auditing and Accountability Journal*, Vol. 15, No. 3, pp. 282–311.

Deegan, C. (2008), 'Towards the implementation of environmental costing to inform capital investment decisions: the case of Australian electricity distributors and their choice of power poles', *Australian Accounting Review*, Vol. 18, No. 44, pp. 2–15.

Deegan, C. (2009a), 'Extended systems of accounting: the incorporation of social and environmental factors within external reporting'. In *Financial Accounting Theory*, Sydney, McGraw-Hill.

Deegan, C. (2009b), 'Unregulated corporate reporting decisions: systems-oriented theories'. In *Financial Accounting Theory*, Sydney, McGraw-Hill.

Deegan, C. and Blomquist, C. (2001), 'Stakeholder influence on corporate reporting: an exploration of the interaction between the World Wide Fund for Nature and the Australian minerals industry', *Third Asian Pacific Interdisciplinary Research in Accounting Conference Proceedings*.

Deegan, C. and Carroll, G. (1993), 'An analysis of incentives for Australian firms to apply for reporting excellence awards', *Accounting and Business Research*, Vol. 23, No. 2, pp. 219–227.

Deegan, C., Rankin, M. and Voght, P. (2000), 'Firms' disclosure reactions to major social incidents: Australia evidence', *Accounting Forum*, Vol. 24, No. 1, pp. 101–130.

Dobbs, S. and Van Standen, C. (2011), 'Motivations for corporate social and environmental reporting: New Zealand evidence', *10th Australasian Conference on Social and Environmental Accounting Research*.

The Economist (2012), 'State capitalism', January, pp. 1–14.

Friedman, M. (1962), *Capitalism and Freedom*, Chicago, University of Chicago Press.

Gao, Y. (2011), 'CSR in an emerging country: a content analysis of CSR reports of listed companies', *Baltic Journal of Management*, Vol. 6, No. 2, pp. 263–291.

Guo, P. (2005), 'Corporate environmental reporting and disclosure in China', www.csr-asia.com/upload/environmentalreporting.pdf.

Hasnas, J. (1998), 'The normative theories of business ethics', *Business Ethics Quarterly*, Vol. 8, No. 1, pp. 19–42.

Hossain, M., Islam, K. and Andrew, J. (2006), 'Corporate social and environmental disclosure in developing countries: evidence from Bangladesh', *Asian Pacific Conference on International Accounting Issues*.

Hu, J. (2005), 'Building up a socialism harmonious society', *Provincial Officer Symposium*.

Hu, J. (2007), 'Hold high the great banner of socialism with Chinese characteristics in order to win new victories in building a moderately prosperous society in the struggle', *17th CPC Congress*.

Ian, B. (2010), 'The end of the free market: who wins the war between states and corporations', *European View*, Vol. 9, No. 2, pp. 249–252.

KPMG (2008a), *KPMG International Survey of Corporate Responsibility Reporting 2008*, Amstelveen: KPMG.

KPMG (2008b), *Sustainable Reporting: A Guide in China*, Amstelveen: KPMG.

KPMG (2011), *KPMG International Survey of Corporate Responsibility Reporting 2011*, Amstelveen: KPMG.

Krippendorff, K. (1980), *Content Analysis: An Introduction to Its Methodology*, London, Sage.

McNally, C.A., Lüthje, B., and Ten Brink, T. (2013), 'Rebalancing China's emergent capitalism: state power, economic liberalization and social upgrading', *Journal of Current Chinese Affairs*, Vol. 32, No. 4, pp. 3–16.

Mohammad, A., Shaila, A. and Md. Shahidul, I. (2009), 'Corporate social responsibility reporting: illustrations from a less-developed country', *Journal of the Asia-Pacific Centre for Environmental Accountability*, Vol. 15, No. 2, pp. 2–12.

Nurhayati, R., Brown, A. and Tower, G. (2006), 'Understanding the level of natural environment disclosures by Indonesian listed companies', *Journal of the Asia Pacific Centre for Environmental Accountability*, Vol. 12, No. 8, pp. 4–11.

Royse, D. (2008), *Research Methods in Social Work*, 5th edition. Belmont, CA: Thomson Higher Education.

Situ, H. and Tilt, C.A. (2012), 'Chinese government as a determinant of corporate environmental reporting: a study of large Chinese listed companies', *Journal Asia-Pacific Centre for Environmental Accountability*, Vol. 18, No. 4, pp. 251–286.

Song, X. and Li, J. (1992), *Accounting for Social Responsibility*, Beijing, China Financial Economics Publisher.

Ten Brink, T. (2013), 'Paradoxes of prosperity in China's new capitalism', *Journal of Current Chinese Affairs*, Vol. 42, No. 4, pp. 17–44.

van den Burg, S. (2008), 'Environmental information disclosure in China', conference proceedings, International Sociological Association.

Wang, X. (2011), 'A preliminary discussion on China's legal construction of "Green Security" policy (浅议我国绿色证券政策的法律构建)' (Electronic), www.lunwen-net.com/thesis/2011/22434.html.

Weber, R.P. (1985), 'Content classification and interpretation', In *Basic Content Analysis*. Newbury Park, CA: Sage.

World Bank and Development Research Center of the State Council (2012), *China 2030: Building a Modern, Harmonious and Creative High-Income Society*, Washington, DC: World Bank.

Xiao, S.F. and Mi, H.Y. (2004), 'Analysis on the survey of enterprises' environmental protection and accounting: views on necessity and feasibility of establishing environmental accounting in China', *Green China*, Vol. 22, pp. 51–54.

Zhang, S. (1993), 'Relation between economic development and corporate social accountability (经济发展与社会责任会计)', *China Agriculture Accounting*, Vol. 2, pp. 22–30.

Zissis, C. and Bajoria, J. (2008), 'China's environmental crisis' (Electronic), www.cfr.org/publication/12608.

12 Education, globalization and rural contexts

Learning for staying, learning for leaving or learning for choice?[1]

R. John Halsey

Introduction

This chapter is based on the premise that the importance of rural communities worldwide is going to increase over the next four decades. The fundamental driver of the premise is population growth. By the middle of the twenty-first century, the world's population will be between nine and ten billion. To bring a personal perspective to the magnitude and impact of these figures, during my working life of nearly 50 years, the world's population has doubled. People being educated in our universities and other tertiary institutions today and into the future, many of whom will play a major role in the policy settings of governments, international bodies like the United Nations and global private sector enterprises, will be advising and deciding on how 'best' to respond to another 40 per cent or more population increase and all of the pressures associated with raising standards of living for the marginalized and those in poverty. As well as population growth, Brugmann (2009) and others have argued that by 2050, up to two-thirds of the world's population will live in urban centres, thus creating unchartered and far-reaching consequences for global, individual nation and community sustainability.

China, with a current population of around 1.36 billion, will likely remain a critical centre for exploring and exemplifying how massive population dimensions impact globally right down to the local rural community/village level. As a point of contrast, Australia, with its very large land mass and distances between major population centres and overall low population density, provides a 'test bed' for how to continue to ensure people can access essential human services regardless of location. From a Western development perspective, natural resources have generally been treated as though they are inexhaustible. A brief examination of a photograph of Earth taken from space reveals, however, a planet that is finite though ironically also imbued with systems and natural laws that have an apparent infinite capacity for regeneration and sustainability.

One of the common characteristics of rural areas in Australia and China, and globally more generally, is the exodus of youth in search of 'greener pastures'. From research undertaken in rural Australia which is helpful for illuminating similar issues in other countries, Alston and Kent (2003) argue that '[t]he lack of meaningful full-time work in rural areas is one of the main reasons for young people leaving rural communities' (p. 6). Limited post-secondary education and training is another significant reason for the exodus of youth from rural areas. Often added to this is a gender imbalance, where young females leave rural areas at a higher rate than young males. There are also challenges associated with the education of indigenous youth so they have choices about their cultural identity, employment opportunities and personal fulfilment.

While this exodus of youth has been happening for centuries and has often been spurred along by fundamental changes in the way societies organize themselves, such as occurred during the Industrial Revolution, it is now one of the most challenging issues confronting rural communities. This is because 'youth are fundamentally future-oriented and, as such, are a critical human resource for re-building and re-energising rural contexts' (Halsey, 2008: 2). As Salt (2004: 68) asserts, '[i]t is the loss of youth and the partial replacement of that demographic by older people that is of most concern ... [because the] structural shift has an impact on the economic wellbeing of a community and also on the sense of [its] vitality'. Put another way, the vibrancy and future of a rural town or community is linked to the choices youth make – to stay, to leave or to return after moving out to experience life elsewhere or to complete education and training not available in the local area.

In addition, with the impact of neoliberalism and its attendant focus on resilience and localization of decision-making, there has been a tendency to play down how important it is for the future of rural towns that locals can access services urban people more or less take for granted. In other words, a strong focus on being competitive, of taking full responsibility for everything that happens in and to a town has a down-side; there is a sense in which the importance of enabling external survival inputs are rendered less visible by overly concentrating on 'what locals can do to solve their problems'. As Cocklin and Dibden (2005: 9–10) have argued:

> In considering sustainability, there is a tendency to focus on the internal (or endogenous) characteristics of a particular community or region – a tendency promoted by contemporary policy discourse of self-reliance. However, a second overarching issue ... is the need to consider the exogenous factors that influence community sustainability and the extent to which a particular location is prospectively impacted by influences operating at other levels. These influences include government policy (for example, in relation to service provision and environmental regulation), commodity prices (which in turn are shaped by shifts in consumer sentiment and international exchange rates), and regional and national environmental agendas.

A few observations on rurality and education in rural Australia and China follow to illustrate some of the diversity of understandings about them and to provide locational and contextual dimensions for the chapter. The concepts of *strong choice* and *weak choice* are then introduced and an amplification of Bernstein's (1971) message system theory about how schools realize their purposes.

Next are theoretical considerations based on Corbett's (2007a) research in a fishing community in Nova Scotia. The final section of the chapter is a brief case study from a rural community in South Australia to inform how strong choice learning may help to retain youth in rural areas and enhance the quality and diversity of education.

Rural

It is widely recognized that there are many definitions and understandings of what is rural, where is rural and who is rural. It is also widely recognized that definitions and understandings vary according to many factors, not the least of which are the physical parameters of the context being considered and its prevailing cultural dimensions. What seems to be less widely recognized, however, is the complexity of rural contexts – as a person who had lived for over 40 years in rural and remote Australia said to me a few years ago: 'When you have visited one rural town, you have visited one rural town!'

Essentially there are instrumental/quantitative definitions of rural, and definitions of a more nuanced and qualitative kind. Quantitative definitions of 'rural' emphasize population size and distance from large centres where there is an extensive range of human services available. Qualitative definitions, on the other hand, while recognizing that population size and distances are contributing elements to what constitutes 'rural', focus on the cultural and relational dimensions of places and people.

In Australia, rural and remote area determinations for government schooling provision are a blend of size of population centre and distance from either the capital city or a major regional centre (Jones, 2000: 12–17). In the Northern Territory, 'country consists of the whole Territory except for areas within a 75 km radius of Darwin and Alice Springs, the two urban centres with a population of 20,000 persons or more' (Jones, 2000: 17). In contrast to this, in South Australia, for example, rural government schools are ones located more than 80 km from Adelaide and non-government rural schools are those more than 50 km from the Adelaide General Post Office (Jones, 2000: 15).

Based upon Lu's (2012) research and analysis of education in rural China, the challenges and hardships of accessing education predominate in terms of defining and encapsulating the overall characteristics of rural locations. Specifically

> rural areas are characterized by relatively high educational costs, limited educational opportunities of lower quality, and a strong gender bias favouring boys … [and] in many rural areas, the lack of local revenues leads to an increase in educational fees, because many schools have to cover costs by charging fees directly to students.
>
> (p. 331)

Brock (2009), while acknowledging the huge advances in education in rural China since the 1950s, draws attention to regional disparities, principally

between East and West. Locational differences also exist in Australia, and as a
'rule of thumb', the more remote the area, the more problematic accessing high-
quality education at all ages and stages of education becomes. Brock also draws
attention to the pressure in rural education to devote as much of the available
funding to personnel as possible, leaving very little for curriculum, materials,
buildings and other consumables. There is also the urban–rural divide in China,
which casts a long shadow over education – namely, 'the trickledown nature of
public funding is evident in the way in which urban projects are prioritised over
rural (especially school building) and funding for key schools (usually in county
towns) consumes disproportionate levels of resources' (Brock, 2009: 454).

Learning for choice

A primary role of education and learning has been, and continues to be, equip-
ping young people with knowledge, skills and dispositions to become autonomous, responsible and productive citizens. In other words, education is critical
in developing and nurturing human agency and for this Giddens' (1993) description of the term agency as 'the lived-through process of everyday conduct'
(p. 81) is particularly relevant. From the perspective of ongoing vibrant and productive rural contexts, a major question flowing from the role of education as
stated is: so what might it translate into for youth, their learning and their mobility? Exploring the question first requires some discussion about the role of
schools and choice.

Schools and education are used to reinforce values and attitudes about
national and international priorities, as well as deal with emerging challenges
and problems. Put another way, schools are used to 'fix problems'. Learning is a
powerful and pervasive resource for perpetuating and for changing ways of
thinking and perceiving; ways of being; ways of doing and responding. Schools
function as they do because of a complex mix of legislative requirements, policies, established practices and expectations about 'what schools should do'. The
'giveness of schools', however, is constructed and therefore is 'open' and 'available' for change. Transforming rural schools to become agents for championing
the vibrancy and sustainability of rural communities through deeply engaging
with questions about the purpose of learning in rural contexts is a major undertaking, which rests most directly with school leaders.

In the Australian context, in the latter half of the twentieth century, choice in
education came to prominence through the work of the Commonwealth Schools
Commission Choice and Diversity in Government Schooling Project. It was
established 'to explore the concept of choice as an approach to educational
improvement' (1980: 7). Through working with the Choice and Diversity
Project, I became involved in thinking about how different framings of choice
might result in improvements for students. While I use the ideas of *weak choice*
and *strong choice* in this chapter, drawn from my experiences with the Choice
and Diversity Project, the Commission's full discussion paper on choice also
refers to 'passive' and 'active' choice, respectively (1980: 16).

For rural young people, a *real* choice of their education and pathways beyond schooling has often been defined and actualized as the choice to move away from their community and leave home. As Corbett (2007b: 775, 776) concluded about youth living in the coastal fishing community in Canada that was the subject of his research: 'community is not a place that can sustain youth throughout their working life'; and '[t]he privilege of being able to choose to stay is fraught with uncertainty'. This in large measure echoes Alston's and Kent's finding about rural contexts, as quoted earlier.

More broadly, choice of education frequently means being able to select between options such as which school to attend, which subjects to study and which career pathway to follow. This concept of choice – of essentially selecting from a programme determined by others – for the purposes of this chapter is called *weak choice*. The consequences of a *weak choice* nevertheless may be beneficial to an individual, such as achieving a high tertiary education rank by selecting subjects taught by teachers who have a track record of 'getting students through Year 12'. The relevant point here is that in a *weak choice* context, the chooser has little or no say about determining the options available to them. The other relevant point about *weak choice* is that it often signifies 'the best as decided by persons other than the student(s)' that can be done with available resources.

Strong choice, on the other hand, is evident when those who need to/want to make choices about their learning participate in constructing the options available to them. A *strong choice* context might well have fewer options than a weak choice context, but the match between learning needs and aspirations and study programme is arguably a better fit. *Strong choice* is characterized more as a partnership – of 'common effort toward common goals' (Seeley, 1981: 65) – than an obligatory set of arrangements set in train as a consequence of choosing from a predetermined range of options.

It might be argued that moving to a *strong choice* approach to learning at a system or even school level would create resource and administrative demands that could not be met. Imagine allowing every student to decide what it is they want to learn, with whom, when and how – a sure recipe for chaos? Two points in response – *strong choice* is not about educators or systems opting out and 'letting things run' with no regard for the consequences. Second, *strong choice* is about creating contexts where learning is negotiated expansively and with the intention of being proactive in addressing issues that impact on learning in-situ. In other words, as a 'local' might say, you roll up your sleeves and work out how to address the issues, to minimize students leaving their home and community, perhaps for good.

What, then, are enabling pieces of education architecture for underpinning *strong choice* and learning for choice, and how might these play out in a rural community to improve the engagement and retention of youth, and thereby potentially enhance community vibrancy and wider sustainability?

Enabling learning for choice

Bernstein (1971), in his seminal paper entitled 'On the classification and framing of educational knowledge' argued that the knowledge functions of education are 'realized through three message systems: curriculum, pedagogy and evaluation' (p. 47). Further, he states that '[c]urriculum defines what counts as valid knowledge, pedagogy defines what counts as a valid transmission of knowledge, and evaluation defines what counts as a valid realization of this knowledge on the part of the taught' (p. 47). These definitions are value-laden, powerful and pervasive in prescribing what schools do and for what purpose(s). While I agree with Bernstein's framing, two other message systems are part of the educational architecture required for creating and nurturing a *strong choice* learning context. They are organizational structures and processes, and location–mobility.

The *organizational structures and processes* message system plays a very important role in highlighting the need for flexibility of learning arrangements. This message system especially focuses on key variables and resources which facilitate access to learning, availability of learning, the affordability of learning and the adaptability of learning. Specifically, when may learning occur, with whom, under what kind of supervisory and mentoring arrangements, where and so forth? The *location–mobility* message system focuses on explicitness about post-school career and living options. It is named separately because it is central to addressing a key problem facing many rural communities as already stated – the loss of youth. Put another way, the location–mobility message system is intended to 'ensure' that discussions and decisions with rural young people about their education and post-education trajectories *always* include meaningful considerations of the possible impacts of their decisions in relation to the local community. As Bandura (1989: 1182) writes, 'people [youth] can generate novel ideas and innovative actions about their past experiences [by] ... bring[ing] influence to bear on their motivation and action in efforts to realize valued futures'.

Second, Corbett's (2007a) seminal research into schooling in a fishing community in Nova Scotia, Canada, provides other powerful tools for looking more deeply and consequentially into learning for choice. Corbett's research is based around a question I believe resonates with all rural teachers and leaders: 'how do some rural youth "learn to leave", while others "learn to stay"?' (p. 9). The theoretical framing for Corbett's research is rich, extensive and especially pertinent for rural educators interested in engaging with a fundamental rethinking of learning in rural locations and what it means for individuals and communities. The heart of it is a fresh engagement with resistance theory from the sociology of education, which draws very substantially on Willis' (1977) pioneering work, *Learning to Labour: How Working Class Kids get Working Class Jobs*, and Bourdieu's 'logic of practice and what he calls "habitus"' (Corbett, 2007a: 45).

While acknowledging limitations and criticisms of Willis' resistance theory, Corbett believes, and I concur, that 'resistance has value ... [especially] in the context of particular locations' (p. 44). This value is strengthened as a theoretical tool for investigating what is going on in the lives of young people when they wrestle with their post-school options and how they might be assisted, by enjoining with Bourdieu's idea of 'habitus', that is, thinking about how different kinds of contexts might influence choices individuals and communities make. Corbett, while greatly valuing Bourdieu's work on habitus, argues that the idea may not be as rigid in practice as that delineated by the author 'because of overlapping discourses' (2007a: 47). Corbett asserts, for instance, that the habitus of families may have a range of valued capitals and the 'spatial turn in social theory [see for example Soja, 1996] has introduced what is now understood as multiple geographies of youth, each containing differential developmental trajectories and patterns of habitus' (2007a: 47).

Many, perhaps most, rural schools are well situated to engage in a *strong choice* approach to education because of their size and proximity to community. In claiming this, two of Corbett's (2007a) research conclusions are pertinent for progressing learning for choice, that is, learning that values and acknowledges the richness of 'the local' as well as 'the universal/global'. The first conclusion is that individuals involved in his study 'detest[ed] and resist[ed] being drawn into abstract systems preferring to remain multi-skilled, hands-on, and community-based' (p. 259). Second, most individuals:

> resist the mobility imperative built in to the idealized education trajectory and remain 'around here'. In the process they build alternative visions of success that involve persistence, survival and resistance to the forces [of modernity] that seek to displace them.

> (p. 259)

Illuminating learning for choice

I have selected a specific location in Australia to develop a brief case-study cum illustration of how privileging learning for choice in education in rural locations might be actualized. As has already been referred to, rural contexts are very diverse and the more so when one contemplates all that might be embraced in an Australia–China amalgam of rural places, spaces and people. Readers are therefore invited to extrapolate and reconstitute as appropriate the ideas put forward for possible implementation in locations and communities known to them.

Karoonda East Murray in South Australia is a rural district of 4,500 square kilometres, with a combined townships and community population of around 1,200. Broad-acre grain and sheep farming is the dominant agricultural focus of the district. The main town, Karoonda, is the administrative centre of local government and also provides retail and commercial services. There is an Area School (combined primary and secondary) in the main town of the district with an enrolment of about 130 students. It was established over 60 years ago through closures and amalgamations of one- and two-teacher rural schools under a general policy of consolidation of education provision in rural areas. Around 80 per cent of students attending the school travel by bus. The enrolment of the school peaked at nearly 400 over 20 years ago. One immediately obvious consequence of this is a very favourable student-to-space ratio. The school is the largest organization in the town and district. Increasingly, students move out of the district for tertiary education and training, and for employment when they have completed school.

The school, like many others trying to maintain curriculum diversity with declining enrolments, uses a combination of face-to-face teaching, distance education services and multi-year-level classes. It also makes students aware of post-school vocational pathways which include some school-based apprenticeship programmes.

Critical to the sustainability of the Karoonda East Murray district is availability of water. While rainfall is the main source of water for broad-acre cereal cropping, most of the agricultural businesses are also very dependent on reliable supplies of quality bore water for stock and for horticulture such as potato, onion and carrot growing. There are 212 water licences representing approximately 400 bores in the Mallee Prescribed Wells Area, which incorporates Karoonda East Murray, as well as several other towns and districts (South Australian Murray–Darling Basin Natural Resources Management Board, 2007–2008).

Living and working in Karoonda East Murray (at the time of data collection) is a person who over 40 years has acquired a very high level of knowledge and expertise about bores, windmills, pumps and reticulation systems. He also has a good working knowledge of the geology and hydrology of the region and, as importantly, knows where to go and who to see when he has questions and issues about these. In discussions with him about his work, a question came to me – who will the primary producers turn to for bore services and advice when he retires or leaves the district? Put another way, can the 'extinction of [local] experience' (Nablan, 1993; cited in Pretty, 2002: 21) be avoided when a working lifetime's worth of knowledge and expertise is taken out of a rural district's bank of human resources? While it is tempting to argue that a demand for bore services will be met by market forces, in rural areas especially this cannot be assumed (Pretty, 2002).

Learning for choice in a *strong choice* context may be a more community-beneficial way of providing an alternative to relying on finding 'someone from outside the district' to provide continuity of bore and water reticulation expertise. Assuming as a given the educational infrastructure outlined above, activating such an approach essentially involves four elements of educational provisioning working together.

First, there needs to be commitment by a school and community to profile and promote employment pathways for youth which include high-quality, high-qualification jobs such as 'bore and ground water expert', which have local as well as wider and global relevance. Second, in promoting and advocating the value of 'local' quality employment, the school and community recognize that youth may want to be mobile and may need to move outside the district for post-secondary education and training. Both of these framing elements highlight the local–global tension which has become a major issue for many, if not most, rural towns (Davison, 2005). The third element is an approach to curriculum and learning that directly engages the learner in what they want to learn and what might be opportune for them to learn. Central to the third element is the school and community being explicit with 'their youth' about the kinds of likely future expertise required so continuation of the local economy, and therefore the community, is optimized and has capacity to respond to flux and changes over time. In relation to the example used of continuity of local bore water supply expertise, this element would include exploring with youth what education and training for a career in this field requires, likely resourcing to start up a small business or take over an existing one, sources of support to do this and, very importantly, introductions to relevant community mentors to help facilitate their transition from the world of a student to the world of a worker/entrepreneur. It would also explicitly include discussions about social and occupational mobility with a view to ensuring that the learners knew about the choices available beyond school. This is essential because youth need to be deeply aware that their post-school life is being negotiated and planned linked to local community needs while also keeping open options of moving out and away from community.

The fourth element focuses on school structures and processes. Preparedness by a school to be flexible about when and where learning occurs, and under what kinds of supervisory arrangements are crucial factors. Challenging the youth of a rural community to think seriously about building their beyond-schooling future around likely local community expertise succession planning requirements is in many ways 'a big ask'. This is particularly so when taking into consideration what is happening in primary industries due to the impact of globalization. As Lawrence (2005: 105) argues, 'many of the changes occurring are not conducive to the retention of natural capital, or to the building of social capital'. Notwithstanding these significant cautions, there are some ameliorating contingencies that can be put in place at a local level. They include building into the overall design and delivery of study programmes for the purposes intended, safeguards for career and life mobility like ensuring that negotiated study plans and expected outcomes meet approved national standards. Put another way, pushing the boundaries of schooling must not expose students to unnecessary risk vis-à-vis their futures. A critical role of schooling is one of opening up rather than closing down or narrowly streaming opportunities, especially when argued from the perspective of *strong choice*.

Figure 12.1 summarizes the main dimensions of *strong choice* and learning for choice.

Summary

The importance of rural communities worldwide is going to increase over the next four decades. Population growth and an increasing preference for urban living linked with the challenges of food sovereignty, water supply, energy needs, environmental health and territorial security underpin this standpoint. In order for rural communities to survive, prosper and be the innovative places and spaces essential for a world with a population of 9–10 billion by 2050, people,

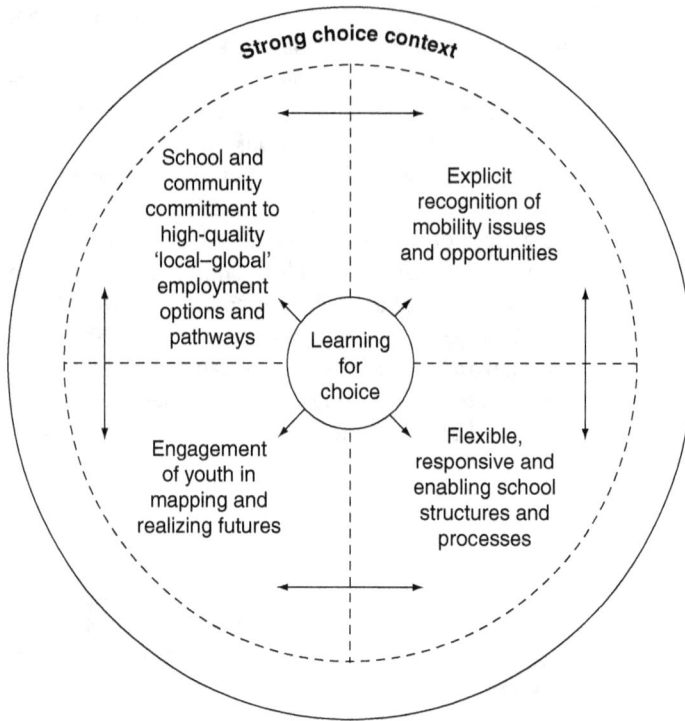

Figure 12.1 Learning for choice.

particularly young people, with a diverse range of knowledge, skills, expertise and commitment to living and working in them are a fundamental requirement. Three key questions about the purposes of learning – for staying, for leaving, for choice – and how they might shape the structuring and processes of a 'typical' rural school have been considered using a South Australian rural context, as a contribution towards what might be done to ensure there are vibrant, productive rural communities.

In Australia, in China and globally, schools and education, as previously stated, are used to reinforce values and attitudes about national priorities as well as deal with emerging challenges and problems. Schools 'fix problems' as well as nurturing the potential of their learners. In rural areas frequently schools have to 'be more than schools', often because they are the one remaining organization in a town with links to all sections of a community. In addition to educating and caring for children and youth, rural schools are social centres, recreation centres, run community libraries, provide health and counselling services, are places for public meetings and voting, are safe refuge centres and so forth. Since the onset of globalization and the accompanying rationalization of human and business services, major demographic changes have occurred and will continue to occur in rural Australia and rural China, albeit in different ways. A particularly significant instance is the out-migration of youth linked with changes to employment and income profiles in rural communities. A *strong choice* approach to education which deeply engages learners in determining what they learn, how, when and for what purposes, embedded in community and connected to wider options and pathways, has the potential to place education at the heart of nurturing the vibrancy and productivity required of rural locations, as world population growth speeds toward nearly ten billion by 2050.

Note

1 Some of the ideas in this chapter were presented in a keynote address to the 2009 Society for the Provision of Education in Rural Australia conference held at Flinders University.

Bibliography

Alston, M. and Kent, J. (2003). Education access for Australia's rural young people: a case of social exclusion. *Australian Journal of Education*, 47(1), pp. 5–17.

Bandura, A. (1989). Human agency in social cognitive theory. *American Psychologist*, 44(9), pp. 1175–1184.

Bernstein, B. (1971). On the classification and framing of educational knowledge. In M.F.D. Young (ed.), *Knowledge and Control: New Directions for the Sociology of Education*. London: Collier-Macmillan.

Brock, A. (2009). Moving mountains stone by stone: reforming rural education in China. *International Journal of Educational Development*, 29, pp. 454–462.

Brugmann, J. (2009). *Welcome to the Urban Revolution: How Cities are Changing the World*. St Lucia, Queensland: University of Queensland Press.

Cocklin, C. and Dibden, J. (eds). (2005). *Sustainability and Change in Rural Australia*. Sydney: University of New South Wales Press.

Choice in Education and Sources of Present Administrative Practice (1980). Choice and diversity in government schooling project. Discussion Paper No. 1, Schools Commission/State Education Departments, Canberra.

Corbett, M. (2007a). *Learning to Leave: The Irony of Schooling in a Coastal Community*. Halifax: Fernwood Publishing.

Corbett, M. (2007b). Travels in space and place and rural schooling. *Canadian Journal of Education*, 30(3), 771–792.

Davison, G. (2005). Rural sustainability in historical perspective. In C. Cocklin. and J. Dibden (eds), *Sustainability and Change in Rural Australia*. Sydney: University of New South Wales Press.

Giddens, A. (1993). *New Rules of Sociological Method*. Cambridge: Polity Press.

Halsey, R.J. (2008). Rural schools and rural revitalisation: blazing new trails. Keynote paper, National Community Education Association Conference, Dallas, TX.

Jones, R. (2000). *Development of a Common Definition of, and Approach to Data Collection on, the Geographic Location of Students to be Used for Nationally Comparable Reporting of Outcomes of Schooling within the 'National Goals for Schooling in the Twenty-First Century'*. Melbourne: Ministerial Council on Education, Employment, Training and Youth Affairs.

Lawrence, G. (2005). Globalisation, agricultural production systems and rural restructuring. In C. Cocklin and J. Dibden (eds), *Sustainability and Change in Rural Australia*. Sydney: University of New South Wales Press.

Lu, Y. (2012). Education of children left behind in rural china. *Journal of Marriage and Family*, 74, pp. 328–341.

Pretty, J. (2002). *Agri-Culture: Reconnecting People, Land and Nature*. London: Earthscan Publications.

Salt, B. (2004). *The Big Shift*. Victoria, Australia: Hardie Grant Books.

Seeley, D.S. (1981). *Education Through Partnership: Mediating Structures and Education*. Cambridge, MA: Ballinger Publishing Company.

Soja, E.W. (1996). *Thirdspace: Journeys to Los Angeles and Other Real-and-Imagined Places*. Malden, MA: Blackwell.

South Australian Murray-Darling Basin Natural Resources Management Board. (2007–2008). *Mallee Prescribed Wells Area: Annual Water Use Report*. Adelaide: Government of South Australia.

Willis, P. (1977). *Learning to Labour: How Working Class Kids Get Working Class Jobs*. New York: Columbia University Press.

13 Why Beijing rules the property market

Rethinking the role of 'five new measures' in regulating the property market under a new era of China's leadership transition

Po-shan Yu, Lei Xu and Mervyn K. Lewis[1]

Introduction

The meltdown of the property market in the US has created a mortgage crisis that ultimately triggered a serious recession – the worst since the Great Depression. In addition, the property sectors of other developed economies, in particular, Spain and Ireland, are still suffering the painful lingering after-effects of the previous years. In contrast, China's economy is much less dependent on external factors than upon government-driven spending in real estate and infrastructure development. As such, there is significant concern as to whether and when the Chinese property market would present the next crisis, in the event that the sub-national government[2] debt or inter-governments loan becomes unsustainable.[3] This chapter aims to elaborate the impacts of the latest 'control measures' to rein in the real estate sector under the existing institutional environment in China (including central government's GDP target policy, land financing, subsidized loans and inter-regional competition), especially when the real estate sector becomes one of the major economic engines in driving today's Chinese GDP growth. With the sub-national governments being highly dependent upon revenue generated from local land sales, which would now be greatly limited by these new 'control measures', the impact of these measures would appear to be directly negative for sub-national governments, and yet the new central leadership is expected to work in cooperation with the sub-national government to balance the interests of stakeholders at all levels. This chapter aims to review these policy changes, examine their underlying rationale and consider the ramifications for Chinese property values. More importantly, the chapter also aims to highlight the symbiotic yet conflicting relationship between the central and sub-national governments and how the collective behaviour (among the sub-national governments, property developers and potential investors) enforce the central government to implement relevant property policies one by one[4] since 2009.

Real-estate 'bubble'

After the Global Financial Crisis, investment in fixed asset investment has often played a significant role in driving Chinese economic growth (as shown in Figure 13.1 and Table 13.1). This effect had been most evident in the Chinese real-estate market, which developed in an extremely rapid, but unsustainable, manner, reaching a level where more than 12 per cent of the 2012 national GDP exists in the residential property sector (as shown in Table 13.1).

In addition, there is a great speculative tendency in Chinese real estate, driven by the unique fundamental characteristics of the structure of the Chinese economy, including an under-developed financial system, which limits channels for investors, low real interest rates in a high-growth environment and a closed capital account. Currently, real estate investment captures a quarter of total fixed asset investment in mainland China (Ahuja *et al.*, 2012), and has been growing at around 30 per cent per annum over 2010 to 2011, representing severe over-investment in a single sector and posing risks to market and financial stability.

The difficulty, however, lies in determining whether a bubble really exists in the Chinese real-estate sector. Paradoxically, the existence of a bubble can only be proven once the bubble bursts. Hence, among academics, it remains a challenge as to exactly how to define and identify a speculative real-estate bubble. Stiglitz (1990: 13) provided the following definition of asset bubbles: 'If the reason that the price is high today is only because investors believe that the

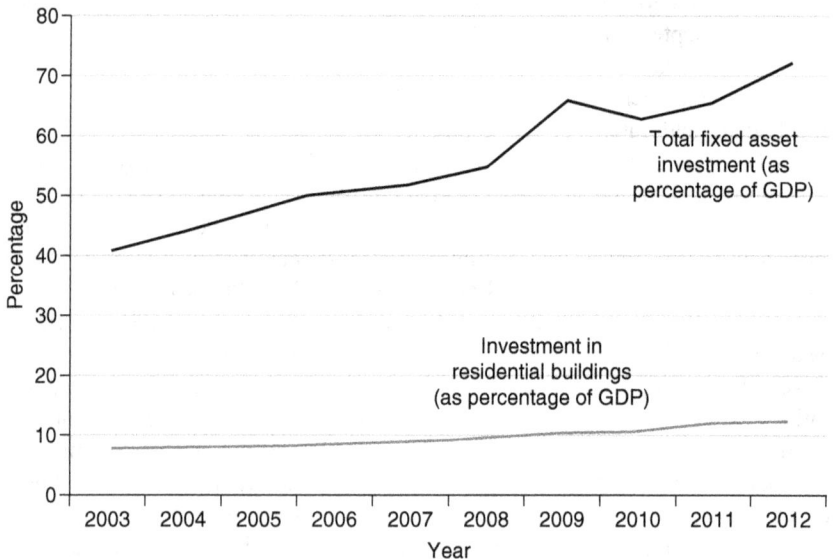

Figure 13.1 Total fixed asset investment and investment in residential buildings (source: compiled by the authors based upon National Bureau of Statistics of China figures).

Table 13.1 Total fixed asset investment and investment in residential buildings

	Percentage of GDP		*In percent of GDP*
	2003		*2004*	
GDP (100 million)	135,822.76		159,878.34	
Investment in residential buildings (100 million)	10,792.30	7.95	13,464.08	8.42
Total fixed asset investment (100 million)	55,566.61	40.91	70,477.43	44.08
	2005		*2006*	
GDP (100 million)	184,937.37		216,314.43	
Investment in residential buildings (100 million)	15,427.23	8.34	19,333.05	8.94
Total fixed asset investment (100 million)	88,773.61	48.00	109,998.16	50.85
	2007		*2008*	
GDP (100 million)	265,810.31		314,045.43	
Investment in residential buildings (100 million)	25,005.01	9.41	30,881.20	9.83
Total fixed asset investment (100 million)	137,323.94	51.66	172,828.40	55.03
	2009		*2010*	
GDP (100 million)	340,902.81		401,512.80	
Investment in residential buildings (100 million)	36,428.23	10.69	45,027.01	11.21
Total fixed asset investment (100 million)	224,598.77	65.88	251,683.77	62.68
	2011		*2012*	
GDP (100 million)	473,104.05		519,470.00	
Investment in residential buildings (100 million)	57,824.43	12.22	64,412.79	12.40
Total fixed asset investment (100 million)	311,485.13	65.84	374,694.74	72.13
	Percentage change 2003–2012			
GDP (100 million)	282.46			
Investment in residential buildings (100 million)	496.84			
Total fixed asset investment (100 million)	574.32			

Source: compiled by authors based upon National Bureau of Statistics of China figures

selling price is high tomorrow – when "fundamental" factors do not seem to justify such a price – then a bubble exists.' Himmelberg *et al.* (2005: 68) further elaborated that

> at least in the short run, the high price of the asset is merited, because it yields a return (capital gain plus dividend) equal to that on alternative assets.

The 'dividend' portion of the return from owning a property comes from the rent the owner saves by living in the property rent-free, and the capital gain from property price appreciation over time.

Further, Krugman (2005) identified a bubble as follows: 'if people think that prices will continue to rise, they become willing to spend even more, driving prices still higher, and so on … prices will keep rising rapidly, generating big capital gains'. Himmelberg *et al.* (2005) and Case and Shiller (2004) held a similar view of a property bubble as being driven by home buyers who are willing to pay inflated prices for property today because they expect unrealistically high property appreciation in the future.

In 2010, Shiller further presented certain criteria in an interview with the New York Times,[5] including:

* Sharp increases in the price of an asset like real estate or dot-com shares
* Great public excitement about said increases
* An accompanying media frenzy
* Stories of people earning a lot of money, causing envy among people who aren't
* Growing interest in the asset class among the general public
* 'New era' theories to justify unprecedented price increases
* A decline in lending standards

All these scholars attempted to interpret what a property bubble is from various grounds. It can be summarized as irrational behaviour, profit driven as well as deviating from the fundamentals.

Using Shiller's 'definition' (2010), one would conclude that speculative bubbles probably do exist in the Chinese tier-one property sector, in cities such as Shenzhen, Guangzhou, Shanghai and Beijing, as shown in Figure 13.2.

However, the fallacy of the 'bubble' argument was elaborated by Himmelberg *et al.* (2005):

the price of a property is not the same as the annual cost of owning; high price growth is not evidence in itself that property is overvalued; differences in expected appreciation rates and taxes can lead to considerable variability in the price-to-rent ratio across markets; the sensitivity of property prices to changes in fundamentals is higher at times when real, long-term interest rates are already low and in cities where expected price growth is high, so accelerating property price growth and outsized price increases in certain markets are not intrinsically signs of a bubble.

Although the Chinese government officials also mentioned that it has a bubble in some of the tier-two and -three cities, for this chapter the authors could not be convinced to borrow the term 'real-estate bubble' from the media or certain

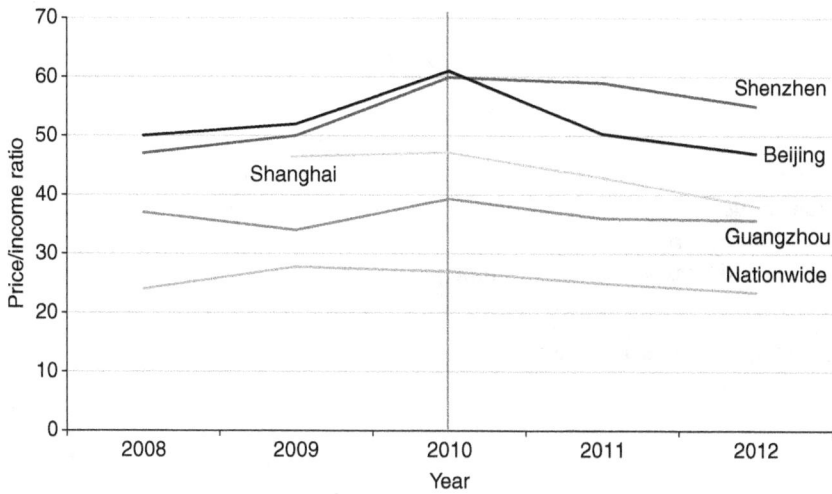

Figure 13.2 Commodity property price to income ratio (source: compiled by authors based upon National Bureau of Statistics of China, Shenzhen Municipal Bureau of Statistics, Guangzhou Municipal Bureau of Statistics, Shanghai Municipal Bureau of Statistics and Beijing Municipal Bureau of Statistics).

authorities to describe what is happening in the unique process of Chinese urbanization.

As per Garber (2000), 'a property bubble is the part of the property price movement that is unexplainable by fundamentals'. However, it is still not that clear, or even arguable, how 'fundamentals' are 'fundamentals', particularly in a unique Chinese economic environment. For example: (1) a leasehold-based property market that would represent an uncertainty at the end of the lease period; and (2) the lack of other investment options that would make Chinese perceive real-estate investment as a unique vehicle to accumulate wealth.

The sustainability of the Chinese property market

To estimate the sustainability of Chinese tier-one cities' residential property sectors during 2008 to 2012, the property price to income (P/I) ratio is used as an indicator or measure of analysing alternative uses of a household's income tied up in a property.

The formula for buying a 100 m² residential property is:

(Average property price per square metre / average annual income) × 100

As shown in Figure 13.2, the ratios of the tier-one cities are higher than the average for the country. From 2008 to 2010, it shows a consistent pattern of Shenzhen and Beijing residential properties. The property prices increased more rapidly than the household's annual income. However, after 2010 it shows an adverse trend; the property price increased slower than annual income. We believe it could be related to the shortage of labour in 2010 (Das and N'Diaye, 2013), which generated upward pressure wages in China. In turn, it is also reflected in the property markets (i.e. income increases faster than property prices).

In addition, when considering the affordability of the property market in China, based upon our P/I calculation, it implies that it takes a household more than 60 years to own a $100\,m^2$ commodity property in Beijing. The period of lease/land-use rights[6] for commercial property in China is 70 years. This implies sustainability issues in Chinese property markets.

The Chinese shadow banking sector

As per Tao and Deng (2013), Chinese shadow banking has the following features:

(1) a complicated structure and poor transparency, with improperly disclosed or undisclosed risks, (2) numerous inter-related products, regardless of their point of origin, (3) excessive deleverage on property and collateral value of land, (4) sensitivity to interest rate movements and property prices, (5) lack of regulation externally and risk management internally, and (6) significantly relying upon a continued influx of capital as well as potential exposure to excess risk if liquidity becomes a problem.

Due to various estimation methods and lack of a generally accepted definition of Chinese shadow banking, there is significant variance when estimating the size of the Chinese shadow banking system (as shown in Table 13.2). The range is from 26 per cent (estimated by UBS) to 198 per cent of the 2012 GDP figure (estimated by Fitch Ratings). Given the capital-intensive nature of property and

Table 13.2 The estimated size of Chinese shadow banking activities

Source	Estimated value (RMB trillion)	Percentage of 2012 GDP*
Citi Research	28	54
Barclays	25.6	49
Moody's	21–29	39–55
Credit Suisse (Median)	22.8	44
UBS	13.7–24.4	26–46
ANZ Bank	15–17	29–33
BAML	14.5	28
Chinese Academy of Social Sciences	15.3–21.1	29–40
J.P. Morgan	36	69
Fitch Ratings	104	198

Source: Thomson Reuters (2013); Zhu (2013).

Notes
* Official 2012 GDP figure for China is RMB52.761 trillion.

infrastructure sectors, China's shadow banking definitely plays a crucial role in the persistent fast-growing real-estate sector. Since 2009, these alternative financing vehicles have rapidly been established to fund real estate and infrastructure construction projects by unsecured developers and sub-national governments who are unable to raise capital through bonds, according to Thomson Reuters (2013). Chinese shadow banking is greatly related to the real-estate sector, and its activities impact upon the property prices. However, the 'Five New Measures' do not impact upon the activities of shadow banking.

Further, the quality and availability of data (for instance, rental prices, land sales revenues, shadow banking activities and vacancy rate, etc.) in China makes it even harder to assess the potential implications of the above-discussed 'fundamentals'. As such, we do not know what a 'bubble' is as such in China. However, we do doubt China will be able to maintain its current property price growth rate per annum. Does that imply it has a bubble? Let us reiterate the answer: we do not know. For us, it only represents that property prices are too high, particularly in certain Chinese cities. It would be unrealistic for this trend to continue.

It is important that the real-estate sector in China is adjusted back to more realistic levels, along with other construction-related sectors, such as steel and cement, which have also developed unsustainably in parallel to the development of real estate.

Following the above discussion, the contributions made by this chapter are to pinpoint how the unique institutional setting in China has significantly driven up property prices, and how the latest 'control measures' introduced by the central government do not directly or intentionally address the issues raised by the institutional environment.

Have property prices achieved a 'harmonious society'?

Introducing the ideology of a socialist harmonious society, China's Communist Party endorsed this political doctrine by the then President Hu Jintao. It calls for the creation of a 'harmonious society', a move that further signalled a shift in the Party's focus from promoting all-out economic growth to solving worsening social tensions (*Washington Post*, 2006). On the one hand, we noticed that the introduction of the new measures is mainly related to the 'harmonized society' ideology; on the other hand, these control measures do not serve its initial objectives, at least not in the short term.

An observation about the Chinese economic transformation is that not only has the net worth of Chinese households expanded over the last decade as property prices have increased, but the net worth of the older generation has also continued to increase. Today, China's elderly tend to have their own property, but their retirement incomes are inadequate (the so-called 'asset rich cash poor'), according to China Economic Net's report (2013). In contrast, those who rent are normally younger households. They are owners-in-waiting who watch the Chinese property markets with significant concern.

As pinpointed by Iley and Lewis (2007), rising real-estate prices do not increase real wealth for society as a whole. The capital gains accruing to home-owners are offset by the increased future living costs borne by those who do not own homes. Wealth is redistributed between these groups, but is not created overall. In this connection, society is not better off as a whole (*The Economist*, 2004). Hence, the impacts of rising property prices for building a 'harmonized society' would become questionable.

The rationale behind the 'five new measures'

In a symposium held at Peking University on April 2013,[7] researchers have accounted for rising property prices in China with the following: (1) land supply in mainland China is highly regulated and supply is limited; (2) regional east–west disparities in population growth due to inter-regional labour migration since the 1990s are putting direct pressure on the property market; (3) resultant rapid growth in per capita income in tier-one and -two Chinese cities is motivating these *nouveau riche* groups to invest in the property market in the absence of other investment opportunities.

Apart from these items, under the one-child policy consideration, Chinese, prior to their retirement ages, tend to believe that buying property as an investment vehicle will often serve the purposes of wealth preservation and appreciation.

In point of fact, these property investments by the wealthy older generation will become bequests to their children. These bequests, to a great extent, are expected by the younger generation, which creates additional upward pressure on real-estate prices. In particular, China has an under-developed financial system which limits channels for investors, low real interest rates in a high-growth environment and a closed capital account.

In the face of persistently high property prices, the central government has introduced a series of measures in the last decade with the aim of taming the market, including the 'Nine-time major rules and regulations enhancement'. The 'five new measures' are the latest rules the central government has brought in to cool the market. However, in spite of successive policies, property prices remain stubbornly high.

It is unclear whether property prices persist in their current state due to demand- or supply-driven factors, but it is evident that this latest policy predominantly targets demand.

'Five new measures'

The 'five new measures' introduced in February 2013 were designed to enhance regulation of the property market. The State Council executive meeting issued five policy measures that require the following. (1) Municipalities and sub-provincial cities, excluding Lhasa, to maintain the fundamental stability of property prices, to annually develop and publish new property price control targets, to establish and improve the accountability of the system which monitors the

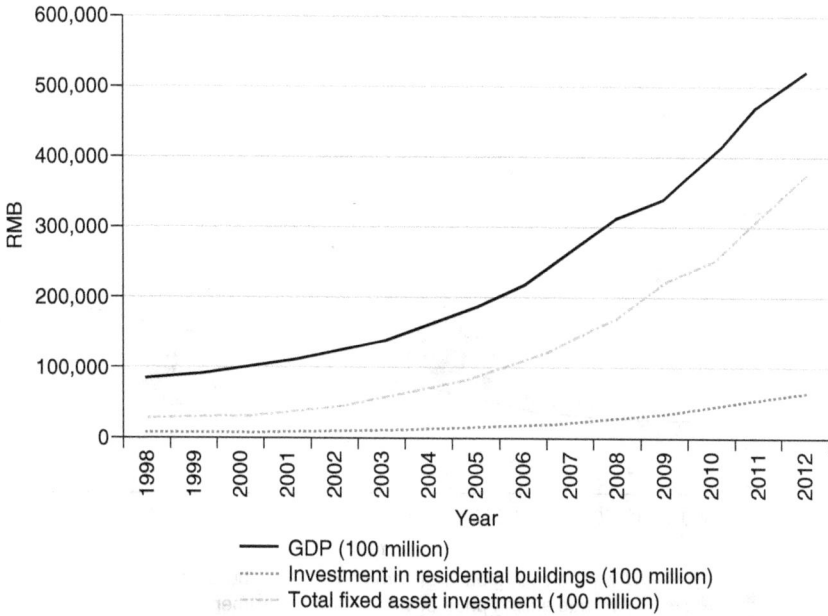

Figure 13.3 GDP, total fixed asset investment and investment in residential buildings (source: National Bureau of Statistics of China).

stability of residential property prices. Sub-national governments to (2) rigorously apply limitations on purchases of 'commodity property',[8] to rein in residential property prices by regulating purchases of different property types by different buyers and to stringently enforce differential property credit policies, as well as expand the scope of individual property tax reform in various cities; (3) increase the supply of ordinary 'commercial property' and land, although the total supply of property land in 2013 is not lower than the average of the past five years; (4) expedite the planning and construction of affordable homes, to plan, construct and deliver necessary supporting facilities simultaneously and to improve and enforce an allocation system to ensure equitable distribution – by the end of 2013, eligible migrant workers in cities of prefecture level and above need to be assisted into local property; (5) strengthen market supervision, monitoring and the management of real-estate sales, strictly implement real-estate sales price marking, reinforce credit management, severely penalize intermediaries engaging in illegal practices and establish urban residential property communication systems to disseminate and manage information distribution.

Chinese real-estate development

How does China transform its real estate development from a planned economy to the mixed one seen today, in which a unique mechanism exists to shape its

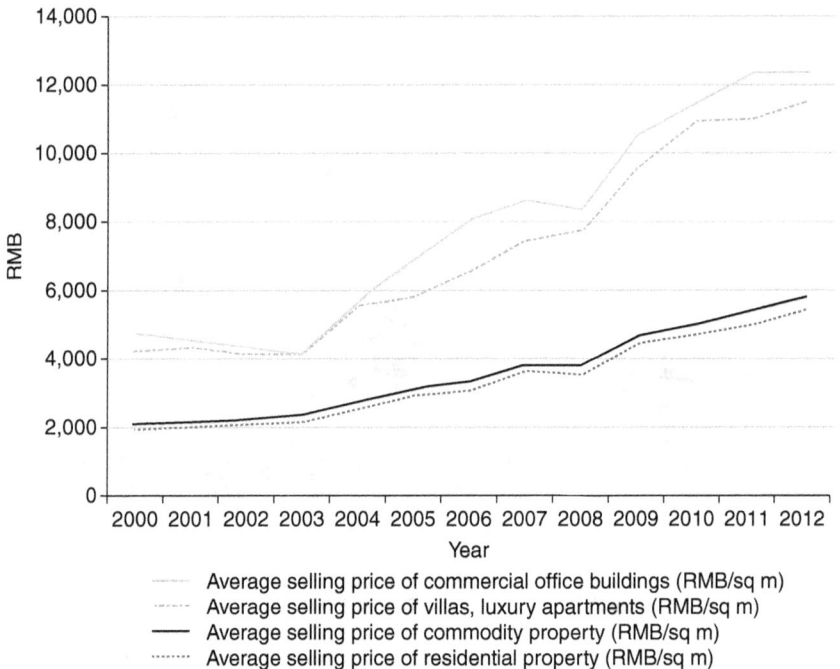

Figure 13.4 The average selling price of various properties (source: National Bureau of Statistics of China).

institutional milieu? Reform is, by definition, an exercise in uncertainty, and China has chosen experimentation as its preferred modus operandi, since it also allows cost minimization via a gradual learning process – a kind of 'piecemeal social engineering' (Chiu and Lewis, 2006).

So what are the most significant and effective regional economic experiments in shaping China's institutions today? How does the central government motivate sub-national governments, but simultaneously monitor and coordinate them in the unique institutional context? In recent years, fiscally stimulated real-estate development has become yet another experiment in Chinese economic history, this time in urbanization.

The inter-linked relationship between central and sub-national governments

Central–provincial government relations

Prior to 1978, China's central government was the ultimate command centre. It controlled the appointment of major provincial officials as well as the fiscal resources of the provinces. This centralized fiscal system was called a 'unified collection and allocation of funds by the state' (*Tongshoutongzhi*). The central government controlled the collection and allocation of fiscal resources.

Between 1978 and 1994, China adopted a more decentralized fiscal responsibility system whereby local authorities took full responsibility for their revenues and expenditures. This system of fiscal federalism was known colloquially as 'fenzaochifan' – literally meaning 'each province eats the rice in its own bowl' (Qian and Weingast 1997), and fundamentally changed China's central–provincial relationship. The central government continued to control the appointment of major officials in the provinces, but it no longer controlled each province's fiscal revenue.

According to Qian and Weingast (1997), Qian and Roland (1998) and Shirk (1993), the introduction of fiscal federalism offered strong incentives for the provinces to develop their own economies. This resulted in most fiscal resources in China being controlled by the provinces. The fiscal capability of the Chinese central government was therefore severely diminished. For instance, in 1993 the share of central government revenue accounted for only 22 per cent of the nation's total tax revenue (Table 13.3).

Table 13.3 Share of central and local governments in government revenue and expenditure (per cent)

Year	Revenue		Expenditure	
	Central	Local	Central	Local
1978	15.50	84.50	47.40	52.60
1980	24.50	75.50	54.30	45.70
1985	38.40	61.60	39.70	60.30
1990	33.80	66.20	32.60	67.40
1991	29.80	70.20	32.20	67.80
1992	28.10	71.90	31.30	68.70
1993	22.00	78.00	28.30	71.70
1994	55.70	44.30	30.30	69.70
1995	52.20	47.80	29.20	70.80
1996	49.40	50.60	27.10	72.90
1997	48.90	51.10	27.40	72.60
1998	49.50	50.50	28.90	71.10
1999	51.10	48.90	31.50	68.50
2000	52.20	47.80	34.70	65.30
2001	52.40	47.60	30.50	69.50
2002	55.00	45.00	30.70	69.30
2003	54.60	45.40	30.10	69.90
2004	54.90	45.10	27.70	72.30
2005	52.30	47.70	25.90	74.10
2006	52.80	47.20	24.70	75.30
2007	54.10	45.90	23.00	77.00
2008	53.30	46.70	21.30	78.70

Source: National Bureau of Statistics of China.

Provincial–local government relations

The tax-sharing system reform in 1994, however, did not extend to the local level. Within a province, local governments still have no autonomy in terms of income generation and expenditure. They remain dependent upon transfer payments from the provincial government. A study by Garnaut *et al.* (2010) found that, in 2004, provincial transfer payments accounted for 71.1 per cent of fiscal expenditure in a county in Sichuan. Higher-level governments are also solely responsible for the nomination of major county officials.

Garnaut *et al.* (2010) thus illustrated a structure in which the higher-level administration holds the reins of power, while local governments are kept weak. This promotes a certain cascade of predatory behaviours practised by all levels of government. The provincial governments engaged in downward vertical financial and political manipulation of the weaker locals, which lacked the ability to oppose these pressures. In turn, the local governments, in an attempt to free themselves from the fiscal tethers of the higher-ups, extract economic rents from the open market, thereby engaging in horizontal predation, being allowed to do so due to an absence of need for government accountability.

The symbiotic yet conflicting relationship between the central and sub-national governments

Sub-national governments are interested in real-estate development for two reasons. First, the central nature of fiscal income and a peripheral/local focus of expenditure cause sub-national governments to seek financial resources, which can easily be found in real estate. Second, real estate provides a ready source of GDP growth, an important economic indicator that is conveniently reportable by government officials. In addition, there is the aesthetic value of real estate – the modernization of a previously decrepit city creates immense *prima facie* political value.

Barth *et al.* (2012) tracked Chinese residential property prices over the past decade. It was found that prices increased up to 2008, when they fell steeply, prior to soaring 23.8 per cent to a record high in 2009, as shown in Figure 13.2. Prices fell 6.7 per cent in the following year. This growth pattern has generated local and international concern as to whether the Chinese residential property boom can be sustained.

However, for the new Xu–Li administration, handling the overheating of the residential property sector and meeting an unprecedented demand for affordable urban property has become a vital task, one which is critical in achieving the lofty goal of the 'harmonized society', as mandated by the previous leadership. Success in attaining these goals would imply that China has transformed from state-driven growth into a market economy. However, any regulatory action would exert a certain degree of negativity upon sub-national governments in terms of their revenue base. Thus, the crucial question remains of how the central government will balance their new regulatory role against appeasing the agenda of their sub-national counterparts.

The institutional context

China has 'crossed the river' of market reforms for the past three decades by 'feeling the stones' – slowly and pragmatically, implementing partial reforms in an experimental manner, walking a fine line between risk and conservativism. As a result, a somewhat unique 'institutional context' has been built. This context defines the 'game rules' of China's economic development and provides guidelines under which the central government coordinate, monitor and motivate the performance of their lower-level counterparts in terms of achieving certain political and economic goals. The significance of this context lies in its role in guiding economic experiments and reforms, as well as deciding various 'incentives' for involved parties (Xu, 2011). Xu also argued that this milieu is frequently misinterpreted by Westerners, who used developed market economies as a reference point, leading to the conclusion that China had poor institutional settings such as insecure property rights, underdeveloped capital markets, poor corporate governance and a lack of democratic accountability. However, if these settings were indeed so inadequate, then China's economic performance would be difficult to explain.

This chapter will try to define this institutional environment in China, an environment which revolves around the central government's policy of GDP targets, land financing, subsidized loans and stimulation of inter-regional competition, and the impact these institutional guidelines have on regional real-estate development. We will also investigate whether this context undermines the effectiveness in the application of the new real-estate regulatory measures.

Land financing and GDP target incentives

According to Ding (2003), the adoption of a land-use rights system in China has had a remarkably positive impact on land development, government finance, real estate and property development, infrastructure provision and urban growth. Land markets began to emerge and land prices started to rationalize land-use allocation and land use (Ding *et al.*, 2000; Xue, 1994).

As per Tao and Wang (2013), since the late 1990s China has implemented a 'new economic growth' model that is significantly dependent upon the system of land management. Land financing is a policy tool used by sub-national governments to use the transaction of land to finance sub-national budgets and extra-budgets. In this connection, sub-national governments seek land-related revenues through three major methods. The first is revenues associated with the supply of land, including the transfer or lease of state-owned land-use rights. The second channel is the tax revenues related to the development of the real-estate sector, e.g. business taxes. The third is the revenues generated by local government financing platforms (LGFPs),[9] such as using land as collateral for loans via LGFP operations.

As previously discussed, sub-national governments are interested in urbanization as their de jure and de facto rights of control of local land and other resources that allow them carte blanche to convert farmland to non-arable usage, thus providing them with fiscal revenue in the form of business taxation (as shown in Figure 13.5). While the central government has, since 1994, reclaimed a substantial share of the tax revenues generated by township and village enterprises and other industries, regardless of ownership, the sub-national government still held exclusive access to the business tax, almost half of which is sourced from the construction and real-estate sectors. This tax has replaced both the value-added tax and enterprise profit tax as a new source of sub-national government revenue (Kung *et al.*, forthcoming).

In addition, large windfall profits are also boosted by the fact that sub-national governments have no obligation to compensate agriculturalists for their land, the reason being that, despite being the nominal owners, farmers only have rights to the agrarian value of their land – i.e. the value of their crop production, which is meagre compared to the proceeds the sub-national government would obtain in land sales if it was to be converted to commercial or residential real-estate use (Kung *et al.*, 2009). This, together with escalating commercial and premium residential land prices, has generated 'windfall profits' for many sub-national governments, particularly those in the rapidly developed coastal regions. While it remains unclear whether high land values drive high property prices, or vice versa, it remains that there is strong motivation for sub-national governments and state-related bodies to become involved in real-estate development.

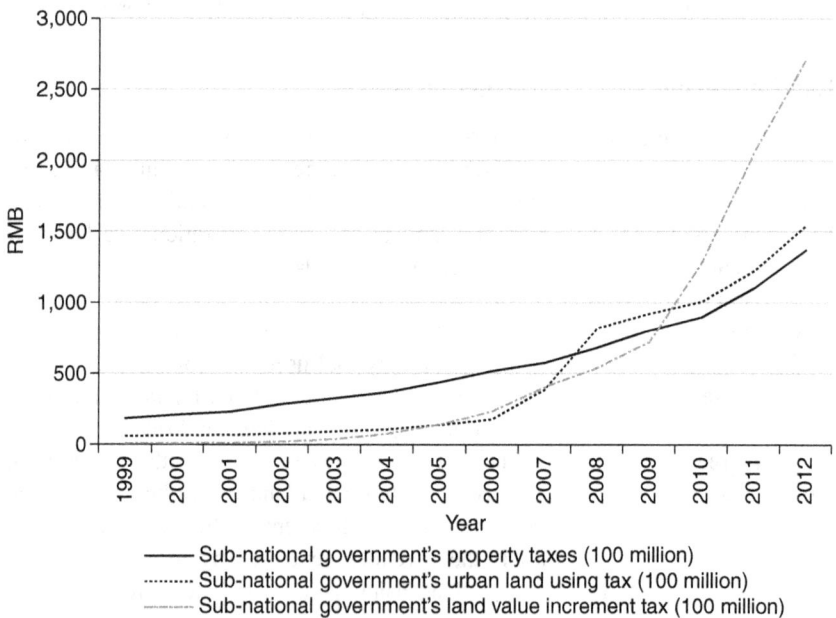

Figure 13.5 Sub-national governments' property-related taxes (source: National Bureau of Statistics of China).

Unfortunately, this 'land-revenue incentive' has not only endangered China's stock of arable land, but also subjected large numbers of farmers to loss of their primary source of livelihood, with minimal compensation.

As also previously discussed, since urbanization spurs local GDP growth and provides important political mileage for local officials in terms of competition (Xu, 2011), then these local officials would, in the interest of self-promotion, be strongly motivated to bolster economic growth for their respective regions (Li and Zhou, 2005).

Once, governments merely set the rules of the game, but now they have also become players. It is not surprising, then, that the majority of the most influential real-estate companies in China all have state-owned backgrounds or connections. In each region there is a coalition of the respective sub-national government, a team of state-owned enterprises (SOEs) and state-owned banks which controls the dominant real-estate development projects. According to Caixin Online, by the end of 2009 the 16 central SOEs accounted for a proportion of total assets, revenue and net profits of the national real-estate sector as shown in Figure 13.6–13.8.

Thus, it is probably in the interests of the sub-national governments not to follow the latest regulatory measures, or to only enforce them in a half-hearted manner. It seems that many are doing so. The Hangzhou, Nanjing and Wuhan regional governments have released a single sentence mentioning the 'five new measures' on their Weibo[10] websites, without any further elaboration. It is more than apparent that there is a huge discrepancy between the efforts of the central leadership and the agenda of the regional governments. In the absence of a fundamental change to the current institutional context, there is doubt as to whether the central government can manipulate their regional cousins into abiding by these new measures.

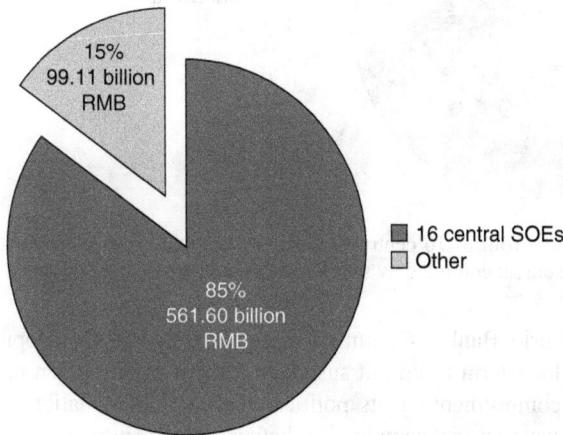

Figure 13.6 Total assets of 16 central SOEs in the national real-estate sector in 2009 (source: compiled by the authors based upon the State-owned Assets Supervision and Administration Commission (SASAC) figures).

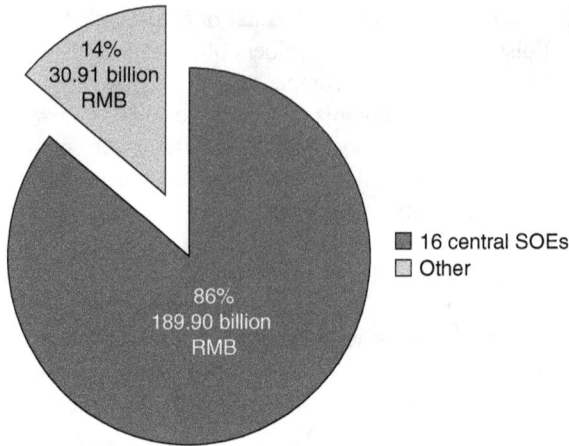

Figure 13.7 Total sales revenue of 16 central SOEs in the national real-estate sector in 2009 (source: compiled by the authors based upon SASAC figures).

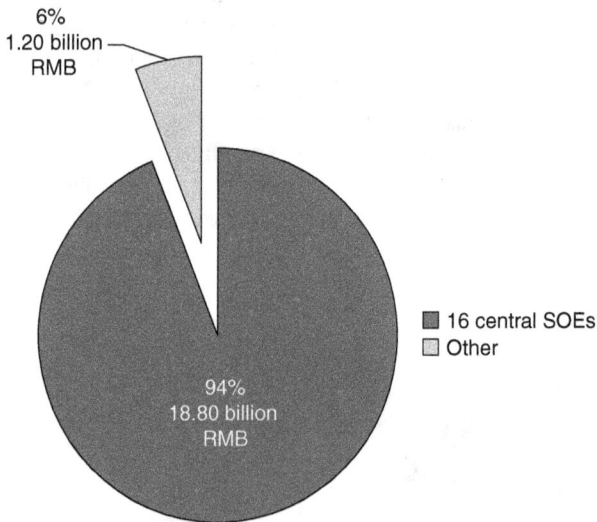

Figure 13.8 Total net profit of 16 central SOEs in the national real-estate sector in 2009 (source: compiled by the authors based upon SASAC figures).

A report by the World Bank's Commission on Growth and Development (2008) states that the long-term rapid but sustained growth of any given nation depends on a strong commitment by its political leaders – both national and regional. The critical question that remains is whether China – in particular, the regional governments with their newfound fiscal powers – will continue to commit to the national experimental strategy that has proven so successful over the past 30 years.

It is probably due to these reasons that the central leadership have become all the more determined to maintain social stability by repeatedly emphasizing and re-introducing various regulations – nine times in ten years – in order to strengthen their ruling mandate and thus continue to drive China's economic development. Their challenge lies in being able to negotiate the minefield of the agendas of the various vested interest groups while attempting to distribute China's newfound wealth.

The effectiveness of the new measures

The effectiveness of the new measures would be greatly dependent on today's unique institutional setting in China, which is a situation of economic reforms without parallel political reforms.

The central government is both powerful and powerless as a regulator. It is powerful as it is an 'undivided power' as a law-maker (Kornai, 1992) in the control of land development. However, it is also powerless because, instead of being enforced, the rules have been contested, circumvented and manipulated by not only land developers and users, but also by state agencies and managers at various local administrative levels due to disparate interests, as discussed above. Similarly – but also ironically – the Communist Party-state is seemingly united on common ideological grounds and integrated through a tightly controlled political system, but this alliance disintegrates when land development is the issue under considera- tion. Thus, the overall power of the 'five new measures' is doubtful.

In the face of these inherent systemic problems, the new leadership can only influence the demand side. Certain measures, such as stipulating higher mort- gage down-payments, pilot implementation of property taxes, prohibitions on purchasing multiple property units and the suspension of non-local purchasing would help cool the market over the immediate to short term. However, the effectiveness of these measures becomes less certain over a more protracted period in the broader environment, where real rates of return on traditional savings vehicles remain negative and alternative investment channels are limited. Hence, we expect these measures would mainly help constrain speculative investments in owner-occupied property. We also believe that the demand-side measures are associated with the active development of state-owned investment in the property sector. Moreover, greater demand-side restrictions would generate unintended consequences for the welfare of non-speculators and dis- courage intra-regional migration, thus putting regional economic growth under pressure.

Conclusion

In summary, demand-side regulations alone will not properly address the prop- erty price issue. However, due to conflicting agendas between the vested interest groups, supply-side measures would not prove politically popular either. Under the existing institutional context, the 'five new measures' gives an impression as being 'unsteady, unbalanced, uncoordinated, and unsustainable'.[11] This can be seen from the fact that advisory capacities, listing registrations, fake divorces[12] and property transaction volumes have trended upwards, and property prices have gone up. The impact of the new measures is clearly inconsistent with the policy intentions.

From a macro policy perspective, however, China must continue to enhance urbanization and urban agglomeration. Unfortunately, neither can be achieved without the support of the real-estate industry. In addition, for China's GDP to maintain a high growth rate, investment in fixed assets must continue. All of these factor mean investment in the real-estate sector cannot be shaken.

In conclusion, the 'five new measures' alone may not be sufficient to effectively address the underlying push behind China's overheating property sector without the central government's vision and the political will to undertake fundamental institutional change.

Notes

1 The authors would like to thank the following people for their insightful comments: Professor David Parker, School of Commerce, University of South Australia; and the participants at the Fourth Sino-Australia Forum 'Changing Economies'.
2 Other than the section of 'Interlinked relationship between central and sub-national governments', for simplicity in this chapter we use 'sub-national' to represent various non-central levels of government in China, e.g. province, city (prefectures, league and autonomous prefecture), county (autonomous county, banner and district under the jurisdiction of the city), district and village (people's commune, town and autonomous country), etc.
3 According to the *Financial Times* of 16 April 2013, the IMF, ratings agencies and investment banks have all raised concerns regarding Chinese government debt. Provinces, cities, counties and villages across China are now estimated to owe between RMB10 trillion and RMB20 trillion (US$1.6 trillion and US$3.2 trillion), equivalent to 20–40 per cent of the size of the economy. Local governments are prohibited from directly raising debt, so they have used special-purpose vehicles to circumvent these rules, issuing bonds under the vehicles' names to fund infrastructure projects.
4 For instance, measures include restrictions upon second and third property purchases, higher minimum down-payments as well as taxation in certain cities on non-locally-owned and multiple properties.
5 http://dealbook.nytimes.com/2010/01/27/schillers-list-how-to-diagnose-the-next-bubble.
6 As per Anglin *et al.* (2013), the leasehold right is '70 years in the case of residential uses, 50 in the case of commercial and 40 in the case of industrial, both the land and any buildings become the property of the lessor, the government'.
7 www.nsd.edu.cn/cn/article.asp?articleid=16856.
8 Individuals buy commodity property via the open market, and the price is based upon the market mechanism.
9 Sub-national governments would use LGFPs as a vehicle to provide off-balance-sheet quasi-fiscal support for their operations, to promote infrastructure development in China, as per Lu and Sun (2013).
10 A Chinese microblogging website.
11 'China's economic growth is unsteady, unbalanced, uncoordinated, and unsustainable'. Premier Wen Jiabao's statement at his press conference following the close of the annual meeting of China's legislature in March 2007.

12 The mortgage officer at the bank recommended divorce as the best way around a new property tax, according to the *Financial Times*: www.ft.com/intl/cms/s/0/602d527a-8640-11e2-8f47-00144feabdc0.html#axzz2UIlzaK00.

References

Ahuja, Ashvin and Alla Myrvoda. 2012, 'The spillover effects of a downturn in China's real estate investment', IMF eLibrary.

Anglin, P., D. Dale-Johnsony, Y. Gaoz and G. Zhux. 2013, 'Patterns of growth in Chinese cities: implications of the land lease', http://zhuguozhong.info/f_research/Ground_Lease_Jan_2013.pdf.

Barth, James R., Michael Lea and Tong Li. 2012, 'China's housing market: is a bubble about to burst?', Milken Institute Research Report.

Caixin Online. 2010, 'Stopping the clock on SOE land sprees', http://english.caixin.com/2010-03-25/100129344.html.

China Economic Net. 2013, 'HSBC survey: mainland residents have inadequate retirement reserve', www.ce.cn/macro/more/201303/01/t20130301_24157426.shtml.

Chiu, Becky and Mervyn K. Lewis. 2006, *Reforming China's State-Owned Enterprises and Banks*. Cheltenham: Edward Elgar.

Commission on Growth and Development. 2008, *The Growth Report Strategies for Sustained Growth and Inclusive Development*, Washington, DC: World Bank.

Das, M. and P. N'Diaye. 2013, 'The end of cheap labor', *Finance & Development*, Vol. 50, No. 2. www.imf.org/external/pubs/ft/fandd/2013/06/das.htm.

Ding, Chengri. 2003, 'Land policy reform in China: assessment and prospects', *Land Use Policy*, Vol. 20, pp. 109–120.

The Economist. 2004, 'The dragon and the eagle: a survey of the world economy', 2 October.

Garber, P.M. 2000, *Famous First Bubbles: The Fundamentals of Early Manias*, Cambridge, MA: MIT Press.

Garnaut, R., Jane Golley and Ligang Song. 2010, *China: The Next Twenty Years of Reform and Development*, Canberra: ANU E Press.

Himmelberg, Charles, Christoph Mayer and Todd Sinai. 2005. 'Assessing high house prices: bubbles, fundamentals, and misperceptions', *Journal of Economic Perspectives*, Vol. 19, No. 4, pp. 67–92.

Iley, Richard A. and Mervyn K. Lewis. 2007, *Untangling the US Deficit*, Cheltenham and Northampton, MA: Edward Elgar.

Kornai, János. 1992. *The Socialist System: The Political Economy of Communism*, Princeton, NJ: Princeton University Press.

Krugman, P. 2005, 'That hissing sound', *New York Times*, 8 August.

Kung, J., Cai, Y. and X. Sun. 2009, 'Rural cadres and governance in China: incentive, institution and accountability', *China Journal*, Vol. 62, pp. 61–77.

Kung, James Kai-Sing, Chenggang Xu, and Feizhou Zhou. Forthcoming. 'From industrialization to urbanization: the social consequences of changing fiscal incentives on local governments' behavior'. In Joseph E. Stiglitz (ed.), *Institutional Design for China's Evolving Market Economy*.

Li, Hongbin and Li-an Zhou, 2005, 'Political turnover and economic performance: the incentive role of personnel control in China', *Journal of Public Economics*, Vol. 89, No. 9–10, pp. 1743–1762.

Lu, Yinqiu and Tao Sun. 2013, 'Local government financing platforms in China: a fortune or misfortune?', IMF Working Paper.

Qian, Y. and Roland, G. 1998, 'Federalism and the soft budget constraint', *American Economic Review*, Vol. 88, No. 5. pp. 1143–1162.

Qian, Y. and Weingast, B. 1997, 'Federalism as a commitment to preserving market incentives', *Journal of Economic Perspectives*, Vol. 11, No. 4, pp. 83–92.

Shiller, Robert J. 2010, 'Shiller's list: how to diagnose the next bubble', *New York Times*, 27 January.

Shirk, Susan L. 1993, *The Political Logic of Economic Reform in China*, Berkeley, CA: University of California Press.

Stiglitz, Joseph E. 1990, 'Symposium on bubbles', *Journal of Economic Perspectives*, Vol. 4, No. 2, pp. 13–18.

Tao, D. and W. Deng 2013, 'China: shadow banking – road to heightened risks', Credit Suisse, https://doc.research-and-analytics.csfb.com/docView?language=ENG&source= emfromsendlink&format=PDF&document_id=1010517251&extdocid=1010517251_1 _eng_pdf&serialid=VLRQ4TgNxWzk%2FTvHinuua9QXHvi9V6lqKh3s0gpV%2 BEA%3D.

Tao, R. and H. Wang. 2013, 'China's urbanization investment and financing model for change', *DF Daily*, www.dfdaily.com/html/8762/2013/3/26/967159.shtml.

Thomson Reuters. 2013, 'Chinese shadow banking', http://accelus.thomsonreuters.com/ sites/default/files/GRC00715_0.pdf.

Washington Post. 2006, 'China's party leadership declares new priority: "harmonious society"', 12 October.

Xu Chenggang. 2011, 'The fundamental institutions of China's reforms and develop-ment', *Journal of Economic Literature*, Vol. 49, No. 5, pp. 1076–1151.

Xue, J. 1994, 'The development trend of the Chinese land market', *Real Estate Market Review*, October, pp. 12–15.

14 China

Accelerating the strategic transformation of foreign trade development mode

Lei Feng and Ai-Ying Jiang

The China's strategic position in the new foreign trade development mode

In the new development mode, China should be positioned as a trading power. We should realize that the requirements of a trading power are different from those of a trading nation.

A trading power strives for development quality in the national economy

A trading nation realizes its goals by expanding trade volume and pursuing a higher ranking in international markets. As trade volume expands at a greater speed than the growth of the national economy, trade dependency rises, which can be as high as 60 per cent or even more. From the positive point of view, China has been integrated into the world economy in accord with the trend of economic globalization. Negatively, the autonomy of the national economy is weakening, and the operation of the macroeconomic policy space is limited by the pursuit of more and more foreign exchange, which has been a goal of China for the past 30 years. In comparison, a trading power pursues quality of national economic development, does not take the expansion of trade itself as a rigid target of macroeconomic policy but as a policy to adjust the national economy and sometimes even makes use of foreign trade policy to suppress trading partners. But a trading power takes imports and huge market potential, rather than exports, as an effective lever to balance trade.

A trading power pursues how to use international resources to serve the country's national economy, and utilizes the domestic resources with a strong selectivity and a wide space

A trading nation is achieved by the expansion of trade, which is characterized by the expansion of exports. The main source of export expansion is the cheap supply of domestic resources. Export expansion can take advantage of low labour costs and cheap domestic resources flowing into export-oriented industries under policy guidance. The price of domestic resources is determined by administrative orders, which underline the international market competitiveness of China's export commodities. Among low-cost resources, international competitiveness improvement and trade expansion, there is a vicious circle which leads to the excessive use of domestic resources. However, in order to achieve national economic take-off, China has to maintain this unreasonable consumption cycle. In contrast, *a trading* power can make full use of foreign resources by imports and save domestic resources through foreign investment.

A new foreign trade development mode, which meets the needs of a trading power and economic power, puts forward some deep questions regarding China's foreign trade. *The new* mode should pay more attention to balanced development of exports and imports, emphasize mutual benefit and win–win results between trading partners, highlight the rational use of resources and environmental protection requirements and pursue a balanced development of scale, structure and benefit.

The strategic priorities of the new foreign trade development mode

Discussions about the new foreign trade development mode

With a basic understanding about the international and national situations which are ahead of China, Chinese foreign trade faces a more opportunity for its development than threat; there will be a very important period of time for it to gain stabilized growth, a harmonized structure and balanced development (Wang, 2012).

China is a large country by trade volume, but a small one by per capita trade volume; a strong country by trade quantity, but a weak one by trade structure; a huge country by exports, but a small one by brand ownership. With the idea of practising the Outlook of Scientific Development to achieve economic and social harmony and sustainable development, China has to change its foreign trade pattern, pay more attention to promotion of export structure, and step up the industrial level of the processing trade, speed up the development of its service trade and focus on the positive impact of imports on economic growth (Meng, 2006).

In 2004 China's foreign trade reached US$1,000 billion, the third highest in the world. Compared to other strong trading countries, China has an extensive growth pattern of trade, but export quality and trade efficiency need to be promoted; these two aspects are rather big gaps for a strong trading country. The only way to solve the problem is to change China's original trade model (Du, 2005).

New growth trade theory, as an important branch of modern international trade theory, discovered the basic principle of the technology factor as a function to promote trade development and trade creation. As international competition is becoming more and more serious, without enough input of technology China's trade industry will be confronted by a critical challenge. The transformation of the trade model would be the solution to this issue (Xu, 1999).

The balanced development of exports and imports

China should change the development mode, promote the balanced development of exports and imports and build a win–win pattern among trading partners.

The balanced development of exports and imports has two implications. The first is to balance export and import scale; the second is to balance the roles imports and exports can play in the development of the national economy.

The balance of exports and imports means that import volume keeps pace with export volume to avoid a drastic fluctuation of the current account. If a huge trade surplus exists in the long term, trade fictions will rise with the trade surplus. Conversely, an excessive trade deficit will weaken the national economy. It is concluded that a balanced development of imports and exports underline a trade pattern in which the trade partners can mutually benefit on a win–win basis.

The balanced roles of imports and exports in the development of the national economy suggest that in order to stimulate the national economy, China depends on not only export expansion, but also requires export structure upgrades and import incentives. In general, a trading power highlights the importance of imports to the national economy.

The reasonable utilization of resources

The transformation of the foreign trade development mode depends on resource stocks. On one hand, we can utilize the domestic resources in an efficient way; on the other hand, the government should balance the use of domestic endowments and international resources.

As we see it, the negotiations on agriculture are not longer a hot issue, but has been overtaken by the matter of the pricing system for international resources, especially energy and mineral resources. In the process of economic globalization, developed nations are investing more and more in manufacturing in developing countries out of strategic consideration of the resources available. Developed countries' investments are mainly related to knowledge and technology factors, and consume the resources of developing countries. When a shortage of resources in developing countries occurs, developed countries dominate international pricing of international resources using a variety of methods in order to take the profits from the manufacturing process out of the developing countries again.

China is a resource-scarce nation, but high-speed economic development leads to huge consumption of resources. What's frequently mentioned is petroleum, over one half of which is imported. China, as the biggest steel producer, consumes a huge amount of iron ore, not only from the domestic market but also imported from other nations. Therefore, the key for the sustainable development of the national economy and foreign trade is to use all kinds of scarce resources in a reasonable way to reduce energy consumption per unit of output and to improve the efficiency of resource use.

In the context of trade itself, imports and exports have different influences on resource consumption. Generally speaking, exports mainly use domestic resources, while imports use international resources. From the perspective of trade policy, a country has more decision-making power regarding domestic resources than international resources. China faces more trouble than other nations because some developed countries impose strict trade restrictions on high-technology product exports to China through the so-called Paris-based Coordinating Committee and Wassenaar Arrangement. Therefore, from the perspective of the rational utilization of resources, trade policy should particularly focus on the development of import trade.

Effective protection to the natural environment

Environmental factors are a hot issue, which were particularly important in the Uruguay Round negotiations. Although most developing countries were against including environmental issues in the negotiation agenda, developed countries were for that because the environmental issues can be used to restrict developing countries from developing their national economies and foreign trade rights. However, the relationship between environmental factors in foreign trade and economic development is an unavoidable question. In essence, the environmental problems faced by developing countries are completely different from those environmental factors which were highlighted by developed countries in trade negotiations.

Environmental problems in developing nations focus on the sustainable development of the national economy and foreign trade. Developing nations should not achieve the development of their national economy and foreign trade at the cost of environmental damage, which to a large extent are caused by the international division of labour and international industrial transfer, dominated by developed countries. The industrial upgrading process means that developed nations transfer highly polluting industries to developing countries, and the host developing nations bear the consequences of environmental pollution.

In the use of foreign direct investment and undertaking international industrial transfer, the government must constantly adjust the foreign investment industrial catalogue and harshly punish domestic enterprises which cause negative environmental impacts. To realize the policy goal, the government should regulate enterprises which do not conform to the environmental regulations and push outdated technology and production techniques out of the market.

The balanced development of scale, structure and benefit

Coordinating the interaction between the trade scale, structure and benefit will promote national medium- and long-term economic development.

Through analysing the relationship between scale, structure and benefits of foreign trade, the government can explore the factors which underline the power to obtain a share of the world market. Comparing production costs with circulation costs and export price with world market prices, we will find that the key factor which determines a country's international competitiveness is social labour productivity; the improvement of productivity will open the road to transformation of China's foreign trade development mode.

The government should adjust the contribution of domestic resources through trade policy and create an institutional framework which can improve factor flows in the realization of the balanced development of scale, structure and benefit.

The two strategic stages of the transformation of foreign trade development mode

The transformation of development mode can be divided into two stages. The first stage focuses on the adjustment of export trade policy; the second stage emphasizes import trade policy adjustment. The two phases have different strategic and realize different strategic objectives.

The first stage is to adjust the export trade policy

The target of this stage is to balance the export volume and import volume. Balanced development of the imports and exports is the essential characteristic of this stage.

A balanced trade does not mean that the volume of export must equal to volume of import. In China's case, it is not wise to solve the problem of a big trade surplus by reducing the volume of export or retaining the volume of export and at the same time increasing the volume of import; a balanced trade means we need to make use of the positive functions or roles of import and export in the development of the Chinese domestic trade and economy.

In the unfair international trade environment, it is wrong to restrain exports or stimulate imports through trade policy adjustment to realize trade balance, and does not conform to the international rational allocation of resources. Against the background of releasing high-tech export limitations to China, China's imports will rise at great speed. At the same time, energy demand driven by economic development will greatly promote the growth of imports. The new international trade environment will change the basic judgement of the trade surplus; the trade surplus of US$100–US$200 billion is a mirage and will disappear with more imports of high-technology products and energy and resource products.

Furthermore, the trade balance should be achieved under domestic and international circumstances with some specific characteristics.

First, we examine the specific characteristics of the international environment, including: a fair trade environment breaking through discriminatory trade restrictions; a reasonable investment environment which can affect trade scale and structure; and an elimination of three terms and conditions at the system level which were unwillingly imposed upon China when entering the WTO.

Second, we explore the characteristics of the domestic economic environment, which concern the contribution of consumption, investment and trade to national economic development and the direction of industry structural adjustment which is not dominated by external demand – in other words, the export-oriented industries will decline in the national economy.

The second stage is to adjust import trade policy

At this stage, the strategic objectives are to grasp the power to coordinate the overall allocation of resources in the domestic market and world market so as to meet the needs of national economic development.

The key point of import trade policy adjustment is to utilize international resources in an more efficient way. On this point, it is important to have the power to influence pricing and to establish a position in the institutional framework of international economy and trade, such as in the WTO, World Bank and IMF. In the end, China will find its voice on trade rules and commodity pricing in the international trading system.

China's industrial structure adjustment and upgrade need international technical support. Technology import (including the import of high-tech commodities and the introduction of new applicable technology) plays an important role in the transformation of trade and national economic development mode, and dominates the high-end international resources trade.

The interaction between two strategic stages

The interaction between the transformation of import and export development mode

The strategic position of the trade mode transformation is to promote China from a trading nation to a trading power. To achieve the trade mode transformation there needs to be a change in the export and import development modes.

Export transformation refers to the basis of national industrial adjustment; the government should move away from over-dependence on labour and resource endowment, stop pursuing export scale blindly, discard the traditional development mode and gradually establish a new mode suitable for a trading power.

Import transformation means that increasing imports can offset the increasing exports, and the huge trade surplus will gradually fall, which leads to tense international economic and trade relations. In the new mode, imports can allocate international and domestic resources in an efficient way and stimulate national economic development.

A trading nation imposes restrictions on imports and discourages them. The role of imports is restrained because excessive imports will offset the trade surplus brought by increasing exports. Because a trade nation only chases rising net exportation instead of export expansion on the basis of import and export balance, imports cannot play a positive role in stimulating national economic development.

The interaction between the two above-mentioned transformations and the national economic development mode

The transformation of export mode and import mode contribute to China's trade development in different ways. The former happens at the level of a trading nation, the latter occurs at the level of a trading power. Correspondingly, they have different characteristics.

First, in the process of export transformation, import trade is taken as a trade balance factor to provide friendly surroundings for export trade.

Second, in the process of import transformation, import trade is taken as an important factor that influences the price of international and domestic markets and the allocations of domestic resource and world resources. The import change is embodied in the transformation of national economic development and the import increase is in accord with the characteristics of national economic development.

The different requirements on export trade and import trade in the two strategic stages

In the first stage, foreign trade should meet the development needs of the national economy; export trade acts as the engine of economic growth and provides the international market space for economic growth. In the second phase, foreign trade should adapt to the development needs of the national economy and import trade plays a more important role and becomes an important approach for allocating domestic and foreign resources and influencing pricing on the domestic and international markets.

The positioning and the choice the foreign trade development mode

It is significant for China's foreign trade and the economy to transform the mode of foreign trade development. The transformation is a strategic measure to ensure foreign trade develops in a sustainable and healthy way, and will guide China's strategic concept of foreign trade development.

The foreign trade development mode is transformed at the strategic and comprehensive level following the adjustment of the guiding ideology. The transformation is to discard the traditional development mode, which is on the basis of export expansion and at the cost of resources and the environment, and to establish a sustainable method of foreign trade development which benefits from environmental protection and resource utilization.

There are many different foreign trade development modes. Because different regional economic development levels and foreign trade development levels exist, different regions have diverse concepts of the transformation of the foreign trade development mode. Consequently, different regions should position their foreign trade development modes according to their economic development level, as well as the specific foreign trade development conditions.

Transformation of foreign trade development mode should allow different regions to establish different foreign trade development goals, choose different paths and adopt different development models

First, because there is a wide gap between China's regional economic development and foreign trade development, transformation of the foreign trade development mode should have diverse but specific goals. The principle should be established that higher trade dependence does not mean a more healthy economy.

Examining Beijing, Shanghai and Guangdong, their economic volumes are great, their industrial foundations are solid and these regions are relatively close to the international level within their industries. After the exploration of the 30-year reform and opening up, foreign trade has experienced different development stages and has played a dominant role in economic development. It is not surprising that foreign trade dependency is more than 100 per cent in these regions. Examining Jiangsu, Zhejiang, Tianjin and Fujian, these regions can take advantage of their geographical location, convenient transportation and a solid industry foundation, and the foreign trade dependency of these regions is around 50 per cent. It is concluded that foreign trade has been playing an important role in the local economy and possesses more potential space to expand. As a result, the transformation should be based on existing advantages, improve the export industry structure, promote a high-end position in the global value chain and fight for the high added-value production and processing with a strategic significance.

The trade dependency of most other regions is in the area of 10–20 per cent, or even below 10 per cent. Because of low trade volume or huge GDP, a lower trade dependency indicates trade development in these regions can't keep up with that of the eastern coastal provinces and cities. This conclusion indicates that these regions are experiencing different stages to those of the eastern, or that export-oriented industries lag behind the international development trend. No matter the situation, the main driving force of economic development in these regions is not foreign trade. A reasonable development strategy should appropriately promote the exploitation of local foreign trade resources, enhance the level of foreign trade development, at least avoid direct reference to the trade goals of the developed areas and a forcible industrial adjustment to the high end of the industrial chain, and then formulate reasonable regional foreign trade development goals on the basis of the actual situation of regional economic development and industrial foundation.

For these areas, although there is no contradiction between the development of foreign trade and the development of local economy, the strategic guiding ideology should be clear which is the priority. In most instances, local economic development is the main task of the local government and is the top priority. In comparison, foreign trade development is only a supporting point in the local economy and not the focal point of even the regional government; it is a task for the whole government.

Second, determining an attainable regional foreign trade development target helps to select the appropriate development path and development mode of foreign trade. Generally, in the process of transformation, disadvantaged areas shouldn't simply imitate developed areas regardless of their own characteristics. The relatively backward areas, whose trade dependency is generally low, should establish an attainable development mode which will promote the local economy and, in turn, the local economic improvements will have a positive effect on the trade dependency. Because the disparity of local economies exists, the outcomes of trade transformation can be different to each other and each region must realize its openness on the basis of the local economic level.

Because the roles of foreign trade in regional economic development are different, the foreign trade development mode should be different. The regions with high trade dependency should focus on the balanced development of exports and imports, emphasize industrial structure upgrades and adjust the trade driving forces; the relatively backward regions with low trade dependency usually put exports at the top of the list of government tasks. The export structure of these regions should be accord with their industrial structure, which is fixed and not in line with the national industrial structure; it should position them appropriately in the national industrial chain and establish an attainable trade development mode *rather than blindly pursue the so-called 'high-end' and 'frontier' industry.* Even if the export trade is unilateral and export pattern is labour-intensive and highly dependent on local resources, the short-term trade pattern should not affect the long-term choice of foreign trade development mode.

Transformation of the national foreign trade development mode should be embodied in the specific roles of regions in national foreign trade development

Some regions benefit from export increases and other areas realize import growth. In some regions, the industrial structure develops at the same pace as international industries, while other areas need to maintain and carry forward the advantages of traditional industries to support exports. Some regions are improving the technology content of exports compared with the regions which only export labour-intensive products. How to avoid resource over-exploitation is a top priority of some areas, but others consider how to take advantage of local natural resources. Some regions highlight further openness while others have to take local economic development as a priority.

One region should establish an attainable trade development mode to meet the requirements of regional economic development, and formulate a concrete plan accordingly. Concerning local foreign trade development, the central government should put forward specific options for foreign trade development and positioning of local economic development, and reserve a policy space for backward areas to develop foreign trade on the basis of their comparative advantage.

References

Du Yongchen. 'Transformation of foreign trade development mode towards a strong trading nation', *Heilongjiang Foreign Economics and Trade*, vol. 11, 2005.

Meng Jianguo. 'Some thinking points on China's transformation of foreign trade development mode', *Commercial Modernization*, vol. 7, 2006.

Wang Shouwen. 'Transforming foreign trade development mode to promote a balanced trade development', *International Trade*, vol. 1, 4–7, 2012.

Xu Ninggang. 'New growth trade theory and transformation of China's foreign trade development mode', *Bulletin of Guangxi Finance College*, vol. 6, 1999.

15 Correlation analysis of trade in services OFDI and industrial structure optimization in China

Jing Tang

Introduction

In the economic globalization era, the proportion of trade in services in international trade has been increasing rapidly. The role of trade in service outwards foreign direct investment (OFDI) for the adjustment of the home industry structure has been of great interest for each country. From the experience of developed countries upgrading their industrial structures by trade in service OFDI, whether it is the US, Japan, South Korea or the newly industrialized Asian countries and regions, they attach importance to the tertiary industries. China's OFDI is highly concentrated in leasing and business services, the resource development industry, processing and manufacturing industry; on the contrary, the proportion of trade in services OFDI in the high-tech industry is quite small.

This chapter is based on annual time series data over the period 2003–2011 in China, and analyses the influence of trade in services OFDI to China's domestic industry structure optimization by the application of the grey relational analysis (GRA) model.

The chapter proceeds as follows. The next section reviews the existing literature on the relationship of trade in services OFDI and industrial structure optimization. The third section presents our empirical strategy, data and results. The final section concludes and discusses policy implications.

Literature review

There are two categories in the literature on correlation analysis of trade in services OFDI and industrial structure optimization, focusing on developed countries and regions on the one hand, and developing countries and regions on the other.

The former puts emphasis on OFDI from developed countries and regions to developing countries and regions – that is OFDI from countries and regions with relatively high-level industrial structures to that of relatively low. The representative theories are 'product lifecycle theory' by Raymond Vernon, 'marginal industrial expansion theory' by Kiyoshi Kojima and 'flying geese model' theory by Akamatsu. Some empirical studies by Fung and Tuan (1997) on Hong Kong's OFDI, and by Barrios *et al.* (2005) on Ireland's OFDI.

The latter gives emphasis on OFDI from developing countries and regions to developed countries and regions. The influential work here is the 'technological innovation and industrial upgrading theory' by Cantwell and Tolentino (1990). Meanwhile, empirical studies cover some countries like Slovenia (Svetlicic *et al.*, 2000) and China, etc. These earlier works have shown that OFDI can prompt investor countries to upgrade their industrial structure through certain mechanisms, like both demand and supply of international production (Jiang and Du, 2002), resource complementation, transfer of traditional industries, emerging production growth, industry associations and radiation and overseas investment income (Wang Qi, 2004).

However, some empirical studies on Chinese OFDI have shown different results. Pan and Liu (2010), for instance, use co-integration theory, Granger causality inspection, and find that China's OFDI cannot promote industrial structure upgrading in the short term, but can in the long term. Liu and Gu (2010) analysed the relationship between OFDI and three industries by regression analysis, and found that the secondary and the tertiary industries were positively correlated with OFDI, while the primary industry showed a negative correlation with OFDI.

Most work empirically adopted the econometric analysis methods on industrial structure on the basis of total amounts of OFDI. From the industry selection angle these studies have not been refined to specific sectors' OFDI, especially in the field of trade in services. Against this background, this chapter builds on and extends this area of research in two ways. First, it includes detailed sector-level services trade OFDI data. Second, it uses the model of grey relative level to analyse the influence of service in trade OFDI on China's industry structure optimization.

Methodology and data

Model specification

The term 'grey' lies between 'black' (meaning no information) and 'white' (meaning full information), and indicates that the information is partially available. It is suitable to unascertained problems with poor information. China's OFDI statistics system was established late in 2002, so the statistical data samples are very limited – only since 2003. This means a large sample statistical model does not apply to the analysis of the relationship between service in trade OFDI and industry structure adjustment in China, while GRA helps to work on such incomplete and unascertained information. GRA has the ability to learn from a small number of cases, which is effective in the context of data-starvation. The draw of GRA is its flexibility to model complex non-linear relationships. It utilizes the work from historical projects of the same area.

The five steps of primary sequence establishment involved in Liu's method are as follows (grey relational grade by Liu *et al.* (2010)):

1   Consider the objective series $X_0 = [x_0(1), x_0(2), \ldots, x_0(n)]$, the reference series $X_i = [x_i(1), x_i(2), \ldots, x_i(n)]$, where $i = 1, 2, 3, \ldots, n$

2   Request the initial image of each sequence:

$$X_i = \frac{X_i}{x_i(1)} = [x_i'(1), x_i'(2), x_i'(3), \ldots, x_i'(n)], \quad \text{where } i = 1, 2, \ldots, m$$

3   Request difference sequence, its max. and min.:

$$\Delta_i = [\Delta_i(1), \Delta_i(2), \Delta_i(3), \ldots, \Delta_i(n)], \text{ where } \Delta_i(k) = |x_o'(k) - x_i'(k)|,$$
$$M = \max_i \max_k \Delta_i(k), \quad m = \min_i \min_k \Delta_i(k)$$

4   Request grey relational coefficient:

$$\gamma_{0i}(k) = \frac{m + \varepsilon M}{\Delta_i(k) + \varepsilon M}, \varepsilon \text{ is identification coefficient,}$$
$$\varepsilon \in (0, 1) \text{ where } \varepsilon = 0.5, k = 1, 2, \ldots, n; \ i = 1, 2, \ldots, m$$

5   Calculate the grey relational grade:

$$\gamma_{0i} = \frac{1}{n} \sum_{k=1}^{n} \gamma_{oi}(k), \quad \text{where } i = 1, 2, \ldots, m$$

Variable selection

1   Objective series (X_0). This chapter takes the industrial structure optimization indicator system by Yang (2006) as the objective series. The design and measurement of this indicator system is based on industrial restructuring of transition countries in the process of marketization. Therefore, it is of great significance to study and analyse China's industrial structure optimization. This system consists of three layers: destination layer, domain layer and index layer. The values in parentheses are the weight of each index (see Table 15.1).

2   Reference series (X_i). This chapter selected the sample of OFDI data from four major sectors of trade in services and three industrial sectors in China from 2003 to 2011 as the reference series. According to statistics in the *Statistical Bulletin of China's Outward Foreign Direct Investment* published by the Ministry of Commerce, Bureau of Statistics and SAFE, The flows and stocks of eight sectors that are the mining industry (X_1), manufacturing (X_2), wholesale and retail services (X_3), transport, storage, postal services (X_4), leasing and business services (X_5), information transmission, computer and software services (X_6) and construction (X_7), which account for over 90 per cent of total OFDI flows and stocks in each year. That means these eight sectors are the main elements when analysing the influence of service in trade OFDI for the home industry structure optimization. This chapter uses the stocks of the above eight sectors as the reference series.

Table 15.1 Industrial structure optimization indicator system and index weight

Destination layer	Domain layer	Index layer
Industrial structure optimization	Three industries development (0.25)	Primary industry growth rate (0.25) Secondary industry growth rate (0.35) Tertiary industry growth rate (0.4)
	Employment distribution structure (0.3)	The ratio of primary industry employment over total employment (0.2)
		The ratio of secondary industry employment over total employment (0.3)
		The ratio of tertiary industry employment over total employment (0.5)
	Industrial department contribution rate (0.45)	The ratio of the increase of primary industry output value over the increase of GDP (0.2)
		The ratio of the increase of secondary industry output value over the increase of GDP (0.3)
		The ratio of the increase of tertiary industry output value over the increase of GDP (0.5)

Data source and calculation

The value of industrial structure optimization indicator is calculated first by using the weight sum method according to the sequence of each layer in Table 15.1. The basic statistical data were obtained from the *China Labour Statistical Yearbook* in each year of 2003–2011, issued by MOHRSS, and *Statistical Bulletin* in each year of 2003–2011, issued by the China Bureau of Statistics. Then the final result of X_0 shown in Table 15.2 is calculated through the initial value of the dimensionless data method.

The data of reference series (X_i) that are the stocks of eight sectors OFDI shown in Table 15.3 are capsulated through the *Statistical Bulletin of China's Outward Foreign Direct Investment* from 2003 to 2011. Then, using the same method of the initial value of the dimensionless data, calculating the comparative sequence of the eight sectors in Table 15.4.

Experimental results

According to the GRA model mentioned above, the calculating results of correlation analysis on the influence of service in trade OFDI to China's industry structure adjustment are as shown in Table 15.5.

Table 15.2 The value of industrial structure optimization indicator and three sub-indicators in 2003–2011

Indicator/year	Three industries development	Employment distribution structure	Industrial department contribution rate	Industrial structure optimization
2003	0.019200	0.09285	0.147301	**0.259351**
2004	0.021950	0.09429	0.153010	**0.26925**
2005	0.022825	0.09540	0.192027	**0.310252**
2006	0.024363	0.09654	0.162635	**0.283538**
2007	0.025438	0.09720	0.143513	**0.266151**
2008	0.021075	0.09804	0.184310	**0.303425**
2009	0.019838	0.09903	0.191291	**0.310159**
2010	0.022863	0.09975	0.168162	**0.290775**
2011	0.020988	0.10098	0.173098	**0.295066**

Conclusion and analysis

Generally speaking, the ranking of GRA results shows that China's OFDI in the seven sectors have played a promotional role in industrial structure adjustment. From the point of view of impact level, we find that the descending order is: information transmission, computer services and software services (X_6) > wholesale and retail services (X_3) > mining industry (X_1) > construction industry (X_7) > manufacturing industry (X_2) > transport, storage, postal services (X_4) > leasing and business services (X_5). There are three sectors belonging to trade in services in the top five. Hence, trade in services OFDI – for example, information transmission, computer services and software services and wholesale and retail services – have a stronger influence on industrial structure adjustment than do secondary industry sectors like mining and manufacturing.

Further analysis is as follows. First, information transmission, computer and software services OFDI is usually for the purpose of obtaining the information technology, which has the characteristics of low cost, high speed, large quantity and lower difficulty. On the basis of the spillover effect, it can make use of foreign advanced technology and experience in business management. In this way, China can reduce the technology gap with developed countries and areas little by little, and create new comparative advantages, which will promote the adjustment and upgrading of domestic industrial structure. Second, wholesale and retail services OFDI is conducive to China enterprises acquiring a better understanding of market conditions and the international advanced concepts on sales and design of products in the host country, which better push domestic products to strengthen the connection to international advanced techniques, and greatly push forward the adjustment and upgrading of the domestic industrial structure. Third, China's OFDI in the construction service sector has played a crucial role in the export expansion of mechanical and electric equipment, raw materials and technical services, which promotes the development of modern banking, civil aviation, insurance

Table 15.3 China's OFDI stocks data of eight major sectors in 2003–2011

Sector	Year								
	2003	2004	2005	2006	2007	2008	2009	2010	2011
Mining	59	59.5	86.5	179	150.1	228.7	405.8	446.6	670
Manufacturing	20.7	45.4	57.7	75.3	95.4	96.6	135.9	178	269.6
Wholesale and retail services	65.3	78.4	114.2	129.6	202.3	298.6	357	420.1	490.9
Transport, storage, postal services	19.9	45.8	70.8	75.7	120.6	145.2	166.3	231.9	252.6
Leasing and business services	19.9	164.2	165.5	194.6	305.2	545.8	729.5	972.5	1,422.9
Information transmission, computer and software services	108.9	11.6	13.2	14.5	19	16.7	19.7	84.1	955.3
Construction	6.6	8.33	12	15.7	16.3	26.8	34.1	61.7	80.5

Note
Unit: 100 million US dollars.

Table 15.4 Results of non-dimensionalization on the sequences of X_0 and X_i

Sector	Year								
	2003	2004	2005	2006	2007	2008	2009	2010	2011
Mining	1	1.008475	1.466102	3.033898	2.544068	3.876271	6.877966	7.569492	11.35593
Manufacturing	1	2.193237	2.78744	3.637681	4.608696	4.666667	6.55217	8.599034	13.02415
Wholesale and retail services	1	1.200613	1.748851	1.984686	3.098009	4.572741	5.467075	6.433384	7.517611
Transport, storage, postal services	1	2.301508	3.557789	3.80402	6.060302	7.296482	8.356784	11.65327	12.69347
Leasing and business services	1	8.251256	8.316583	9.778894	15.33668	27.42714	36.65829	48.86935	71.50251
Information transmission, computer and software services	1	0.10652	0.121212	0.13315	0.174472	0.153352	0.1809	0.772268	8.772268
Construction	1	1.262121	1.818182	2.378788	2.469697	4.060606	5.166667	9.348485	12.19697

Table 15.5 The grey relational analysis result

Sector	Mining	Manufacturing	Wholesale and retail services	Transport, storage, postal services	Leasing and business services	Information transmission, computer and software services	Construction
Grey relational grade	0.9231	0.9016	0.9354	0.879	0.667	0.9611	0.9217
Ranking	3	5	2	6	7	1	4

service sectors and the relative sectors of transportation, electric power, electronic communications, etc.

In conclusion, in order to change the backward condition of industrial structure, China shall bring the role of OFDI in promoting industrial structure adjustment into full play, and give a clear direction to OFDI industries. At the present stage of economic development, China's government should encourage enterprises to choose investments in those sectors with strong intra-industry linkages and technology-intensive industries, which in turn result in upgrades of the domestic industrial structure.

References

Barrios S., H. Gorg and E. Strob. 'Foreign direct investment, competition and industrial development in the host country'. *European Economic Review*, 2005, 49, 1761–1784.

Cantwell, J. and P.E. Tolentino, 'Technological accumulation and third world multi-national'. Discussion paper in International Investment and Business Studies, 1990, University of Reading.

Fung-Yee. N.G. (Linda) and Chyau Tuan. 'Evolving outward investment, industrial concentration and technology change: implications for post-1997 Hong Kong'. *Journal of Asian Economics*, 1997, 8 (2), 315–332.

Jiang, X.J. and L. Du. 'FDI theory and implications for China'. *Review of Economic Research*, 2002, 73, 32–44.

Liu, D. and G.D. Gu. 'The relationship between FDI and industrial structure: an empirical investigation in China', *Market Forum*, 2010, 1, 12–13.

Liu, S.F., Y.G. Dang, Z.G. Fang and N.M. Xie. *Grey System Theory and Its Application.* Beijing: Beijing Science Press, 2010.

Pan, Y. and Liu Huihuang, 'An empirical study on relationship between OFDI and industrial structure in China'. *Statistics and Decision*, 2010, 2, 102–104.

Svetlicic, Marjan, Matija Rojec and Andreja Trtnik. 'The restructuring role of outward foreign direct investment by Central European firms: the case of Slovenia', in Attila Yaprak and Hulya Tutek (eds), *Globalization, the Multinational Firm, and Emerging Economies*, JAI, New York, 2000.

Wang Qi 'The adjustment effect and its conduction mechanism of FDI to investment country's industry structure'. *Journal of International Trade*, 2004, 5, 73–77.

Yang, X.M., 'Analysis on regional difference of measurement of market-oriented process in transforming countries: design and review based on the index of industrial structure adjustment'. *World Economy Study*, 2006, 1, 72–78.

16　Conclusion and discussion

Lei Feng

Under the 'changing economies' theme of the Fourth Sino-Australia Forum which led to this volume, the presentations were extensive and promoted academic exchange, discussions and even arguments among Sino-Australian scholars concerning China's economic development, trade liberalization, energy development, tourism development, social welfare and many other fields. All of those different views and arguments illustrate the need for further communication.

The following discussion is a brief review, as a closing chapter of this book.

Chinese labour costs

Michael Schiavone's chapter (Rising labour costs in China: a problem or an opportunity) poses a crucial question. The success of China's economic reforms and opening up to some extent is thanks to the so-called 'demographic dividend', i.e. the continuous transferring of agricultural surplus labour to the manufacturing sector for its development has provided a competitive labour supply. Now, many analysts believe that China's 'demographic dividend' has disappeared and relying on the 'demographic dividend' for economic growth is no longer sustainable. Rather, 'reform dividend' has become a key driving force for economic development.

Back to the question itself, Michael thought, on the whole, that the advantage of China's labour costs will help Chinese businesses and government. It should be said that this judgement is reasonable. Justification for this judgement can also be seen as follows.

First, the other economic implication of rising labour costs is the growth in spending power, which is consistent with the efforts of the Chinese government policy to have domestic demand promote economic growth. Second, the inclusion of labour income covering the fields of expenditure continues to expand its range of content – housing, education and medical care is increasingly provided through market channels instead of government channels, and gradually into the category of expenditure in labour income. Third, expanding consumer demand in areas such as travel expenses, recreation, sports and high-end cultural activities reflects the rising income of workers. In addition, the rise of labour costs and the direction of adjustment of industrial structure maintains a consistent direction, closely related to the use of high-technology equipment and high-level industry, requiring higher labour skills or proficiency of workers; but also with the implementation of China's 'go abroad' strategy being consistent featured, it is one of the factors promoting international industrial shift.

The contribution of CDM for China to deal with climate change and sustainable development

China's response to global climate change and sustainable development has many aspects, one of which is the use of the Clean Development Mechanism (CDM) in a global participatory way, with a depth of cooperation in capital and technology equipment between developed and developing countries. The Chinese government, enterprises and the public have an awareness of sustainable development, not only reflected in CDM knowledge, but also in the understanding of the circular economy. The circular economy concept is not only for the rational use of resources and effective protection of the environment, but also for industry selection and industrial structure adjustment; the circular economy is not only the rational allocation of the industrial chain, but also includes strategic positioning of the regional economic structure; the circular economy is not only to commit to the resources and environment, but also to promote the transformation of economic development strategically.

Han Lin's chapter (The contribution of the Clean Development Mechanism towards China's climate change mitigation and sustainable development) tries to clarify this point of view. If the difference between these three different concepts could be fully clarified, one could more clearly see the significance of CDM to China's sustainable economic development. In addition, the effects of CDM to China's sustainable economic development can also be more intuitively displayed from the reality of statistical data analysis.

Confucianism in China's environmental governance

Confucianism, Taoism and Buddhism are three major philosophical systems that also have an expanding space in the governance of the national economy and environment. A harmonious society and harmonious world is the core concept of Confucianism. However, the specific content of the above and the standard of harmonious transactions at different times and under different social backgrounds may not quite be the same. Environmental governance in China is difficult to understand if placed within other countries' systems of values. Han Lin and Jeffrey Gil's chapter (Confucian principles to enhance China's environmental governance) has a certain depth of understanding about the link between Confucianism and China's environmental governance issues.

The use of the state of the world's awareness of the philosophy of Confucianism, Buddhism and Taoism for environmental governance requires skill – both a reasonable grasp of the integrated nature of environmental governance and also a thorough understanding of the essence of Confucianism. Although we cannot deny cross-disciplinary studies, it is perhaps more realistic to limit the problem to be discussed to a more specific range of subjects.

Real-estate market: the so-called 'five new measures'

Po-shan Yu, Lei Xu and Mervyn K. Lewis' article (Why Beijing rules the property market: rethinking the role of 'five new measures' in regulating the property market under a new era of China's leadership transition) discusses the impact of the so-called 'five new measures' on the Chinese real estate market.

The timeliness of a strong policy evaluation is a certain risk. Simply put, because the effect of the policy has not been fully displayed and because of the nature of the policy in effect, whether it is valid or invalid is not yet known.

Housing prices in China's economic transition period is an extremely complex issue, and using univariate or multivariate analyses will often lead to different conclusions. Hence, it is necessary to conduct a structural analysis of the relations between the many factors, and the economic development objectives of these factors will be, *mutatis mutandis*, possible to understand in terms of their pros and cons.

When it comes to local government reliance on the land market, one can also consider the debt burden of local governments, considered along with economic growth, expanding the size of the public expenditure, tax distribution system architecture of the central and local governments and a series of push-chain of relations between.

Factors analysis on China's venture investment decision model

Risk investment decision models depend mainly on the socio-economic environment. It is beyond doubt that business models should follow customer service, customer demand for a given service and adaptation to the environment. This general conclusion is not hard to prove.

Different entrepreneurial success factors will come from the different factors' impacts on risk investment decisions. An analysis or a study of different factors in risk investment decisions may dig into a collection of entrepreneurial success factors and structure in a specific socio-economic environment, thus one may be able to provide more effective advice for the mode of operation of venture capital.

One of the characteristics of China's transitional economy is that the social and economic system is rapidly changing. The level of internationalization of the venture capital companies and the persons employed, and the venture capital industry itself will, to a large extent, be key factors affecting the risk investment decisions. These factors may be something overseas researchers need to be aware of. Finding possible problems in the economy from a special preference decision-making model of venture capital is both reasonable and constructive.

Regional mobility of labour, the nature of workers and family in China and Australia

Helen McLaren's chapter (Geographic labour mobility, workers and family in China and Australia) compares labour flows among regions between China and Australia. China and Australia are both vast, with an uneven distribution of their national populations, and have some common concerns in labour mobility and so on. However, the difference between the two countries is also very obvious.

Australia's labour usually has a shorter period of travel time compared with that in China. In Australia, commuting is common and workers rarely change their place of work into a residence. The Chinese labour migration cycle is longer, often on an annual basis, where the work is relatively stable. They leave their homes, become residents where they work, and this in turn underpins China's rapid urbanization.

Different factors also determine labour mobility between the two countries. In Australia employment in the mining industry is the main reason; in China, industry concentration is not obvious, and China's 'dual economy' means the movement is from rural areas to towns or industrial areas.

In China, migrant workers send home remittances to help improve the economic situation of the families left behind. The living standard of both migrant workers and their family members has led to many social problems, which gets the attention of government and society.

Some migrant workers return home afterwards to create their own business, and this plays a huge role for their hometowns' development. Other migrant workers settle as residents where they work, and this has a great impact on their families. Sooner or later this will lead to their family members' mobility, and this raises problems for the provision of local social services, for example in housing, utilities, transportation, health care, education and so on, and needs to be considered by local governments.

Private equity and transferring management power through generations in a family-run business

Private equity (PE) practice in China is generally seen as a more market-oriented investment and financing manner, although this approach does not preclude its use by family businesses. But it is not common enough to solve the problem of transferring management power through generations in a family-run business.

China's practice is generally not to use professional managers for family businesses that continue through generations. Rather, family members learn business skills through various forms of business schools. The vast majority of Chinese family businesses are SMEs, and for them family members take over the business. In the future the preferred route and updating of large family-run businesses perhaps means the involvement of professional managers, and PE is an option that cannot be avoided for family business to achieve sustainable development in the future.

Pi-Shen Seet *et al.*'s chapter (Inter-generational transitions of family businesses using private equity: lessons for China and Australia from Chinese family-owned enterprises in Singapore) provides a PE experience of Chinese overseas family businesses in Singapore, which provides Chinese family business options for the future, but also for the future development of PE.

China's banking sector after WTO entry efficiency gains

Kai Du's chapter (WTO accession and efficiency gains: evidence from China's banking sector) uses DEA to describe the impact of WTO accession on the efficiency of China's banking sector. We endorse its conclusion; that is, in opening China to foreign investment, the Chinese banking sector has improved, directly or indirectly, its overall efficiencies.

People are more concerned about the volume of foreign capital flowing into the banking sector. From 2000 to 2009, during the key stage of China's rapid economic development, various reform measures were rolled out, including the RMB exchange rate management system, investment and financing system, the development of private enterprises, treasury management system, and the efforts of interest rate marketization. One of the key components here is how the management system affects the efficiency of the banking sector.

What changes in the Chinese banking sector have led to efficiencies? If entering the WTO is a single variable, the relationship between the two is very clear. According to the data, from 2000 to 2007, the Chinese banking sector's efficiency increased, but from 2008 to 2009 it decreased. The explanation may be the consequence of the Global Financial Crisis triggered by the US subprime mortgage crisis, and the Chinese government's response.

Strategic transformation of the trade development mode

Discussion of China's foreign trade development mode conversion from a strategic perspective is of great significance for the development of China's national economy. Lei Feng and Ai-Ying Jiang's chapter (China: accelerating the strategic transformation of foreign trade development mode) conducts a useful exploration and description of China's foreign trade development mode, and describes the key tasks for its two transition phases.

For a better understanding of the meaning and significance of strategic transformation of China's foreign trade development mode, we need to put it in the domestic and international environment of China's economic development, and to be aware of China's specific economic development. Investment, as the driving force of China's national economic development in the 1980s through to the mid-1990s, has played an important role, but reform of the investment system has lagged, bringing a lack of investment, low efficiency and other serious problems. These include foreign trade, especially export trade, that played a significant role for nearly 20 years and created a great chance for the excess agricultural labour force to move away from that industry, and for the coastal regional economic development to receive a continuous labour force supply. But China's comparative advantage in labour is gradually weakening and China's international competitiveness has been eroded. The stimulation of consumption has been a weakness of China's economic development for a long time and the income growth mainly from expanding exports has not created a clear consumer-driven economy. One can provide more choice for the consumer through the purchase of imports, and this also helps to promote China's shift from a trading nation to a trading power.

China's overseas investment of service industries and industrial restructuring

Jing Tang's chapter (Correlation analysis of trade in services OFDI and industrial structure optimization in China) verifies the relationship between overseas investment experiences of four services sectors and three manufacturing industries, and industrial structure adjustment in China. It will be an important issue for China in the long term, whether to receive benefits from optimizing the industrial structure for overseas investment of the service sector or from service sectors' overseas investment for industrial structure adjustment.

China's industrial restructuring has continued through the whole process of the reform and opening up. The industrial structure adjustment shift to a market economy has undergone a transition from a planned economy, and the coastal areas have enjoyed relatively open economic development. The international transfer of industry to China brought about by large-scale foreign investment was particularly characterized by the influx of foreign investment in manufacturing. Foreign investment in the services sector is now becoming a potential positive factor for China's industrial structure adjustment.

Adjustment of industrial structure and energy efficiency

Jiajun Liu's chapter (Spatial analysis on the contribution of industrial structural adjustment to regional energy efficiency: a case study of 31 provinces across China) analyses China's industrial restructuring and its contribution to the level of energy efficiency. Industrial structure adjustment of China's economic development is very important, but for many years the problem has not been solved.

There is need for further discussion, between the regional industrial structure adjustment and energy efficiency, and the link between regional economic development goals and China's economic development goals and energy efficiency objectives. If you simply consider the adjustment of industrial structure of a region and its corresponding energy efficiency, which should be considered the priority? Industrial structure seems to be more local, with high switching costs between regions; regional levels of production and efficiency of energy use by transportation or delivery seems to be inter-regional and optimized. Generally speaking, eliminating backward production capacity, introducing high-tech equipment (especially the use of low-power technology and equipment or processes) and improvements in energy efficiency are reasonable.

To improve energy efficiency in terms of the different levels of development between different regions of China, relatively backward areas can benefit from industrial restructuring, especially in the manufacturing sector's contribution to industrial restructuring. More developed regions will be more significant in their contribution to energy efficiency where the manufacturing sector is giving way to the services sector. Of course, these claims require a more sophisticated analysis of the data in order to be verified.

China's environmental issues

Environmental protection is a common issue facing countries in their economic development. China needs to pay more attention to environmental protection while it moves towards sustained and rapid economic development and industrialization. Thankfully, China, in environmental protection legislation and its implementation, has made quite outstanding achievements.

Through the analysis of Corporate environmental reporting (CER) of sample companies and the Measures of Disclosure of Environmental Information (MDEI), Hui Situ *et al.*'s chapter (Changing economies for a more sustainable future: the influence of stakeholders and environmental reporting developments in transforming Chinese corporate practices) found that the Chinese government-led model is different from the environmental community governance model, which has broad participation in most developed countries. State-owned enterprises are much better than non-state-owned enterprises in information disclosure using corporate environmental reporting. The effect of the government's environmental policies in influencing corporate environmental behaviour is clearly significant. The chapter notes that environmental protection needs all aspects of society's participation and it will be possible to constrain enterprises' behaviour, which is driven by the 'invisible hand'.

Transition economies have features, in governance for social and economic affairs, of a combined mode of the government's 'visible hand' and the market's 'invisible hand'. Both are required in order to reach the optimum levels of a two-governance configuration, namely an optimal and efficient governance of socio-economic affairs. It should be noted that in the transformation of the economic development process, the issue of concerned citizens and their importance in developed economies is quite different from developing ones, and this may help people to understand why environmental concerns of part of the Chinese community at the current stage are still at a relative low level.

Rural development issues

R. John Halsey's chapter (Education, globalization and rural contests: learning for staying, learning for leaving or learning for choice) regarding rural education raises three questions – access to education, the question of whether to leave the countryside or stay, or improve freedom of choice and the ability of the educated – all of which lead to the determined challenge of rural education goals for rural development. When people gain their education after leaving the rural areas, this may lead to excessive urbanization and a hollowing out of rural areas, as well as problems of food security, water supply, inefficient use of energy and poor environmental protection.

The purpose of studying rural education, according to the stages of development in different countries, is to adjust its focus. China's economic development faces long-term so-called 'three rural' issues (i.e. peasant life, agricultural production and rural development). In developing countries such as China, the target of rural education has two basic considerations; the first is to improve the cultural knowledge of the rural population and to reduce illiteracy; the second is to spread knowledge of agricultural production technology to improve agricultural productivity. Of these two objectives, Chinese rural education in the past half-century has made great achievements. It is on the basis of this success, along with China's economic development, that a large amount of agricultural surplus labour force has found employment in urban areas. Hence the level of urbanization in China continues to increase. However, there are some people who have returned to rural areas to start their own businesses and to promote rural economic development.

Development and harmony: Xinjiang

Gary Groot's chapter (The contradictions of developmentalism and the Chinese Party-state's goal of ethnic harmony: the case of Xinjiang) talked about some of the disharmony in China's rapid economic development that shows the importance of focusing on addressing social development issues at the same time as encouraging economic development. To some extent these discussions also echo the Chinese government's comprehensive demands in economic, political, cultural and social development.

Only the development of thinking is incomplete and unreasonable. The naive view is that as long as there is development, then problems will be solved. However, the idea that problems can be solved without economic development is unrealistic as well. China is a developing country, and the significance of development for China is far greater than for developed countries – development is a basic condition for solving many problems.

Research on China's economic, political, social and cultural issues should follow the track of the existing Chinese practice. China's pace of development is not only in its economic growth, but also in greater awareness among Chinese citizens of the country's economic, political, social and cultural development. If they are aware, then Chinese people can better adapt to, and deal with, the many problems facing the so-called transition economies.

Any studies on China, using international comparisons, needs to be done very carefully. Over the past 30 years China has experienced a very different way forward in its development from other countries, and a simple comparison is not sufficient to explain China's issues.

Index

Page numbers in *italics* denote tables, those in **bold** denote figures.

For Product Safety Concerns and Information please contact our EU
representative GPSR@taylorandfrancis.com
Taylor & Francis Verlag GmbH, Kaufingerstraße 24, 80331 München, Germany

www.ingramcontent.com/pod-product-compliance
Lightning Source LLC
Chambersburg PA
CBHW050409280326
41932CB00013BA/1791